ASIAN ECONOMIC INTEGRATION REPORT 2016

WHAT DRIVES FOREIGN DIRECT INVESTMENT IN ASIA AND THE PACIFIC?

ASIAN DEVELOPMENT BANK

50 YEARS

ADB

© 2016 Asian Development Bank
6 ADB Avenue, Mandaluyong City, 1550 Metro Manila, Philippines
Tel +63 2 632 4444; Fax +63 2 636 2444
www.adb.org; openaccess.adb.org

Some rights reserved. Published in 2016.
Printed in the Philippines.

ISBN 978-92-9257-683-7 (Print), 978-92-9257-684-4 (e-ISBN)
Publication Stock No. RPT168560-2

Cataloging-In-Publication Data

Asian Development Bank.
    Asian Economic Integration Report 2016: What Drives Foreign Direct Investment in Asia and the Pacific?
Mandaluyong City, Philippines: Asian Development Bank, 2016.

1. Regionalism.   2. Subregional cooperation.   3. Economic development.   4. Asia.   I. Asian Development Bank.

Contents

Foreword.. v
Acknowledgments... vi
Definitions... vii
Abbreviations.. viii
Highlights.. x

1. Economic Outlook and Resilience.. 1
   Economic Outlook... 2
   Economic Shocks and Risks... 3
   Building Economic Resilience... 4
   Correlates of Economic Resilience... 9
   Policy Consideration.. 13
   References... 13

   Box
   1.1 Drivers of Asian Output... 5

2. Trade and Global Value Chain.. 15
   Recent Trends in Asia's Trade... 16
   Analysis of Global and Regional Value Chains............................ 24
   Diagnosing Channels of the Brexit Impact: Trade and Investment Linkages........ 25
   Updates on Regional Trade Policy.. 29
   Annexes.. 42
   References... 44

   Boxes
   2.1. Gravity Model Estimation of Bilateral Exports....................... 20
   2.2 Impact of Foreign Exchange Rate on Trade........................... 22
   2.3 Rising Protectionism.. 33
   2.4 Impact of Nontariff Measures on Trade Flows........................ 39

3. Financial Integration.. 45
   Quantity Indicators... 46
   Price Indicators.. 62
   Financial Spillover.. 67
   Capital Flow Volatility... 72
   References... 75

Boxes
3.1 The Recent Rise in Nonperforming Loans in Asia and Policy Considerations   58
3.2 Asia's Financial Integration Initiatives—Then and Now.   69
3.3 Asia's Financial Market Infrastructure Development and Its Role in Financial Integration   74

4. Movement of People   77
    Remittances and Tourism Receipts   78
    Migration Updates.   86
    Drivers of Migration   91
    References   96

    Boxes
    4.1 Impact of Migration on Remittances   90
    4.2 Impact of Migration   92
    4.3 Can Migration Help Solve Population Aging in Asia and the Pacific?.   94

5. Subregional Cooperation Initiatives.   99
    Central and West Asia: Central Asia Regional Economic Cooperation Program   100
    Southeast Asia: Greater Mekong Subregion Program   105
    East Asia: Support to CAREC and GMS Programs   110
    South Asia: South Asia Subregional Economic Cooperation Program.   114
    The Pacific: Framework for Pacific Regionalism   118
    References   122

    Boxes
    5.1 PRC Involvement in Greater Mekong Subregion   112
    5.2 Belt and Road Initiative   112

6. Special Theme: What Drives Foreign Direct Investment in Asia and the Pacific?   123
    Introduction   124
    Trends and Patterns of FDI for Asia and the Pacific.   126
    Asia's Investment Patterns in the Age of Global Value Chains   138
    FDI Drivers by Mode of Entry.   151
    GVC–FDI: More Greenfield Investment or M&As?.   155
    Policy Implications.   158
    Special Section: The Role of International Investment Policy.   159
    Annexes   169
    Background Papers   173
    References   173

    Boxes
    6.1 Identifying GVC-FDI in the Data   130
    6.2 GVC–Trade in Asia.   139
    6.3 Special Economic Zones as Instruments for Attracting FDI—Case Study from Thailand.   143
    6.4 Product Fragmentation and GVC–FDI—Regression Results   151
    6.5 Analyzing the Link between GVC–FDI and Mode of Entry.   157
    6.6 Double Taxation Treaty with BITs and RTIAs   166

7. Statistical Appendix.   177

Foreword

Regional cooperation and integration (RCI) in Asia and the Pacific continues to evolve, creating an important source for the region's dynamic growth. This report assesses the RCI progress against (i) the growing uncertainty following the United Kingdom's referendum on leaving the European Union and the United States election, (ii) the sluggish global economic recovery, and (iii) the ongoing economic restructuring in the People's Republic of China (PRC) and growth moderation.

The region's trade and financial integration continues to strengthen—the intraregional trade share rose to 57.1% of the region's total trade in 2015, while intraregional cross-border asset holdings rose to 26.1% of the region's total cross-border asset holdings in 2014. However, the report also notes that trade growth in the region decelerated further in 2015 and, while trade links within subregions remain strong—especially East Asia—links between subregions have weakened. Regional financial integration still lags far behind trade integration.

The slower-than-expected global economic recovery continues to take its toll on international trade. Against this backdrop, trade growth in Asia and the Pacific decelerated to 2.3% in 2015, below the 2.7% rate of global trade, and falling further behind growth in its gross domestic product. Developing Asia's exports grew 3.0% in 2015, on par with advanced economies, yet imports grew a meager 1.7%. In addition to anemic global growth, a slowdown in global value chain expansion and the PRC's economic shift away from export-oriented manufacturing contributed.

On the bright side, Asia and the Pacific remains the world's top destination for foreign direct investment (FDI), attracting $527 billion in 2015, up 9.0% from 2014. FDI helps achieve inclusive growth and regional integration. It contributes to economic development through physical and human capital accumulation as well as technological and knowledge transfers.

The report also notes the steady progress in the region's financial integration. Asia's greater financial openness saw its cross-border portfolio investment and bank claims increase from $3 trillion in 2001 to $11 trillion in 2015. However, the intraregional share remains low at 20% of the total cross-border portfolio investment and bank claims by residents—compared with the EU's 59% intraregional share.

Remittances and tourism receipts are increasingly important and stable sources of external finance for many developing Asian economies. In 2015, however, remittances to South Asia and Central Asia fell sharply as share of GDP due to soft oil prices and the economic slump in the Middle East and the Russian Federation. This trend is expected to continue in 2016. Migration is the most important driver of remittances for developing Asia. Inter-subregional migration can help mitigate shortages of labor and skills in host economies while remittances can contribute to foreign exchange earnings in source countries.

Faced with heightened uncertainty, the region's policy makers need to continue to strengthen RCI to prop up regional trade and investment amid the weak global recovery while effectively managing spillovers from the PRC's economic shift.

Juzhong Zhuang
Deputy Chief Economist and Deputy Director General,
Economic Research and Regional Cooperation Department

Acknowledgments

The *Asian Economic Integration Report (AEIR) 2016* was prepared by the Regional Cooperation and Integration Division (ERCI) of ADB's Economic Research and Regional Cooperation Department (ERCD), under the overall supervision of ERCI Director Cyn-Young Park. Jong Woo Kang coordinated overall production assisted by Mara Claire Tayag. ERCI consultants under Technical Assistance 9121: Asian Economic Integration—Building Knowledge for Policy Dialogue contributed data compilation, research, and analysis.

Contributing authors include James Villafuerte and Joy Blesilda Sinay with data support from Pilar Dayag (Economic Outlook and Resilience); Jong Woo Kang, Mara Claire Tayag, Suzette Dagli, Dorothea Ramizo, and Paul Mariano (Trade and Global Value Chain); Junkyu Lee, Peter Rosenkranz, and Ana Kristel Molina (Financial Integration); and Fahad Khan and Grendell Vie Magoncia (Movement of People). The chapter "Subregional Cooperation Initiatives" is contributed by regional departments of ADB: Giovanni Capannelli and Ronaldo Oblepias (Central and West Asia); Greater Mekong Subregion Secretariat (Southeast Asia); Yuebin Zhang, Cris Lozano, and Ying Qian (East Asia); Ronald Antonio Butiong (South Asia); and Paul Curry and Rommel Rabanal (Pacific). The regional value chain analysis in "Trade and Global Value Chain" benefitted from construction of input-output tables by a team headed by Mahinthan J. Mariasingham from ERCD's Development Economics and Indicators Division.

Fahad Khan, Junkyu Lee, and Jong Woo Kang coordinated and contributed to the production of the "Special Theme: What Drives Foreign Direct Investment in Asia and the Pacific?" Background papers were provided by Natalia Ramondo, Hyun-Hoon Lee, Rodolphe Desbordes, and Julien Chaisse. Benjamin Endriga, Ma. Concepcion Latoja, Jesson Pagaduan, and Suzette Dagli provided research support.

Guy Sacerdoti, James Unwin, and Eric van Zant edited the manuscripts. Ariel Paelmo typeset and produced the layout, Erickson Mercado created the cover design and assisted in typesetting, and Cherry Zafaralla proofread the manuscript. Support for *AEIR 2016* printing and publishing was provided by the Printing Services Unit of ADB's Office of Administrative Services and by the publishing team of the Department of External Relations. Paulo Rodelio Halili, Carol Ongchangco, Pia Asuncion Tenchavez, Maria Criselda Aherrera, and Susan Monteagudo provided administrative and secretarial support, and helped organize the AEIR workshop. Erik Churchill of the Department of External Relations coordinated dissemination of *AEIR 2016*.

Definitions

The economies covered in the *Asian Economic Integration Report 2016* (AEIR 2016) are grouped by major analytic or geographic group.

- Asia refers to the 48 Asia and the Pacific members of the Asian Development Bank (ADB), which includes Japan and Oceania (Australia and New Zealand) in addition to the 45 Developing Asian economies.
- Developing Asia comprises the 45 developing members of ADB as listed below:
  - Central Asia comprises Armenia, Azerbaijan, Georgia, Kazakhstan, the Kyrgyz Republic, Tajikistan, Turkmenistan, and Uzbekistan.
  - East Asia comprises the People's Republic of China; Hong Kong, China; the Republic of Korea; Mongolia; and Taipei,China.
  - South Asia comprises Afghanistan, Bangladesh, Bhutan, India, the Maldives, Nepal, Pakistan, and Sri Lanka.
  - Southeast Asia comprises Brunei Darussalam, Cambodia, Indonesia, the Lao People's Democratic Republic, Malaysia, Myanmar, the Philippines, Singapore, Thailand, and Viet Nam.
  - The Pacific comprises the Cook Islands, Fiji, Kiribati, the Marshall Islands, the Federated States of Micronesia, Nauru, Papua New Guinea, Palau, Samoa, Solomon Islands, Timor-Leste, Tonga, Tuvalu, and Vanuatu.

Unless otherwise specified, the symbol "$" and the word "dollar" refer to US dollars. ADB recognizes "China" as the People's Republic of China; "Hong Kong" as Hong Kong, China; "Korea" as the Republic of Korea; and "Vietnam" as Viet Nam.

Abbreviations

ABCI	Almaty–Bishkek Corridor Initiative
ABF	Asian Bond Fund
ABO	AsianBonds Online
ABIF	ASEAN Banking Integration Framework
ABMF	ASEAN+3 Bond Market Forum
ABMI	Asian Bond Markets Initiative
ACMF	ASEAN Capital Markets Forum
AEC	ASEAN Economic Community
AFC	Asian financial crisis
AFIF	ASEAN Financial Integration Framework
AMBIF	ASEAN+3 Multi-currency Banking Integration Framework
AMRO	ASEAN+3 Macroeconomic Research Office
ASEAN	Association of Southeast Asian Nations (Brunei Darussalam, Cambodia, Indonesia, the Lao People's Democratic Republic, Malaysia, Myanmar, the Philippines, Singapore, Thailand, and Viet Nam)
ASEAN+3	ASEAN plus the People's Republic of China, Japan, and the Republic of Korea
ASP	ASEAN Surveillance Process
BIMSTEC	Bay of Bengal Initiative for Multi-sectoral Technical and Economic Cooperation
BIT	bilateral investment treaty
CAREC	Central Asia Regional Economic Cooperation
CASP	Core Agriculture Support Program
CEPII	Centre d'Etudes Prospectives et d'Informations Internationales (Institute for Research on the International Economy)
CGIF	Credit Guarantee and Investment Facility
CIS	Collective Investment Scheme
CMI	Chiang Mai Initiative
CMIM	Chiang Mai Initiative Multilateralization
CSIF	Cross-border Settlement Infrastructure Forum
DCC	dynamic conditional correlation
DMCs	Developing Member Countries
DTT	double taxation treaty
DVA	domestic value added
ECB	European Central Bank
EMEAP	Executives' Meeting of East Asia Pacific
EPA	Economic Partnership Agreement
ERPD	Economic Review and Policy Dialogue
EU	European Union (Austria, Belgium, Bulgaria, Croatia, Cyprus, Czech Republic, Denmark, Estonia, Finaland, France, Germany, Grece, Hungary, Ireland, Italy, Latvia, Lithuania, Luxembourg, Malta, the Netherlands, Poland, Portugal, Romania, Slovak Republic, Slovenia, Spain, Sweden, and the United Kingdom)
euro area	Austria, Belgium, Cyprus, Estonia, Finland, France, Germany, Greece, Ireland, Italy, Latvia, Lithuania, Luxembourg, Malta, the Netherlands, Portugal, Slovak Republic, Slovenia, and Spain
FDI	foreign direct investment

FMI	financial market infrastructure
FSL	Fianancial Service Liberalization
FSM	Federated States of Micronesia
FTA	free trade agreement
FVA	foreign value added
G3	Group of Three (euro area, Japan, and the United States)
GDP	gross domestic product
GFC	global financial crisis
GMS	Greater Mekong Subregion
GUH	global ultimate headquarters
GVC	global value chain
IIA	international investment agreement
IMF	International Monetary Fund
ICT	information and communications technology
ISDM	investor-state dispute mechanism
M&A	merger and acquisition
NPL	nonperforming loan
OECD	Organisation for Economic Co-operation and Development
OLS	ordinary least squares
PDC	purely double-counted terms
PPML	Poisson Pseudo-Maximum Likelihood
PRC	People's Republic of China
RCEP	Regional Comprehensive Economic Partnership
RDV	returned value added
REER	real effective exchange rate
RER	real exchange rate
ROW	rest of the world
RTA	regional trade agreement
RTGS	real-time gross settlement
RTIA	regional trade and investment agreement
SAARC	South Asian Association for Regional Cooperation
SASEC	South Asia Subregional Economic Cooperation
SEZ	special economic zone
SPS	sanitary and phytosanitary
TAPI	Turkmenistan-Afghanistan-Pakistan-India
TBT	technical barriers to trade
TPP	Trans-Pacific Partnership
TUTAP	Turkministan-Uzbekistan-Tajikistan-Afghanistan-Pakistan
UNCTAD	United Nations Conference on Trade and Development
UNESCAP	United Nations Economic and Social Commission for Asia and the Pacific
UNWTO	United Nations World Tourism Organization
UK	United Kingdom
US	United States
VIX	Chicago Board Options Exchange's Volatility Index
WGI	World Governance Indicators
WTO	World Trade Organization
y-o-y	year-on-year

Highlights

Trade and Investment

- **With the continued anemic global economic recovery, trade growth in Asia and the Pacific decelerated in 2015, falling further behind growth in gross domestic product.** Asia's trade growth by volume decelerated to 2.3% in 2015, below the 2.7% growth in global trade, and falling further below the region's gross domestic product (GDP) growth rate of 5.3%.[1] Developing Asia's exports grew 3.0% in 2015, on par with advanced economies. But imports grew a meager 1.7% compared with 4.5% in advanced economies. The slower-than-expected global economic recovery was the main culprit, but other structural and policy factors also played a role—including a slowdown in global value chain (GVC) expansion and the People's Republic of China (PRC)'s economic shift away from low-cost manufacturing. Rising protectionism has become an increasing concern to international trade prospects. The number of antidumping duty cases against the region's exporters increased from 181 in 2011 to 279 in 2015.

- **Trade linkages within subregions have continued to strengthen, while inter-subregional trade linkages weakened.** Asian economies traded with regional partners well beyond what geographical, cultural, or economic proximity can explain; with 57.1% of total trade intraregional. By subregion, trade integration—measured by the share of intraregional trade in total trade—is strongest in East Asia, followed by Southeast Asia and Central Asia. However, trade across subregions weakened.

- **The effect of exchange rates on trade has softened in recent years partly due to the expansion of GVCs, while the negative impact from nontariff barriers has become more significant.** After the global financial crisis (GFC), a 1% depreciation in exchange rate is estimated to have increased export volumes by just 0.27%, less than half the level prior to the GFC—and the effect is more short-lived. The use of foreign inputs associated with the region's GVC participation may partly offset the impact of exchange rate movements on exports. However, nontariff measures have become major obstacles to trade. The number of trade remedies (such as antidumping and countervailing duties and safeguards), sanitary and phytosanitary (SPS) measures, and technical barriers to trade has been rising, with negative effects on developing Asia's exports. Agriculture trade is particularly susceptible to adverse impact of SPS measures.

---

[1] In this report, Asia refers to the 48 Asia and the Pacific members of the Asian Development Bank (ADB), including the region's three advanced economies —Australia, Japan, and New Zealand, while developing Asia refers to ADB's 45 developing member economies..

- **Asia continues to be the world's top destination for foreign direct investment, attracting $527 billion in 2015, up 9.0% over 2014.** Global foreign direct investment (FDI) increased to a record $1.8 trillion in 2015, with nearly 30% going to the region. Outward FDI from Asia and the Pacific declined to $418 billion, down 9.4% from 2014. Intraregional FDI (from and to Asia and the Pacific) has increased over time (about 52.6% of total FDI inflows to the region in 2015). East Asia received 60% of total intraregional inflows in 2015, with Southeast Asia attracting 24%. FDI in Asia is driven predominantly by export-oriented multinationals investing in manufacturing (See "Special Theme: What Drives Foreign Direct Investment in Asia and the Pacific?").

Finance

- **Financial integration continues to increase gradually in the region; but still lags far behind trade integration.** With greater financial openness, Asia's cross-border portfolio investment and bank claims increased from $3.0 trillion in 2001 to $11.0 trillion in 2015. However, Asia's share in global cross-border portfolio investment and bank claims remained a modest 16.2% in 2015, slightly up from 14.1% in 2001. The degree of regional financial integration also pales when compared with regional trade integration. In 2015, while intraregional trade was nearly 60% of Asia's total trade, intraregional cross-border portfolio investment and bank claims were just about 20% of the region's total.

- **Asia's financial links with the rest of the world remain stronger than those within the region.** Asia's cross-border portfolio investment and bank claims primarily go to a few large economies outside the region. As of 2015, the main destinations for the region's portfolio investment were the United States (US) (37.7%) and the European Union (EU) (25.4%) for debt; and the US (25.8%), Cayman Islands (25.0%), and the EU (14.6%) for equity. The intraregional investment share remained low at 17.9% for debt and 19.8% for equity—compared with the EU's intraregional share at 65.5% for debt and 55.7% for equity. Asia's cross-border bank claims are also mainly directed outside the region—29.4% to the US and 27.2% to the EU. Asia's cross-border bank liabilities are primarily concentrated in the EU (36.9%) and the US (32.9%).

- **Financial flows have become more stable since the GFC.** Capital flow volatility (measured by standard deviation normalized by GDP) across all types of investment flows—equity, debt, FDI, and other investment flows— declined in the 2009–2015 post-GFC period compared with the 1999–2007pre-GFC period. The drop in volatility suggests more stable capital flows to the region, which may have benefited from various regional initiatives. These include macroprudential and capital flow management measures aimed at strengthening financial stability and deepening the regions' capital markets—particularly local currency bond markets. Other contributing factors could be strengthened capital and liquidity standards, enhanced supervision, and the improving quality of financial market infrastructure.

Movement of People

- **Migration from Asia increased between 2010 and 2015—although the increase was directed more to outside Asia than within the region.** Asia and the Pacific is the largest source of international migrants (83.3 million), accounting for more than a third of the 243.7 million migrants worldwide as of 2015.[2] Asia and the Pacific is also a host to more than 42 million international migrants—up from around 40 million in 2010. However, Asia's intraregional migration (30.6 million) as a proportion of its total outbound migration decreased slightly—from 38.0% in 2010 to 36.7% in 2015.

- **Economic factors—such as better living conditions and job opportunities—are often behind the attraction of voluntary international migration.** Among seven Asian economies with 2015 GDP per capita above $20,000, six posted net inbound migration—the exception was the Republic of Korea. By contrast, those with GDP per capita below $20,000 showed net outbound migration. Migration is a significant determinant of home country remittances. A 1 percentage point increase in a given economy's outward migrant stock as share of total population is estimated to increase remittances as a share of GDP by almost 0.3 percentage point.

- **Remittances and tourism receipts play an important role in economic growth and development in many Asia and the Pacific economies.** Remittances and tourism receipts are an increasingly important and stable source of external financing for many developing Asian economies. On average, remittances in 2015 accounted for 1% of GDP ($271.1 billion) in Asia and the Pacific including the region's more advanced economies. South Asia and Central Asia are most dependent on remittances—for example, the remittance receipts in Nepal and Tajikistan reached 31.5% and 28.9% of their respective GDP in 2015. A slowdown in remittances from the Middle East and the Russian Federation due to the oil price plunge and the economic slump underscores the growing challenges of economic diversification and strengthening competitiveness in these subregions. In 2014, Asia and the Pacific received the second largest amount of tourism receipts ($341.8 billion, or 24% of the global total) after the EU ($470.4 billion, or 33%). Tourism receipts in the Pacific reached almost 6% of GDP, compared with the regional average of 1.4%. Smaller island nations such as the Maldives, Palau, and Vanuatu are most vulnerable to volatility in tourist flows with more than 30% of GDP coming from tourism receipts.

Special Theme: What Drives Foreign Direct Investment in Asia and the Pacific?

Characteristics of FDI in Asia and the Pacific

- **FDI contributes to inclusive growth and development by facilitating trade along with technology and skill transfer.** FDI's contribution to output by stimulating investment in new infrastructure, other facilities, and boosting production is widely recognized. However, benefits are not automatic and vary by "type" of FDI and subject to the specific economy contexts—the host economy's development stage, absorptive capacity, and investment climate, among others. For example, FDI in extractive industries often proved less beneficial to the host economy, which might have been the cases for unsuccessful FDI experiences in some Central Asian economies. Economic, institutional, and policy factors also exert considerable influence over a firm's decision on whether or how to invest.

---

[2]   The United Nations Population Division defines "migrants" as foreign-born population (see "Chapter 4: Movement of People").

- **Greenfield investments have been preferred to merger and acquisitions (M&As) as a mode of entry for FDI in Asia and the Pacific.** FDI can be made through (i) greenfield investments (investments in new assets) or (ii) M&As (takeovers or acquiring existing firms). Firm-level data suggest that, historically, greenfield investments have been the dominant mode of entry for multinationals investing in Asia, although M&As have increased rapidly in recent years. Greenfield FDI is the more common mode of entry in manufacturing, with M&As favored more for services.

- **Asian multinationals tend to engage more in GVC-FDI than those outside the region.** FDI can be categorized by the multinational's investment motivation: (i) to avoid trade barriers and gain better access to local markets by replicating production activities done elsewhere (horizontal FDI); or (ii) to lower costs by placing specific production stages where there is comparative advantage (vertical FDI). Together, vertical and export-oriented FDI can be viewed as GVC investment (GVC-FDI). Firm-level data show most GVC-FDI in Asia is in manufacturing. Japan is the largest source of GVC-FDI in Asia, followed by the Republic of Korea.

- **"Factory Asia" still helps explain GVC-FDI in Asia and the Pacific.** Empirical findings suggest product specialization near the final stage of production processes helps attract GVC-FDI in the region. Developing economies can take advantage of relatively low wages and abundant labor to attract more GVC-FDI.

Determinants of FDI in Asia and the Pacific

- **Institutional quality matters for FDI, particularly M&As.** Among the factors associated with comparative advantage, institutions (or governance), the business environment, and regional integration, the most important driver of FDI in Asia is the quality of institutions measured by perception-based governance indicators. The effect of institutional quality is greater for M&As, although it is significant and positive for greenfield FDI as well. By source economy, FDI from high-income economies is most sensitive to the level of governance in destination economies. By sector, FDI targeting resources are least sensitive.

- **A better business environment can complement the level of governance quality in destination economies.** The business environment—as measured by the Ease of Doing Business indicator—has a positive impact on FDI, with the impact even greater where there is a relatively lower level of governance. Among indicators of the business environment, the ease of "registering property" is most important for attracting greenfield investments, while the ease of "getting credit" matters most for attracting M&As.

- **Regional Trade Agreements help attract north-south FDI.** Regional trade agreements increase greenfield FDI from high-income to low-income economies, perhaps by helping improve the business environment and cutting trade costs. Meanwhile, its effect is negative for greenfield FDI among developing economies—particularly in manufacturing and services—suggesting that FDI among developing economies might be driven more by tariff jumping and market seeking rather than the desire for an export platform for external trade. Nonetheless, the effect of longer-term trade and investment promotion is expected to outweigh a more short-term substitution effect.

- **Greater domestic production fragmentation helps attract more GVC-FDI.** Production fragmentation entails compartmentalizing the production process into small incremental steps. Deepening input-output linkages among parent companies and their industry affiliates not only expands domestic value chains but strengthens an industry's GVC linkages. This helps promote trade in intermediate components and the vertical FDI typically associated with GVCs. Low trade barriers of the host economy also help attract GVC-FDI.

- **Bilateral investment treaties (BITs) are important international policy tools in spurring FDI.** Despite the growing heterogeneity in the scope and depth of BITs, the treaties generally help both greenfield FDI and M&As. Empirical findings suggest that having investor-state dispute mechanisms (ISDMs) is most effective for BITs to attract FDI—it can increase the number of FDI projects by 35.3%. Separately, nondiscrimination provisions—such as national treatment and most-favored nation clauses in regional trade agreement investment chapters—are the most effective element in attracting FDI.

Policy Implications

- **Determinants of FDI vary by mode of entry, a firm's motivation for entering, industrial sector, and the characteristics of source and host economies.** Policymakers need to carefully consider the different types of investment that may best suit their development strategies when devising FDI policy on incentives and facilitation in the context of an economy's development stage, comparative advantage, and industrial structure.

- **Strong political will and commitment help attract FDI in developing Asia.** Good governance and quality institutions of the host economy are the most important determinants of a multinational's FDI decisions. Credible policy reforms creating better governance and institutions maximize the host economy's chances of attracting productive FDI. Also, the inclusion of ISDMs into BITs signals a government's commitment to honoring the interests of foreign investors and their investments.

- **A good investment climate is vital in fostering productive private investment—either domestic or foreign.** Creating an investment friendly environment encourages private investment that is key to strong economic growth and rapid poverty reduction. Upgrading the business environment is particularly important for economies with relatively weaker institutions to attract FDI inflows, as improving the general quality of institutions would often require comprehensive and painstaking reforms.

- **Developing economies need to further develop domestic value chains in manufacturing to attract GVC-FDI.** Building strong backward and forward linkages among domestic firms in manufacturing could help facilitate GVC-FDI from multinationals. This could be particularly relevant to economies in Central Asia and South Asia, which have yet to adequately link their manufacturing industries to international production networks.

1 | Economic Outlook and Resilience

Economic Outlook and Resilience

Economic Outlook

Despite an unfavorable external environment, developing Asia is expected to maintain 5.7% growth in 2016 and 2017, buoyed by resilience in the region's largest economies, the People's Republic of China and India.

The recovery in the Group of Three (G3) economies of the euro area, Japan and the United States (US), continues to stall. The US growth in the first half of 2016 was softer on low investment and weak trade. Going forward, there are lingering concerns that significant policy changes by the Trump government—repeal of the Dodd-Frank law, restructuring of energy and immigration policies, and imposing more trade restrictions—could affect growth prospects. In Japan, growth improved, although the rising yen in the second half of 2016 weighed heavily on exports. While the growth outlook in the euro area held steady in 2016, political uncertainties have added to downside risks (Table 1.1).

Growth in the People's Republic of China (PRC) in the first half of 2016 eased to 6.7% from 7.0% in the same period last year, as reforms to restructure the economy away from export-led growth toward consumption continued. Private consumption and services contributed most to growth, in line with the government's goal of attaining balanced and sustainable growth. In India, steady progress of reforms boosted its growth prospects. In June 2016, the approval of wage and pension increases enhanced private consumption; and a new law creating a national value added tax are expected to strengthen India's fiscal position and lift investor confidence.

Table 1.1: Regional GDP Growth (%, y-o-y)

	2013	2014	2015	Forecast 2016	Forecast 2017
Developing Asia	6.5	6.3	5.9	5.7	5.7
Central Asia	6.6	5.2	3.0	1.5	2.6
East Asia	6.8	6.6	6.1	5.8	5.6
People's Republic of China	7.8	7.3	6.9	6.6	6.4
South Asia	6.2	6.7	7.0	6.9	7.3
India	6.6	7.2	7.6	7.4	7.8
Southeast Asia	5.0	4.5	4.4	4.5	4.6
The Pacific	3.9	9.4	7.2	2.7	3.5
Major Industrialized Economies					
Euro area	-0.2	1.1	1.9	1.5	1.4
Japan	1.4	-0.1	0.6	0.6	0.8
United States	1.7	2.4	2.6	1.5	2.4

GDP = gross domestic product, y-o-y = year-on-year.
Notes: Developing Asia refers to the 45 regional members of ADB, while subregional groupings are based on ADB's *Asian Development Outlook*. Aggregates weighted by gross national income levels (Atlas method, current $) from World Development Indicators, World Bank. Figures are based on ADB estimates except for the People's Republic of China, India, euro area, Japan, and the United States, which are actual values. ADB forecasts from *Asian Development Outlook Update 2016*.
Sources: ADB calculations using data from ADB (2016b); CEIC; World Bank. World Development Indicators. http://data.worldbank.org/data-catalog/world-development-indicators (accessed October 2016).

Strong growth is expected to continue in Southeast Asia on higher export prices for commodities and rising infrastructure investment. This should offset the impact of the drought that caused agriculture to contract during the first half of 2016 across the region, except in Indonesia. In Central Asia, low oil prices continue to cloud growth forecasts. The recession in the Russian Federation is affecting growth in remittance-dependent economies. In the Pacific's large economies, cyclone damage and fiscal difficulties are weighing heavily on growth this year, although stronger tourism receipts could help stimulate growth in South Pacific economies in 2017.

Economic Shocks and Risks

Asia has been hit by a multitude of shocks with high cost implications.

Natural disasters, economic and financial crises, and oil and food price shocks affected Asian economies over the last half-century. Some of these shocks ended in loss of lives, economic and social dislocations, and financial losses and economic costs (Figure 1.1). The frequency of these shocks appears to have increased, with nine shocks hitting the region since 2005. While there is no simple way to quantify the full impact of these shocks,

anecdotal evidence suggests the costs of these shocks are increasing. For instance, the $70 billion estimated annual average damage to the region from natural disasters since 2005 is almost double the estimated $36.6 billion in annual average damage recorded since 1975 (both in 2010 prices).

Table 1.2 presents a peak versus trough analysis of the cumulative impact economic shocks had on Asia's gross domestic product (GDP) growth.[1] It clearly shows these shocks brought down average GDP growth in the region by 4–13 percentage points, with the largest decline in growth (almost 28 percentage points) observed during the 1997/98 Asian financial crisis. The effects of these

Figure 1.1: GDP Growth, Shocks, and Cost of Natural Disasters—Asia

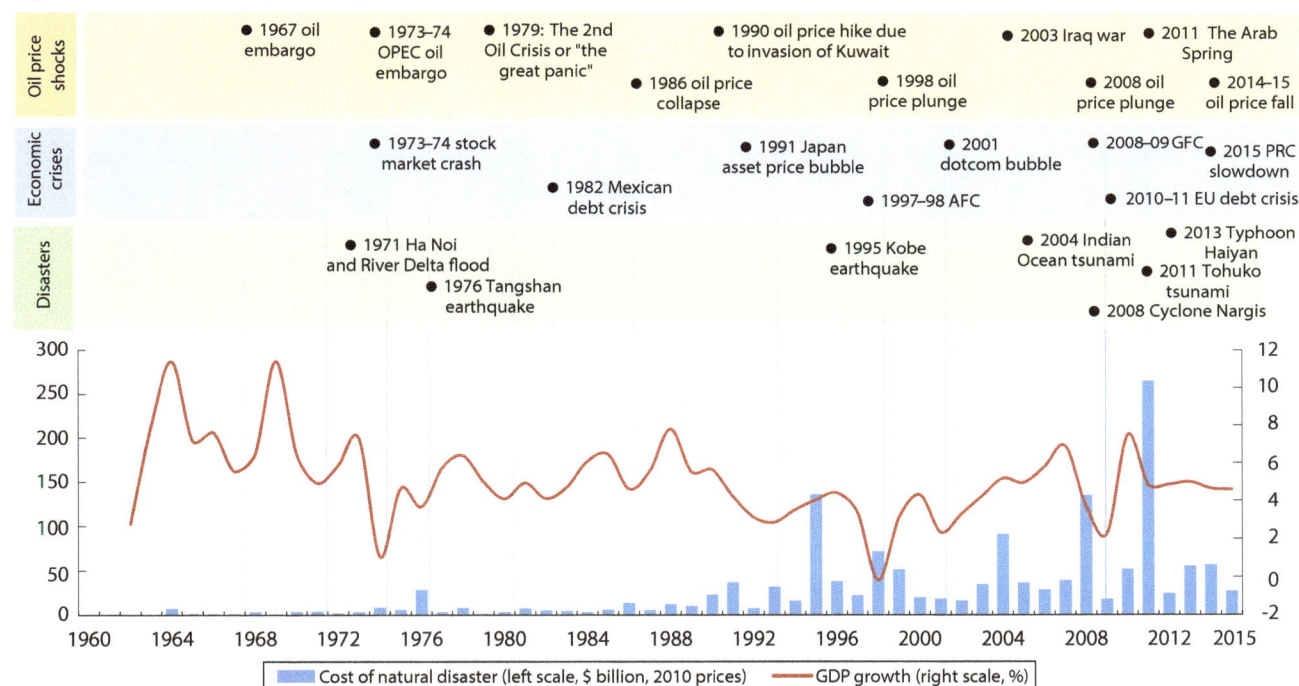

AFC = Asian financial crisis, PRC = People's Republic of China, EU = European Union, GDP = gross domestic product, GFC = global financial crisis, OPEC = Organization of the Petroleum Exporting Countries.
Notes: Aggregate GDP growth weighted using gross national income (Atlas method current $). Natural disasters include epidemic, insect infestation, extreme temperature, drought, flood, mass movement (wet and dry), wildfires, earthquakes, volcanic eruptions, and storms. Total damage costs hold direct (e.g., damage to infrastructure, crops, housing) and indirect (e.g., loss of revenues, unemployment, market destabilization) consequences for the local economy.
Sources: ADB calculations using data from Centre for Research on the Epidemiology of Disasters. EM-DAT The International Disaster Database. http://www.emdat.be/database; and International Monetary Fund. World Economic Outlook April 2016 Database. https://www.imf.org/external/pubs/ft/weo/2016/01/weodata/index.aspx (both accessed September 2016).

[1]   The peak versus trough analysis is applied to huge shocks that affected the output growth of economies in the region. The analysis compares the highest growth prior to the occurrence of a shock with the lowest growth after the shock. The impact is then calculated as the growth differential in percentage points and the duration as the number of quarters before the lowest point of the growth path is reached.

Table 1.2: GDP Growth Impact of Economic Crises on Developing Asia (peak versus trough)

Crisis	Drop in GDP growth[a] (y-o-y, % points)			Duration of Impact[b] (no. of quarters)		
	Average	Minimum	Maximum	Average	Minimum	Maximum
1991 Japan asset price bubble	−4.0	−0.8	−13.2	4	2	7
1997/98 Asian financial crisis	−12.9	−3.1	−27.8	6	3	9
2001 dotcom bubble	−7.1	−0.8	−14.5	6	3	8
2008/09 global financial crisis	−10.7	−4.2	−17.5	6	5	9
2010/11 EU debt crisis	−8.1	−0.8	−15.9	8	5	11

EU = European Union, GDP = gross domestic product; y-o-y = year-on-year.
[a]The drop in GDP growth was computed as the difference between peak and trough during each crisis period.
[b]The duration of impact is the number of quarters covering the peak and trough during each crisis period.
Notes: Minimum, maximum, and average values across sample economies in developing Asia, which includes the People's Republic of China; Hong Kong, China; India; Indonesia; the Republic of Korea; Malaysia; the Philippines; Singapore; Taipei,China; and Thailand. For each shock, the drop in GDP growth and duration from the peak up to trough was computed.
Source: ADB calculations using data from Oxford Economics.

shocks persisted for nearly six quarters on average. Their magnitude and duration have also fluctuated, with big shocks observed during the Asian financial crisis and the global financial crisis, and smaller shocks recorded in between. Some economies in the region cope better with shocks than others.

Downside risks to the outlook could disrupt the region's growth trajectory.

Externally, the slow recovery in the euro area, Japan, and the US continues to pose downside risks to developing Asia's projected economic growth. Interest rate hikes by the US Federal Reserve, though the timing remains uncertain, could disrupt the region's capital flows and complicate the macroeconomic environment. The pushback against globalization and increasing political pressures against trade openness could create more hurdles to the trade environment, potentially slowing the progress of regional integration. More so, recent political events—such as the Brexit vote in June 2016 and Trump's victory in the US election—suggest a rising tide of anti-globalization and anti-establishment sentiment among parts of the electorate worldwide. These events could increase global uncertainty and erode confidence on global institutions.

The slowdown in the PRC continues to cast a shadow on trade growth in the region (Box 1.1). Private sector debt—incurred either through direct borrowing or intercompany lending—continues to rise in many economies. Alongside borrowing by Asian companies, growing household debt

is also an increasing concern in some economies. These debts could prove unsustainable should interest rates rise sharply.

Given these frequent and costly shocks, economies need to build economic resilience in the region through early identification of potential vulnerabilities.[2]

Building Economic Resilience

The concept of economic resilience is complex and can mean many things to many people.

Broadly speaking, the word resilience comes from the Latin word *resilire—to recoil or leap back.*

In economics, resilience refers to an economy's ability to withstand the impact of exogenous shocks such as those arising from financial contagion, commodity price volatility, or external demand shocks. This is similar to dampening the amplitude or the degree of change in economic activity arising from a shock (Duval et al. 2007). The literature refers to this as enhancing the

---

[2]   In this section, the discussion is confined to economic shocks arising from economic interdependence and global and regional spillovers. Necessarily, the notion of building resilience will also be limited to measures that can help economies mitigate the impact of these types of economic shocks.

Box 1.1: Drivers of Asian Output

A vector autoregression model is used to estimate the effects of external shocks on business cycles in emerging Asia. Asian business cycles are measured as the de-trended gross domestic product using a Hodrick-Prescott filter. External factors represent global and regional economic conditions that affect output in regional economies, including (i) the United States (US) output shock, a proxy of business cycle in advanced economies; (ii) the Chicago Board Options Exchange's Volatility (VIX) index, a measure of global financial risk; (iii) world trade growth; and (iv) an output shock in the People's Republic of China (PRC). These external factors are assumed unaffected by contemporaneous domestic shocks. Further, shocks to external factors are assumed to be transmitted in the same order as above.

The result from the variance decomposition shows that external factors drive most of the variation in output among the region's economies. This was particularly evident following the 1997/98 Asian financial crisis, when the impact of both US and PRC output shocks increased and became more persistent.

Share of Asia ex-PRC Output Variance Due to External and Local Factors (%, x-axis = number of quarters)

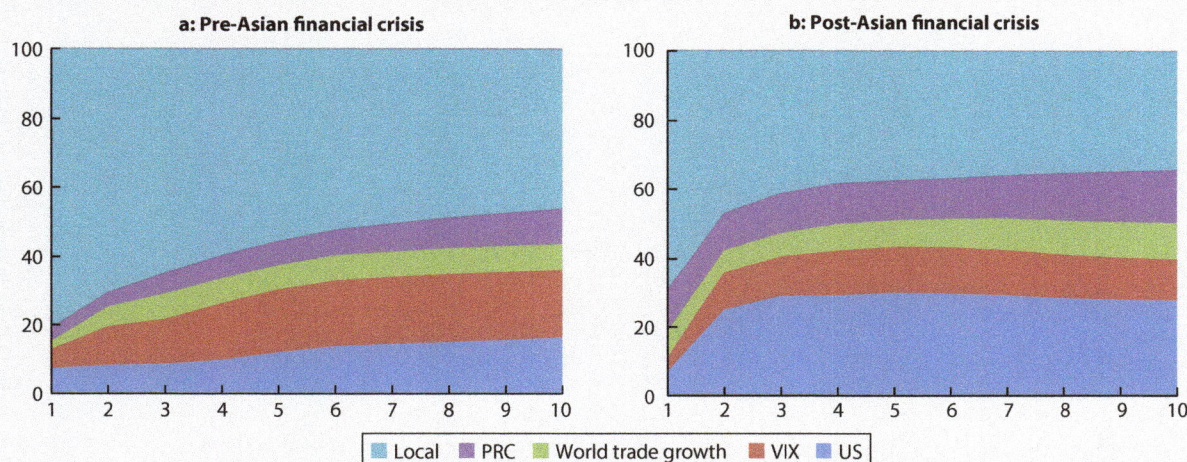

Asia ex-PRC = Asia excluding the PRC, PRC = People's Republic of China, US = United States, VIX = Chicago Board Options Exchange's Volatility Index.
Note: Pre-Asian financial crisis covers Q1 1987 up to Q1 1997. Post-Asian financial crisis covers Q1 1999 up to Q2 2016. Asia ex-PRC includes Hong Kong, China; Indonesia; the Republic of Korea; Malaysia; the Philippines; Singapore; Taipei,China; and Thailand. US, PRC, and individual Asia ex-PRC (local) output based on the Hodrick-Prescott filtered seasonally adjusted gross domestic product at constant prices.
Source: ADB calculations using data from Bloomberg; CEIC; Oxford Economics; and World Bank. World Development Indicators. http://data.worldbank.org/data-catalog/world-development-indicators (accessed November 2016).

absorptive capacity for resilience. Similarly, resilience could also be used to refer to an economy's ability to quickly recover from a shock and return to its long-term equilibrium. This is similar to minimizing the persistence of a shock and has been referred to as increasing the adaptive capacity for resilience.

An alternative notion of resilience is the ability of an economy to enhance and restructure its productive capacity so that the system improves its ability to deal with future shocks—sometimes called the transformative capacity for resilience.

Based on these definitions, Asia can build economic resilience by (i) improving the absorptive capacity of an economy to withstand shocks (ii) enhancing the adaptive capacity of an economy to recover or bounce back from shocks and (iii) strengthening the transformative capacity of an economy to upgrade and restructure its systems to boost economic resilience to future shocks.

Evidence suggests that good policies can enhance resilience to better cope with unforeseen economic shocks.

Briguglio et al. (2008) argue that policies contributing toward greater macroeconomic stability, microeconomic market efficiency, good governance, and social protection underpin economic resilience.

Figure 1.2 presents an economic framework for building economic resilience. In addition to policies already mentioned above, the framework incorporates the role of global and regional cooperation, and provides concrete policies as illustrations. In this framework, good governance and institutions serve as a platform or fulcrum to help implement good policies or deliver programs that can buttress economic resilience.

Figure 1.2: Building Economic Resilience—A Framework

		Absorptive capacity	Adaptive capacity	Transformative capacity	
Quality governance and strong institutions	**Macroeconomic policy**				
	Fiscal policy	Countercyclical fiscal policy (stimulus)	Budget strategy and tax system	Government spending on health and education	
	Infrastructure investment	Rebuilding and reconstruction	Investing in efficient and world class infrastructure		
	Monetary policy	Countercyclical monetary policy (interest rate cuts)	Enhancing monetary policy transmission	Deepening capital markets	
			Promoting financial inclusion		
	Exchange rate	Flexible exchange rate	Macroprudential policy		
	Microeconomic policy				
	Labor market	Labor regulations (contractualization, hiring, and firing)	Enhancing labor mobility (training and employment promotion)	Policy reform to enhance flexibility in the labor, capital, and product markets	Industrial labor relations
	Product market	Price controls and regulation Subsidies	Tax system Competition policy		Industrial policy
	Capital market		Financial inclusion (support to micro-enterprises and small and medium-size enterprises)		Capital market reform
	Technology and innovation		Programs to raise productivity	Fostering innovation	
	Social policy				
	Education	Cash transfer to support education and health	Inclusive and accessible education and health services	Access to education services	
	Health			Access to health and medical services	
	Social protection	Transfers and subsidies	Temporary employment programs	Insurance programs	
	Global and regional cooperation				
	Financial assistance and cooperation	Liquidity support, standby facilities, and swap arrangements		Official development assistance, grants, and loans	
	Economic surveillance and policy dialogue	Economic surveillance			
		Global and Regional Policy dialogues			

Source: ADB.

Macroeconomic Policy

In the short run, policymakers use countercyclical macroeconomic policies to cushion or mitigate the impact of economic shocks.

Sound macroeconomic policies can build resilience by enhancing an economy's absorptive capacity to withstand shocks. A good example is the set of prudent macroeconomic and flexible exchange rate policies often employed to boost aggregate demand and spark economic recovery. During the global financial crisis—amid dwindling external demand for Asian exports and tightening global liquidity—many economies cut interest rates to boost domestic consumption and investment, and ease liquidity in the system. They also supported a flexible exchange rate—which helped by altering the return differential between assets denominated in foreign currencies and those denominated in local currency—to stabilize economic fluctuations due to volatile capital flows. These coordinated actions helped create greater economic resilience to soften the crisis impact.

Another set of useful policy tools are countercyclical fiscal policies that help prop domestic demand in times of crisis. Sometimes, fiscal stimulus comes in the form of temporary employment programs through public (re)construction. Or it could come via natural stabilizers—policies and programs that help reduce fluctuations in economic activity through price movements; or by introducing offsetting adjustments in taxes or subsidies, for example. There are discretionary fiscal policies as well, such as unemployment assistance or subsidies. These instruments can cushion an economy from changes in the business cycle as they alter business costs and allow for some income redistribution, thereby helping businesses and households endure the impact of a shock.

Microeconomic Policy

Policies that enhance the flexibility of labor, capital, and product markets can also contribute to greater economic resilience.

Microeconomic policies that facilitate the reallocation of resources to more productive uses is one way to help raise the productivity of factors of production, and make the product market more efficient. In doing so, these policies enable the economy to recover more quickly from a shock and push the economy back toward its potential growth path. Augmented by strong institutions, these microeconomic policies can also raise market efficiency and help macroeconomic policies become more effective. For instance, financial sector and domestic capital market development can increase the efficiency of financial intermediation and boost productivity. Equally important, financial sector innovation—that creates new financial instruments or invests in high-technology financial infrastructure—can also enhance monetary and financial policy effectiveness, thereby increasing resilience. Similarly, flexible labor market institutions and policies can improve the effectiveness of automatic stabilizers, and multiply the impact of discretionary fiscal policy aimed at stimulating specific sectors (Sanchez et al. 2015).

Structural Reform Policy

Building resilient systems requires "sound and forward-looking policy options" to cope with future economic shocks.

Berkes (2007) describes how to build resilience—by improving the organization, internal processes, and production efficiency—to deal with change characterized by uncertainty and surprises. Consistent with this notion, many East and Southeast Asian economies are pursuing a range of reforms to make their economies more resilient in the aftermath of the global financial crisis. For instance, an analysis of over 10,000 firms in 13 developing economies in Asia confirms that obstacles like judicial bias, unequal access to finance, excessive labor regulation, poor electricity supply, and corruption impede the efficient allocation of factors across firms. Therefore, structural reforms to remove these obstacles can enhance firm efficiency, support economic dynamism, and move economies toward their frontier potential growth (ADB 2016a).

While some policies build a system's absorptive capacity, it could also weaken future adaptive capacity and undermine its ability to cope with shocks.

A good example is employment protection. In the face of an economic shock, this policy helps agents absorb the impact of a shock because their jobs remain secure. And if this is further linked to well-designed training programs, it will spark transformation toward a more resilient labor market system. However, employment protection could also weaken the system's adaptive capacity because it hinders the efficient reallocation of resources toward its most productive use. For instance, it has been pointed out that shūshin koyō—or the ancient practice of providing permanent employment—has weakened the ability of Japan's economy to rebound from economic recession, as companies are unable to reduce their staff complement and labor costs and become more competitive.

While pursuing structural reforms to boost resilience is good, they can also be very difficult to implement.

First, the gains from structural reforms are often not visible to everyone—making it difficult for policymakers to push the reform efforts. For example, the imposition of a duty on housing transactions in an attempt to manage a growing property bubble and make the housing market more resilient to potential shocks. Initially, imposing a duty would raise the cost of owning a house and would affect first home buyers, making it an unpopular policy. Second, there are also short-run adjustment costs associated with structural reform that distort perceptions on the gains from reform. For instance, while a more flexible labor market policy can strengthen an economy's resilience through faster reallocation of labor resources, it can be perceived as contributing to greater job insecurity. Finally, the costs and benefits of a reform might accrue to different groups of people—with some benefiting more than others. This would encourage greater opposition from those who would lose from reform efforts.

Global and Regional Cooperation

Asia needs to cooperate more to boost national and regional economic resilience.

To the extent that global and regional integration raises the probability of negative spillover effects through trade and finance, economic and financial policy cooperation is important to manage the risks arising from the integration process. Cooperation can focus on rule-making and monitoring to minimize negative spillovers. A good example is cooperation on establishing financial safety nets to mitigate the risks of contagion-exacerbating crises. Cooperation to increase the cross-border flows of goods, services, and people can also enhance resilience by expanding markets and improving resource allocation. This in turn helps economies diversify their markets and get better returns on their labor or capital. For instance, at the height of the global financial crisis, when external demand was weak, the big economies in the region provided alternative sources of demand for exports. Cooperation to enhance infrastructure connectivity and manage regional public goods (and public "bads") can also strengthen many aspects of regional resilience. For one, infrastructure connectivity facilitates the flow of goods, services, and people, raising overall productivity. Managing regional "public goods" allows economies to account for the social costs in providing public goods to help optimize outcomes (ADB 2013).

Regional policy dialogue allows authorities to prepare for global or regional contagion by better understanding its origins and transmission mechanisms.

Regional dialogue aims to prevent financial crises by (i) promoting information sharing, policy dialogue, and coordination; (ii) collaborating on financial, monetary, and fiscal issues of common interest; (iii) detecting early macroeconomic and financial vulnerabilities; and (iv) implementing swift, remedial policies. There are already many forums for regional economic information exchange, analysis, and policy dialogue, among them, the Association of Southeast Asian Nations (ASEAN) Surveillance Process for finance ministers; the Economic Review and Policy Dialogue process for ASEAN+3 (ASEAN plus the PRC, Japan, and the Republic of

Korea) finance ministers and central bank governors; transregional processes such as the Asia-Pacific Economic Cooperation finance ministers' meeting; and the Asia-Europe Meeting of finance ministers. Cooperation between regional and global policy dialogue is also a good idea.

Governance and Institutions

Political stability, good governance, and strong institutions are needed to support gains from good economic policies and programs and build resilience.

Good policies are only meaningful if they are appropriate, well-timed, effectively implemented, and delivered to those most vulnerable. This increasingly depends on political stability, quality of governance, and the presence of strong institutions.

Correlates of Economic Resilience

Vulnerability to international spillovers and contagion can be measured in several ways. For instance, trade openness or financial openness can be used to capture vulnerabilities arising from global shocks or those originating in major trade or financial centers, such as the US, the euro area, or the PRC (Röhn et al. 2015). In the context of disaster, size can also be associated with vulnerability as it limits the distribution of losses, meaning resilience could be higher if losses can be more widely distributed or shared across a bigger population or geographic area. Similarly, infrastructure can also gauge susceptability to macroeconomic shocks as it is key in supply-chain networks and during reconstruction (World Bank 2013). On the policy front, Briguglio et al. (2008) noted that resilience can be captured through macroeconomic stability, microeconomic efficiency, good governance, and social protection policies, among others.

Output and consumption growth volatility is examined below as a measure of vulnerability to international spillovers and contagion. The correlation of economy

characteristics and economy policy instruments with these volatility measures are then examined to identify whether there are economy characteristics or policy instruments that can help mitigate volatility in output and consumption growth.

Size and reliance on resources appear to contribute to greater economic vulnerability as measured by output and consumption growth volatility.

The volatility of GDP and consumption growth was plotted against size (measured by population) and reliance on resources (measured by terms of trade) (Figure 1.3).[3] The results—size is inversely correlated to GDP and consumption growth volatility while terms of trade is positively correlated—are not surprising and are generally consistent with economic theory (Figure 1.4).

Generally, small economies tend to be highly concentrated in a narrow set of economic activities, making them more vulnerable to natural disasters like cyclones or economic shocks (such as the global financial crisis). Many small economies also tend to face higher costs—due to limited scale—for providing

Figure 1.3: Volatility of Output and Consumption Growth versus Population, 2006–2015

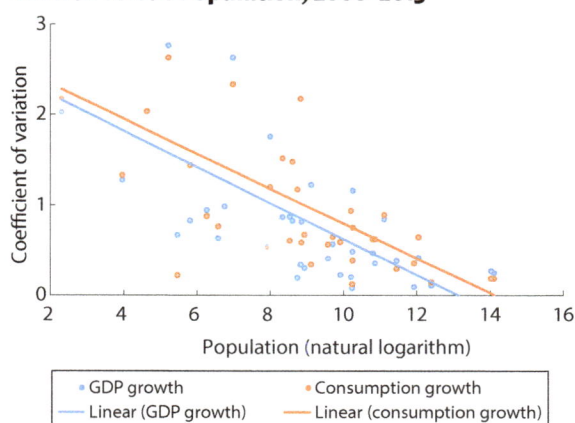

GDP = gross domestic product.
Sources: ADB calculations using data from United Nations Statistics Division. http://unstats.un.org/unsd/default.htm; and World Bank. World Development Indicators. http://data.worldbank.org/data-catalog/world-development-indicators (both accessed October 2016).

---

3   In this report, volatility is measured through the coefficient of variation in GDP growth and household consumption growth.

infrastructure such as power, health, and education. Size also coincides with geographical remoteness or sea- or land-locked economies. Thus, prices for food and energy will tend to be higher for small economies, making them more vulnerable to shocks. Similarly, relying on exports of natural resources could propel an economy toward greater output and consumption growth

Figure 1.4: Volatility of Output and Consumption Growth versus Terms of Trade, 2006–2015

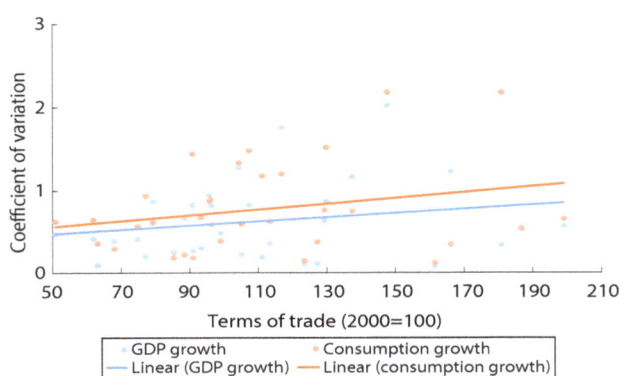

GDP = gross domestic product.
Notes: The terms of trade is the percentage ratio of the export unit value index to the import unit value index. The value index is the current value of exports or imports converted to the United States dollars and expressed as a percentage of the base period (2000).
Sources: ADB calculations using data from United Nations Conference on Trade and Development. http://unctadstat.unctad.org/EN/Index.html; and United Nations Statistics Division. http://unstats.un.org/unsd/default.htm (both accessed October 2016).

volatility, as prices of natural resources tend to exhibit greater volatility, which is also captured in output and consumption volatility.

Openness through trade and financial flows seems to increase economic exposure to the effects of global or regional shocks, increasing the volatility of output and consumption growth.

As seen in Figure 1.5, the volatility of GDP and consumption growth increases with both trade and capital account openness. Capital account openness shows a stronger positive link to volatility in both output and consumption growth. This result seems to confirm that capital flow volatility has become an important driver of economic vulnerability in Asia and the Pacific. Prior to the global financial crisis, Asia received strong capital inflows from nonresidents, reaching almost 10% of GDP of emerging Asian economies in 2007. However, during the crisis, in the fourth quarter of 2008, the region saw massive capital outflows equivalent to 14% of GDP. With open capital accounts, the region became more vulnerable to changes in risk appetite and global uncertainty, which affected output and consumption growth volatility (Box 1.1).

Figure 1.5: Volatility of Output and Consumption Growth versus Economic Openness, 2006–2015

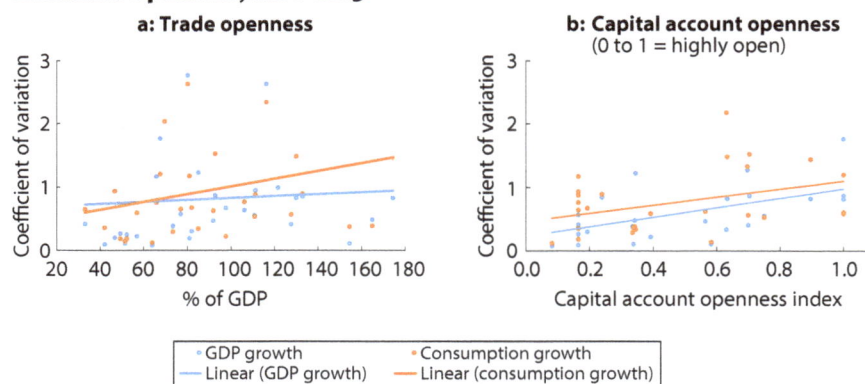

GDP = gross domestic product.
Notes: Trade openness is estimated as the sum of exports and imports of goods and services as a share of GDP. The capital account openness index or Chinn-Ito index is calculated using data on restrictions on cross-border financial transactions reported in the International Monetary Fund's Annual Report on Exchange Arrangements and Exchange Restrictions (AREAER). Coefficients of variation of GDP growth and consumption growth cover the period from 2006–2015; trade openness from 2006–2015; and capital account openness index from 2006–2014.
Sources: ADB calculations using data from United Nations Statistics Division. http://unstats.un.org/unsd/default. htm (accessed October 2016); and Chinn and Ito (2006).

A favorable pattern of structural transformation, from agrarian to modern industrial economy, for example, also contributes to greater economic resilience.

Clearly, structural transformation can contribute to resilience in many ways. Increasing the share of industrial employment, for example, tends to reduce output and consumption growth volatility (Figure 1.6). First, by their very nature, employment and income from agriculture tend to vary more than industry or manufacturing given

changes in weather and the increasing impact of climate change. Productivity levels in industry and manufacturing are also higher than in agriculture, such that switching employment toward manufacturing will lead to a more stable form of employment and income—contributing to greater economic resilience. This consequently supports the observation that to sustain growth, end poverty, and make economies more resilient, resources should be moved from low productivity (agriculture) to higher productivity (manufacturing) sectors.

Greater private savings and available credit can help provide greater economic resilience.

Dipping into savings or going into debt (some examples of household's coping strategies) can help smooth output and consumption growth volatility during economic shocks (Reyes et al. 2011) (Figure 1.7). Other coping strategies with similar impact include liquidating assets, seeking additional work, or looking for overseas employment.

Inadequate and low-quality infrastructure can undermine economic resilience.

Economic resilience can also be affected by the quality and availability of infrastructure and infrastructure services (Figure 1.8). Based on the scatterplots, it appears that economies with higher infrastructure scores—meaning they have better infrastructure, quality

Figure 1.6: Volatility of Output and Consumption Growth versus Employment Industry, 2006–2015

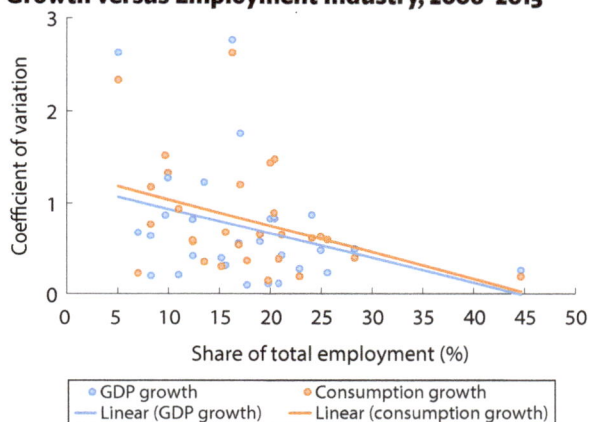

GDP = gross domestic product.
Sources: ADB calculations using data from United Nations Statistics Division. http://unstats.un.org/unsd/default.htm; and World Bank. World Development Indicators. http://data.worldbank.org/data-catalog/world-development-indicators (both accessed October 2016).

Figure 1.7: Volatility of Output and Consumption Growth versus Saving and Debt, 2006–2015

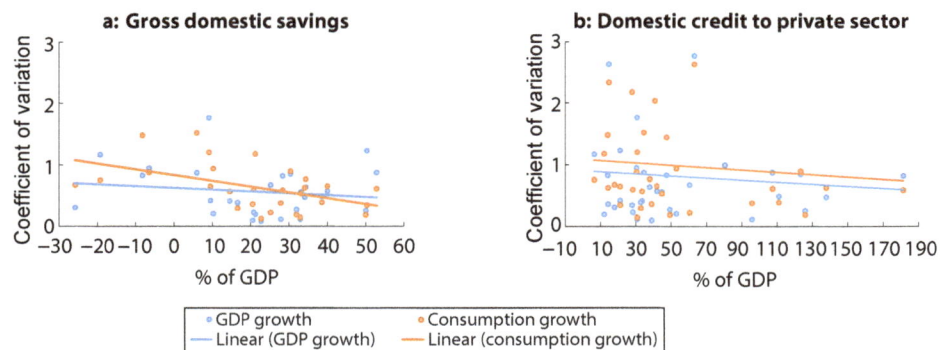

GDP = gross domestic product.
Notes: Gross domestic savings is GDP less total consumption. Domestic credit to private sector refers to financial resources provided to the private sector by financial corporations that establish a claim for repayment. For some economies, these claims include credit to public enterprises.
Sources: ADB calculations using data from United Nations Statistics Division. http://unstats.un.org/unsd/default.htm; and World Bank. World Development Indicators. http://data.worldbank.org/data-catalog/world-development-indicators (both accessed October 2016).

Figure 1.8: Volatility of Output and Consumption Growth versus Infrastructure Quality

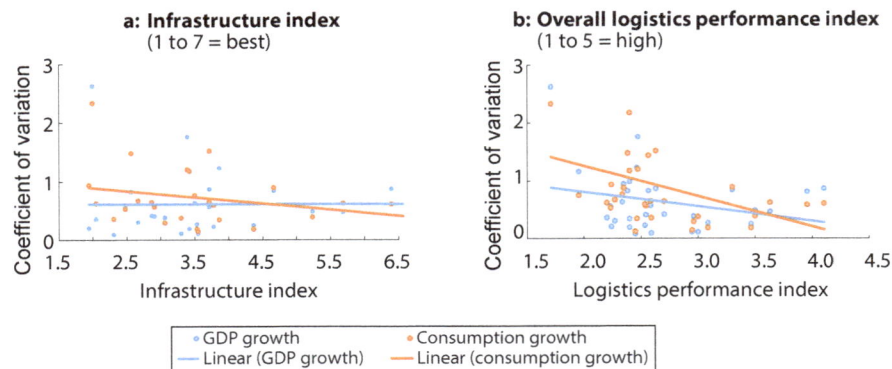

a: Infrastructure index
(1 to 7 = best)

b: Overall logistics performance index
(1 to 5 = high)

GDP = gross domestic product.
Notes: The infrastructure index is the arithmetic mean of transport, electricity, and telephone quality and availability indicators included in the second pillar of the Global Competitiveness Index. The overall logistics performance index reflects perceptions of a economy's logistics based on efficiency of customs clearance process, quality of trade- and transport-related infrastructure, ease of arranging competitively priced shipments, quality of logistics services, ability to track and trace consignments, and frequency with which shipments reach the consignee within the scheduled time. Coeffients of variation of GDP growth and consumption growth cover the period from 2006–2015; infrastructure index covers the peroid from 2007–2015; and logistics performance index include data from 2007, 2010, 2013, and 2014.
Sources: ADB calculations using data from United Nations Statistics Division. http://unstats.un.org/unsd/default.htm; World Economic Forum. Global Competitiveness Index. http://reports.weforum.org/global-competitiveness-index/; and World Development Indicators. http://data.worldbank.org/data-catalog/world-development-indicators (all accessed October 2016).

of trade and transport-related infrastructure, logistics performance index, and competence and quality of logistics services—exhibit lower volatility in output and consumption growth. These results are not surprising given that connectivity through infrastructure—particularly highways, roads, and bridges—is important when responding to natural disasters and economic shocks. But an even more important point is the need to build resilient infrastructure that can withstand shocks from natural disasters or black-swan events.

Good governance and social safety nets help build economic resilience.

Based on preliminary analysis, good governance—government effectiveness, rule of law, and regulatory quality—seems to be associated with lower volatility in output and consumption grow*th* (Figure 1.9). This is consistent with the general observation that good governance has always supported and reinforced gains from a range of economic policy reforms. In particular, without political stability, good governance, and strong institutions—key foundations for effective policy

implementation—good policies alone cannot contribute effectively to economic resilience.

Social protection policies as measured by the adequacy of social protection and labor programs seem to be positively associated with increased volatility in output and consumption growth (see Figure 1.9).

At first glance, this appears counterintuitive as social protection programs would be expected to offset the volatility in output and consumption growth. However, to the extent that social protection programs respond to economic shocks—function as ex-ante mechanisms—it follows that economies with greater volatility in output and consumption growth will also spend more on social protection. Hence, this result supports the observation that effective safety nets are needed to ensure food and job security, especially among vulnerable groups, during periods of economic shock.

Figure 1.9: Volatility of Output and Consumption Growth versus Governance and Social Protection, 2006–2015

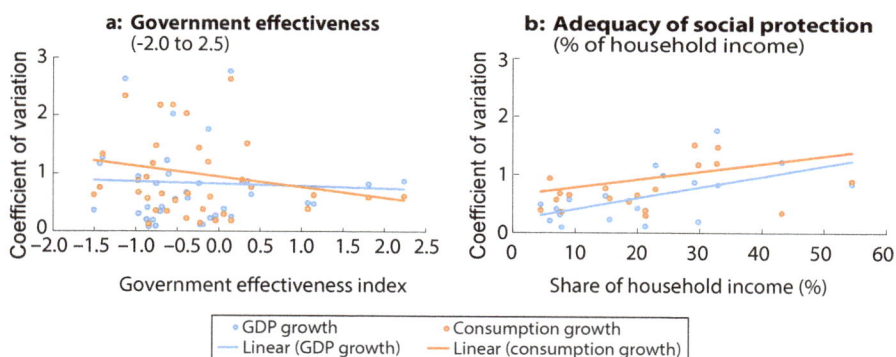

a: Government effectiveness (-2.0 to 2.5)

b: Adequacy of social protection (% of household income)

- GDP growth
- Consumption growth
- Linear (GDP growth)
- Linear (consumption growth)

GDP = gross domestic product.
Notes: Government effectiveness index captures perception of the quality of public services, the quality of the civil service and the degree of its independence from political pressures, the quality of policy formulation and implementation, and the credibility of the government's commitment to such policies. Adequacy of social protection and labor programs is measured by the total transfer amount received by the population participating in social insurance, social safety net, and unemployment benefits and active labor market programs as a share of their total welfare. Welfare is defined as the total income or total expenditure of beneficiary households.
Sources: ADB calculations using data from United Nations Statistics Division. http://unstats.un.org/unsd/default.htm; World Bank. World Development Indicators. http://data.worldbank.org/data-catalog/world-development-indicators; and World Bank. Worldwide Governance Indicators. http://data.worldbank.org/data-catalog/worldwide-governance-indicators (all accessed October 2016).

Policy Considerations

From the foregoing discussions, building economic resilience will entail building the resilience of various components and systems that make up the economy. It underscores the importance of appropriate interventions (through policies, programs, and projects) to develop economic resilience that is absorptive, adaptive, and transformative.

There are five important policy considerations that can help economies respond to large and unpredictable changes in demand: strong macroeconomic fundamentals, a flexible microeconomic structure, structural reform policies, social policies and programs, and strong global and regional cooperation. It will also require good governance and strong institutions to translate these good policies into action.

Finally, resilience can only be strengthened through the collective effort of policymakers from national and regional bodies, the academe, research, the private (and business) sector, and civil society to strengthen resilience thinking, risk analysis, and risk management.

References

ADB. 2013. *Regional Integration and Cooperation in a Changing World*. Manila.

———. 2016a. *Asian Development Outlook 2016: Asia's Potential Growth*. Manila.

———. 2016b. *Asian Development Outlook 2016 Update: Meeting the Low-Carbon Growth Challenge*. Manila.

F. Berkes. 2007. Understanding Uncertainty and Reducing Vulnerability: Lessons from Resilience Thinking. *Natural Hazards*. 41 (2): 283–295.

L. Briguglio et al. 2008. Economic Vulnerability and Resilience: Concepts and Measurements. *UNU-WIDER Research Paper*. No. 2008/55. Helsinki: United Nations University – World Institute for Development Economics Research.

M. Chinn, and H. Ito. 2006. What Matters for Financial Development? Capital Controls, Institutions, and Interactions. *Journal of Development Economics*. 81(1). pp.163–92.

R. Duval, J. Elmeskov, and L. Vogel. 2007. Structural Policies and Economic Resilience to Shocks. *OECD Economics Department Working Papers*. No. 567. Paris: Organization for Economic Cooperation and Development.

C. Reyes et al. 2011. The Impact of the Global Financial Crisis on Poverty in the Philippines. In C. Reyes and M. Baris Jr., eds. *Monitoring the Impacts of the Global Crisis at the Community Level*. Manila: De La Salle University.

O. Röhn et al. 2015. Economic Resilience: A New Set of Vulnerability Indicators for OECD Countries. *OECD Economics Department Working Papers*. No. 1249. Paris: Organization for Economic Cooperation and Development.

A. C. Sanchez, M. Rasmussen, and O. Röhn. 2015. Economic Resilience: What Role for Policies? *OECD Economics Department Working Papers*. No. 1251. Paris: Organization for Economic Cooperation and Development.

World Bank. 2013. *World Development Report 2014: Risk and Opportunity Managing Risk for Development*. Washington, DC.

2 | Trade and Global Value Chain

Trade and Global Value Chain

Recent Trends in Asia's Trade

Asia's trade growth in 2015 continued to slow below world trade growth; it also fell further below GDP growth.

Trade growth by volume fell from 3.5% in 2014 to 2.3% in 2015 in Asia and the Pacific, much sharper than the decline in global trade from 2.8% to 2.7% in the same period. In comparison, North America's trade growth fell 0.8 percentage points to 3.7%, and Africa's by 0.4 percentage points to 0.7%. Latin America's total trade continued to contract (from a rate of −2.0% in 2014 to −2.3% in 2015). By contrast, trade growth accelerated to 4.3% from 2.7% in the European Union (EU) and to 3.3% from 1.5% in the Middle East.

Asia's trade growth has consistently fallen below output growth since 2012, consistent with the global trend (Figures 2.1a, 2.1b).

By volume, both export and import growth has slowed in Asia and the Pacific since 2011, after a rebound in 2010 following the global financial crisis. Worldwide growth deceleration was more pronounced in developing economies than developed economies. Developing Asia's export growth slowed sharply to 3.0% in 2015 from 6.4% in 2013 and 4.6% in 2014, compared with the gradual recovery in developed economies' export growth to 3.0% in 2015 from 1.7% in 2013 and 2.5% in 2014 (Figures 2.2a, 2.2b). Import growth has been below that in developed economies since 2014—a meager 1.7% in 2015 against 4.5% growth in developed economies. While sluggish import growth may have helped economies with current account deficits shore up current account balances, it also reflected the domestic demand weakness across

Figure 2.1: Merchandise Trade and GDP Growth—Asia and World (%, y-o-y)

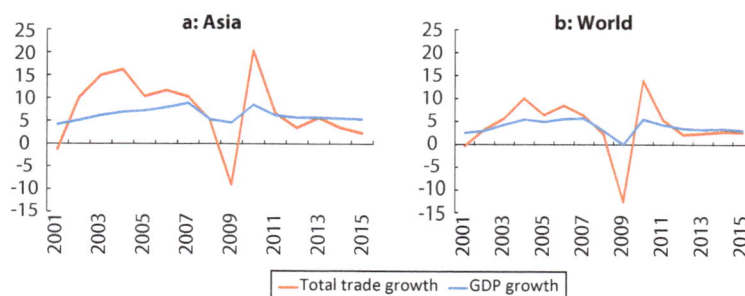

GDP = gross domestic product, y-o-y = year-on-year.
Note: Real GDP growth is weighted using GDP at purchasing power parity. Total trade growth is the average of export volume growth and import volume growth.
Sources: ADB calculations using data from International Monetary Fund. World Economic Outlook April 2016 Database. https://www.imf.org/external/pubs/ft/weo/2016/01/weodata/index.aspx; World Trade Organization Statistics database. http://stat.wto.org (accessed September 2016).

Figure 2.2: Export and Import Volume Growth—Developed Economies and Developing Asia (%, y-o-y)

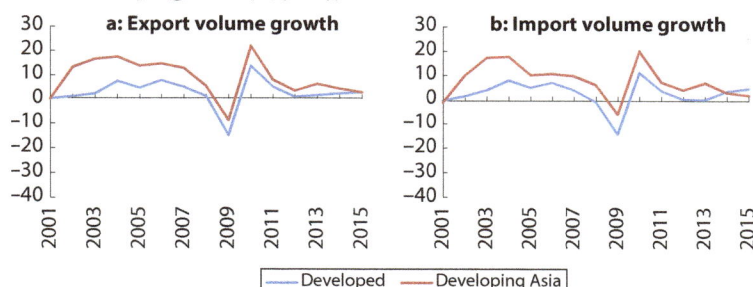

y-o-y = year-on-year.
Notes: Economies were grouped into "developed" and "developing" based on country classification of the United Nations. The computations included 37 developed economies (European Union [EU], non-EU, Asia, and North America) and 146 developing economies (from non-EU, Africa, Asia, Middle East, and Latin America and the Caribbean). Developing Asia includes ADB's 45 developing member economies.
Source: Source: ADB calculations using data from World Trade Organization Statistics database. http://stat.wto.org (accessed October 2016).

Figure 2.3: PRC and Asia ex-PRC Trade Volume Growth (%, y-o-y)

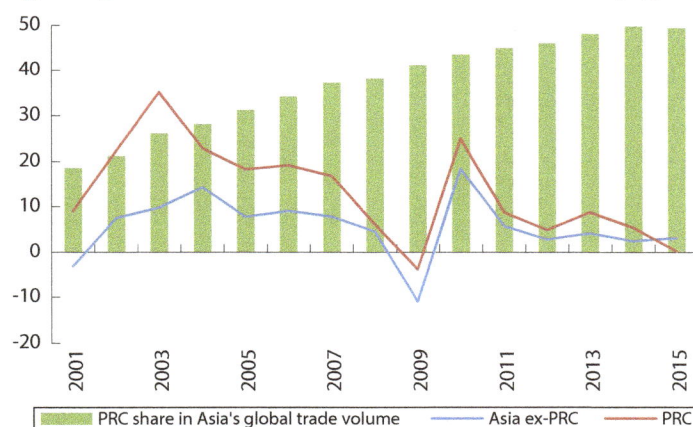

PRC = People's Republic of China, y-o-y = year-on-year.
Source: ADB calculations using data from World Trade Organization Statistics database. http://stat.wto.org (accessed October 2016).

developing Asia, further complicating the challenge of sustaining economic growth momentum beyond tepid export growth.

Asia's trade slowdown was driven by weaker trade in the People's Republic of China (PRC) and slower intermediate goods trade growth in the region.

The PRC's trade slowdown worsened in 2015, with trade volume growth plunging to just 0.2% from 5.4% in 2014 (Figure 2.3). PRC's exports continued to grow, but much slowly, down to 4.8% in 2015 from 6.8% in 2014, as reforms continue to steer the economy

away from export-oriented growth to more domestic demand-driven growth—slower yet more sustainable and balanced. Imports contracted 4.2%, reversing the 4% growth in 2014. With the PRC accounting for the bulk of the region's total trade, the PRC trade slowdown pulled down Asia's total global trade. Excluding the PRC, Asia's aggregate trade volume growth rose to 3.1% from 2.5% in 2014.

By value, intermediate goods trade contracted 13.2% in 2015, affecting Asia's overall trade performance as well. Intermediate goods—particularly processed goods—remain a major component of Asian exports and imports—accounting for about 58% of its total

Figure 2.4: Total Trade by Commodity Groups—Asia

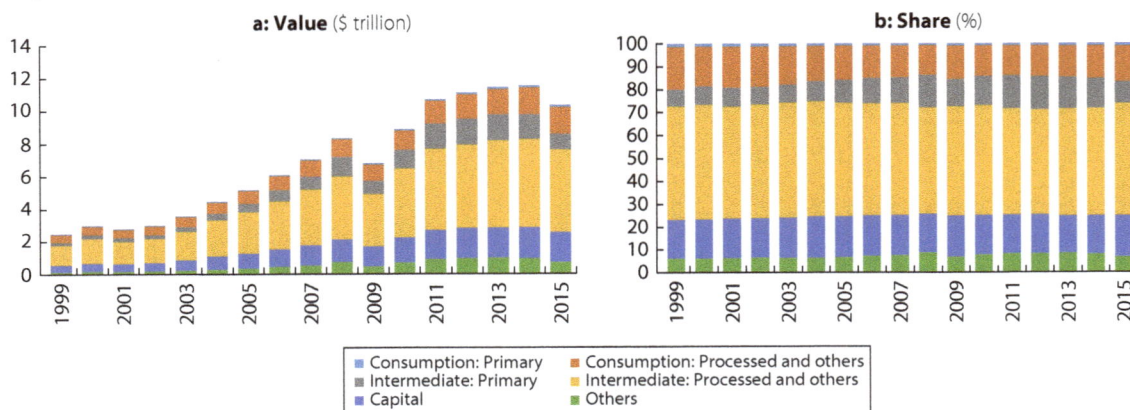

a: Value ($ trillion)

b: Share (%)

Legend:
- Consumption: Primary
- Consumption: Processed and others
- Intermediate: Primary
- Intermediate: Processed and others
- Capital
- Others

Note: Based on Broad Economic Categories.
Source: ADB calculations using data from United Nations. Commodity Trade Database. https://comtrade.un.org (accessed October 2016).

trade (Figures 2.4a, 2.4b). Beginning in 2010, growth of processed intermediate goods fell rapidly from 31% to 1.3% in 2014 and contracted 6.8% in 2015. Consumption goods growth also declined, but not as much—by 1.9% in 2015; while capital goods fell 3.6%. Detailed commodity level data show that the fall in intermediate goods trade value had nearly equal drops in both price and volume.[4] Falling intermediate goods trade growth could indicate stagnating or loosening global and regional value chains (see "Analyzing Global and Regional Value Chains" for more details).

Asia's Intraregional Trade

Despite the slowdown in overall trade, Asia's intraregional trade share increased in 2015 given its declining trade with non-Asian economies.

Intraregional trade in Asia and the Pacific increased to 57.1% in 2015, up from an average 55.8% during 2010–2014 (Figure 2.5). By comparison, intraregional trade in the European Union (EU) and North America is 63% and 25%, respectively.

Figure 2.5: Intraregional Trade Shares—Asia, European Union, North America (%)

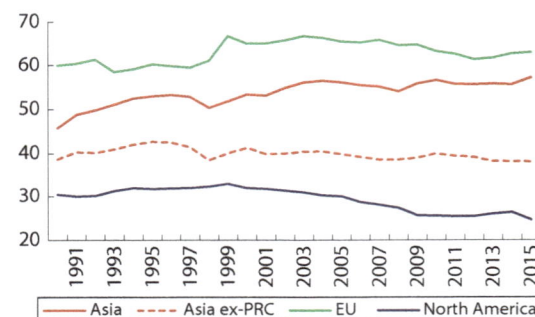

Legend: Asia — Asia ex-PRC — EU — North America

EU= European Union, PRC= People's Republic of China.
Notes: EU refers to the aggregate of 28 EU members. North America covers Canada, Mexico, and the United States.
Sources: ADB calculations using data from CEIC; and International Monetary Fund. Direction of Trade Database. https://www.imf.org/en/Data (accessed August 2016).

However, intraregional trade by value declined by 7.4% in 2015 after growing only 1.3% in 2014. Indeed, intra-Asia trade share increased in 2015 because of an even sharper drop in Asia's trade with non-Asian economies (down by 13%). Excluding the PRC, intraregional trade growth fell even more sharply at 10% in 2015, while Asia's trade with the PRC contracted 3% (Figure 2.6).

---

[4]   The United Nations Commodity Trade Database lists exports up to a six-digit product level.

Figure 2.6: Trade Value Growth—Asia By Partner
(%, y-o-y)

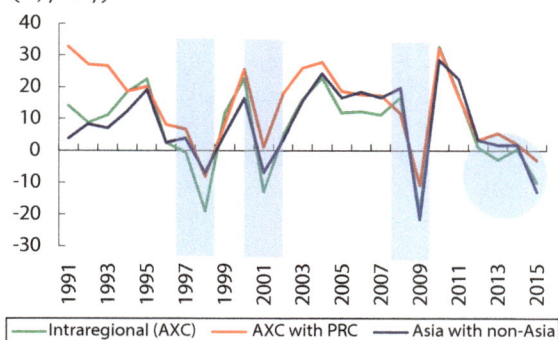

AXC = Asia excluding the PRC, PRC = People's Republic of China,
y-o-y = year-on-year.
Source: ADB calculations using data from International Monetary
Fund. Direction of Trade Database. https://www.imf.org/en/Data
(accessed August 2016).

Figure 2.7: Intra-subregional Trade Shares—Asia (%)

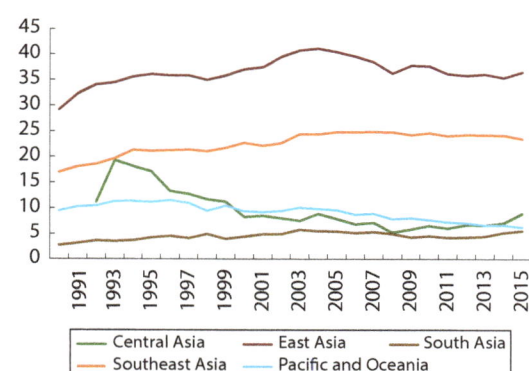

Source: ADB calculations using data from International Monetary
Fund. Direction of Trade Database. https://www.imf.org/en/Data
(accessed August 2016).

Figure 2.8: Inter-subregional Trade Shares—Asia (%)

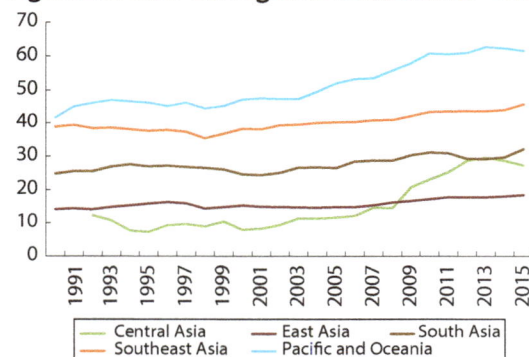

Source: ADB calculations using data from International Monetary
Fund. Direction of Trade Database. https://www.imf.org/en/Data
(accessed August 2016).

Trade share mostly strengthened within subregions, but declined across subregions— also confirmed by gravity model estimation results based on bilateral trade data.

While the intra-subregional trade shares of Central Asia, East Asia, and South Asia rose in 2015 from 2014, those of Southeast Asia and the Pacific and Oceania fell (Figure 2.7).[5] Intra-subregional trade shares remain the highest in East Asia and Southeast Asia. Central Asia outpaced the Pacific and Oceania in 2015 and now occupies the third position. South Asia still has the lowest share, but not too far behind the Pacific and Oceania.

Inter-subregional trade shares—trade across subregions within Asia—declined in Central Asia and the Pacific and Oceania, and slightly rebounded in East Asia. Inter-subregional trade shares increased in South Asia and Southeast Asia. The Pacific and Oceania continues to engage in significantly more trade with other subregions in Asia than within itself, with the highest inter-subregional trade share among Asian subregions (Figure 2.8).

After controlling for economic size and geographic, cultural, and economic proximity, Asia's intraregional exports are significantly higher than exports to non-Asian economies (Box 2.1). From gravity model estimation results based on data for 2011–2015, the most recent

period, intraregional trade bias declined to 0.96 from 1.16 in 2010–2014.[6]

Gravity model is also a useful tool to assess the impact of foreign exchange rate on trade. The volatility of exchange rate has grown significantly recently. However, weaker local currency does not seem to contribute to export growth as much as before (Box 2.2).

---

5   The Pacific and Oceania includes ADB's Pacific developing member economies plus Australia and New Zealand.

6   Intraregional trade bias refers to the coefficient of the intra-Asia dummy in the gravity model of bilateral export flows. A positive and significant coefficient means that Asia's trade with itself is higher than its trade with non-Asian economies.

Box 2.1: Gravity Model Estimation of Bilateral Exports

In traditional gravity models, trade flows (either exports or imports) are determined by the size of the respective source and destination economies and distance, which appears to be an overall proxy for trade costs. However, this simple specification fails to capture the unobserved multilateral trade resistance. Multilateral trade resistance measures the cost of country *i* to export to country *j* relative to the cost of exporting to other economies (outward multilateral resistance) or the cost of country *i* to import from country *j* relative to the cost of importing from all possible import sources (inward multilateral resistance).

Because of the structural weakness of the intuitive gravity model in assessing trade flows, international trade literature uses the Anderson and van Wincoop (2003) gravity model specifications that account for multilateral trade resistance. To account for time-varying characteristics of each trading partner, the gravity model is augmented with country fixed effects interacted with year dummies.

Results of gravity model estimation using annual data covering 2011–2015 and 2010–2014 are shown in box table 1. This 5-year rolling regression, updated annually, provides a snapshot of progress

1: Gravity Model Estimation Results

Dependent Variable: Log(bilateral exports)	All Goods	Capital Goods	Consumption Goods	Intermediate Goods
Log(distance)	-1.79***	-1.72***	-1.90***	-1.83***
	(0.02)	(0.02)	(0.02)	(0.02)
Colonial relationship dummy	0.82***	0.73***	0.93***	0.84***
	(0.11)	(0.10)	(0.12)	(0.11)
Common language dummy	0.98***	0.92***	1.04***	0.82***
	(0.04)	(0.05)	(0.05)	(0.05)
Contiguity dummy	0.91***	0.94***	0.99***	0.95***
	(0.12)	(0.11)	(0.12)	(0.12)
Regional dummies (base: Asia to ROW)				
Both in Asia dummy	0.96***[1.16***]	0.11 [0.51]	0.48 [0.90**]	0.15 [0.47]
	(0.32)	(0.36)	(0.40)	(0.37)
Importer in Asia dummy	0.92	-0.22	0.09	0.81
	(0.61)	(0.82)	(0.65)	(0.76)
Both in ROW dummy	-0.61	-0.93	-1.27***	0.03
	(0.46)	(0.70)	(0.45)	(0.61)
Sample size	148,780	148,780	148,780	148,780
Censored observations	40,292	76,499	58,922	54,211
Uncensored observations	108,488	72,281	89,858	94,569

*** = significant at 1%, **= significant at 5%, *= significant at 10%, robust standard errors in parentheses.
ROW = rest of the world.
Notes: Based on annual data covering 2011–2015. Numbers in brackets are the coefficients of the regional dummies for gravity model estimation results using annual data covering 2010–2014. Time-varying economy dummies are included but not shown for brevity. Heckman sample selection estimation was used to account for missing economy-pair data. Data cover 173 economies, of which 43 are from Asia. Trade data based on Broad Economic Categories.
Sources: ADB calculations using data from Institute for Research on the International Economy. http://www.cepii.fr/CEPII/en/cepii/cepii.asp; and United Nations. Commodity Trade Database. https://comtrade.un.org (both accessed October 2016).

in regional trade integration. The coefficient of "both in Asia" dummy can be viewed as a trade integration index.

In terms of intra-subregional trade bias, East Asia still stands out, followed by Southeast Asia and Central Asia. South Asia continues to engage in significantly more trade with other subregions within Asia, although its inter-subregional bias weakened slightly (box table 2). While Asia's intra-subregional bias remained high for both estimation periods (2011–2015 and 2010–2014) in all goods across most subregions, inter-subregional bias weakened. Subregional trade integration seems to be progressing steadily, centered on subregional specific integration initiatives such as the Greater Mekong Subregion, Central Asia Regional Economic Cooperation, South Asia Subregional Economic Cooperation, and the Pacific Islands Forum. While this is encouraging for advancing regional integration, weak inter-subregional trade links suggest more work is needed to improve inter-subregional connectivity and trade facilitation across subregions (beyond subregional level efforts).

2: Gravity Model Estimation Results: Intra- and Inter-subregional Trade

Dependent Variable: Log(bilateral exports)	Central Asia	East Asia	South Asia	Southeast Asia	Pacific and Oceania
Intra-subregional Trade Dummy					
All goods	4.53***[4.44***]	6.63***[6.74***]	1.33**[1.48***]	4.65***[4.81***]	1.07**[0.75]
Capital goods	3.16***[3.98***]	3.35***[3.84*]	0.57[0.85*]	3.06***[2.77***]	0.13 [0.47]
Consumption goods	5.48***[5.02***]	5.64***[5.03***]	0.72[1.29***]	4.79***[4.04***]	0.44 [-0.09]
Intermediate goods	3.59***[3.62***]	6.94***[7.27***]	0.85*[1.04***]	4.91***[5.46***]	0.13 [0.07]
Inter-subregional Trade Dummy					
All goods	0.62 [0.90**]	0.65*[0.77**]	3.89***[4.13***]	0.83**[1.02***]	-2.05***[-1.16*]
Capital goods	-0.60 [-0.06]	-0.28 [0.11]	1.94***[1.61***]	0.07 [0.39]	-1.04 [-0.56]
Consumption goods	0.21 [1.10*]	0.24 [0.58]	4.32***[3.59***]	0.12 [0.54]	-0.57 [-0.13]
Intermediate goods	-0.52 [-0.03]	-0.15 [0.10]	3.48***[4.14***]	0.28 [0.58]	-3.43***[-2.09***]

*** = significant at 1%, **= significant at 5%, *= significant at 10%. Estimates for 2010–2014 are in brackets.
Note: Base category (benchmark) is the subregion's trade with economies outside Asia. A separate regression was estimated for "all goods" and for each commodity group. The usual gravity model variables and time-varying economy dummies are included but, for brevity, not shown. Heckman sample selection estimation was used to account for missing bilateral economy-pair data. Data cover 173 economies, of which 43 are from Asia. Trade data are based on Broad Economic Categories.
Sources: ADB calculations using data from Institute for Research on the International Economy. http://www.cepii.fr/CEPII/en/cepii/cepii.asp; and United Nations. Commodity Trade Database. https://comtrade.un.org (both accessed October 2016).

Box 2.2: Impact of Foreign Exchange Rate on Trade

Analyzing recent trade growth patterns reveals some interesting changes—a slump in trade growth or convergence toward moderate, longer-term growth rates. Given conventional wisdom—that exchange rate appreciation contributes to an increase in imports and decreased exports, with depreciation acting vice versa—the box examines how the change in exchange rate affected trade flows in the 2000s. Examining exchange rate movements over time, the analysis shows that variations in real effective exchange rate (REER) movements across economies decreased before the global financial crisis (box figure 1a). However, exchange rate variations across economies rapidly increased after the crisis (box figure 1b).

On the other hand, the trade response to exchange rate changes has been smaller since the global financial crisis. Many more economies had lower elasticity of both exports and imports

relative to changes in REER after the global financial crisis than before (box figures 2a, 2b).

Given the main focus on trade volume growth—excluding the volatile price factor—the empirical analysis investigates how real exchange rate movements lead to changes in trade volumes. While much of the literature tests the impact of exchange rate volatility on trade flows, not much examines the impact of the exchange rate level itself on trade, particularly trade volume. In investigating the relationship between changes in trade and exchange rates, a panel gravity model is employed with various fixed effects included to control for omitted variable bias and its associated endogeneity.

$$\ln X_{ijt} = \beta_0 + \beta_1 \ln xrate_{ijt} + \beta_2 \ln GDP_{jt} + \beta_3 R_{ij} + \gamma_{it} + \delta_j + \phi_{ijt}$$

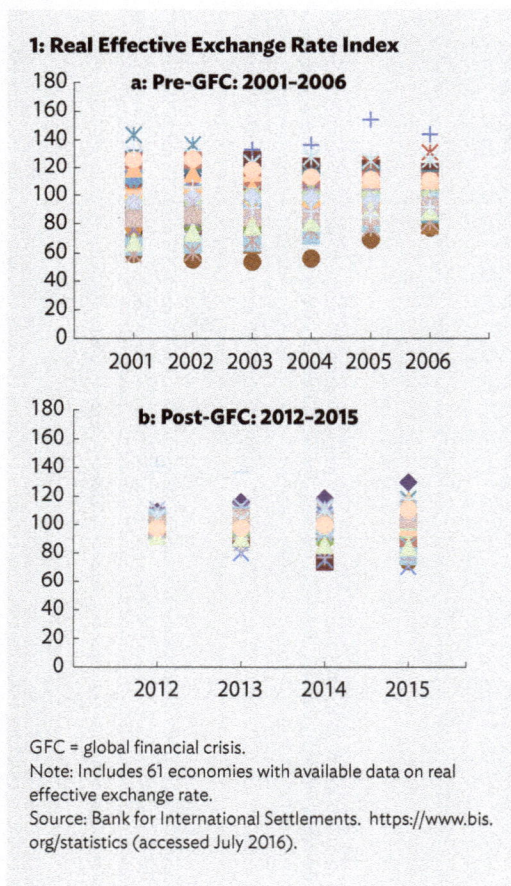

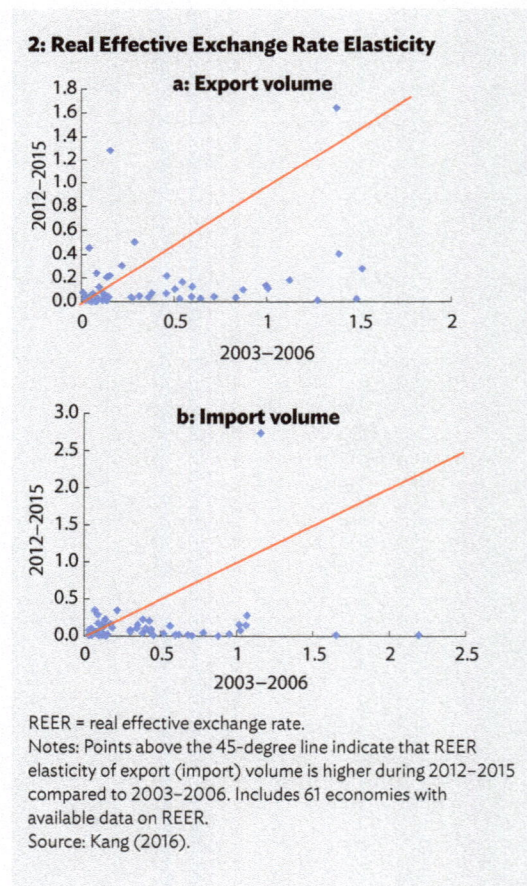

1: Real Effective Exchange Rate Index

a: Pre-GFC: 2001–2006

b: Post-GFC: 2012–2015

2: Real Effective Exchange Rate Elasticity

a: Export volume

b: Import volume

GFC = global financial crisis.
Note: Includes 61 economies with available data on real effective exchange rate.
Source: Bank for International Settlements. https://www.bis.org/statistics (accessed July 2016).

REER = real effective exchange rate.
Notes: Points above the 45-degree line indicate that REER elasticity of export (import) volume is higher during 2012–2015 compared to 2003–2006. Includes 61 economies with available data on REER.
Source: Kang (2016).

where the subscript i and j denote the importer and exporter, respectively, and t denotes time. X is the annual bilateral export volume, calculated by deflating the export value by producer price index of the exporting economy. *xrate* is the bilateral real exchange rate, calculated by $\text{nxrate} \times \frac{CPI_i}{CPI_j}$, where *nxrate* is the nominal exchange rate, and CPI_i and CPI_j are consumer price indexes of importing and exporting economies, respectively. GDP_{jt} denotes the real GDP of exporting economies, and R_{ij} controls the usual gravity variables, including distance, colonial relationship, common language, and geographical contiguity. γ_{it} is time-varying importer fixed effects to control for remaining importer specific factors on trade, such as tariffs and other nontariff barriers, and δ_j are exporter fixed effects. Finally, ϕ_{ijt} is an error term. The model tests the impact of exchange rate on exports for 2001–2015 and separately for 2003–2006 (before the global financial crisis), 2007–2010 (global financial crisis), and 2012–2015 (after the crisis). In addition to the level of real exchange rate, we test the impact of its one and two-lagged values (box Table 1). This can help estimate the longer-term impact of exchange rate and also addressing potential simultaneity problem.

1: Gravity Model Estimation Results: Impact of Real Exchange Rates on Bilateral Exports

Period	Log (RER)	Log (RER$_{t-1}$)	Log (RER$_{t-2}$)
Full Period	0.13***	0.06***	0.04***
Pre-GFC	0.66***	0.22***	0.05
GFC	0.09***	0.03	0.01
Post-GFC	0.27***	0.20	0.07

*** = significant at 1%, ** = significant at 5%, * = significant at 10%. Dependent Variable: Log(bilateral exports volume).
GFC = global financial crisis, RER = real exchange rate.
Notes: Full-period covers 2001–2015, 2003–2006 is the period before the global financial crisis, 2007–2010 is the global financial crisis period, and 2012–2015 after the crisis. The usual gravity model variables were included but for brevity are not shown. For the complete gravity model estimation results, please see Annex 2a. Data cover 166 economies, of which 40 are from Asia.
Sources: ADB calculations using data from Institute for Research on the International Economy. http://www.cepii.fr/CEPII/en/cepii/cepii.asp; United Nations. Commodity Trade Database. https://comtrade.un.org; and World Bank. World Development Indicators. data.worldbank.org/data-catalog/world-development-indicators (accessed September 2016).

First, trade resistance factors point to the significance and expected direction of influence on trade volume. For 2001–2015, the real exchange rate (RER) effect of the year is positive and significant at the 1% level, suggesting the weaker an exporter's currency, the larger the export volume relative to trading partners. A 1% depreciation of an exporter's RER

on average leads to a 0.13% increase in export volume of the same year. When the lagged variable of the RER is considered, the magnitude of the impact decreases over time. The term structure of the RER impact on trade reveals interesting, consistent patterns. First, the size of the RER coefficient shrinks from level RER to lag(1) and lag(2) RERs. Even the significance of the RER is not retained for lag(2) RER across all three periods. This indicates the effect of the real exchange rate over export volume is greatest during the contemporaneous year and dissipates over time. There is no indication of a J-curve effect.

Second, the magnitude of the RER coefficient is consistently larger for the periods before and after the global financial crisis and much smaller during the global financial crisis. The exchange rate effect was significantly dampened during the crisis period.

Third, compared with the pre-global financial crisis period, the exchange rate effect on export volume in the period after the crisis was less than halved during the same year and its lagged impact has become even insignificant. The results show the exchange rate effect significantly weakened.

One potential cause of the subdued impact of exchange rate on trade is a deepening global value chain (GVC) worldwide. For example, while depreciation of the local currency may induce greater exports by increasing the price competitiveness of exported goods, the impact could be dampened if the exported goods embed a large portion of intermediates, as these demands could be undermined by the depreciation, obscuring the net impact of currency depreciation. Additionally, some adjustments were made to test this GVC factor hypothesis, by averaging export, GDP, and exchange rate variables for 2001–2003, 2006–2008, 2009–2011, and 2012–2014, and including the data of domestic value added (DVA) share out of gross bilateral exports for the years 2000, 2005, 2008, and 2011, given the available value added decomposition data for these years. This can also measure the persistent effect of GVC participation spreading over multiple years. box table 2 presents both summary results under a base-line model without time-varying importer fixed effects and an extended model with time-varying importer fixed-effects.

Overall, a larger DVA share leads to less bilateral exports. This indicates that deepening GVCs can induce greater trade, confirming the hypothesis that rapid expansion of GVCs has contributed to international trade growth. The impact of average real exchange rate on exports becomes negative

Box 2.2. continued.

after considering the GVC impact, although the sizes of the coefficients are very small. Further, the interaction between DVA share and exchange rates reveals a positive coefficient. These suggest deepening GVCs could have dampened the traditional mechanism of exchange rate levels influencing trade. Nevertheless, the coefficient of the interaction term indicates the impact of exchange rate could still be positive for the exports of an economy with higher than 77% of DVA share based on the basic model and 70% based on the extended model. These results suggest not that the GVC is the only factor that might have induced the weakening impact of exchange rate on trade, but that it could be one of the structural factors.

2: Regression Results

	Base Model	Extended Model
DVA share	-0.355*** (0.144)	-0.279** (0.155)
Average RER	-3.74e-05*** (1.85e-05)	-2.98e-05** (1.73e-05)
DVA*(average RER)	4.85e-05*** (2.14e-05)	4.26e-05*** (1.85e-05)

*** = significant at 1%, ** = significant at 5%. Dependent variable: Log(bilateral exports volume).
DVA = domestic value added, RER = real exchange rate.
Notes: Results for other gravity model variables, for brevity, are not presented. DVA share is the share of domestic value added in total exports for 47 economies with available data from the ADB Multi-Regional Input-Output Tables, with 14 economies from Asia (Australia; Bangladesh; People's Republic of China; India; Indonesia; Japan; the Republic of Korea; Malaysia; Mongolia; the Philippines; Sri Lanka; Taipei,China; Thailand; and Viet Nam). Bilateral RER is deflated by the ratio of consumer price indexes of importer over that of exporter.
Sources: ADB calculations using data from ADB Multi-Regional Input-Output Tables based on methodology by Wang, Wei, and Zhu (2014); Institute for Research on the International Economy. http://www.cepii.fr/CEPII/en/cepii/cepii.asp (accessed July 2016); United Nations. Commodity Trade Database. https://comtrade.un.org (accessed September 2016); and World Bank. World Development Indicators. data.worldbank.org/data-catalog/world-development-indicators (accessed September 2016).

Analysis of Global and Regional Value Chains

The expansion of global and regional value chains has slowed.

The *Asian Economic Integration Report 2015* referred to maturing global and regional value chains as one of the potential causes of trade growth slowdown since 2012. The recent International World Input-Output data supports this argument.[7] Among the components of gross world exports, the value of DVA increased 2.6 times between 2000 and 2011 and 1.1 times between 2011 and 2015. For the same periods, foreign value added (FVA) increased 2.8 and 0.8 times, respectively; returned domestic value added (RDV), 2.1 and 0.9 times; and purely double-counted terms (PDC), 3.2 and 0.5 times. While DVA still increased between 2011 and 2015, all other components that capture an expanding production network through multiple border-crossing have decreased in absolute value. As shown in Figure 2.9a, the DVA portion out of gross exports declined between 2000 and 2011, while other components' shares grew, except for RDV during this period, indicating a deepening GVC. This trend reversed between 2011 and 2015, with the DVA portion accounting for a much larger portion.

As a major contributor to international trade and the deepening of the GVC, Asia is no exception. Value-added decomposition of Asia's gross exports also points to deepening integration into the GVC between 2000 and 2011, which reversed the direction between 2011 and 2015 (Figure 2.9b).

Asia's GVC participation as measured by the share of value added contents of gross exports used for further processing through cross-border production networks also attests to this. The GVC participation ratio rose from 63.2% to 65.5% between 2000 and 2011 but declined to 58.7% in 2015 (see Figure 2.9).[8]

---

[7] The ADB Multi-Regional Input-Output Table covers 47 economies, with 14 from Asia and Pacific (Australia; Bangladesh; the PRC; India; Indonesia; Japan; the Republic of Korea; Malaysia; Mongolia; the Philippines; Sri Lanka; Taipei,China; Thailand; and Viet Nam).
[8] The GVC participation ratio is measured as: [gross exports − (T1+T9+T10+T15+T16)]/gross exports. Please refer to Annex 2b for the components of decomposed gross exports.

Figure 2.9: Components of Gross Exports (%)

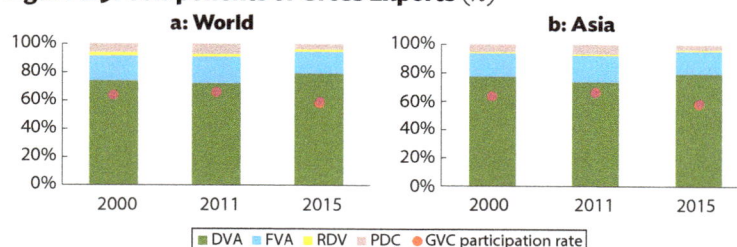

DVA = domestic value added, FVA = foreign value added, PDC = purely double-counted terms, RDV = returned domestic value added.
Note: The GVC participation ratio is measured as: [gross exports – (T1+T9+T10+T15+T16)]/gross exports. Please refer to Annex 2b for the components of decomposed gross exports.
Sources: ADB calculations using ADB Multi-Regional Input-Output Tables and methodology by Wang, Wei, and Zhu (2014).

Regional value chains have strengthened over time, while progress varies across subregions.

For the geographical linkage of value chains in Asian subregions from a forward-linkage perspective, we find that East Asia is becoming more integrated outside the region than inside, reflecting its strong outward orientation. Out of gross exports, DVA export share to the region has fallen slightly, from 34.4% in 2000 to 33.5% in 2015, while the share outside the region increased from 65.5% to 66.5% (Table 2.1). This phenomenon is more pronounced when the progress of vertical specialization is examined. In East Asia, 37% of FVA exports went outside the region in 2000 and jumped to 56% by 2015. The RDV and PDC also indicate a similar trend, albeit to a lesser extent.

In contrast, South Asia's value chain linkage strengthened inside the region. South Asia's DVA export share for the region grew from 20.1% to 25.5% between 2000 and 2015. The regional share for other components went even further in South Asia, reflecting its relatively closer value chain linkage inside the region. For example, the regional share for FVA increased from 22.3% to 38.4%. South Asia's overall intra-subregional linkage weakened overtime. Instead its value chain linkage with other subregions strengthened, particularly with Southeast Asia. The share of Southeast Asia in South Asia's FVA exports, for example, rose from just 9.7% in 2000 to 19.1% in 2015.

Southeast Asia does not show much change over time between regional and extra-regional value chain linkages. At the subregional level, however, its linkage has strengthened with South Asia in particular. Oceania, represented only by Australia in our data, reveals fast-growing value chain linkage with the region. East Asia's share is the largest for Oceania, while the share of other subregions has also grown in general.

Among select Asian economies, Viet Nam shows the highest FVA export portion of gross exports, at 31.0% in 2015, followed by Taipei,China at 25.4%; Malaysia at 25.3%; and Thailand at 24.7% (Table 2.2). This indicates significant amounts of processing manufacturing. While Malaysia's FVA export portion drastically declined from 40.2% in 2000 to 25.3%, its weight on processing manufacturing remains significant. The PRC's FVA export share edged up, from 13.8% in 2000 to 14.1% in 2015. Japan's FVA grew significantly, from 6.6% to 12.1% in the period, which could have benefitted from expanding production offshoring activities of parts and components, driven by strengthening outward foreign direct investment (FDI).

Diagnosing Channels of the Brexit Impact: Trade and Investment Linkages

The Brexit impact on Asia through trade and investment linkages may not be sizeable; but some economies may face additional costs due to value chain and indirect investment linkages.

The United Kingdom's (UK) decision to leave the EU (Brexit) rattled the global financial market, triggering a flight to safe-haven assets such as the United States

Table 2.1: Asia's Link to Global and Regional Value Chains (% of total per component)

Exporter/ Importer	2000					2015				
	East Asia	South Asia	Southeast Asia	Oceania	Rest of the World	East Asia	South Asia	Southeast Asia	Oceania	Rest of the World
Domestic Value Added										
East Asia	24.3	1.0	7.3	1.8	65.5	21.1	3.7	6.5	2.2	66.5
South Asia	11.3	3.1	4.1	1.6	79.8	9.3	5.4	8.8	2.0	74.5
Southeast Asia	29.6	1.4	11.4	2.7	55.0	26.9	4.8	11.2	4.1	52.9
Oceania	41.1	1.2	8.9	—	48.8	49.4	4.3	12.3	—	34.0
Foreign Value Added										
East Asia	37.5	0.3	23.4	1.5	37.3	33.6	0.8	7.9	1.4	56.4
South Asia	10.9	0.8	9.7	0.9	77.7	14.6	3.1	19.1	1.6	61.6
Southeast Asia	29.3	0.5	38.6	3.9	27.7	35.2	2.9	27.8	4.7	29.4
Oceania	45.5	0.9	16.0	—	37.7	66.7	2.1	14.0	—	17.2
Returned Domestic Value Added										
East Asia	23.3	1.0	7.0	1.9	66.8	20.4	3.8	6.6	2.2	67.1
South Asia	10.8	3.2	3.9	1.6	80.5	9.3	5.4	8.8	2.0	74.6
Southeast Asia	32.4	1.5	10.8	3.4	51.9	27.8	4.9	11.3	4.5	51.5
Oceania	41.4	1.2	8.8	—	48.6	49.9	4.3	12.0	—	33.9
Purely Double-Counted Terms										
East Asia	27.4	1.2	4.6	1.9	64.9	20.7	4.1	5.9	2.3	67.1
South Asia	14.0	3.0	3.9	1.9	77.2	8.7	6.3	7.4	2.2	75.5
Southeast Asia	25.0	1.4	11.6	1.6	60.4	23.5	4.9	10.2	2.9	58.4
Oceania	38.7	1.4	8.4	—	51.5	41.9	5.7	15.7	—	36.7

— = data unavailable.
Note: Data for the Pacific unavailable.
Sources: ADB calculations using ADB Multi-Regional Input-Output Tables and methodology by Wang, Wei, and Zhu (2014).

Table 2.2: Select Individual Asian Economies Export Component (% of total exports)

2000	AUS	PRC	IND	INO	JPN	KOR	MAL	TAP	THA	VIE
DVA (% of total)	86.5	81.6	85.1	80.2	89.1	69.4	47.6	63.7	59.2	75.6
FVA (% of total)	10.1	13.8	11.9	15.0	6.6	22.8	40.2	26.7	33.6	20.4
RDV (% of total)	0.3	0.8	0.2	0.2	1.9	0.3	0.1	0.3	0.2	0.1
PDC (% of total)	3.1	3.8	2.9	4.6	2.4	7.5	12.1	9.3	6.9	4.0
2015	**AUS**	**PRC**	**IND**	**INO**	**JPN**	**KOR**	**MAL**	**TAP**	**THA**	**VIE**
DVA (% of total)	90.2	81.5	86.1	90.6	83.9	72.8	68.8	65.8	71.1	65.7
FVA (% of total)	7.3	14.1	11.8	7.3	12.1	21.4	25.3	25.4	24.7	31.0
RDV (% of total)	0.4	1.5	0.3	0.4	0.9	0.3	0.2	0.2	0.2	0.1
PDC (% of total)	2.1	2.9	1.7	1.7	3.1	5.5	5.7	8.6	4.1	3.2

AUS = Australia; DVA = domestic value added; FVA = foreign value added; IND = India; INO = Indonesia; JPN = Japan;
KOR = Republic of Korea; MAL = Malaysia; PDC = purely double-counted terms; PRC = People's Republic of China;
RDV = returned domestic value added; TAP = Taipei,China; THA = Thailand; VIE = Viet Nam.
Sources: ADB calculations using ADB Multi-Regional Input-Output Tables and methodology by Wang, Wei, and Zhu (2014).

(US) dollar and Japanese yen, and tightened financial markets. The global financial market quickly stabilized, however, supported by ultra-loose monetary policy in major advanced economies and slimmer prospects for further increases in the US interest rates in the near future. The International Monetary Fund (IMF), in its July 2016 *World Economic Outlook*, estimated minimal global spillover from Brexit, particularly in large economies such as the PRC and the US. However, it noted that the negative impact could be larger in "downside" or "severe" scenarios with tighter financial conditions and lower business and consumer confidence than the baseline; or where financial stress intensifies, especially in advanced European economies, leading to sharp tightening of financial conditions and a drop in confidence (IMF 2016).

Macroeconomic repercussions and financial market spillovers caused by the anticipated lengthy procedures culminating in the UK departure from the EU could themselves pose risks to the global economy and individual economies with relatively close UK economic ties. But the actual Brexit impact on the real sector will likely appear through trade and investment channels. The UK is one of the most open economies in the world. For non-EU trading partners, Brexit implies higher transaction costs. Before Brexit, country A in Figure 2.10 faced a common trade regime with the EU with the UK as a part, which included common tariffs and other trade-related systems. If a country already has a free trade agreement (FTA) with the EU, it could enjoy preferential treatment trading with the EU, including the UK.

With Brexit, however, country A faces a different trade regime from the EU's when trading with the UK. Even if the UK provides the same or similar treatment as the EU to country A, it would still face higher transaction costs due to separate compliance requirements for trading with the UK, including separate documentation of certificates of origin, and so on. The same applies to the country's trade with the EU, though to a lesser extent. If the country has an existing FTA with the EU, it loses flexibility in using UK resources and inputs in qualifying for EU preferential treatment, thus having to use non-UK-produced inputs in manufacturing final products to avail of EU preferential treatment. This implies additional transaction costs. As depicted below, shifting from a single transaction point to multiple ones entails higher costs to the trading partner both with the UK and the EU.

Figure 2.10: Trade and Investment Channels of Brexit Impact

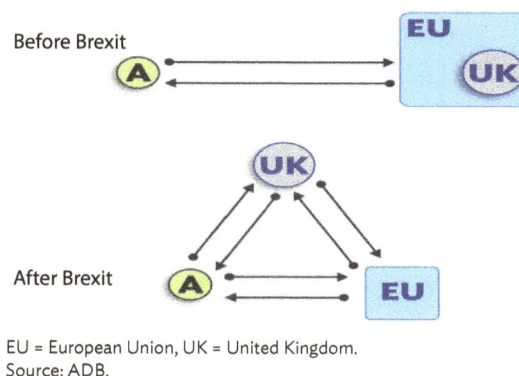

EU = European Union, UK = United Kingdom.
Source: ADB.

Brexit impact: Trade channel

We now examine which economies in the EU and Asia could be more affected by Brexit by investigating their value chain linkages with the UK. We use the gross export decomposition methodology by Wang, Wei, and Zhu (2014), using the ADB Multi-Regional Input-Output tables. It covers 27 EU members, 14 Asian economies, Brazil, Canada, Mexico, the Russian Federation, Turkey, and the UK. If an economy in the EU or Asia has a deeper value chain linkage with the UK by sharing segments of a production network, the economy will likely suffer more from Brexit because transaction costs will rise due to the need for separate trading engagements with the UK, the increase in costs exacerbated by multiple border-crossings of products with respect to the UK.

In exports to the UK in 2015, Malta and Ireland are the EU economies with higher value chain linkage with the UK relative to gross export linkage (Table 2.3). In Figure 2.11, economies above the 45-degree line have higher value chain linkage than linkage through gross exports.

Among Asian economies' value chain linkages with the UK, several are exposed to greater value added export linkages with the UK than others (Table 2.4). However, Asian economies overall are much less exposed to value chain linkages with the UK than EU economies. Sri Lanka has the highest export weight for the UK in gross terms, but its weight is around a half in terms of value chain linkages. Others with relatively higher value chain linkages with the UK are India and Australia (Figure 2.12).

Table 2.3: Top 10 EU Exporters to UK, 2015

Exporter	Gross Exports to UK (%)[a]	FVA+RDV+ PDC Exports (%)[b]	FVA+RDV+ PDC Exports (%)[c]
Malta	13.6	19.2	14.8
Ireland	13.7	18.8	13.8
Netherlands	11.9	9.5	7.2
Belgium	8.8	6.2	8.4
Denmark	7.2	6.2	4.9
Cyprus	8.5	5.7	2.2
Sweden	8.0	5.5	4.4
France	8.2	5.0	3.6
Germany	6.3	4.8	5.4
Portugal	7.9	4.3	3.2

EU = European Union, FVA = foreign value added, RDV = returned domestic value added, PDC = purely double-counted terms, UK = United Kingdom.
[a] Share in gross exports to the world.
[b] Share of FVA + RDV + PDC exports to the world.
[c] Share of gross exports to the UK.
Sources: ADB calculations using ADB Multi-Regional Input-Output Tables and methodology by Wang, Wei, and Zhu (2014).

Table 2.4: Top Asian Exporters to the UK, 2015

Exporter	Gross Exports to UK (%)[a]	FVA+RDV+ PDC Exports (%)[b]	FVA+RDV+ PDC Exports (%)[c]
Sri Lanka	10.1	5.4	1.4
India	6.4	3.6	1.8
Australia	7.9	3.0	1.2
Philippines	4.4	2.7	2.7
Thailand	3.9	2.6	4.3
Bangladesh	4.3	2.6	1.8
Malaysia	2.3	1.8	6.9
PRC	2.9	1.0	2.2
Taipei,China	2.2	1.0	5.4
Indonesia	3.1	0.9	0.8
Republic of Korea	1.8	0.9	4.1
Japan	1.8	0.9	2.7
Viet Nam	1.7	0.9	3.5
Mongolia	0.7	0.4	6.1

PRC = People's Repblic of China, FVA = foreign value added, PDC = purely double-counted terms, RDV = returned domestic value added, UK = United Kingdom.
[a] Share in gross exports to the world.
[b] Share of FVA + RDV + PDC exports to the world.
[c] Share of gross exports to the UK.
Source: ADB calculations using ADB Multi-Regional Input-Output Tables and methodology by Wang, Wei, and Zhu (2014).

Figure 2.11: Global Value Chain Link (Exports) and Gross Exports of EU to UK, 2015
(% of world total)

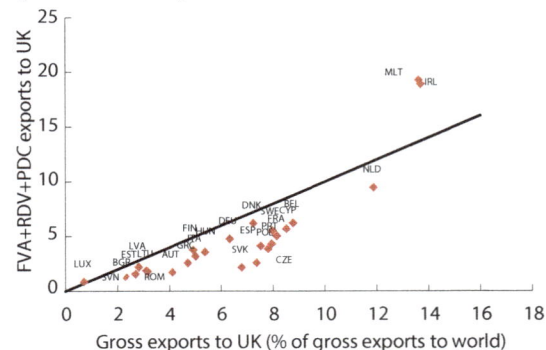

AUT=Austria, BEL=Belgium, BGR=Bulgaria, CYP=Cyprus, CZE=Czech Republic, DEN=Denmark, EST=Estonia, FIN=Finland, FRA=France, FVA=foreign value added, GER=Germany, GRC=Greece, HUN=Hungary, IRE=Ireland, ITA=Italy, LTU=Lithuania, LUX=Luxembourg, LVA=Latvia, MLT=Malta, NET=Netherlands, PDC=purely double-counted terms, POL=Poland, POR=Portugal, RDV=returned domestic value added, ROM=Romania, SPA=Spain, SVK=Slovak Republic, SVN=Slovenia, SWE=Sweden, UK = United Kingdom.
Sources: ADB calculations using ADB Multi-Regional Input-Output Tables and methodology by Wang, Wei, and Zhu (2014).

Figure 2.12: Global Value Chain Link (Exports) and Gross Exports of Asia to UK, 2015
(% of world total)

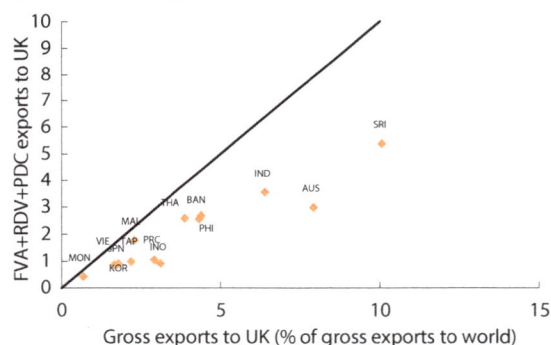

AUS = Australia; BAN = Bangladesh; PRC = People's Republic of China; FVA = foreign value added; IND = India; INO = Indonesia; JPN = Japan; KOR = Republic of Korea; MAL = Malaysia; MON = Mongolia; PHI = Philippines; PDC = purely double-counted terms; RDV = returned domestic value added; SRI = Sri Lanka; TAP = Taipei,China; THA = Thailand; VIE = Viet Nam, UK = United Kingdom.
Sources: ADB calculations using ADB Multi-Regional Input-Output Tables, and methodology by Wang, Wei, and Zhu (2014).

Brexit impact: FDI channel

The higher transaction costs to Asian investors after Brexit include those associated with "passporting rights", which for now facilitate the economy's FDI into the EU through the UK and vice versa. In this sense, examining indirect FDI routes through the EU and the UK is useful in determining how much an economy could be exposed to additional transaction costs, including potential relocation costs if needed, which is not captured by sheer FDI exposure. In this analysis, indirect FDI refers to investments by a parent company through a subsidiary. We look at indirect investments from Asia to the UK through any member of the EU, and to any member of the EU through the UK. For example, Appco Group, a UK-based company, invested in business services in France in 2015. Appco is a subsidiary of Cobra Group International, which is incorporated and headquartered in Hong Kong, China. In this case, Hong Kong, China is the source of indirect investments to France through the UK.

Among major Asian investors to the UK, Japan and India show the largest number of "greenfield" investments in 2015—$3.9 billion and $3.1 billion, respectively (Figure 2.13).[9] The Republic of Korea and Singapore greenfield FDI are geared more toward non-UK, EU economies. For indirect FDI into the UK and EU, India was relatively high in 2015, heading mainly to the EU through the UK (amounting to $1.5 billion in 2015). The Republic of Korea appears different: most indirect FDI went through the EU to the UK.

Updates on Regional Trade Policy

While trade liberalization is advancing centered on continued efforts to reach bilateral and regional free trade agreements, concern is growing about rising protectionism globally and regionally.

Recent FTA trends

As of August 2016, based on the Regional Trade Agreements Information System Database of the World Trade Organization (WTO), which covers FTAs of all WTO members, only one FTA—Japan-Mongolia Economic Partnership Agreement (EPA) —entered into force in the first half of 2016 (Figure 2.14).

Free trade agreement activities in Asia remain robust, although the global trend on launching new FTAs stagnated after agreement on the Trans-Pacific Partnership (TPP)—a "mega FTA"—and amid ongoing negotiations on the Regional Comprehensive Economic Partnership (RCEP), another regional mega FTA[10] (Figures 2.15, 2.16). In addition to the Japan–Mongolia FTA, the Republic of Korea–Colombia FTA came into force in July 2016. Another, the Viet Nam–Eurasian Economic Union FTA takes effect in October 2016.[11] In addition, seven FTAs had been proposed or launched for negotiation as of August 2016 (Table 2.5).

Trans-Pacific Partnership

After 5 years of negotiations, the TPP—a free trade and investment agreement—was signed by Australia, Brunei Darussalam, Chile, Canada, Japan, Malaysia, Mexico, New Zealand, Peru, Singapore, the US, and Viet Nam on 4 February 2016 in Auckland, New Zealand. The next step is for TPP member legislatures to pass the agreement and to ratify it within 2 years. If one or more members miss the ratification deadline, the TPP can survive if at least six original signatories—accounting for 85% of the region's 2013 GDP—complete the ratification, preferably but not necessarily within 2 years. Failure by either Japan or the US to ratify the agreement,

---

9   A greenfield investment is a form of foreign direct investment where a parent company builds its operations in a foreign country from the ground up. In addition to the construction of new production facilities, these projects can also include the building of new distribution hubs, offices, and living quarters.

10   Based on the World Trade Organization Regional Trade Agreements database. Of the nine FTAs that came into force in 2015, seven involve Asia. RCEP member economies include (1) Australia, (2) Brunei Darussalam, (3) Cambodia, (4) Indonesia, (5) the Lao People's Democratic Republic, (6) Malaysia, (7) Myanmar, (8) the People's Republic of China, (9) the Philippines, (10) Singapore, (11) Thailand, (12) Viet Nam, (13) India, (14) Japan, (15) the Republic of Korea, and (16) New Zealand.

11   The FTA consists of Armenia, Belarus, Kazakhstan, the Kyrgyz Republic, and the Russian Federation.

Figure 2.13: Direct and Indirect Greenfield Foreign Direct Investment to the UK and EU from Asian Economies, 2015

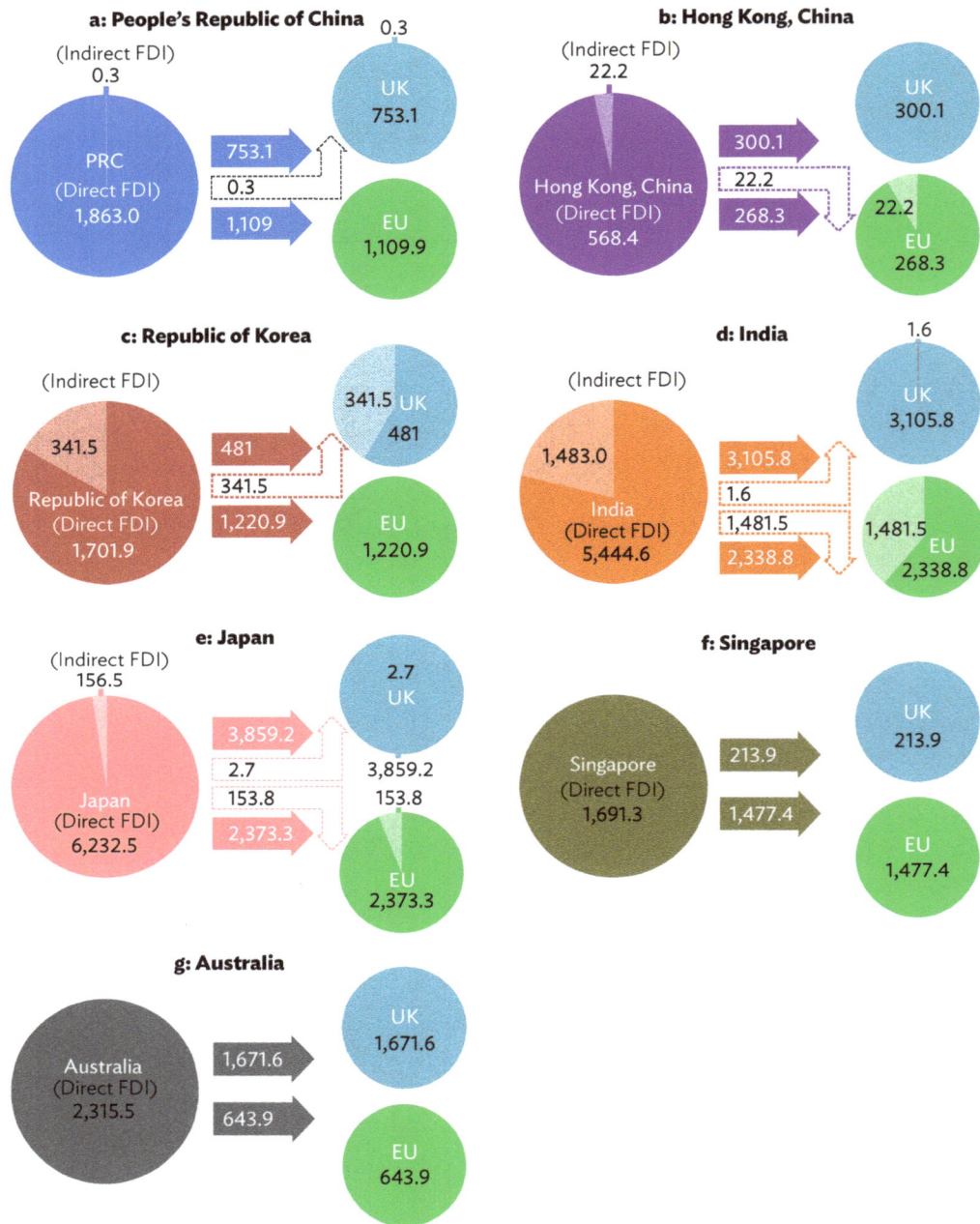

EU = European Union, FDI = foreign direct investment, PRC = People's Republic of China, UK = United Kingdom.
Notes: Indirect FDI refers to investment by a parent company through a subsidiary. fDi Markets tracks greenfield FDI by source economy, which is the location of the parent company, and by investing company information. In the analysis, we look at indirect investments from Asia to the UK through any EU member and to any member of the EU through the UK. Values are in $ million.
Source: ADB calculations using data from Financial Times. fDi Markets.

Figure 2.14: Number of Newly Effective FTAs—World

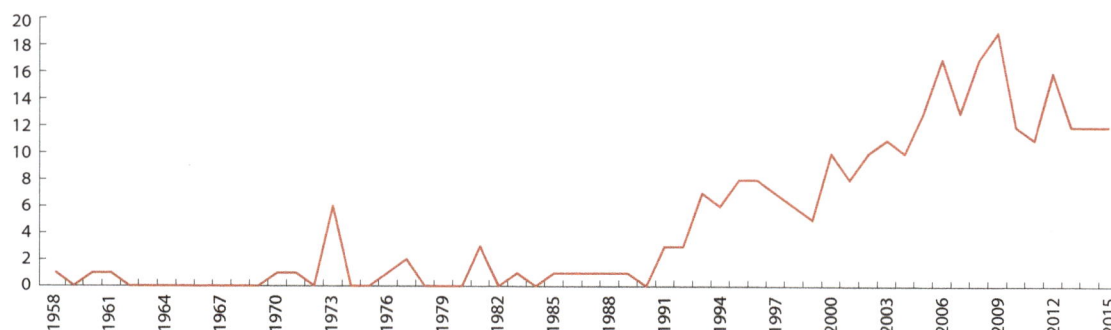

FTA = free trade agreement.
Source: World Trade Organization. Regional Trade Agreement Information System. http://rtais.wto.org (accessed August 2016).

Figure 2.15: Number of Signed FTAs—Asia (cumulative since 1975)

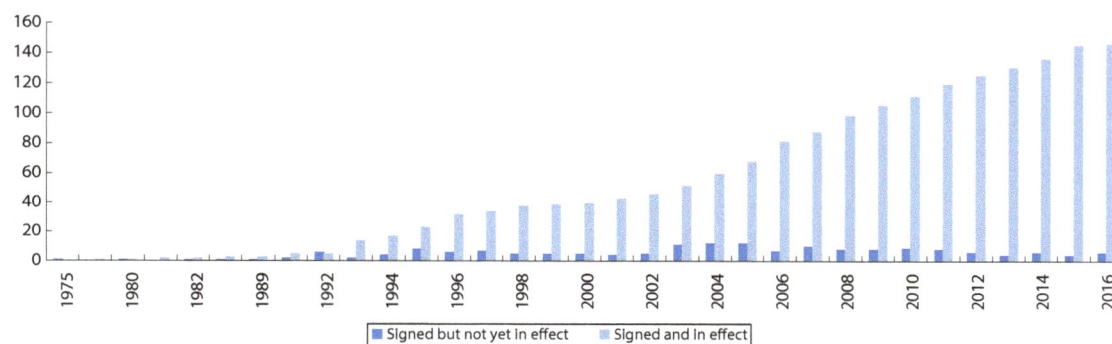

FTA = free trade agreement.
Notes: Includes bilateral and plurilateral FTAs with at least one of ADB's 48 regional members as signatory. The year 2016 covers FTAs that came into effect from January to July and FTAs that are expected to come into force within the year based on official statements.
Source: ADB. Asia Regional Integration Center FTA Database. https://aric.adb.org/fta (accessed September 2016).

Figure 2.16: Number of FTAs Proposed and Signed by Year—Asia

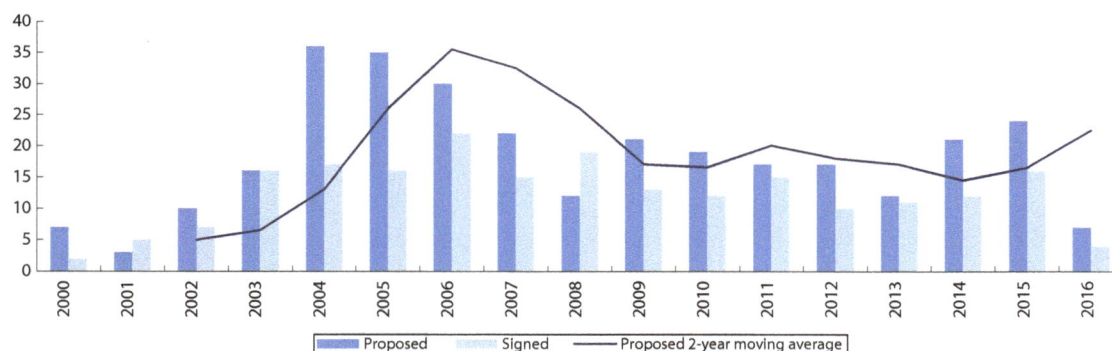

FTA = free trade agreement.
Notes: Includes bilateral and plurilateral FTAs with at least one of ADB's 48 regional members as signatory. The year 2016 covers FTAs that came into effect from January to July, and FTAs that are expected to come into force within the year based on official statements. "Signed" includes FTAs that are signed but not yet in effect, and signed and in effect. "Proposed" includes FTAs that are (i) proposed (the parties consider an FTA, governments or ministries issue a joint statement on the FTA's desirability, or establish a joint study group and joint task force to conduct feasibility studies); (ii) framework agreement signed and under negotiation (the parties, through ministries, negotiate the contents of a framework agreement that serves as a framework for future negotiations); and (iii) under negotiation (the parties, through ministries, declare the official launch of negotiations, or start the first round of negotiations).
Source: ADB. Asia Regional Integration Center FTA Database. https://aric.adb.org/fta (accessed September 2016).

Table 2.5: Recently Proposed FTAs in Asia

2013	2014	2015	2016
Japan–EU	ASEAN–Hong Kong, China	EEU–Iran	Hong Kong, China–Georgia
Japan–Turkey	Indonesia–Chile	India–EEU	Hong Kong, China–Maldives
Pakistan–Thailand	Indonesia–Peru	India–Iran	Singapore–Sri Lanka
Pakistan–Republic of Korea	Pakistan–US	Japan–Sri Lanka	Republic of Korea–Israel
PRC–Japan–Republic of Korea	Peru–India	Philippines–Canada	Nepal–PRC
PRC–Israel	Philippines–Australia	Philippines–Chile	Thailand–Sri Lanka
RCEP	Philippines–EU	Philippines–Mexico	Indonesia–EU
Thailand–EU	Philippines–EFTA	PRC–Maldives	
Thailand–Colombia	PRC–EU	PRC–Georgia	
Viet Nam–EEU	PRC–Sri Lanka	Thailand–Jordan	
	New Zealand–EU	Pakistan–Viet Nam	
	Singapore–Turkey	Pakistan–EEU	
	Taipei,China–India	Australia–EU	
		Singapore–EEU	

ASEAN = Association of Southeast Asian Nations, EEU = Eurasian Economic Union, EFTA = European Free Trade Association, EU = European Union, FTA = free trade agreement, PRC = People's Republic of China, RCEP = Regional Comprehensive Economic Partnership, US = United States.
Source: ADB. Asia Regional Integration Center FTA Database. https://aric.adb.org/fta (accessed September 2016).

constituting slightly less than 80% of total GDP of all TPP members, would effectively block the agreement.

United States. While President Barack Obama unequivocally supports TPP ratification, President-elect Donald Trump does not, and it is unlikely the US plans to take up the issue anytime soon. Neither Republicans nor Democrats have given clear indication of their support. Recent developments suggest bleak prospect of the US ratifying the agreement soon.

Nonetheless, a diverse group of US economic and industry leaders has endorsed the agreement, including the National Association of Manufacturers, the Business Roundtable, the US Chamber of Commerce, the National Small Business Association, and the American Farm Bureau Federation. The groups recognize the TPP's economic benefits, which range from substantial tariff elimination to protecting innovation (Office of the United States Trade Representative 2016).

Japan. Although some economic sectors are against the TPP—particularly agriculture, which fears competition with imports from Australia and the US—Japan strongly supports the TPP. In July 2016, the economy top business leaders asked Prime Minister Shinzo Abe to push for the ratification of the TPP during the Diet session in

September (Prime Minister of Japan and His Cabinet 2016a). Prime Minister Abe reiterated his determination for quick ratification, calling the agreement "pivotal" to Japan's economic growth.[12] He also urged the US government to secure ratification as soon as possible, stressing that the success or failure of the agreement "will sway the direction of the global free trade system" (Prime Minister of Japan and His Cabinet 2016b). Japan's lower house of Parliament voted to ratify the TPP on 10 November 2016.

New Zealand parliament has also passed the bill that allows the government to ratify the TPP. Meanwhile, leaders of TPP member economies have indicated the possibility that TPP membership could expand.

Regional Cooperation Economic Partnership

Another mega trade deal, the RCEP, is also being negotiated. As noted, the RCEP would bind the 10 ASEAN members and six economies with which ASEAN

---

[12] This is the response of Prime Minister Abe to questions against TPP during debate in the Diet sessions where TPP ratification is under deliberation (*Japan Times* 2016).

has existing FTAs. These 16 states have agreed to conclude negotiations before the end of 2016 (Malaysia Ministry of International Trade and Industry 2016). However, according to the latest reports, RCEP will miss its agreed timeframe for concluding negotiations. The Joint Leader's Statement on RCEP released 8 September 2016 reiterated "the importance of advancing negotiations" and calls to "intensify negotiations in a cooperative manner for the swift conclusion of the RCEP negotiations" (ASEAN 2016). But the statement indicates no timeframe on concluding talks.

Several complex issues, including on services, are holding back the negotiations. Although members have now agreed to a single-tier system of tariff relaxation from the earlier three-tier system, talks have been slow (Business Standard 2016).

According to officials, RCEP participants are planning to accelerate negotiations by holding rounds of talks through the end of 2016 (Bangkok Post 2016). As of October 2016, 15 rounds of negotiations, which include working groups on trade in goods, trade in services, and investment, have been conducted since 2013 (Ministry of Foreign Affairs of Japan 2016). The sixteenth round of negotiations will be held on 2–10 December 2016 in Indonesia (Australian Government Department Foreign Affairs and Trade 2016).

Trade Remedies

Rising protectionism worldwide attracts increasing attention from policy makers and academia (Box 2.3). While the *Asian Economic Integration Report* 2015 highlighted a fast-growing number of trade remedies amid the slowdown in international trade, this trend continued in 2015 (Figure 2.17). Antidumping duties are the most prevalent trade remedies imposed on Asian exporters (Table 2.6). There was a spike in the number of trade remedies involving Asia in 2013–2015. Base metals and chemicals are the most affected sectors in the

Box 2.3: Rising Protectionism

The World Trade Organization recently downgraded its forecast for world trade growth to 1.7% in 2016 from 2.8% in April. It also cut its growth projections for 2017 to 1.8%–3.1% from the previous forecast of 3.6%. Tepid world trade growth does not bode well for a still sluggish global economic recovery marked by weak domestic demand, unable to offset slack external demand.

More worrying is the bleak landscape surrounding the future of international trade. Rising protectionism in the run-up to the peak of election cycles and on the back of growing geopolitical tensions arising out of refugee and migration issues is looming over international trade. If history is any guide, protectionism in the 1930s—through increased tariff barriers and the forming of currency blocs—exacerbated conflicts that led to World War II. Nevertheless, politics, which are prone to weigh short-term (and domestic) benefits against long-term gains, tend to be susceptible to populist sentiments that blame globalization for growing income inequality and diminishing job opportunities in domestic economies. Making matters worse, the phenomenon seems to have a domino effect, be it through political rhetoric or more frequent issuance of nontariff barriers.

Given the multipolar international trade environment, growing tensions in trade may trigger a downward spiral of negative-sum games, prompting mutual retaliation through administrative trade policy tools and undermining the nascent status of global economic growth. Those administrative trade measures, such as trade remedies and nontariff barriers, are legitimate policy tools to restore a level playing field with the former and to protect national health and environment with the latter, including sanitary or phytosanitary measures and technical barriers to trade. But they are susceptible to the vested interests of domestic stakeholders and, thus, protectionism for the sake of safeguarding national interest at the expense of others.[a]

Given the public good nature of open and liberalized international trade, the importance of concerted effort from the international community cannot be overemphasized—particularly at this juncture. In this context, the role that the Group of 20 and other international forums can play in upholding the growth of international trade by averting creeping protectionism and further supporting trade liberalization and facilitation efforts should be strengthened.

---

[a] For more on rising protectionism, see Kang and Legal (2016).

Figure 2.17: Number of Trade Remedy Measures Affecting Asia
(by type)

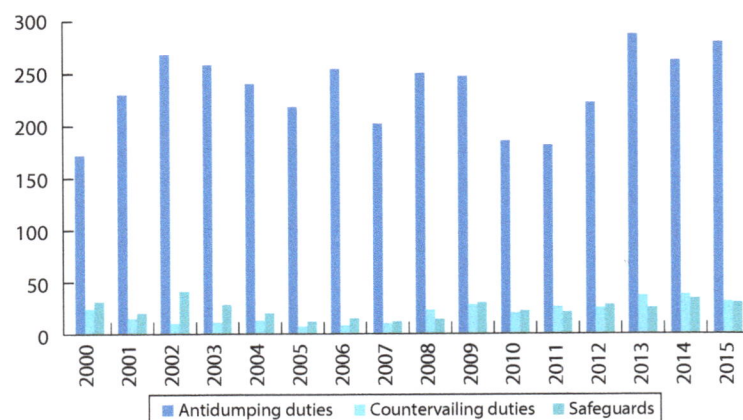

Note: Trade remedy measures include both "initiated" and "in force."
Safeguard measures are imposed on all members of the World Trade Organization; no bilateral data available.
Source: ADB calculations based on data from WTO. Integrated Trade Intelligence Portal.
https://www.wto.org/english/res_e/statis_e/itip_e.htm (accessed August 2016).

Table 2.6: Trade Remedy Measures and WTO Cases, 2010–2016

Agreement	World Total	Asia[a] Total	Asia (Complainant) ROW (Respondent)	ROW (Complainant) Asia (Respondent)	Asia (Complainant) Asia (Respondent)
Antidumping (Article VI of GATT 1994)					
Number of measures implemented	888	719	346	103	270
Number of cases	33 (4%)	25 (3.5%)	14	7	4
Countervailing Measures					
Number of measures implemented	78	67	52	7	8
Number of cases[b]	27 (35%)	19 (28%)	9	9	1
Safeguards[c]					
Number of measures implemented[d]	59	33	26	33	33
Number of cases	12 (20%)	5 (15%)	3	0	2
Total					
Number of measures implemented	1025	819	424	143	311
Number of cases	72 (7%)	49 (6%)	26	16	7

ROW = rest of the world, WTO = World Trade Organization.
[a] Asia as implementing or affected region, which is equivalent to the global number of trade remedy measures less ROW-ROW (not shown in table).
[b] Includes cases involving complaints on grant of subsidies and countervailing measures.
[c] Safeguard measures are imposed on all WTO members; no bilateral data available.
[d] Includes safeguard measures affecting all WTO members.
Note: Trade remedies include measures in force.
Sources: ADB calculations based on data from WTO. Integrated Trade Intelligence Portal.
https://www.wto.org/english/res_e/statis_e/itip_e.htm; WTO. Disputes by Agreement. https://www.wto.org/english/tratop_e/dispu_e/dispu_agreements_index_e.htm (accessed August 2016).

Table 2.7: Number of Trade Remedy Measures Affecting Asia, 2010–2016

HS Product Description	Total	Anti-dumping Duties	Countervailing Duties	Safeguards
Base metals and articles	491	379	71	41
Products of the chemical and allied industries	202	173	16	13
Resins, plastics and articles; rubber and articles	147	125	12	10
Machinery and electrical equipment	109	91	11	7

HS = harmonized system.
Note: Trade remedy measures include both initiated and in force.
Source: ADB calculations based on data from WTO. Integrated Trade Intelligence Portal.
https://www.wto.org/english/res_e/statis_e/itip_e.htm (accessed August 2016).

Table 2.8: Number of Implemented Trade Remedy Measures—Top Affected Asian Economies, 2010–2016

Economy Affected	Number of Measures Implemented		
	ROW	Asia	Total
PRC	253	136	389
Republic of Korea	56	66	122
Taipei,China	58	63	121

PRC = People's Republic of China, ROW = rest of the world.
Notes: Trade remedies include measures in force. Safeguard measures are applied to all WTO members, hence the number of measures implemented include measures that are applied to all WTO members.
Source: ADB calculations based on data from WTO. Integrated Trade Intelligence Portal.
https://www.wto.org/english/res_e/statis_e/itip_e.htm (accessed August 2016).

region (Table 2.7). The PRC; the Republic of Korea; and Taipei,China are the Asian economies most affected by trade remedies (Table 2.8).

Sanitary and Phytosanitary and Technical Barriers to Trade Measures

An important goal for governments is to guarantee the safety of food for consumers and prevent or limit the spread of pests, outbreak of diseases among plants and animals, and other health risks arising from residues (of pesticides or veterinary drugs), contaminants (heavy metals), toxins or disease-causing organisms in food, beverages, or feed. Policies with these objectives are generally referred to as sanitary (human and animal health) and phytosanitary (plant health) measures, more commonly known as sanitary and phytosanitary (SPS) measures, which include all relevant laws, decrees, regulations, requirements and procedures.

In response to consumer demand for greater product safety and stricter environmental protection, governments have tightened existing rules or implemented new policies. Economies have therefore increased technical regulations (which are mandatory) and standards (which are voluntary). These regulations and standards, also known as technical barriers to trade (TBTs), define either the specific characteristics of a product (for example, shape, size, or design and performance) or can pertain to the process and methods used in production (WTO 2012).

Despite their legitimate national heath and security rationale, stringent SPS and TBT measures and delays in unexpected procedures concerned could harm trade flows by acting as nontariff barriers, due to high compliance costs for businesses and the perishable nature of some exported products. The incidence of SPS and TBT measures has grown. As of August 2016, 14,123 SPS measures and 21,399 TBT measures had been notified to the World Trade Organization (WTO). Figures 2.18 and 2.19 show the number of notifications to the WTO and the number of notifying economies since 1995 for SPS and TBT measures—both trending upward.

The majority of SPS and TBT measures are imposed on all WTO members, although some are bilateral. On average, 46 WTO economies were notified as imposing SPS measures from 1995–2015; 30% from Asia. For the same period, an average of 59 WTO economies

Figure 2.18: Number of SPS Measures

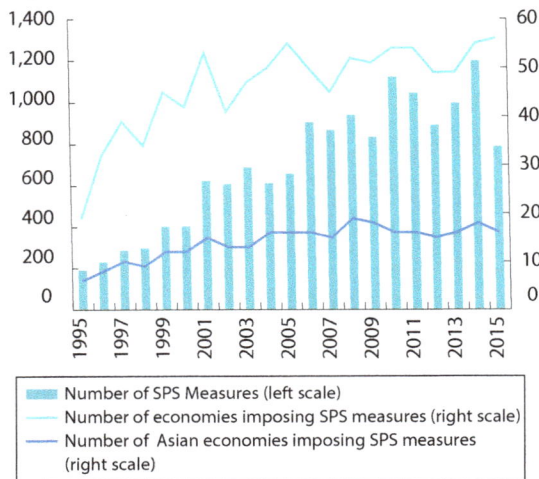

SPS = sanitary and phytosanitary, TBT = technical barriers to trade
Note: SPS and TBT measures include both initiated and in force.
Source: ADB calculations based on data from World Trade Organization. Integrated Trade Intelligence Portal. https://www.wto.org/english/res_e/statis_e/itip_e.htm (accessed August 2016).

Figure 2.19: Number of TBT Measures

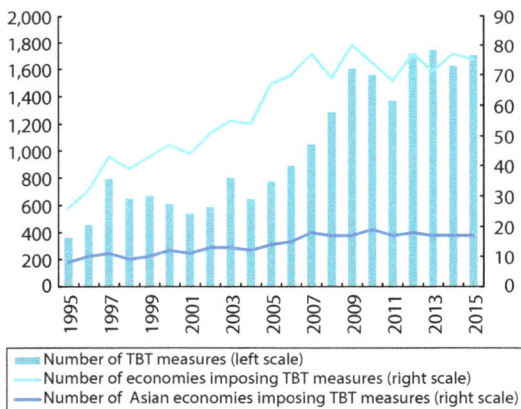

SPS = sanitary and phytosanitary, TBT = technical barriers to trade,
Note: SPS and TBT measures include both initiated and in force.
Source: ADB calculations based on data from World Trade Organization. Integrated Trade Intelligence Portal. https://www.wto.org/english/res_e/statis_e/itip_e.htm (accessed August 2016).

Figure 2.20: Number of Specific Trade Concerns Raised to the WTO SPS Committee

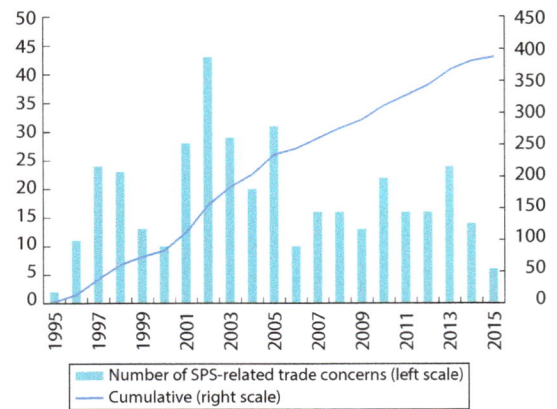

SPS = sanitary and phytosanitary, WTO = World Trade Organization.
Source: ADB calculations based on data from WTO. Integrated Trade Intelligence Portal. https://www.wto.org/english/res_e/statis_e/itip_e.htm (accessed August 2016).

Figure 2.21: Number of Specific Trade Concerns Raised to the WTO TBT Committee

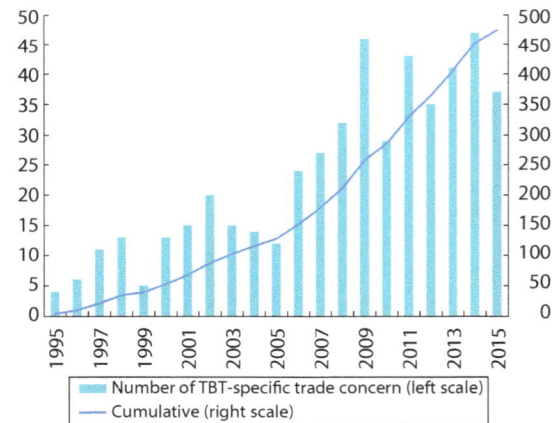

TBT = technical barriers to trade, WTO = World Trade Organization.
Source: ADB calculations based on data from WTO. Integrated Trade Intelligence Portal. https://www.wto.org/english/res_e/statis_e/itip_e.htm (accessed August 2016).

notified imposing TBT measures, with a quarter of these from Asia.

The evidence of upward trends in the number of SPS and TBT measures notified is supported by complaint-based information contained in the Specific Trade Concerns Database (Figures 2.20, 2.21). Trends also show that more TBT than SPS measures were imposed, and that more

economies imposed TBT measures than SPS measures. Asia imposed the most TBT (4,948) and SPS (4,297) measures, followed by North America, with 4,001 SPS measures and 2,337 TBT measures. Asia was most targeted by bilateral SPS measures (282) or SPS measures

Figure 2.22: Number of SPS Measures Imposed by Region, 1995–2015

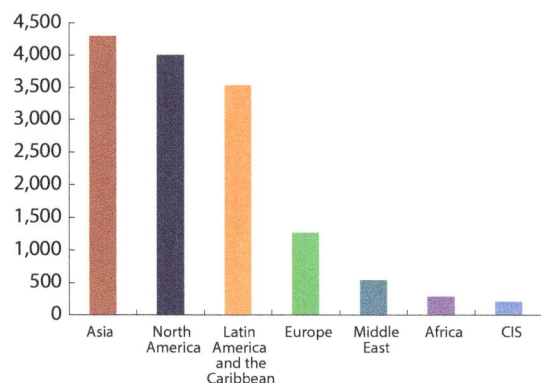

CIS = Commonwealth of Independent States, SPS = sanitary and phytosanitary.
Note: SPS measures include both initiated and in force.
Source: ADB calculations based on data from World Trade Organization. Integrated Trade Intelligence Portal. https://www.wto.org/english/res_e/statis_e/itip_e.htm (accessed August 2016).

Figure 2.23: Number of Bilateral SPS Measures Affecting Each Region, 1995–2015

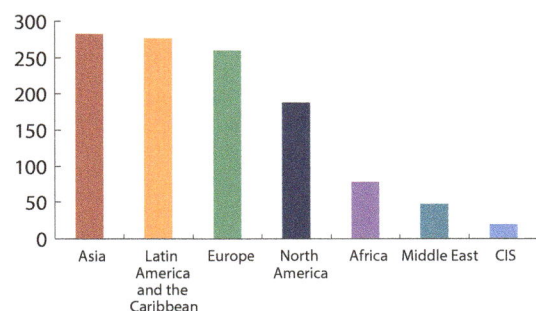

CIS = Commonwealth of Independent States, SPS = sanitary and phytosanitary.
Note: SPS measures include both initiated and in force.
Source: ADB calculations based on data from World Trade Organization. Integrated Trade Intelligence Portal. https://www.wto.org/english/res_e/statis_e/itip_e.htm (accessed August 2016).

Figure 2.24: Top 10 Economies Imposing SPS, 1995–2015 (number of measures)

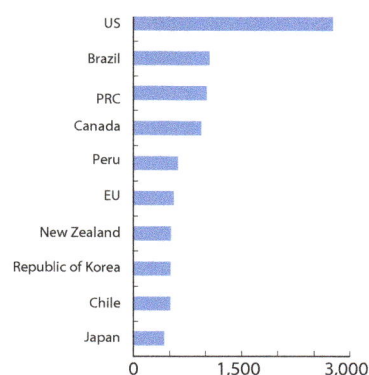

PRC = People's Republic of China, EU = European Union, SPS = sanitary and phytosanitary, US = United States.
Note: SPS measures include both initiated and in force.
Source: ADB calculations based on data from World Trade Organization. Integrated Trade Intelligence Portal. https://www.wto.org/english/res_e/statis_e/itip_e.htm (accessed August 2016).

Figure 2.25: Top 10 Economies Imposing TBT, 1995–2015 (number of measures)

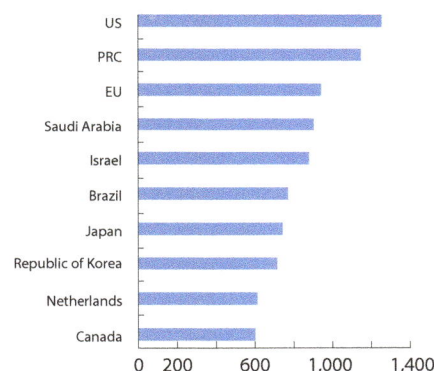

PRC = People's Republic of China, EU = European Union, TBT = technical barriers to trade, US = United States.
Note: TBT measures include both initiated and in force.
Source: ADB calculations based on data from World Trade Organization. Integrated Trade Intelligence Portal. https://www.wto.org/english/res_e/statis_e/itip_e.htm (accessed August 2016).

that are imposed on a particular economy and not on all WTO members (Figures 2.22, 2.23).[13]

The US has imposed the most number of SPS (2,769) and TBT (1,256) measures. The PRC is second in TBT measures and third in SPS measures. Japan and the Republic of Korea are in the top 10 economies

---

[13]   No bilateral data are available on TBT measures.

Figure 2.26: Number of SPS and TBT Measures Imposed on Product Groups, 1995–2015

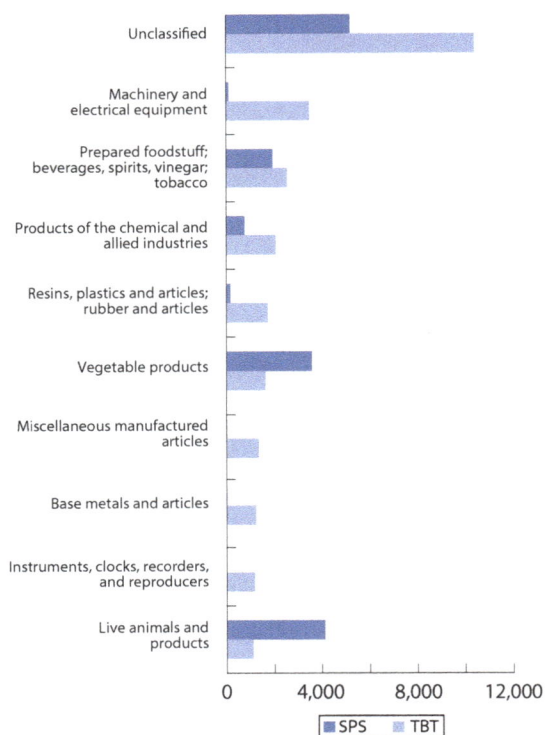

SPS = sanitary and phytosanitary, TBT = technical barriers to trade.
Note: SPS and TBT measures include both initiated and in force.
Source: ADB calculations based on data from World Trade Organization. Integrated Trade Intelligence Portal. https://www.wto.org/english/res_e/statis_e/itip_e.htm (accessed August 2016).

imposing the most number of SPS and TBT measures (Figures 2.24, 2.25).

Product groups subject to large numbers of SPS measures include (i) live animals and products; (ii) vegetable products; (iii) prepared foodstuff, beverages, spirits, vinegar, tobacco; (iv) products of the chemical and allied industries; and (v) animal and vegetable fats, oils and waxes (Figure 2.26).

Product groups subject to high numbers of TBT measures include (i) machinery and electrical equipment; (ii) prepared foodstuff; beverages, spirits, vinegar; tobacco; (iii) products of the chemical and allied industries; (iv) resins, plastics and articles; rubber and articles; and (v) vegetable products.

Despite their growing importance, there is a dearth of knowledge on the impact of SPS and TBT measures on

trade. Economic theory offers no straightforward forecast of how these measures impact international flows of goods. Instead, theory proposes that the effect of SPS and TBT measures on trade may vary and does not always reduce trade. For example, Thilmany and Barrett (1997) differentiate informative and non-informative regulatory measures. The former contains information addressing consumer concerns about product quality or safety; the latter does not. Evaluating the diverse effects of SPS and TBT measures remains an empirical issue.

SPS and TBT measures are estimated to forge significantly negative impact on exports from developing economies, particularly on Asia's intraregional trade in agricultural products.

SPS and TBT agreements require WTO members to notify the WTO Secretariat on the SPS and TBT measures they impose. These notifications are collected, complemented by information based on national sources, and analyzed by the United Nations Conference on Trade and Development, which are available through the World Bank's World Integrated Trade Solution. For economies with no SPS and TBT data available under the World Integrated Trade Solution, we gather data from WTO's Integrated Trade Intelligence Portal (I-TIP).

Using these data, we estimate various econometric models on the trade impact of SPS and TBT measures (Box 2.4). Model estimation results show that the positive impact of SPS and TBT on trade flows is mainly driven by exports of advanced economies, followed by Asian exports, while the majority of developing and least developed economies in the rest of the world face negative impacts from SPS and TBT. We further examine whether different impacts of SPS and TBT on trade exist by separately testing the impact of SPS and TBT. The results indicate that positive impacts largely stem from TBT, while the impact of SPS is insignificant. Developing Asia's exports, in particular, are negatively affected by SPS measures. Developing Asia's exports in agriculture sector are even more susceptible to SPS measures. Further, intraregional trade among developing Asia is also being hurt by SPS measures. These results suggest policy makers in the region need to act more proactively in resolving nontariff barriers across borders, in particular, by focusing on SPS. Stronger regional cooperation through subregional and regional dialogue should help.

Box 2.4: Impact of Nontariff Measures on Trade Flows

Following Feenstra (2004), which measured the impact of sanitary and phytosanitary (SPS) and technical barriers to trade (TBT) measures on trade in agriculture, we estimate the gravity equation model using fixed effects for each exporting and importing economy. These fixed effects consider the size effects, including the price and number of varieties of the exporting economy for each sector and the size of demand and the price index of the importing partner. To control for various types of economy and sector-specific factors that may affect trade flows, we include a set of importer, exporter, and sector fixed effects, which can also mitigate potential endogeneity problems.

To measure transport costs, bilateral distance between both partners (d) are used. These distances are obtained from the CEPII database. In addition, a dummy variable "contiguity" (contig), which equals one if both economies share a border, is also included. Bilateral trade can be enhanced by economies' cultural proximity. We therefore control for this proximity by introducing two dummy variables, respectively equal to 1 if there is a common official or primary language spoken in both economies (comlang_off) or if both partners have had colonial ties (col). Data are also derived from the CEPII database. The dependent variable x refers to bilateral import data of country j (importer) from country i (exporter) at the four-digit level of the Harmonized System classification. The source is the United Nations Commodity Trade database. Notifications and tariff data are compiled from 2012 to 2014 in our sample. To address the problem that the error terms are likely to exhibit correlation patterns for a given country-pair, we cluster the robust standard errors at the country-pair and four-digit product code level. Our model specification is analogous to the Disidier et al. (2008) approach.

The estimated base equation using pooled ordinary least squares (OLS) and panel regression method is

$$\ln x_{ijt}^{hs_4} = \mu_i f e_i^{hs} + \alpha_j f e_j^{hs} + \delta_1 \ln GDP_{it} + \delta_2 \ln GDP_{jt} + \delta_3 \ln d_{ij} \\ + \delta_4 \text{contig}_{ij} + \delta_5 \text{comlang\_off}_{ij} + \delta_6 \text{col}_{ij} + \delta_7 tar_{ijt}^{hs_4} + \delta_8 NTM_{ijt}^{hs_4} + \varepsilon_{ij}^{hs_4}$$

To investigate the impact of SPS and TBT measures on the exports of different exporter and importer groups and income groups, we also add regional and income group dummy for different regression models.

The regression results across all models confirm the expected impact of gravity factors. Gross domestic product (GDP) levels of both exporter and importer have significantly positive impact on trade. The same applies to border contiguity, use of common language, and historical colonial ties. Geographical distance

shows highly significant and negative effect on bilateral trade flows. As expected, ad valorem equivalent bilateral applied tariff rate (weighted average) exert a significantly negative impact on trade.

As shown in box table 1a, existence of SPS or TBT increases trade in both pooled OLS and panel regressions. According to the basic model, SPS and TBT increase average worldwide bilateral trade by 15% to 19%. Regional differences are revealed in the regression results under columns (3) and (4). Compared with economies of the Organisation for Economic Co-operation and Development (OECD), Asia's exports to the world are more positively affected by the SPS and TBT measures of importers. On the other hand, exports of non-Asia, non-OECD economies are hurt by SPS and TBT measures, as evidenced by the significant, negative coefficient of –0. 38 (in pooled OLS) and –0.17 (in the panel regression). On average, exports of non-Asia, non-OECD economies are 13% lower due to SPS and TBT measures of importers, according to the pooled OLS regression. It is worth noting that, in our analysis, non-Asia, non-OECD economies constitute the largest sample, with 91 economies in Africa, the Middle East, Latin America, and Eastern Europe.

The regression results presented for the agriculture sector reveal interesting implications (box table 1b). When importers are OECD economies, the positive impact of SPS and TBT on exports from Asia and non-Asian, non-OECD economies are very much subdued, while OECD-to-OECD trades are greatly boosted. For Asian importers, the positive impact of SPS and TBT on exports from OECD economies in the agriculture sector is much smaller, at 27%. While this positive impact is significantly boosted for imports from non-Asia, non-OECD economies, the impact for imports from Asian economies is significantly dampened by SPS and TBT measures, making the overall impact –7%. For agriculture, SPS and TBT measures hurt intraregional trade in Asia.

Testing the impact of SPS and TBT separately reveals interesting results (box table 2). While Asia's exports to the world are hurt by SPS measures of importing economies particularly in agricultural sector, TBT measures have positive impact on exports. The opposite results are demonstrated for non-Asia, non-OECD economies. Their exports are significantly larger due to SPS measures of importers, but are significantly lower due to TBT measures. When the effects of SPS and TBT are tested separately, SPS measures show large negative impact on intraregional trade. Intraregional trade among developing Asian economies is being hurt by SPS.

Box 2.4. continued.

1a: Influence of SPS/TBT—Full Sample, 2012–2014

Dependent variable: Log(bilateral imports)	(1) Pooled OLS	(2) Panel–Random Effects	(3) Pooled OLS	(4) Panel - Random Effects
Importer	All WTO member economies		All WTO member economies	
Exporter	All WTO member economies		All WTO member economies	
Bilateral applied tariff AVE(weighted average)	−0.01*** (0.00)	−0.01*** (0.00)	−0.01*** (0.00)	−0.01*** (0.00)
SPS/TBT dummy (at least 1 SPS or TBT at HS6 level)[a]	0.19*** (0.01)	0.15*** (0.01)	0.27*** (0.01)	0.18*** (0.01)
Exporter dummy (base = OECD)				
Asia			0.67*** (0.10)	1.24*** (0.07)
Non-Asia, non-OECD			2.94*** (0.14)	−1.54*** (0.11)
Interaction: SPS/TBT dummy and exporter dummy				
Asia			0.09*** (0.02)	0.08*** (0.02)
Non-Asia, non-OECD			−0.38*** (.02)	−0.17*** (0.02)
Number of observations	2,448,182	2,448,182	2,448,182	2,448,182
R-squared	0.39	0.31	0.39	0.31

1b: Influence of SPS/TBT—Agriculture Sector, 2012–2014

Dependent variable: Log(bilateral imports)	(5)	(6)	(7)	(8)
Importer	OECD Economies		Asian Economies	
Exporter	All WTO Member Economies		All WTO Member Economies	
Bilateral applied tariff AVE (weighted average)	−0.003*** (0.00)	−0.003*** (0.00)	−0.001*** (0.00)	−0.001*** (0.00)
SPS/TBT dummy (at least 1 SPS or TBT at HS6 level)[a]	0.90*** (0.13)	1.35*** (0.13)	0.38*** (0.04)	0.27*** (0.06)
Exporter dummy(base = OECD)				
Asia		0.31 (0.34)		1.03*** (0.40)
Non-Asia, non-OECD		−3.05*** (0.80)		−2.11* (1.09)
SPS/TBT dummy X exporter dummy				
Asia		−0.70*** (0.11)		−0.34*** (0.12)
Non-Asia, non-OECD		−1.01*** (0.10)		0.79*** (0.12)
Number of observations	157,006	157,006	146,137	146,137
R-squared	0.32	0.32	0.24	0.25

*** = significant at 1%, ** = significant at 5%, * = significant at 10%.

AVE = ad valorem equivalent, HS = harmonized system, OECD = Organisation for Economic Co-operation and Development, OLS = ordinary least squares, SPS = sanitary and phytosanitary, TBT = technical barriers to trade, WTO = World Trade Organization.

[a] To clarify, four-digit level of the harmonized system (HS) classification is considered equal to 1 if the importing economy notifies at least one SPS or TBT measure at the six-digit level, which is under the four-digit level of the HS classification.

Note: Robust standard errors in parentheses. Based on pooled OLS, models (1) and (3) include exporter, importer, and sector (four-digit level) fixed effects (no interaction). Panel regression (random effects) models (2) and (4) include exporter, importer, and sector (two-digit level) fixed effects (no interaction). Pooled OLS models 5–8 include exporter and sector (two-digit level) specific importer fixed effects (with interaction) in all estimations. Usual gravity model variables were included, but not shown for brevity.

Sources: ADB calculations using data from Institute for Research on the International Economy. http://www.cepii.fr/CEPII/en/cepii/cepii.asp; United Nations. Commodity Trade Database. https://comtrade.un.org; World Bank. World Integrated Trade Solution. https://wits.worldbank.org; and WTO. Integrated Trade Intelligence Portal. https://www.wto.org/english/res_e/statis_e/itip_e.htm (all accessed August 2016).

Box 2.4. continued.

2: Influence of SPS and TBT Separately, 2012–2014

Dependent variable: Log(bilateral imports)	(1) SPS	(2) TBT	(3) SPS	(4) TBT	(5) SPS	(6) TBT	(7) SPS	(8) TBT
Importer			All WTO members				Developing Asia	
Exporter			All WTO members				All WTO members	
Sector		All sectors			Agriculture		All sectors	
Bilateral applied tariff AVE (weighted average)	−0.02*** (0.00)	−0.02*** (0.00)	−0.02*** (0.00)	−0.02*** (0.00)	−0.02*** (0.00)	−0.02*** (0.00)	−0.06*** (0.00)	−0.06*** (0.00)
SPS (TBT) dummy[a]	−0.002 (0.02)	0.09*** (0.04)	−0.03 (0.02)	0.34*** (0.04)	−0.20*** (0.04)	0.67*** (0.07)	−0.37*** (0.02)	0.32*** (0.00)
Exporter dummy (base = OECD)								
Developing Asia			1.28*** (0.48)	0.89* (0.48)	7.02*** (1.06)	6.55*** (1.07)	2.22 (3.33)	2.44 (3.33)
Non-Developing Asia, non-OECD			1.82*** (0.57)	2.82*** (0.58)	9.68*** (1.22)	10.26 (1.22)	3.51 (3.83)	4.74 (3.83)
Interaction: SPS (TBT) dummy and exporter dummy								
Developing Asia			−0.50*** (0.04)	0.20*** (0.08)	−0.39*** (0.09)	0.04 (0.12)	−0.51*** (0.10)	0.42*** (0.13)
Non-Developing Asia, non-OECD			0.47*** (0.04)	−1.07*** (0.07)	0.29*** (0.08)	−0.93*** (0.11)	0.31*** (0.10)	−0.41*** (0.12)
Number of observations	271,280	271,280	271,280	271,280	60,151	60,151	19,182	19,182
R-squared	0.38	0.38	0.38	0.38	0.16	0.16	0.44	0.44

*** = significant at 1%, ** = significant at 5%, * = significant at 10%.

AVE = ad valorem equivalent, HS = harmonized system, OECD = Organisation for Economic Co-operation and Development, OLS = ordinary least squares, SPS = sanitary and phytosanitary, TBT = technical barriers to trade, WTO = World Trade Organization.

[a] To clarify, four-digit level of the harmonized system (HS) classification is considered equal to 1 if the importing economy notifies at least one SPS (TBT) measure at the six-digit level, which is under the four-digit level of the HS classification.

Note: Robust standard errors in parentheses. Based on panel regression which includes exporter, importer, and sector (four-digit level) fixed effects (no interaction). For brevity, the results of coefficients for usual gravity factors are not presented. Pooled regression was also done to confirm and compare the results.

Sources: ADB calculations using data from Institute for Research on the International Economy. http://www.cepii.fr/CEPII/en/cepii/cepii.asp; United Nations. Commodity Trade Database. https://comtrade.un.org; World Bank. World Integrated Trade Solution. https://wits.worldbank.org; and WTO. Integrated Trade Intelligence Portal. https://www.wto.org/english/res_e/statis_e/itip_e.htm (all accessed August 2016).

Annexes

Annex 2a: Gravity Model Estimation Results: Impact of Real Exchange Rates on Exports

Dependent Variable: Log (bilateral exports volume)	Full Period	Pre-Global Financial Crisis	Global Financial Crisis	Post-Global Financial Crisis	Full Period	Pre-Global Financial Crisis	Global Financial Crisis	Post-Global Financial Crisis	Full Period	Pre-Global Financial Crisis	Global Financial Crisis	Post-Global Financial Crisis
Log(real GDP of exporter)	0.433*** (0.0692)	0.707** (0.316)	0.286 (0.188)	0.117 (0.310)	0.334*** (0.0680)	0.562* (0.322)	0.260 (0.189)	0.304 (0.311)	0.326*** (0.0691)	0.445 (0.314)	0.246 (0.190)	0.299 (0.319)
Log(distance)	−1.728*** (0.0286)	−1.736*** (0.0322)	−1.802*** (0.0322)	−1.699*** (0.0340)	−1.749*** (0.0286)	−1.737*** (0.0323)	−1.806*** (0.0324)	−1.716*** (0.0341)	−1.748*** (0.0289)	−1.730*** (0.0323)	−1.803*** (0.0331)	−1.702*** (0.0336)
Colonial relationship dummy	0.601*** (0.126)	0.722*** (0.134)	0.602*** (0.137)	0.553*** (0.141)	0.586*** (0.125)	0.723*** (0.134)	0.596*** (0.137)	0.559*** (0.140)	0.571*** (0.127)	0.725*** (0.135)	0.603*** (0.138)	0.562*** (0.138)
Common language dummy	0.867*** (0.0549)	0.741*** (0.0636)	0.845*** (0.0642)	0.864*** (0.0657)	0.848*** (0.0550)	0.738*** (0.0640)	0.849*** (0.0645)	0.854*** (0.0662)	0.861*** (0.0555)	0.746*** (0.0642)	0.841*** (0.0652)	0.874*** (0.0661)
Contiguity	0.513*** (0.151)	0.511*** (0.164)	0.458*** (0.170)	0.507*** (0.172)	0.583*** (0.152)	0.509*** (0.164)	0.458*** (0.173)	0.534*** (0.173)	0.593*** (0.153)	0.510*** (0.163)	0.446** (0.174)	0.579*** (0.174)
Log(real exchange rate)	0.130*** (0.0109)	0.661*** (0.112)	0.0878*** (0.0339)	0.274*** (0.0817)								
Log(real exchange rate$_{t-1}$)					0.0576*** (0.00915)	0.222*** (0.0676)	0.0256 (0.0176)	0.197 (0.147)				
Log(real exchange rate$_{t-2}$)									0.0416*** (0.00872)	0.0458 (0.0412)	0.00925 (0.0197)	0.0726 (0.0549)
Constant	13.72*** (1.905)	4.515 (7.949)	15.95*** (5.407)		11.40*** (1.606)	6.971 (7.241)		9.978 (6.952)	12.08*** (1.633)	9.641 (7.117)		7.831 (7.451)
Observations	128,046	32,361	33,863	30,407	127,716	32,151	33,682	31,295	119,989	31,933	33,514	31,707
Number of country-pairs	10,319	8,856	9,400	8,815	10,512	8,801	9,332	8,699	10,505	8,743	9,250	8,766

*** = significant at 1%, ** = significant at 5%, * = significant at 10%.

Note: Full-period covers 2001–2015, pre-global financial crisis covers 2003–2006, global financial crisis covers 2007–2010, and post-global financial crisis covers 2012–2015.

Sources: ADB calculations using data from Institute for Research on the International Economy. http://www.cepii.fr/CEPII/en/cepii/cepii.asp; United Nations. Commodity Trade Database. https://comtrade.un.org; and World Bank. World Development Indicators. data.worldbank.org/data-catalog/world-development-indicators (accessed September 2016).

Annex 2b: Decomposition of Gross Exports

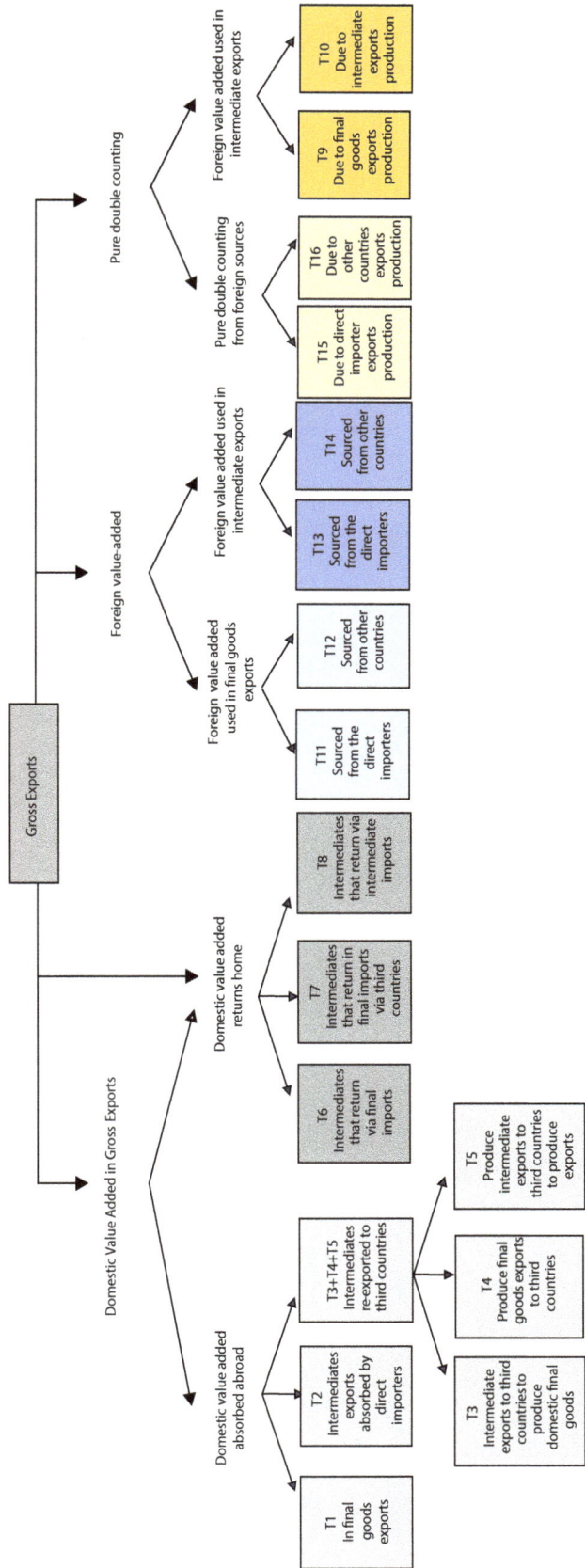

Source: Wang, Wei, and Zhu (2014).

References

ADB. 2015. How can Special Economic Zones Catalyze Economic Development? *Asian Economic Integration Report 2015*. Manila.

J.E. Anderson and E.V. Wincoop. 2003. Gravity And Gravitas: A Solution To The Border Puzzle. *American Economic Review*. 93(1). pp. 170-192.

Association of Southeast Asian Nations (ASEAN). 2016. ASEAN Joint Leaders' Statement on the Regional Comprehensive Economic Partnership. https://www.asean2016.gov.la/kcfinder/upload/files/Joint%20 Leaders%E2%80%99%20Statement%20%20on%20 the%20Regional%20Comprehensive%20Economic%20 Partnership%20(RCEP).pdf

Australian Government Department Foreign Affairs and Trade. 2016. Regional Comprehensive Economic Partnership. http://dfat.gov.au/trade/agreements/rcep/Pages/regional-comprehensive-economic-partnership.aspx

Bangkok Post. 2016. RCEP Leaders to Skip 2016 Completion Target. 7 September. http://www.bangkokpost.com/business/news/1080409/rcep-leaders-to-skip-2016-completion-target

Business Standard. 2016. RCEP Talks May Miss December 2016 Deadline, Enter 2017: Nirmala. 24 August. http://www.business-standard.com/article/pti-stories/rcep-talks-may-miss-december-2016-deadline-enter-2017-nirmala-116082401240_1.html

DBS Group Research. 2016. Japan: Rising Direct Investment in Southeast Asia. 18 March. https://www.dbs.com/aics/pdfController.page?pdfpath=/content/article/pdf/AIO/160318_insights_japan_looks_to_southeast_asia_for_growth.pdf.

A. C. Disdier, L. Fontagné, and M. Mimouni. 2008. The Impact of Regulations on Agricultural Trade: Evidence from the SPS and TBT Agreements. *American Journal of Agricultural Economics*. 90 (2). pp.336–50.

R. Feenstra. 2004. *Advanced International Trade: Theory and Evidence*. Princeton, New Jersey: Princeton University Press.

International Monetary Fund (IMF). 2016. *World Economic Outlook Update: Uncertainty in the Aftermath of the UK Referendum*. Washington, DC: International Monetary Fund.

Japan Times. 2016. Abe Goes Toe-to-toe Over TPP as Diet Debate Heats Up. 27 September. http://www.japantimes.co.jp/news/2016/09/27/national/politics-diplomacy/abe-goes-toe-toe-tpp-diet-debate-heats/#.V-s59_I96Uk

J.W. Kang and M. Legal. 2016. Rising tides of protectionism will cause more harm than good. Asian Development Blog. 25 May. https://blogs.adb.org/blog/rising-tides-protectionism-will-cause-more-harm-good

Malaysia Ministry of International Trade and Industry. 2016. Media Statement: ASEAN Committed Towards Preserving Centrality and Meeting the 2016 Deadline of Regional Comprehensive Economic Partnership (RCEP) Negotiations. http://www.miti.gov.my/index.php/pages/view/3048

Ministry of Foreign Affairs of Japan. 2016. Negotiations on Regional Comprehensive Economic Partnership (RCEP). http://www.mofa.go.jp/policy/economy/page2e_000001.html

Office of the United States Trade Representative. 2016. TPP Endorsements: Diverse Coalition of American Businesses, Farmers, and Manufacturers Call for TPP Passage to Help Boost Made in America Exports, Level the Playing Field. https://ustr.gov/about-us/policy-offices/press-office/press-releases/2016/january/Diverse-Coalition-American-Businesses-Farmers-Manufacturers-Call-for-TPP-Passage#

Prime Minister of Japan and His Cabinet. 2016a. Proposal from Economic Organizations on Seeking the Early Realization of the TPP Agreement. http://japan.kantei.go.jp/97_abe/actions/201607/13article2.html

Prime Minister of Japan and His Cabinet. 2016b. Address by Prime Minister Shinzo Abe at the Seminar "Investment Opportunities in Japan toward the New Asia-Pacific Era." http://japan.kantei.go.jp/97_abe/actions/201607/13article2.html

D.D. Thilmany and C.B. Barrett. 1997. Regulatory Barriers in an Integrating World Food Market. *Review of Agricultural Economics*. 19 (1). pp. 91–107.

Z. Wang, S.J. Wei, and K. Zhu. 2014. Quantifying International Production Sharing at the Bilateral and Sector Levels. *NBER Working Paper*. No. 19677. Cambridge: National Bureau of Economic Research.

World Trade Organization. 2012. Trade and public policies: A closer look at non-tariff measures in the 21st century. Geneva.

3 | Financial Integration

Financial Integration

Recent developments in Asian financial markets show financial integration continues to increase gradually in the region; but still lags far behind the level of trade integration. Quantity indicators show the level of intraregional cross-border asset holdings and liabilities have remained relatively low since 2001, although the pace of intraregional financial integration is gradually increasing. Intraregional cross-border asset holdings are concentrated in a few Asian economies, though with increasing participation of other economies in the region. Asia's financial links with the rest of the world remain stronger than those within the region.

Compared with 2014, total outward portfolio investment from Asia in 2015 increased by $303.6 billion. Outward portfolio investment to the United States (US) increased significantly—by $178.6 billion—coinciding with a drastic $108.1 billion drop in investment to the European Union (EU). Price indicators reveal that despite being more globally integrated, Asia's equity markets are increasingly integrated regionally; with bond market integration lagging behind equity markets. Volatility across all types of financial flows has declined since the 2008/09 global financial crisis (GFC) compared with pre-crisis levels.

Quantity Indicators

Asian investors increased cross-border asset holdings between 2010 and 2014.

In 2014, Asia's cross-border asset holdings totaled $14.1 trillion—14.5% of total global cross-border asset holdings—an increase of $2.7 trillion compared with

2010.[14] Bank claims overseas accounted for the largest share of Asia's total cross-border assets, at $4.0 trillion or 28.4% of the region's total cross-border asset holdings, followed by the stock of outward foreign direct investment (FDI), which accounted for $3.5 trillion or 25.1%. Cross-border portfolio debt assets accounted for 25.1% at $3.5 trillion and cross-border portfolio equity assets for the smallest share at 21.5%.

An analysis of Asia's cross-border asset and liability holdings finds that Asia's financial links with the rest of the world remain stronger than those within the region.

Intraregional asset holdings—the share of Asian financial assets in Asia's total cross-border holdings—were 26.1% (or $3.7 trillion in value) in 2014 (Figure 3.1). The intraregional share increased compared with 2010 (20.6%) indicating the gradual regional financial integration; but it remained relatively low, suggesting greater room for improvement.

The intraregional share in Asia's total cross-border asset holdings has increased since 2010 for all asset classes except for portfolio equities. Although Asia's total cross-border portfolio equity assets increased from $1.9 trillion in 2010 to $3.0 trillion in 2014, the share of intraregional equity holdings declined from 24.9% to 20.8%. This suggests that the majority of recent cross-border equity investment was directed to the rest of the world. The intraregional share of Asia's cross-border debt asset holdings increased from 12.1% to 18.8%, but this remained lowest among all asset categories in 2014. The intraregional share of Asia's cross-border bank claims

---

[14] Throughout this chapter, Asia's cross-border asset holdings refer to the stock of outbound portfolio debt, portfolio equity, and FDI, as well as cross-border bank claims. FDI stock data available only for 2009-2014.

Figure 3.1: Cross-border Assets—Asia

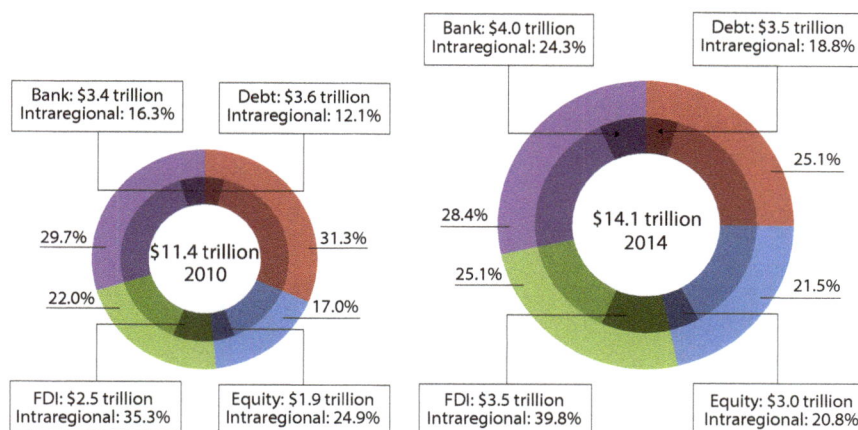

Bank: $3.4 trillion
Intraregional: 16.3%

Debt: $3.6 trillion
Intraregional: 12.1%

29.7%

31.3%

22.0%

17.0%

$11.4 trillion
2010

FDI: $2.5 trillion
Intraregional: 35.3%

Equity: $1.9 trillion
Intraregional: 24.9%

Bank: $4.0 trillion
Intraregional: 24.3%

Debt: $3.5 trillion
Intraregional: 18.8%

25.1%

28.4%

25.1%

21.5%

$14.1 trillion
2014

FDI: $3.5 trillion
Intraregional: 39.8%

Equity: $3.0 trillion
Intraregional: 20.8%

FDI = foreign direct investment.
Notes: FDI assets refer to FDI outward holdings. Bank assets refer to bank claims data. FDI stock data available for 2009–2014. Asia includes all the 48 regional ADB members for which data are available.
Sources: ADB calculations using data from International Monetary Fund. Coordinated Portfolio Investment Survey. http://cpis.imf.org (accessed September 2016); International Monetary Fund. Coordinated Direct Investment Survey. http://cdis.imf.org (accessed April 2016); and Bank for International Settlements. Banking Statistics. https://www.bis.org/statistics/bankstats.htm (accessed September 2016).

increased to 24.3% in 2014 from 16.3% in 2010, the biggest increase relative to other asset classes during the period. The intraregional share of Asia's outward FDI in stock also increased from 35.3% in 2010 to 39.8% in 2014.

Asia's gross cross-border liabilities exceed its gross cross-border assets, highlighting the region's attractiveness as an investment destination.

In 2014, Asia's total cross-border liabilities—inward investment—reached $14.8 trillion, an increase of $3.3 trillion compared with 2010 (Figure 3.2). Asia's total cross-border liabilities are larger than its cross-border asset holdings. Asia's cross-border liabilities were significantly skewed toward inward FDI, which accounted for 44.7% of Asia's total cross-border liabilities in 2014. The cross-border portfolio equity liabilities, bank liabilities, and portfolio debt liabilities accounted for 24.8%, 15.7%, and 14.9% of the region's total cross-border liabilities, respectively.

Asia's intraregional liabilities amounted to $4.7 trillion or 31.6% of its total cross-border liabilities in 2014, up from $3.4 trillion or 29.5% in 2010. As in the case of intraregional asset holdings, Asia's financial linkages on liabilities were also stronger with the rest of the world than within the region. Still, the intraregional share of total cross-border liabilities increased compared with 2010, suggesting a gradual increase in the level of regional financial integration for Asia's cross-border liability holdings.

The intraregional share of Asia's total cross-border liabilities is 43.5% for the stock of inward FDI, followed by 30.0% for portfolio debt liabilities, 21.7% for bank liabilities and 17.1% for portfolio equity liabilities. The intraregional shares of cross-border liabilities increased for all asset classes compared with 2010, confirming the trend toward more regionally integrated financial markets in Asia.

Figure 3.2: Cross-border Liabilities—Asia

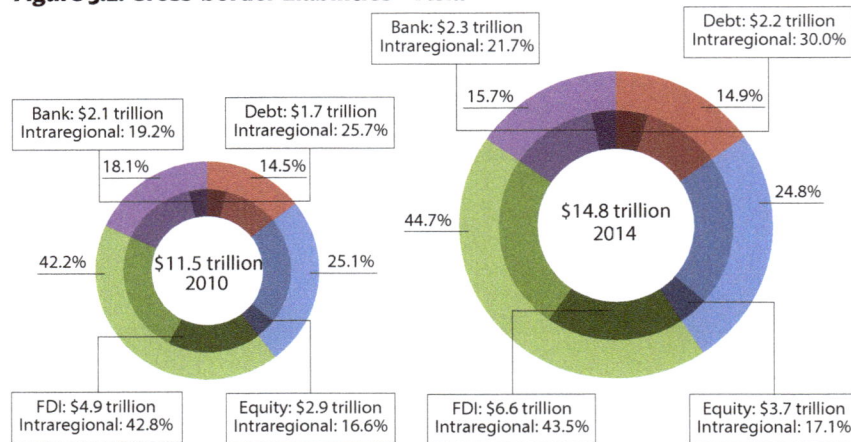

Bank: $2.1 trillion Intraregional: 19.2%
Debt: $1.7 trillion Intraregional: 25.7%
Bank: $2.3 trillion Intraregional: 21.7%
Debt: $2.2 trillion Intraregional: 30.0%
18.1% 14.5% 15.7% 14.9%
42.2% $11.5 trillion 2010 25.1%
44.7% $14.8 trillion 2014 24.8%
FDI: $4.9 trillion Intraregional: 42.8%
Equity: $2.9 trillion Intraregional: 16.6%
FDI: $6.6 trillion Intraregional: 43.5%
Equity: $3.7 trillion Intraregional: 17.1%

FDI = foreign direct investment.
Notes: FDI liabilities refer to FDI inward holdings. FDI stock data available only for 2009–2014.
Asia includes all the 48 regional ADB members for which data are available.
Sources: ADB calculations using data from International Monetary Fund. Coordinated Portfolio Investment Survey. http://cpis.imf.org (accessed September 2016); International Monetary Fund. Coordinated Direct Investment Survey. http://cdis.imf.org (accessed April 2016); and Bank for International Settlements. Banking Statistics. https://www.bis.org/statistics/bankstats.htm (accessed September 2016).

Portfolio Debt Holdings

In 2015, Asia recorded net outward portfolio debt investment, as its outward debt investment exceeded inward debt investment.

The main destinations for Asia's outward portfolio debt investment remained the EU and the US, whereas the top destinations for intraregional portfolio debt investment were the People's Republic of China (PRC), Australia, and the Republic of Korea, respectively. Hong Kong, China was the largest regional source of debt investment in Asia.

Global outward portfolio debt investment increased from $7.2 trillion in 2001 to $24.4 trillion in 2015 (Figure 3.3). In 2015, the largest investors for global outward portfolio debt investment were the EU (44.8%), Asia (14.9%), and North America (12.1%). Latin America, the Middle East, and Africa had a combined contribution of only 1.2%, even though it has grown rapidly.[15]

Asia's contribution to global outward portfolio debt investment in 2015 indicated a slight recovery compared

Figure 3.3: Portfolio Debt Investment—World ($ trillion)

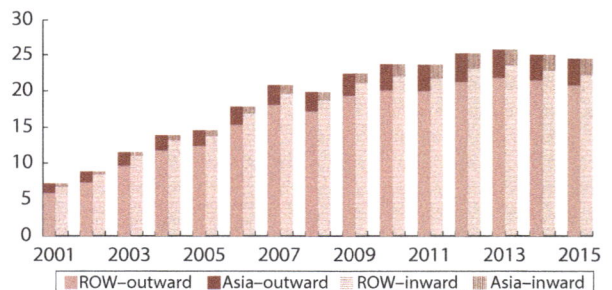

ROW–outward Asia–outward ROW–inward Asia–inward

ROW = rest of the world.
Note: Asia includes all the 48 regional ADB members for which data are available.
Source: ADB calculations using data from International Monetary Fund. Coordinated Portfolio Investment Survey. http://cpis.imf.org (accessed September 2016).

with its 13.2% share during the GFC. But its share remained lower than the peak of 15.6% during the surge in capital outflows in 2012. North America's share increased to 12.1% from 8.3% during the GFC, even surpassing its 10.0% share in 2001. The EU remained the largest contributor, but outward portfolio debt investment declined to 44.8% in 2015, its lowest share since 2001.

The EU (46.9%), North America (29.0%), and Asia (9.1%) still attracted the most of global inward portfolio debt

---

[15] The remaining 26.9% was contributed by economies outside these regions.

investment. Latin America, the Middle East, and Africa had a combined contribution of only 3.0%. Similar to outward portfolio investment, they have grown rapidly from a small base.

Asia's share of total inward portfolio debt investment has substantially increased from 5.5% share in 2008, as has North America, from its GFC low of 24.6%. However, the EU's 46.9% share in 2015 was below its 56.0% GFC level.

Asia's outward portfolio debt investment remains substantially skewed toward the rest of the world, but the bias toward non-Asian economies appeared to be weakening.

Asia's outward portfolio debt investment increased from $1.3 trillion in 2001 to $3.6 trillion in 2015 (Figure 3.4). But Asia's outward portfolio debt investment to Asia—intraregional portfolio debt investment—was only $650 billion, or 17.9% of the 2015 total. While the intraregional share fell slightly from 18.8% in 2014, it has increased significantly since its 7.8% share in 2001 and 10.3% share in 2008.[16]

While Asia's intraregional share of its total outward portfolio debt investment in 2015 (17.9%) remained well

below the EU's (65.5%)—a region characterized by mainly two currencies (the euro and British pound sterling)—it remained comparable to the intraregional shares of the Middle East (21.3%), and North America (19.2%), and was significantly above the shares in Africa (7.2%), and Latin America (9.2%).

In fact, Asia's intraregional portfolio investment declined $11.9 billion between 2014 and 2015, with Japan and New Zealand accounting for $6.9 billion of the decline.[17] Its outward portfolio debt investment to the rest of the world—excluding the EU and the US—increased $70.5 billion in 2015 compared with 2014.[18]

Ongoing yield differences between the EU and the US prompted a shift in Asia's outward investment portfolio for debt securities.

Asia's outward portfolio debt investment to the EU declined in 2015 by $89.7 billion, but less than its 2014 decline of $163.1 billion (Figure 3.5).[19] This coincided with a sharp increase in Asia's outward portfolio debt investment to the US by $149.0 billion, up further from its $50.1 billion rise in 2014.[20] This trend in outward portfolio debt adjustments was not unique to Asia. Global outward portfolio debt investment to the US also rose $430.9 billion in 2015, while global outward portfolio debt investment to the EU dropped a dramatic

Figure 3.4: Outward Portfolio Debt Investment—Asia

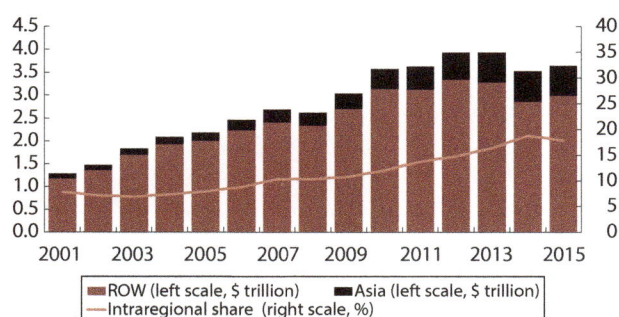

ROW = rest of the world.
Note: Asia includes all the ADB 48 regional members for which data are available.
Source: ADB calculations using data from International Monetary Fund. Coordinated Portfolio Investment Survey. http://cpis.imf.org (accessed September 2016).

---

16   This excludes data for the PRC in 2015. If the PRC data were included, Asia's total portfolio debt outward investment in 2015 would be $3.7 trillion, and intraregional portfolio debt outward investment would be $685 billion, or 18.3% of Asia's total portfolio debt outward investment. No data for the PRC are available for 2001–2014.

17   This excludes data for the PRC in 2015. If the PRC data were included, the change in Asia's intraregional portfolio debt outward investment in 2015 would have increased by $23.1 billion. No data for the PRC are available for 2001–2014.

18   This excludes data for the PRC in 2015. If the PRC data were included, the change in Asia's portfolio debt investment to the rest of the world excluding the EU and the US and the EU in 2015 would have increased by $89.1 billion. No PRC data are available for 2001–2014.

19   This excludes data for Australia's investment to the United Kingdom, as data for 2015 was recorded as 'confidential' by the data source. This also excludes data for the PRC in 2015. If both were included, the decline in Asia's portfolio debt outward investment to the EU in 2014 would have been $167.7 billion, and the decline in Asia's portfolio debt outward investment to the EU in 2015 would have been $96.6 billion. No data for the PRC are available for 2001–2014.

20   This excludes data for the PRC in 2015. If the PRC data were included, the change in Asia's portfolio debt outward investment to the US in 2015 would have increased by $198.5 billion. No PRC data are available for 2001–2014.

Figure 3.5: Change in Outward Portfolio Debt Investment—Asia ($ billion)

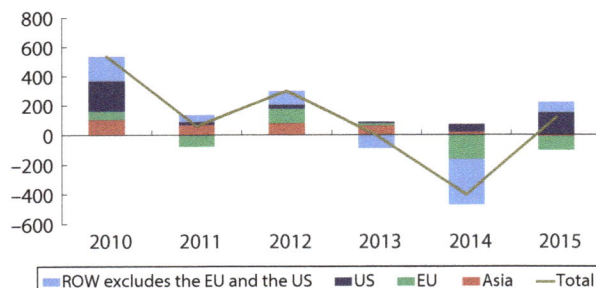

EU = European Union, ROW = rest of the world, US = United States.
Note: Asia includes all the ADB 48 regional members for which data are available.
Source: ADB calculations using data from International Monetary Fund. Coordinated Portfolio Investment Survey. http://cpis.imf.org (accessed September 2016).

$980.0 billion.[21] Yield-seeking investors may have shifted from EU portfolio debt assets to the US portfolio, with negative interest rates in the euro area since June 2014 and the expected interest rate rise in the US.

The European Central Bank (ECB) has pushed interest rates down further after launching its large-scale quantitative easing asset purchase program in March 2015. Weak European macroeconomic fundamentals, combined with an intensifying crisis in Greece, further pressured the euro. In contrast, with the US economy performing better and US Federal Reserve raising its key policy rate in December 2015 (for the first time since the GFC), Asian investors flocked to the US. The gap between the US and the EU 10-year government bond yields began to rise during the November 2011 euro crisis, peaking in March 2015 at the start of the ECB's massive quantitative easing. With the improving US economy, investors had already rebalanced their portfolios even before the US policy-rate increase in December 2015. The decline of $89.7 billion in Asia's outward portfolio debt investment in the EU came primarily from Australia ($22.2 billion) and Japan ($73.9 billion). The increase of $149 billion in Asia's outward portfolio debt investment to the US was primarily from Japan ($105.0 billion), as

well as the region's two financial hubs, Hong Kong, China ($24.7 billion) and Singapore ($19.3 billion).

Asia's outward portfolio debt investment continued to go mostly to the US and the EU in 2015, although the more attractive destination between the two has changed from the EU in 2010 to the US in 2015 (Table 3.1). Asia's outward portfolio debt investment was limited to a few economies, whether within or outside the region. In 2010, much of Asia's intraregional portfolio debt investment went to Australia, the PRC, and the Republic of Korea, comprising 8.0% of its total global cross-border debt asset holdings and 67.9% of its intraregional debt asset holdings. These were the same top destinations in 2015, with share to total global and intraregional holdings at 11.0% and 61.7%, respectively. Hong Kong, China, meanwhile, held 95.6% of the PRC's debt securities in 2010 and 73.3% in 2015.

By subregion, the source of Asia's intraregional portfolio debt investment is primarily East Asia. However, its share to total intraregional investment declined from 70.6% in 2001 to 66.7% in 2015 (Figure 3.6). Southeast Asia, another primary source, increased its share from 24.9% in 2001 to 28.6% in 2015. This indicates that while financial integration remained concentrated in just a few economies, it is nonetheless broadening.

By economy, top sources of Asia's intraregional portfolio debt investment in 2015 were Hong Kong, China; Japan; and Singapore. Their combined share increased to 25.5% in 2015 from 23.5% in 2010. Outside Asia, the EU and the US continue to be the top sources for inward portfolio debt investment to the region. Along with international organizations, which invest heavily in Japan's and Republic of Korea's cross-border debt, the combined share of the EU, the US, and international organizations totaled 60.7% of Asia's inward portfolio debt investment. This again shows nonregional economies were the primary source of inward portfolio investment in the region, although their relative share declined between 2010 and 2015 (Table 3.2).

The share of intraregional inward portfolio debt investment increased from 25.7% in 2010 to 29.2% in 2015 (see Table 3.2), accompanied by an increase in Asia's inward portfolio debt investment from $1.7 trillion in 2010 to $2.2 trillion in 2015 (Figure 3.7). While the

---

21   These exclude data for the PRC, as there is no PRC data for 2001–2015. These also exclude data for the Bahamas, Ireland, and Isle of Man, as data for 2015 is unavailable. And they exclude Australia's investment to the United Kingdom, as data for 2015 was recorded as "confidential" by the data source.

Table 3.1: Destinations of Asia's Outward Portfolio Debt Investment ($ billion)

	2015		2010		% Change
Asia					
People's Republic of China	185	(5.1%)	53	(1.5%)	▲
Australia	157	(4.3%)	169	(4.7%)	▼
Republic of Korea	59	(1.6%)	64	(1.8%)	▼
Other Asia	249	(6.8%)	145	(4.0%)	▲
Asia's outward portfolio debt investment to Asia	650	(17.9%)	430	(12.1%)	▲
Non-Asia					
United States	1,370	(37.7%)	1,116	(31.2%)	▲
European Union	925	(25.4%)	1,142	(32.0%)	▼
Not specified (including confidential)	199	(5.5%)	45	(1.3%)	▲
Other non-Asia	514	(14.1%)	837	(23.4%)	▼
Asia's outward portfolio debt investment to non-Asia	2,990	(82.1%)	3,140	(87.9%)	▼
Asia's total outward portfolio debt investment	**3,640**	**(100.0%)**	**3,570**	**(100.0%)**	

Source: ADB calculations using data from International Monetary Fund. Coordinated Portfolio Investment Survey. http://cpis.imf.org (accessed September 2016).

Figure 3.6: Asia's Intraregional Portfolio Debt Investment by Subregion ($ billion)

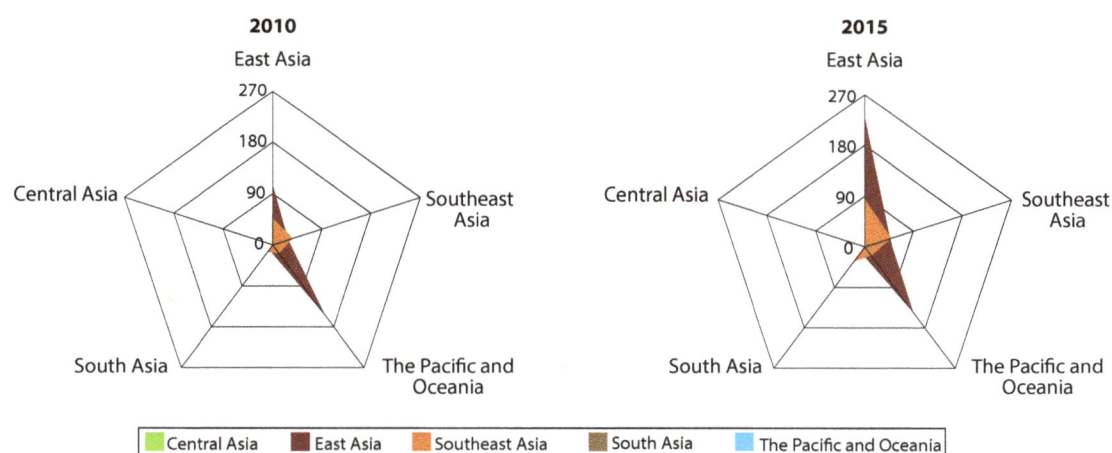

Note: Subregions in legend refer to the source. Subregions on the chart axis refer to the destination.
Source: ADB calculations using data from International Monetary Fund. Coordinated Portfolio Investment Survey. http://cpis.imf.org (accessed September 2016).

Table 3.2: Sources of Asia's Inward Portfolio Debt Investment ($ billion)

	2015		2010		% Change
Asia					
Hong Kong, China	239	(10.7%)	146	(8.7%)	▲
Japan	178	(8.0%)	150	(9.0%)	▼
Singapore	151	(6.8%)	96	(5.8%)	▲
Other Asia	82	(3.7%)	38	(2.3%)	▲
Asia's inward portfolio debt investment from Asia	650	(29.2%)	430	(25.7%)	▲
Non-Asia					
European Union	605	(27.1%)	520	(31.0%)	▼
United States	419	(18.8%)	320	(19.1%)	▼
International Organizations	330	(14.8%)	290	(17.3%)	▼
Other non-Asia	225	(10.1%)	113	(16.8%)	▲
Asia's inward portfolio debt investment from non-Asia	1,579	(70.8%)	1,244.	(74.3%)	▼
Asia's total inward portfolio debt investment	**2,229**	**(100.0%)**	**1,674**	**(100.0%)**	

Source: ADB calculations using data from International Monetary Fund. Coordinated Portfolio Investment Survey. http://cpis.imf.org (accessed September 2016).

Figure 3.7: Inward Portfolio Debt Investment—Asia

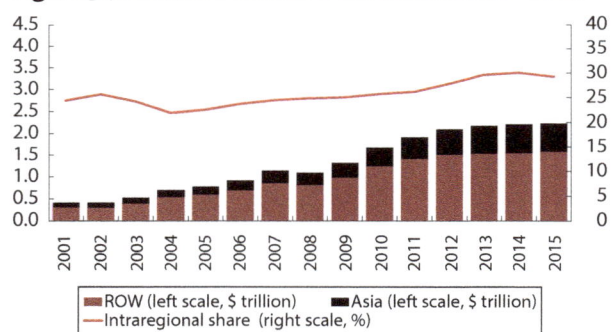

ROW = rest of the world.
Note: Asia includes all the ADB 48 regional members for which data are available.
Source: ADB calculations using data from International Monetary Fund. Coordinated Portfolio Investment Survey. http://cpis.imf.org (accessed September 2016).

Figure 3.8: Change in Inward Portfolio Debt Investment—Asia ($ billion)

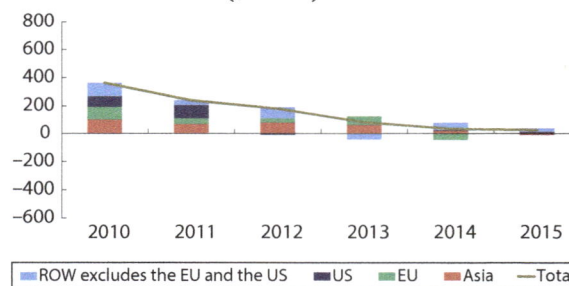

EU = European Union, ROW = rest of the world, US = United States.
Note: Asia includes all the ADB 48 regional members for which data are available.
Source: ADB calculations using data from International Monetary Fund. Coordinated Portfolio Investment Survey. http://cpis.imf.org (accessed September 2016).

amount in 2015 was more than 5 times what it was in 2001, Asia's inward portfolio debt investment remained lower than outward portfolio debt investment by $1.4 trillion.

Asia's inward portfolio debt investment increased by $23.8 billion in 2015 from the previous year, albeit at a moderating pace of increase over 2010–2015

(Figure 3.8). The decline in Asia's intraregional inward investment ($11.9 billion), primarily due to Hong Kong, China-PRC investment (a $38.4 billion decline), was offset by an increase in investment from the rest of the world, excluding the US and the EU ($23.3 billion).

Portfolio Equity Holdings

Asia's cross-border equity investment remained concentrated in a few large economies outside the region.

According to 2015 data, the main destinations of Asia's outward portfolio equity investment were the US (25.8%), Cayman Islands (25.0%), and the EU (14.6%). The intraregional share for outward portfolio equity investment fell to 19.8% in 2015 from 24.9% in 2010, while the share for inward investment rose to 17.5% in 2015 from 16.6% in 2010. The top destinations for intraregional outward portfolio equity investment were the PRC (8.8%), Japan (2.0%), and Hong Kong, China (1.4%) while Singapore was the largest regional source of equity investment (5.9%) in Asia in 2015.

Asia's gross inward equity investment exceeded its gross outward investment, making the region a net recipient in cross-border portfolio equity investment.

Global outward portfolio equity investment increased from $5.0 trillion to $21.6 trillion between 2001 and 2015 (Figure 3.9). In 2015, similar to the trend in outward portfolio debt investment, the EU (38.3%), North America (35.7%), and Asia (14.9%) were the three biggest contributors to global outward portfolio equity

investment. Latin America, Middle East, and Africa had a combined share 2.5%.

Asia's share in global outward equity investment has recovered from its 11.4% level during the GFC in 2008, reaching 14.9% in 2015. North America marginally increased its share to 35.7% of global outward portfolio investment in 2015, from its 33.1% share during the GFC. The EU, however, while still the largest contributor to global portfolio equity investment, saw its share decline from 43.7% in 2008 to 38.3% in 2015. On the other hand, the EU (41.4%), North America (19.8%), and Asia (16.8%) attracted the most global inward equity investment.

Unlike portfolio debt investment, Asia was a net receiving region in cross-border portfolio equity investment. While its share of inward equity investment to the global total in 2015 (16.8%) declined from the capital flow surge in 2012 (18.5%), it still increased from its 2001 share (12.9%). The EU's inward portfolio equity investment declined to 41.4% in 2015 from 50.8% in 2001. It reached a low of 39.6% in 2011 during the European debt crisis. North America's share to global total also declined to 19.8% in 2015 from 21.3% in 2001. It had reached a low of 16.7% in 2007, just before the onset of the GFC.

Asia's outward portfolio equity investment was destined more outside than inside the region.

Asia's total outward portfolio equity investment increased from $424 billion in 2001 to $3.2 trillion in 2015 (Figure 3.10).[22] However, intraregional equity investment was only $633.9 billion, 19.8% of Asia's total cross-border equity holdings. The share of intraregional equity holdings in 2001 was 11.9%. Intraregional equity asset holdings peaked at 28.7% in 2007. While Asia's intraregional share in 2015 was lower than the EU's (55.7%), it is significantly higher than other regions that do not share a common currency—Africa (1.9%), Latin America (2.2%), the Middle East (8. 3%) and North America (11.5%).

Figure 3.9: Portfolio Equity Investment—World
($ trillion)

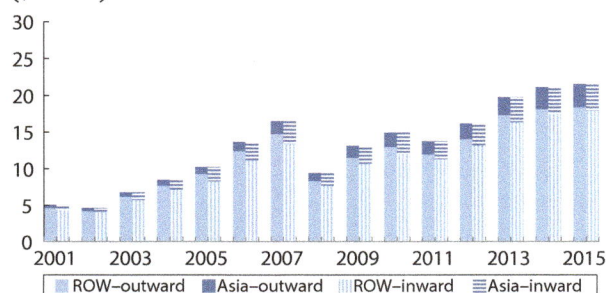

ROW = rest of the world.
Note: Asia includes all the ADB 48 regional members for which data are available.
Source: ADB calculations using data from International Monetary Fund. Coordinated Portfolio Investment Survey. http://cpis.imf.org (accessed September 2016).

22 This excludes data for the PRC in 2015. If the PRC data were included, Asia's total portfolio equity outward investment in 2015 would have been $3.4 trillion, and intraregional portfolio equity outward investment $685 billion, or 20.3% of Asia's total outward portfolio equity investment. No data for the PRC are available for 2001–2014.

Figure 3.10: Outward Portfolio Equity Investment—Asia

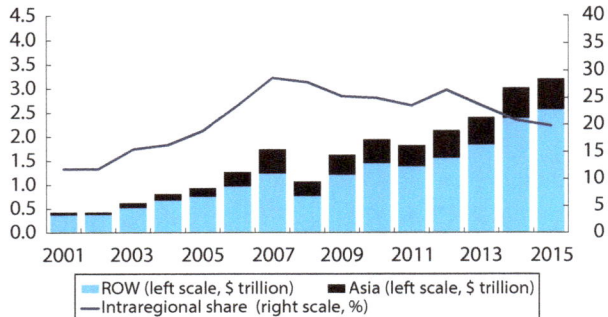

ROW = rest of the world.
Note: Asia includes all the ADB 48 regional members, for which data are available.
Source: ADB calculations using data from International Monetary Fund. Coordinated Portfolio Investment Survey. http://cpis.imf.org (accessed September 2016).

Figure 3.11: Change in Outward Portfolio Equity Investment—Asia ($ billion)

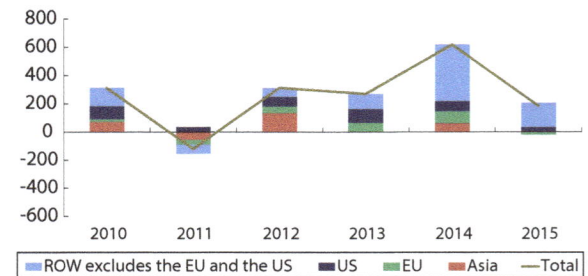

EU = European Union, ROW = rest of the world, US = United States.
Note: Asia includes all the ADB 48 regional members, for which data are available.
Source: ADB calculations using data from International Monetary Fund. Coordinated Portfolio Investment Survey. http://cpis.imf.org (accessed September 2016).

Between 2014 and 2015, Asia's outward portfolio equity investment rose $185.8 billion, with its destinations broadened and diversified (Figure 3.11). While Asia's investment in EU portfolio equity assets dropped $18.3 billion, its investment in other regions increased.[23] Asia's investment to the rest of the world excluding the EU and the US increased $168.5 billion in 2015.[24] Asia's intraregional investment and Asia's investment in the US equity assets increased $5.9 billion and $29.6 billion, respectively.[25] Asia's outward portfolio equity investment to the EU fell perhaps due to downward pressure on the euro against the US dollar, associated with the intensifying crisis in Greece. In contrast, the increased outward portfolio equity investment to the US was mainly from Japan ($30.8 billion) and New Zealand ($12.2 billion). The improved US economic outlook could have made its equity market more attractive than that of the EU.

[23] This excludes data for Australia's investment to the United Kingdom, as data for 2015 was recorded as 'confidential' by data source. This also excludes data for the PRC in 2015. If both were included, the decline in Asia's portfolio equity outward investment to the EU in 2015 would have been $28.9 billion. No data for the PRC are available for 2001–2014.

[24] This excludes data for the PRC in 2015. If the PRC data were included, the change in Asia's portfolio equity investment to the rest of the world excluding the US and the EU in 2015 would have increased by $196.0 billion. No data for the PRC are available for 2001–2014.

[25] This excludes data for the PRC in 2015. If the PRC data were included, the change intraregional outward portfolio equity investment in 2015 would have increased by $56.5 billion. Asia's outward portfolio equity investment to the US increased by $91.2 billion. No data for the PRC are available for 2001–2014.

The intraregional shares of both outward and inward portfolio equity investment suggest significantly higher regional integration in cross-border equity investment than in debt.

The US remained the most popular destination for Asia's outward portfolio equity investment in 2015, while Cayman Islands replaced the EU as the second most popular destination (Table 3.3). The EU dropped to third. Similar to the region's outward portfolio debt investment, Asia's outward portfolio equity investment was more destined to the rest of the world than to the region. Unlike the region's outward portfolio debt investment, its outward portfolio equity investment in non-Asian economies increased between 2010 and 2015.

The primary regional destinations for Asia's outward portfolio equity investment are the PRC; Hong Kong, China; and Japan. These economies received 62.0% of intraregional equity investment in 2015, up from 60.3% in 2010, indicating more concentration in intraregional equity investment (see Table 3.3).

By subregion, the source of Asia's portfolio equity investment was also primarily East Asia (Figure 3.12). Half of Asia's intraregional outward portfolio equity investment came from East Asia. East Asia's intra-subregional share of 80.5% has driven much of intraregional equity market integration, with its remaining outward portfolio equity investment going to the Pacific and Oceania (8.4%), and Southeast Asia (8.2%). Southeast Asia contributed 38.2%

Table 3.3: Destinations of Asia's Outward Portfolio Equity Investment ($ billion)

	2015		2010		% Change
Asia					
People's Republic of China	282	(8.8%)	204	(10.5%)	▼
Hong Kong, China	45	(1.4%)	41	(2.1%)	▼
Japan	65	(2.0%)	47	(2.4%)	▼
Other Asia	241	(7.5%)	192	(9.9%)	▼
Asia's outward portfolio equity investment to Asia	634	(19.8%)	483	(24.9%)	▼
Non-Asia					
United States	826	(25.8%)	523	(27.0%)	▼
Cayman Islands	801	(25.0%)	295	(15.2%)	▲
European Union	466	(14.6%)	328	(16.9%)	▼
Other non-Asia	475	(14.8%)	309	(15.9%)	▼
Asia's outward portfolio equity investment to non-Asia	2,568	(80.2%)	1,455	(75.1%)	▲
Asia's total outward portfolio equity investment	**3,202**	**(100.0%)**	**1,938**	**(100.0%)**	

Source: ADB calculations using data from International Monetary Fund. Coordinated Portfolio Investment Survey. http://cpis.imf.org (accessed September 2016).

Figure 3.12: Asia's Intraregional Portfolio Equity Investment by Subregion ($ billion)

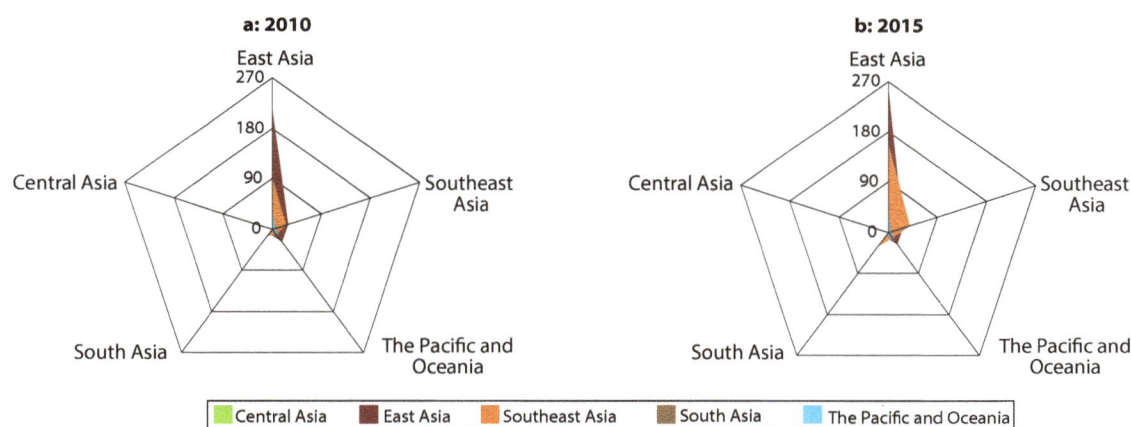

Note: Subregions in legend refer to the source. Subregions on the chart axis refer to the destination.
Source: ADB calculations using data from International Monetary Fund. Coordinated Portfolio Investment Survey. http://cpis.imf.org (accessed September 2016).

to intraregional outward portfolio equity investment, which primarily went to East Asia (65.8%), its own subregion (16.4%), and South Asia (13.0%). The Pacific and Oceania also contributed 11.0% to intraregional portfolio investment, with half of their contribution going to East Asia.

Asia's top sources of inward portfolio equity investment in 2010 were Hong Kong, China; Singapore; and Japan (Table 3.4). By 2015, the order changed to Singapore; Hong Kong, China; and Japan. The intraregional share of Asia's total inward portfolio equity investment edged up

to 17.5% in 2015 from 16.6% in 2010. At the same time, its top source, the US, increased its investment to Asia from 44.3% in 2010 to 45.0% in 2015. The EU remained Asia's second top source of investment despite a decline in its relative share from 27.5% in 2010 to 24.3% in 2015. Canada contributed 3.6% of Asia's total inward portfolio investment in 2015.

Inward portfolio equity investment to Asia rose from $653.4 billion in 2001 to $3.6 trillion in 2015, with the intraregional share also increasing from 7.7% in 2001 to 17.5% in 2015 (Figure 3.13).

Table 3.4: Sources of Asia's Inward Portfolio Equity Investment ($ billion)

	2015		2010		% Change
Asia					
Singapore	214	(5.9%)	128	(4.4%)	▲
Hong Kong, China	207	(5.7%)	166	(5.7%)	▲
Japan	83	(2.3%)	84	(2.9%)	▼
Other Asia	131	(3.6%)	105	(3.6%)	▲
Asia's inward portfolio equity investment from Asia	634	(17.5%)	483	(16.6%)	▲
Non-Asia					
United States	1630	(45.0%)	1285	(44.3%)	▲
European Union	880	(24.3%)	798	(27.5%)	▼
Canada	129	(3.6%)	93	(3.2%)	▲
Other non-Asia	351	(9.7%)	242	(8.3%)	▲
Asia's inward portfolio equity investment from non-Asia	2,989	(82.5%)	2,418	(83.4%)	▼
Asia's total inward portfolio equity investment	**3,623**	**(100.0%)**	**2,901**	**(100.0%)**	

Source: ADB calculations using data from International Monetary Fund. Coordinated Portfolio Investment Survey. http://cpis.imf.org (accessed September 2016).

Figure 3.13: Inward Portfolio Equity Investment—Asia

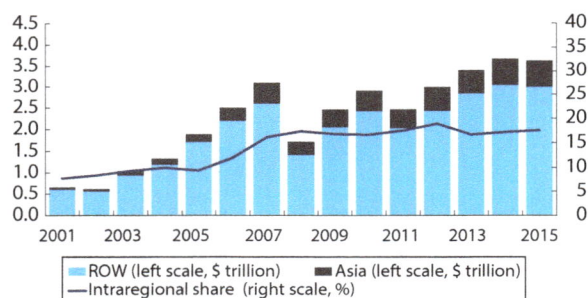

ROW = rest of the world.
Note: Asia includes all the ADB 48 regional members for which data are available.
Source: ADB calculations using data from International Monetary Fund. Coordinated Portfolio Investment Survey. http://cpis.imf.org (accessed September 2016).

Figure 3.14: Change in Inward Portfolio Equity Investment—Asia ($ billion)

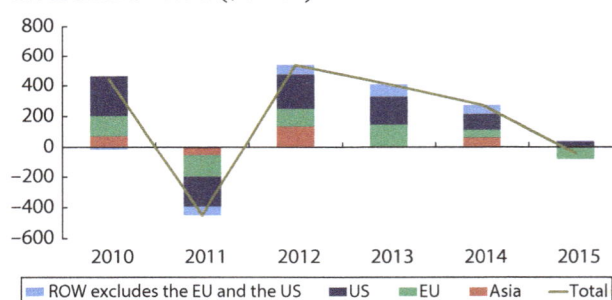

EU = European Union, ROW = rest of the world, US = United States.
Note: Asia includes all the ADB 48 regional members for which data are available.
Source: ADB calculations using data from International Monetary Fund. Coordinated Portfolio Investment Survey. http://cpis.imf.org (accessed September 2016).

Portfolio equity investment going to Asia fell $42.0 billion between 2014 and 2015, largely due the decline of $80.8 billion in inward investment from the EU (Figure 3.14). Much of the decline was in investments going to Hong Kong, China ($14.8 billion) and the PRC ($14.1 billion). This coincided with the depreciation of the PRC yuan in August 2015, followed by the PRC stock market slump.

Bank Holdings

Asia's cross-border bank claims and liabilities are mainly directed outside the region, with the EU and US holding the major shares.

Asia's cross-border bank claims were destined mostly outside the region—29.4% to the US and 27.2% to the EU. Its cross-border bank liabilities were also primarily

Figure 3.15: Cross-border Bank Holdings—World ($ trillion)

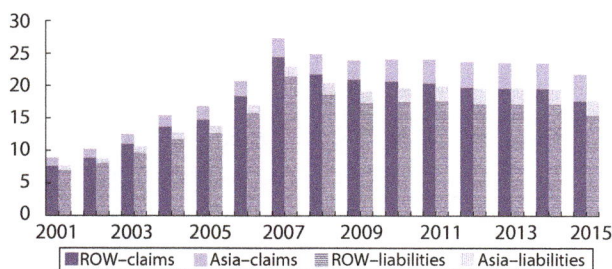

ROW = rest of the world.
Note: Asia reporters include Australia; Japan; the Republic of Korea; and Taipei,China.
Source: ADB calculations using data from Bank for International Settlements. Banking Statistics. https://www.bis.org/statistics/bankstats.htm (accessed September 2016).

Figure 3.16: Cross-border Bank Claims—Asia

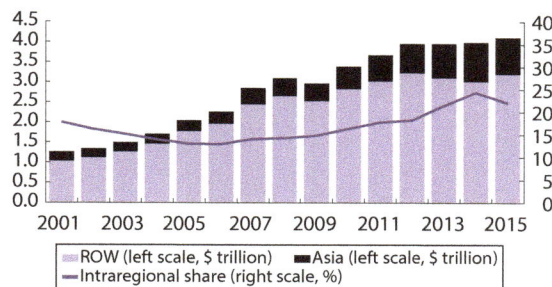

ROW = rest of the world.
Note: Asia includes all the 48 regional members of ADB for which data are available.
Source: ADB calculations using data from Bank for International Settlements. Banking Statistics. https://www.bis.org/statistics/bankstats.htm (accessed September 2016).

Figure 3.17: Change in Bank Claims—Asia ($ billion)

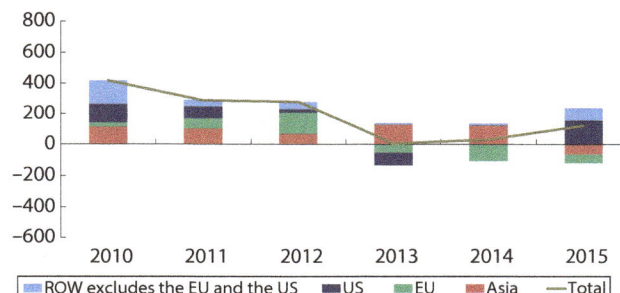

EU = European Union, ROW = rest of the world, US = United States.
Note: Asia includes all the ADB 48 regional members for which data are available.
Source: ADB calculations using data from Bank for International Settlements. Banking Statistics. https://www.bis.org/statistics/bankstats.htm (accessed September 2016).

concentrated in the EU (36.9%) and the US (32.9%). While Asian banks' claims and liabilities remained more linked to the rest of the world, their intraregional shares rose significantly over 2010–2015—from 16.3% to 22.1% for bank claims and 19.2% to 23.1% for bank liabilities, respectively.[26] As for the region's source economies for cross-border bank claims, Japan held the largest share in 2015 (76.6%)—down from 91.8% in 2001—while Australia and the Republic of Korea increased their shares considerably.

Global cross-border bank claims increased from $8.4 trillion in 2001 to $21.8 trillion in 2015 (Figure 3.15). However, this remained below its 2007 peak of $27.3 trillion. In 2015, the EU continued to hold the biggest share (58.3%), followed by Asia (18.9%) and North America (16.0%). Africa and Latin America's combined share was 0.7%.[27] In global cross-border bank liabilities, the EU (51.1%), North America (23.0%), and Asia (12.9%) accounted for the three largest shares in 2015. Latin America and Africa had a combined 1.3% share of the total.

Asia's cross-border bank claims increased from $1.3 trillion in 2001 to $4.3 trillion in 2015. While the intraregional share of cross-border bank claims increased

from 17.8% to 22.1%, this is below its 24.3% peak in 2014 (Figure 3.16).

Asia's bank claims have continued to increase since 2010, although the pace of increase slowed in recent years. Cross-border bank claims increased to $121.9 billion in 2015, with the largest share going to the US ($158.3 billion). This was primarily due to an exceptional rise in Japanese bank claims ($121.8 billion), in particular from its official sector.[28] Asia's bank claims on the EU declined by $55.3 billion in 2015 (Figure 3.17). Yield-seeking investors likely rebalanced their bank claims as the gap between the US and the EU primary rates widened.

[26] Asia's reporting economies of locational banking statistics–statistics that comprise bilateral bank claims–are Australia; Japan; the Republic of Korea; and Taipei,China.
[27] There were only 29 economies that reported bilateral bank claims as of end-2015. None are from the Middle East. The remaining 6.1% was contributed by Guernsey; the Isle of Man; Jersey; Macau, China; and Switzerland.
[28] The official sector comprises the general government sector, the central bank sector, and international organizations.

Box 3.1: The Recent Rise in Nonperforming Loans in Asia and Policy Considerations

Asia needs to monitor both the type of financial assets flowing into the region to minimize volatility and the quality of financial assets held in the region to ensure stability. Increased regional integration in banking claims—and its closer financial links globally than regionally—are raising concerns over nonperforming loans (NPLs).

NPLs are generally defined as past due loans—unpaid past their due date. The 1997/98 Asian financial crisis (AFC)—characterized by currency and maturity mismatches—caused many loans to go bad and created an NPL crisis. The asset quality of banks since then has grown much better because of regulatory safeguards and strengthened supervision, the design and use of asset management companies (AMCs) in resolving NPLs, growth in nominal income, and increased financial inclusion.

However, since 2013, NPLs have been rising in many economies in Asia—Bangladesh and India (in South Asia); the People's Republic of China (PRC); Hong Kong, China; and Mongolia

(East Asia); and in Cambodia, Indonesia, Malaysia, and Thailand (Southeast Asia). As percentage of total loans, NPLs averaged 4.8% in 2015 (box figure). Those with NPLs between 4.8% and 10.0% include Armenia, Azerbaijan, Bangladesh, India, Kazakhstan, the Kyrgyz Republic, and Samoa. Asian banking systems with NPL ratios above 10% include Afghanistan, Bhutan, the Maldives, Pakistan, and Tajikistan (box table).

The ongoing economic slowdown combined with intensified global risk aversion and tighter financing conditions might have contributed to rising NPLs and heightened credit risks. Empirical estimates generally confirm that lower output growth is associated with rising NPLs. With slower economic growth, creditors' debt servicing capacity weakens, causing NPLs to surge. Economic literature also suggests the existence of moral hazard (Klein, 2013; and Keeton and Morris, 1987). Estimates indicate a negative relationship between equity-to-asset ratios and NPLs—that is, poorly capitalized banks tend to have allowed lending to riskier clients. The risk-taking behavior is also shown through the direct relationship between loan-to-deposit ratios and NPLs. While past

NPLs and NPL Ratios of Selected Asian Economies

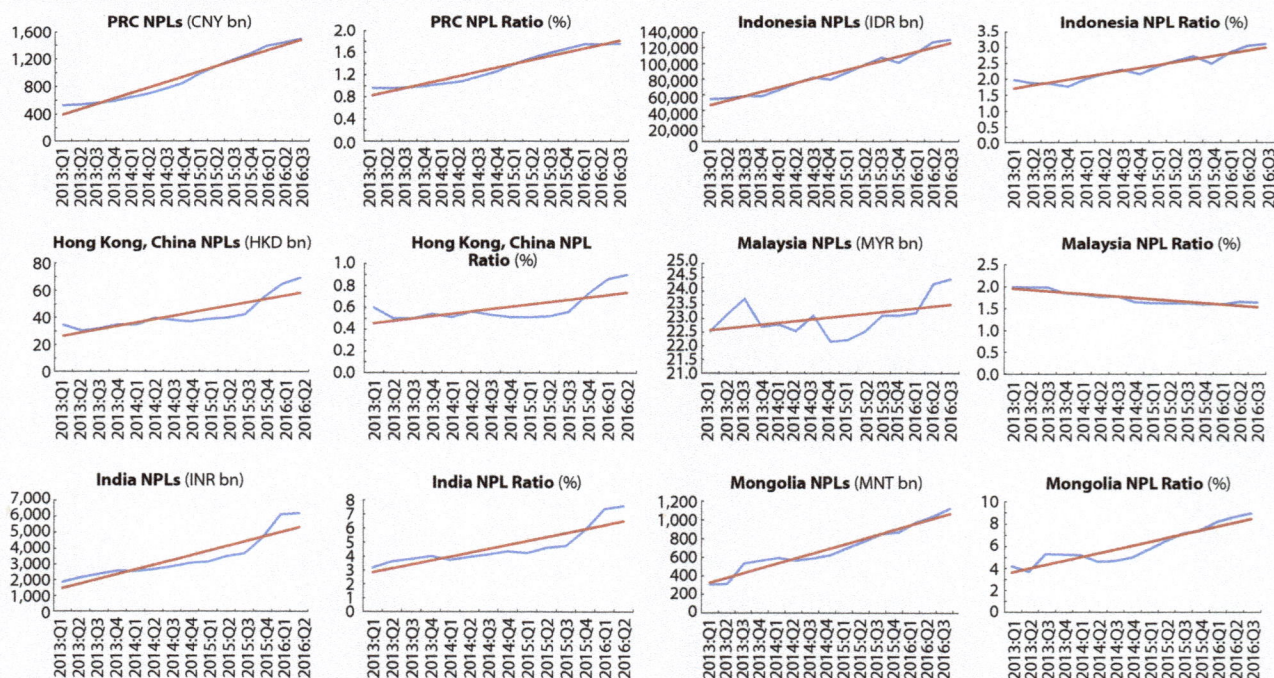

CNY = PRC yuan; HKD = Hong Kong, China dollars; IDR = Indonesian rupiah; INR = Indian rupee; MNT = Mongolian tögrög; MYR = Malaysian ringgit; NPLs = Nonperforming Loans; PRC = People's Republic of China.
Sources: ADB calculations using data from CEIC; and Haver Analytics.

excessive lending as measured by lagged loan growth is positively related to NPLs, profitability (measured by return on equity) is negatively related to NPLs (Makri et al 2013 and Klein 2013). Profitable banks have less incentive to get into high-risk activities. Past episodes of financial crisis offer strong lessons that rising NPLs must be addressed quickly. Early "clean-up" of NPLs from bank balance sheets is essential to ensure quality and productive loans. can continue.

NPL Ratios of Selected Asian Economies

Economy	NPL Ratio (%)	Year
Below 5%		
Turkmenistan	0.01	2014
Brunei Darussalam	0.4	2015
Uzbekistan	0.4	2015
Republic of Korea	0.6	2014
New Zealand	0.6	2015
Hong Kong, China	0.7	2015
Singapore	0.9	2015
Australia	1.0	2015
People's Republic of China	1.5	2015
Cambodia	1.6	2015
Japan	1.6	2015
Malaysia	1.6	2015
Fiji	1.8	2015
Philippines	1.9	2015
Georgia	2.7	2015
Thailand	2.7	2015
Viet Nam	2.9	2014
5% to below 10%		
Samoa	5.3	2015
Kyrgyz Republic	7.1	2015
Armenia	7.9	2015
Kazakhstan	8.0	2015
Bangladesh	9.3	2015
Above 10%		
Pakistan	11.4	2015
Bhutan	11.9	2015
Afghanistan	12.3	2015
Maldives	14.1	2015
Tajikistan	19.1	2015

Sources: World Bank. World Development Indicators. http://data.worldbank.org/data-catalog/world-development-indicators (accessed September 2016).

Intraregional bank claims also decreased $63.3 billion in 2015 from 2014, driven largely by the PRC's $49.9 billion contribution. This was most likely underpinned by the PRC economic slowdown coupled with a rise in PRC non-performing loans (NPLs) (Box 3.1). Nonetheless, the PRC remained one of the top destinations of Asia's intraregional bank claims.

In 2015, Hong Kong, China; Singapore; and the PRC ranked as top regional destinations for Asia's cross-border bank claims with Australia following closely (Table 3.5). Their combined share of Asia's intraregional bank claims was 63.3%, whereas their share of Asia's total cross-border bank claims was 14.1%. Although regional banking market integration appears to be making gradual progress, Asian banking markets remained more linked to the rest of the world than to the region. The US remained the top destination of Asia's bank claims, although its relative share declined from 30.3% in 2010 to 29.4% in 2015. The EU's share of Asia's total bank claims also declined, but remained the second top destination in 2015. There has been a significant increase in Asia's bank claims on the Cayman Islands—$543 billion in 2015, with 96.1% ($522 billion) coming from Japan.

Data on Asia's cross-border bank claims by reporter were derived from four economies—Australia, Japan, the Republic of Korea, and Taipei,China. Among them, Japan held the largest share in 2015, at 76.6%, down from 91.8% in 2001 (Figure 3.18). As Japan's relative contribution declined, the other economies increased their share—in 2015, Australia held 10.7%, the Republic of Korea 4.3%, and Taipei,China 8.5%.[29]

Asia's cross-border bank liabilities also increased from $655 billion in 2001 to $2.3 trillion in 2015 (Figure 3.19). While absolute levels increased between 2001 and 2015, the intraregional share of cross-border bank liabilities fell from 35.4% in 2001 two 23.1% in 2015, indicating that Asia borrowed increasingly more from economies outside the region than within the region over the period. The intraregional share recovered modestly from its 19.2%

---

[29]   Hong Kong, China began reporting in December 2014. This is not shown in Figure 14 as it shows a dramatic increase, beginning that month, distorting the analysis. The Republic of Korea began reporting in December 2005. India, Indonesia, Malaysia, and Singapore also report total bank claims, but do not provide a bilateral breakdown.

lowest point in 2010 despite the overall decline over 2001–2015.

Asia's cross-border bank liabilities have been falling since 2013, with its largest contraction of $70.5 billion in 2013 (Figure 3.20). Liabilities fell by $19.7 billion in 2014 and again by $29.7 billion in 2015. This drop was driven by the EU's decline by $49.0 billion in 2014 and by $100.9 billion in 2015. The rising intraregional change in bank liabilities

in 2015 was mainly driven by an increase in Hong Kong, China ($18.3 billion) and the PRC ($15.3 billion). The economic slowdown accompanied by the rise in NPLs in the PRC could have prompted domestic investors to borrow elsewhere in the region.

In 2015, Hong Kong, China; Singapore; and the PRC were Asia's top three borrowers from the region's banks (Table 3.6). Japan ranked fourth. Their combined

Table 3.5: Destination of Asia's Bank Claims ($ billion)

	2015		2010		% Change
Asia					
Hong Kong, China	204	(5.0%)	117	(3.5%)	▲
Singapore	187	(4.6%)	138	(4.1%)	▲
People's Republic of China	184	(4.5%)	48	(1.4%)	▲
Other Asia	333	(8.1%)	248	(7.3%)	▲
Asia Bank Claims, Asia	907	(22.1%)	551	(16.3%)	▲
Non-Asia					
United States	1,210	(29.4%)	1,025	(30.3%)	▼
European Union	1,118	(27.2%)	1,124	(33.2%)	▼
Cayman Islands	543	(13.2%)	322	(9.5%)	▲
Other non-Asia	332	(8.1%)	360	(10.6%)	▼
Non-Asia Bank Claims, Asia	3,203	(77.9%)	2831	(83.7%)	▼
Total Cross-border Bank Claims, Asia	**4,110**	**(100.0%)**	**3,383**	**(100.0%)**	

Source: ADB calculations using data from Bank for International Settlements. Banking Statistics. https://www.bis.org/statistics/bankstats.htm (accessed September 2016).

Figure 3.18: Cross-border Bank Claims—Asia by Reporter ($ trillion)

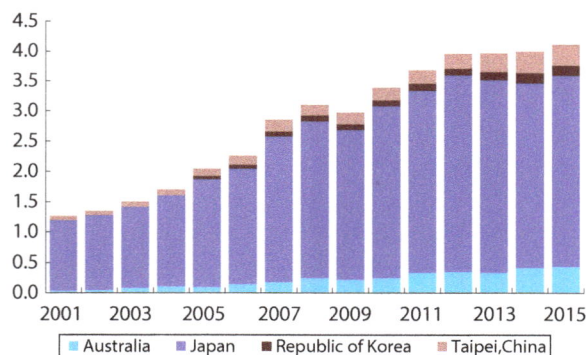

Note: Asia partners include all the ADB 48 regional members for which data are available.
Source: ADB calculations using data from Bank for International Settlements. Banking Statistics. https://www.bis.org/statistics/bankstats.htm (accessed September 2016).

Figure 3.19: Cross-border Bank Liabilities—Asia

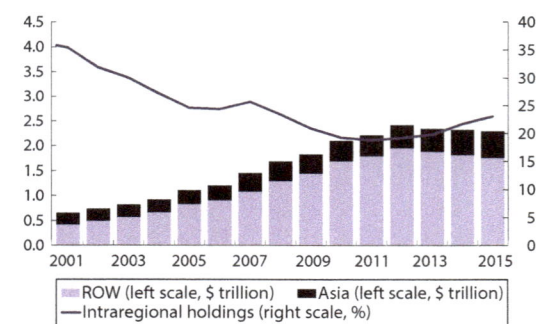

ROW = rest of the world.
Note: Asia includes all the ADB 48 regional members for which data are available.
Source: ADB calculations using data from Bank for International Settlements. Banking Statistics. https://www.bis.org/statistics/bankstats.htm (accessed September 2016).

share of Asia's intraregional bank liabilities was 74.1%, equivalent to just 17.1% of Asia's total. In 2010, Asia's top three borrowers were Hong Kong, China; Singapore; and Japan with the PRC ranked fourth. Similar to the trend in portfolio investment, Asia's banks borrow more from the rest of the world than within the region. But Asia's bank borrowing from non-Asian economies has decreased, primarily due to the large decline in Asia's bank borrowing from the EU as well as from the Cayman Islands. Its borrowing from the US, however, increased in both absolute and relative terms.

Similar to Asia's cross-border bank claims by reporter, data on Asia's cross-border bank liabilities by reporter comprise the same four economies—Australia; Japan; the Republic of Korea; and Taipei,China. Japan explains more than half of Asia's cross-border bank liabilities (52.5%) in 2015 (Figure 3.21). Australia; the Republic of Korea; and Taipei,China accounted for 30.9%, 8.7%, and 7.9%, respectively. Australia's share rose from 17.9% in 2001 to 30.9% in 2015; the Republic of Korea's from 5.2% to 8.7%; and Taipei,China's from 4.3% to 7.9%.

Figure 3.20: Change in Bank Liabilities—Asia ($ billion)

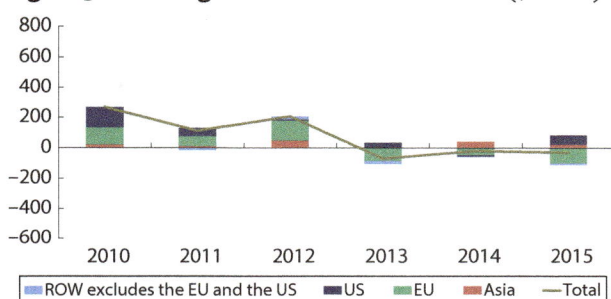

EU = European Union, ROW = rest of the world, US = United States.
Note: Asia includes all the ADB 48 regional members for which data are available.
Source: ADB calculations using data from Bank for International Settlements. Banking Statistics. https://www.bis.org/statistics/bankstats.htm (accessed September 2016).

Figure 3.21: Sources of Bank Liabilities ($ trillion)

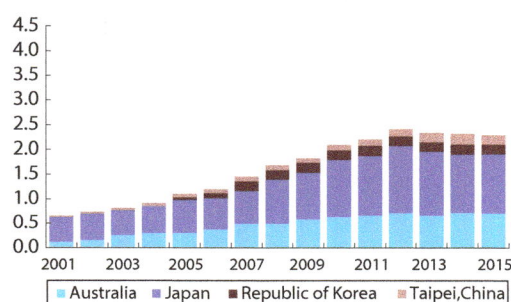

Note: Asia partners include all the ADB 48 regional members for which data are available.
Source: ADB calculations using data from Bank for International Settlements. Banking Statistics. https://www.bis.org/statistics/bankstats.htm (accessed September 2016).

Table 3.6: Sources of Asia's Bank Liabilities ($ billion)

	2015		2010		% Change
Asia					
Hong Kong, China	207	(9.0%)	141	(6.7%)	▲
Singapore	126	(5.5%)	132	(6.3%)	▼
People's Republic of China	59	(2.6%)	16	(0.8%)	▲
Other Asia	137	(6.0%)	114	(5.4%)	▲
Asia Bank Liabilities, Asia	529	(23.1%)	402	(19.2%)	▲
Non-Asia					
European Union	846	(36.9%)	887	(42.4%)	▼
United States	754	(32.9%)	613	(29.3%)	▲
Cayman Islands	44	(1.9%)	81	(3.9%)	▼
Other non-Asia Liabilities	119	(5.2%)	110	(15.2%)	■
Non-Asia Bank Liabilities, Asia	1,763	(76.9%)	1,691	(80.8%)	▼
Total Cross-border Bank Liabilities, Asia	**2,292**	**(100.0%)**	**2,093**	**(100.0%)**	

Source: ADB calculations using data from Bank for International Settlements. Banking Statistics. https://www.bis.org/statistics/bankstats.htm (accessed September 2016).

Price Indicators

Despite being more integrated globally, Asia's equity markets are increasingly integrated regionally.

Although the correlation of Asian intraregional equity returns has increased since the GFC, it remains below its correlation with global equity returns. Asian bond markets remain much less integrated than their equity market counterparts—both regionally and globally. While deepening financial integration is a welcome development for better resource allocation regionally, it may also increase vulnerability to financial contagion, capital flow reversals, and greater output volatility.

Equity

Price-based indicators for equity market integration suggest that Asia's equity markets are increasingly integrated both regionally and globally.

Weekly data on equity returns from January 1999 to September 2016 show that return comovements between

Asia and Asia as well as between Asia and world equity markets have increased (Table 3.7). The average simple correlation of Asian equity returns with the region increased from 0.28 before the GFC to 0.36 afterward—a trend shared by all subregions. The simple correlation of Asian equity returns with the world also increased from 0.32 to 0.43.[30]

Particularly notable is the increased correlation of Central Asian equity markets with the region after the GFC, while there was hardly any correlation before the crisis. Central Asia's increased correlation with world equity markets is also significant because, again, it was barely correlated with the global markets before the GFC. Both regional and global correlation of Asian equity returns peaked during the crisis. Equity market correlations tend to spike during crises, likely caused by increased spillover effects (Hinojales and Park 2010).

Equity return correlations between Asia and the PRC have increased noticeably from a very low base before the GFC, a trend shared among all subregions (Table 3.8). Equity return correlations between Asia and Japan also increased, though from a higher base than the pre-GFC Asia–PRC correlation. With increased equity market comovements, the economic slowdown and stock market

Table 3.7: Average Simple Correlation of Stock Price Index Weekly Returns—Asia with Asia and World

Region	Asia			World		
	Pre-GFC Q1 1999–Q3 2007	**GFC Q4 2007–Q2 2009**	**Post-GFC Q3 2009–Q3 2016**	**Pre-GFC Q1 1999–3Q2007**	**GFC Q4 2007–Q2 2009**	**Post-GFC Q3 2009–Q3 2016**
Central Asia	0.09	0.15	0.19	0.02	0.14	0.24
East Asia	0.35	0.61	0.48	0.42	0.57	0.57
Southeast Asia	0.33	0.72	0.43	0.34	0.64	0.48
South Asia	0.14	0.32	0.15	0.15	0.31	0.18
Oceania	0.38	0.74	0.55	0.57	0.77	0.70
Asia	0.28	0.53	0.36	0.32	0.50	0.43

GFC = global financial crisis.
Central Asia includes Georgia, Kazakhstan, and the Kyrgyz Republic. East Asia includes the People's Republic of China; Hong Kong, China; Japan; the Republic of Korea; Mongolia; and Taipei,China. Southeast Asia includes Indonesia, the Lao People's Democratic Republic, Malaysia, the Philippines, Singapore, Thailand, and Viet Nam. South Asia includes Bangladesh, India, Nepal, Pakistan, and Sri Lanka. Oceania includes Australia and New Zealand. Asia includes all economies from each subregion.
Notes: Values refer to the average of pair-wise correlations. Weekly returns are computed as the natural logarithm difference between weekly average of daily stock price index for the current week, and the weekly average of the daily stock price index from the previous week.
Sources: ADB calculations using data from Bloomberg; CEIC; Stooq. http://stooq.com/q/d/?s=^sti (accessed August 2016); and World Bank. World Development Indicators http://data.worldbank.org/data-catalog/world-development-indicators (accessed September 2016).

[30] The "Asia index" of each economy is created using the weighted sum of the index of individual economies, excluding the economy of interest. The current GDP in US dollar terms serves as weights for the Asia indexes. This methodology is based on Park and Lee (2011).

Table 3.8: Average Simple Correlation of Stock Price Index Weekly Returns—Asia with the PRC and Japan

Region	PRC			Japan		
	Pre-GFC Q1 1999–Q3 2007	GFC Q4 2007–Q2 2009	Post-GFC Q3 2009–Q3 2016	Pre-GFC Q1 1999–3Q2007	GFC Q4 2007–Q2 2009	Post-GFC Q3 2009–Q3 2016
Central Asia	0.00	0.07	0.11	0.15	0.15	0.17
East Asia	0.08	0.33	0.30	0.31	0.52	0.39
Southeast Asia	0.09	0.37	0.21	0.29	0.67	0.34
South Asia	0.06	0.17	0.10	0.13	0.30	0.14
Oceania	0.06	0.32	0.25	0.41	0.76	0.56
Asia	0.07	0.27	0.20	0.26	0.49	0.30

GFC = global financial crisis, PRC = People's Republic of China.
Central Asia includes Georgia, Kazakhstan, and the Kyrgyz Republic. East Asia includes the PRC; Hong Kong, China; Japan; the Republic of Korea; Mongolia; and Taipei,China. Southeast Asia includes Indonesia, Lao People's Democratic Republic, Malaysia, the Philippines, Singapore, Thailand, and Viet Nam. South Asia includes Bangladesh, India, Nepal, Pakistan, and Sri Lanka. Oceania includes Australia and New Zealand. Asia includes all economies from each subregion.
Notes: Values refer to the average of pair-wise correlations. Weekly returns are computed as the natural logarithm difference between weekly average of daily stock price index for the current week, and the weekly average of the daily stock price index from the previous week.
Sources: ADB calculations using data from Bloomberg; CEIC and Stooq. http://stooq.com/q/d/?s=^sti (accessed August 2016).

Table 3.9: Average Simple Correlation of Stock Price Index Weekly Returns—Asia with the EU and the US

Region	EU			US		
	Pre-GFC Q1 1999–Q3 2007	GFC Q4 2007–Q2 2009	Post-GFC Q3 2009–Q3 2016	Pre-GFC Q1 1999–3Q2007	GFC Q4 2007–Q2 2009	Post-GFC Q3 2009–Q3 2016
Central Asia	–0.01	0.17	0.15	–0.03	0.10	0.21
East Asia	0.38	0.55	0.50	0.34	0.49	0.52
Southeast Asia	0.29	0.64	0.40	0.28	0.54	0.44
South Asia	0.11	0.34	0.14	0.10	0.28	0.17
Oceania	0.53	0.79	0.65	0.51	0.72	0.66
Asia	0.27	0.51	0.36	0.25	0.43	0.39

GFC = global financial crisis; EU = European Union; US = United States.
Central Asia includes Georgia, Kazakhstan, and the Kyrgyz Republic. East Asia includes the People's Republic of China; Hong Kong, China; Japan; the Republic of Korea; Mongolia; and Taipei,China. Southeast Asia includes Indonesia, the Lao People's Democratic Republic, Malaysia, the Philippines, Singapore, Thailand, and Viet Nam. South Asia includes Bangladesh, India, Nepal, Pakistan, and Sri Lanka. Oceania includes Australia and New Zealand. Asia includes all economies from each subregion.
Notes: Values refer to the average of pair-wise correlations. Weekly returns are computed as the natural logarithm difference between weekly average of daily stock price index for the current week, and the weekly average of the daily stock price index from the previous week.
Sources: ADB calculations using data from Bloomberg; CEIC and Stooq. http://stooq.com/q/d/?s=^sti (accessed August 2016).

slump in the PRC may present a risk to the region's equity markets.

The return correlation of Asia's equity markets with the EU increased from 0.27 before the GFC to 0.36 afterward (Table 3.9). The return correlation of Asia's equity markets with the US also increased after the crisis, from 0.25 to 0.39. These increased global linkages suggest potential vulnerability of Asian equity markets to increased market volatility in the EU—for example through Brexit—or in the US during its monetary tightening cycle.

As seen in the correlation table over different sample periods, the simple correlations can be subject to large variation during the crisis. To correct for the shortcomings of measuring integration using average simple correlation, a dynamic conditional correlation (DCC) model can be used (Hinojales and Park 2010). This model, proposed by Engle (2002), incorporates time-varying volatilities instead of simple correlations. A higher time-varying correlation indicates larger comovement between equity

Figure 3.22. Conditional Correlations of Equity Markets—Asia with Select Economies and Regions

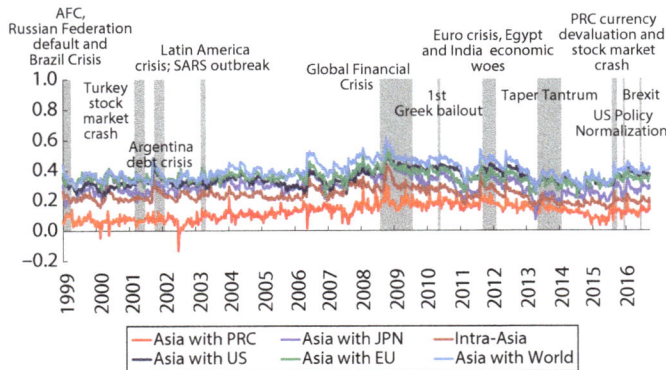

AFC = Asian financial crisis; PRC = People's Republic of China; JPN = Japan; EU = European Union; US = United States; SARS = Severe Acute Respiratory Syndrome.
Note: Asia includes Australia; Bangladesh; the PRC; Georgia; Hong Kong, China; India; Indonesia; Japan; Kazakhstan; the Kyrgyz Republic; the Republic of Korea; the Lao People's Democratic Republic; Malaysia; Mongolia; Nepal; New Zealand; Pakistan; the Philippines; Singapore; Sri Lanka; Taipei,China; Thailand; and Viet Nam.
Sources: ADB calculations using data from Bloomberg; CEIC; Stooq. http://stooq.com/q/d/?s=^sti (accessed August 2016); and methodology by Hinojales and Park (2010).

markets at a point in time.[31] Consistent with the results from simple correlation, these results indicate that Asia's DCCs with the region and world are increasing (Figure 3.22). Also in line with the results from simple correlation, Asia's equity markets remain more integrated with world markets than the region's. Similar to the results from simple correlation, Asia's equity markets are more correlated with the world than those of the EU and the US. Almost all correlations of Asia's equity markets

---

[31] Estimates of the conditional correlations use the GARCH (1,1)-DCC model in which a two-step estimation procedure is applied. First, equity return residuals of individual economies are estimated using a univariate GARCH model. These residuals are subsequently used to get the conditional correlation of each economy's equity returns with that of another economy. The correlation estimator is defined as

$$\rho_{i,j,t} = \frac{q_{i,j,t}}{\sqrt{q_{i,i,t} \; q_{j,j,t}}}$$

where $\rho_{i,j,t}$ is the conditional correlation between the equity asset returns of economies i and j at time t, and $q_{i,j,t}$ is the off-diagonal elements of the variance–covariance matrix.

The GARCH(1,1) process followed by the qs is as follows:

$$q_{i,j,t} = \overline{\rho_{i,j}} + \alpha\left(\varepsilon_{i,t-1}\varepsilon_{j,t-1} - \overline{\rho_{i,j}}\right) + \gamma\left(q_{i,t-1}q_{j,t-1} - \overline{\rho_{i,j}}\right)$$

where $\rho_{i,j,t}$ is the unconditional expectation of the cross product $\varepsilon_{i,t}-1 \; \varepsilon_{j,t-1}$.

with Japan remain higher than those with the region. Their correlation with the PRC remains the lowest—though it increased after the GFC.

Having decreased since the GFC, conditional correlations of Asian equity markets with global and regional markets have picked up recently. The most noticeable recent increase has been with the PRC market since 2015, although the Asia-PRC correlation is yet to recover to its GFC level.

Debt

Price-based indicators for bond market integration suggest that Asia's local currency bond market integration is gaining momentum.

Data on weekly bond returns from January 2005 to September 2016 show that, post-GFC, Asia's bond market is more correlated with the region's bond markets than with the world's (Table 3.10). Increased regional correlations are mainly due to the increased regional correlations of India, Indonesia, the Republic of Korea, Malaysia, Singapore, and Thailand.[32] While regional correlations increased noticeably, the correlation of Asian economies with the world remained unchanged post-GFC. Especially, the PRC's correlation with the region's bond market increased from 0.01 pre-GFC to 0.28 post-GFC, whereas its pre- and post-GFC correlation with world bond market remained unchanged.

The simple correlations of Asian bond markets with the PRC and Japan also increased following the GFC (Table 3.11). Particularly noteworthy is the increased correlation of individual Asian economies with the PRC—from 0.00 pre-GFC to 0.18 post-GFC. The correlations of India, Indonesia, the Republic of Korea, and Singapore with the PRC turn positive after the crisis from negative beforehand. Australia, Malaysia, and Thailand's correlations with the PRC also increased noticeably after the crisis.

Asia's correlation with Japan marginally increased, from 0.19 before the crisis to 0.20 afterward. The region's more

---

[32] The regional bond market is computed using the same methodology as the regional equity market.

Table 3.10: Average Simple Correlation of Weekly Bond Return Index—Asia with Asia and World

Economies	Asia			World		
	Pre-GFC Q1 2005–Q3 2007	GFC Q4 2007–Q2 2009	Post-GFC Q3 2009–Q3 2016	Pre-GFC Q1 2005–Q3 2007	GFC Q4 2007–Q2 2009	Post-GFC Q3 2009–Q3 2016
Australia	0.38	0.37	0.32	0.41	0.34	0.38
PRC	0.01	0.24	0.28	0.04	0.09	0.04
Japan	0.08	0.31	0.06	0.23	0.28	−0.04
Indonesia	−0.15	−0.06	0.16	0.02	0.24	0.25
India	0.28	0.33	0.17	0.29	0.52	0.41
Republic of Korea	0.15	0.36	0.32	0.37	0.23	0.26
Malaysia	0.22	0.31	0.29	0.13	0.27	0.13
Philippines		0.30	0.21		0.14	0.15
Singapore	0.29	0.41	0.42	0.27	0.31	0.46
Thailand	0.20	0.53	0.30	0.29	0.32	0.24
Asia	0.16	0.31	0.26	0.23	0.27	0.23

GFC = global financial crisis; PRC = People's Republic of China.
Notes: Values refer to the average of pair-wise correlations. Weekly returns are computed as the natural logarithm difference between weekly average of daily bond return index for the current week, and the weekly average of the daily bond return index from the previous week. All bond return indexes are comprised by local currency government-issued bonds.
Sources: ADB calculations using data from Bloomberg; and World Bank. World Development Indicators http://data.worldbank.org/data-catalog/world-development-indicators (accessed September 2016).

Table 3.11: Average Simple Correlation of Weekly Bond Return Index—Asia with the PRC and Japan

Economies	PRC			Japan		
	Pre-GFC Q1 2005–Q3 2007	GFC Q4 2007–Q2 2009	Post-GFC Q3 2009–Q3 2016	Pre-GFC Q1 2005–Q3 2007	GFC Q4 2007–Q2 2009	Post-GFC Q3 2009–Q3 2016
Australia	0.06	0.11	0.26	0.59	0.56	0.42
PRC	0.00	0.00	0.00	0.07	−0.05	0.11
Japan	−0.09	0.47	0.22	0.06	0.18	−0.03
Indonesia	−0.12	0.06	0.13	−0.25	−0.06	0.11
India	0.07	−0.05	0.11	0.00	0.00	0.00
Republic of Korea	−0.06	0.29	0.24	0.16	0.18	0.35
Malaysia	0.10	0.25	0.22	0.21	0.07	0.09
Philippines		0.17	0.03		0.24	0.10
Singapore	−0.09	0.08	0.15	0.32	0.40	0.38
Thailand	0.11	0.28	0.21	0.37	0.28	0.22
Asia	0.00	0.19	0.18	0.19	0.20	0.20

GFC = global financial crisis; PRC = People's Republic of China.
Notes: Values refer to the average of pair-wise correlations. Weekly returns are computed as the natural logarithm difference between weekly average of daily bond index for the current week, and the weekly average of the daily bond index from the previous week. All bond indexes are comprised by local currency government-issued bonds.
Source: ADB calculations using data from Bloomberg.

Table 3.12: Average Simple Correlation of Weekly Bond Return Index—Asia with the EU and the US

Economies	EU			US		
	Pre-GFC Q1 2005–Q3 2007	**GFC Q4 2007–Q2 2009**	**Post-GFC Q3 2009–Q3 2016**	**Pre-GFC Q1 2005–Q3 2007**	**GFC Q4 2007–Q2 2009**	**Post-GFC Q3 2009–Q3 2016**
Australia	0.75	0.68	0.38	0.75	0.69	0.73
PRC	0.13	0.02	0.14	0.05	0.09	0.17
Japan	0.26	0.28	0.17	0.21	0.38	0.09
Indonesia	−0.23	−0.14	0.18	−0.18	0.00	0.09
India	0.62	0.60	0.28	0.52	0.56	0.49
Republic of Korea	0.26	0.17	0.33	0.29	0.21	0.46
Malaysia	0.18	0.22	0.20	0.16	0.25	0.19
Philippines		0.01	0.20		0.21	0.15
Singapore	0.32	0.50	0.40	0.35	0.55	0.63
Thailand	0.34	0.45	0.27	0.33	0.44	0.35
Asia	0.29	0.28	0.26	0.28	0.34	0.33

EU = European Union; GFC = global financial crisis; PRC = People's Republic of China; US = United States
Notes: Values refer to the average of pair-wise correlations. Weekly returns are computed as the natural logarithm difference between weekly average of daily bond index for the current week, and the weekly average of the daily bond index from the previous week. All bond indexes are comprised by local currency government-issued bonds.
Source: ADB calculations using data from Bloomberg.

advanced economies (including Australia, the Republic of Korea, and Singapore) are relatively more positively correlated with Japan than other regional economies.

While the correlation of Asian economies with the world bond market remain unchanged pre- and post-GFC, its correlation with the US increased and its correlation with the EU decreased (Table 3.12). The heightened correlation with the US post-GFC is attributed to the increased correlation between the US and the Republic of Korea, as well as between the US and Singapore. The drop in correlation with the EU is due to a decline in correlation between the EU and Australia, and between the EU and India, and between the EU and Japan.

Estimating Asia's bond market DCC shows that its correlation with the region and selected economies is below Asia's equity market correlation with the region and corresponding selected economies (Figure 3.23). This suggests that Asia's equity markets are more integrated both regionally and globally than Asia's bond markets. The correlation of the EU and the US bond markets with Asia's is highest among the selected economies, except during 2011–2013. During this period, the EU's bond market correlation with Asia dipped, but recovered during the onset of the "taper tantrum" in 2013–2014. Similar to the equity market, Asia's bond market correlation with the PRC's bond market remains lowest among the select economies, but exhibits an upwards trend.

Figure 3.23: Conditional Correlations of Bond Markets— Asia with Select Economies and Regions

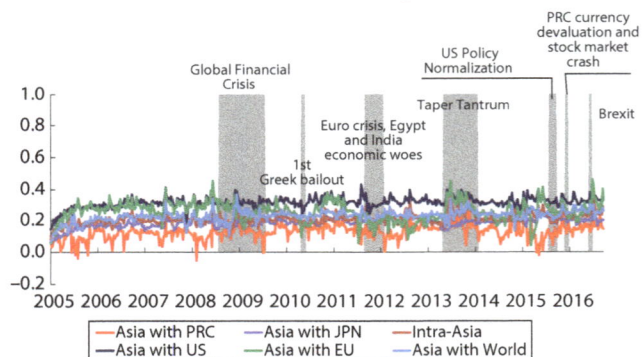

PRC = People's Republic of China; JPN = Japan; EU = European Union; US = United States.
Asia includes Australia, the PRC, India, Indonesia, Japan, the Republic of Korea, Malaysia, the Philippines, Singapore, and Thailand.
Sources: ADB calculations using data from Bloomberg and methodology by Hinojales and Park (2010).

More importantly, the DCC of Asia's bond markets shows sharp rises for specific economies during crises. During the European sovereign debt crisis and Brexit, for instance, Asia's bond market correlation with the EU bond market increased sharply. Immediately before the PRC currency devaluation, its correlation with selected global bond markets again increased. Its correlation with the PRC bond market was in stark contrast—a pronounced negative correlation.

Financial Spillovers

Equity

Asia's equity markets are more vulnerable to global equity market volatility than regional volatility.

The correlations between Asia's equity markets with the region, the world, and other selected markets provide a glimpse of Asia's global and regional linkages. However, they do not provide sufficient information on risk spillovers originating from any specific region. The increased correlation of equity markets with the region and the world can also increase the contagion of booms and busts in the region. The variance decomposition of Asia's equity returns shows Asia's integration with both the region and the world has increased from pre- to post-GFC periods (Figures 3.24a and 3.24b).[33]

The results indicate that Asia's equity markets are more vulnerable to volatility from the global equity market than to volatility from regional equity markets. Figures 3.24a and 3.24b shows global shocks explain a dominant share of variance in Asia's local equity returns both pre- and post-GFC. The variance of Asian equity returns are increasingly subject more to global market volatility than

Figure 3.24: Share of Variance in Local Equity Returns Explained by Global and Regional Shocks (%)

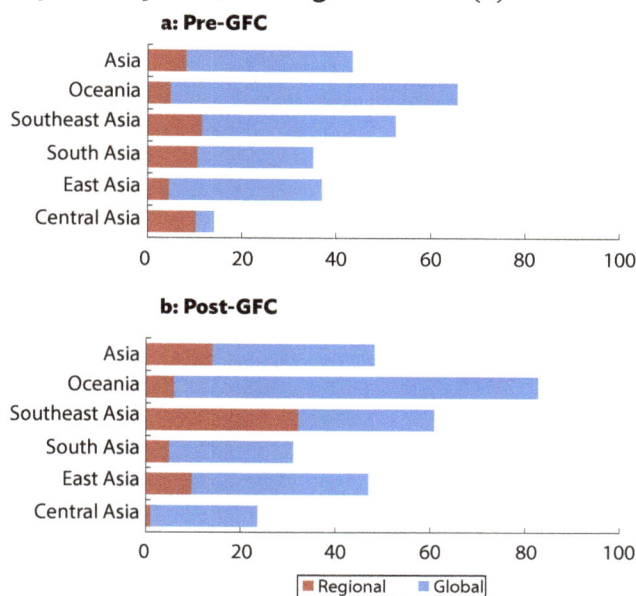

a: Pre-GFC

b: Post-GFC

GFC = global financial crisis.
Notes: Pre-GFC = January 1999 to September 2007. Post-GFC = July 2009 to September 2016.
Central Asia includes Georgia, Kazakhstan, and the Kyrgyz Republic. East Asia includes the People's Republic of China; Hong Kong, China; Japan; the Republic of Korea; Mongolia; and Taipei,China. Southeast Asia includes Indonesia, the Lao People's Democratic Republic, Malaysia, the Philippines, Singapore, Thailand, and Viet Nam. South Asia includes Bangladesh, India, Nepal, Pakistan, and Sri Lanka. Oceania includes Australia and New Zealand. Asia includes Central Asia, East Asia, South Asia, Southeast Asia and Oceania.
Sources: ADB calculations using data from Bloomberg; World Bank. World Development Indicators http://data.worldbank.org/data-catalog/world-development-indicators (accessed September 2016); and methodology by Lee and Park (2011).

to regional volatility, confirming Asian equity markets' greater global than regional integration—as indicated in the earlier quantity analysis as well as simple correlation and DCC analysis.

However, compared with the pre-GFC period, the combined share of variance explained by global and regional shocks substantially increased. Although the share of global shock in local equity return variance is still much greater post-GFC, the share of regional shocks in the equity return variance also increased, suggesting gradual progress in Asian equity market integration.

---

[33] The formula to arrive at the regional and the global variance decomposition are as follows:

$$VR_{c,t}^{G} = \frac{(\beta_{c,t}^{G})^2 \sigma_{G,t}^2}{\sigma_{c,t}^2} \qquad VR_{c,t}^{EA} = \frac{(\beta_{c,t}^{EA})^2 \sigma_{EA,t}^2}{\sigma_{c,t}^2}$$

where $VR_{c,t}^{EA}$, and $VR_{c,t}^{G}$ are the regional and global variance of economy c, at time t, respectively. $\beta_{c,t}^{EA}$ and $\beta_{c,t}^{G}$ are the economy-specific sensitivity to the regional and global beta at time t, respectively. These were obtained from the following equation –

$$\varepsilon_{c,t} = \alpha_{c,t} + \beta_{c,t}^{EA}\varepsilon_{EA,t} + \beta_{c,t}^{G}\varepsilon_{G,t}$$

The formula was applied on a rolling basis, with 78 weekly data points. and are the regional conditional variance and global conditional variance, estimated from the above equation. They are assumed to follow a standard asymmetric GARCH (1, 1) process. $\varepsilon_{c,t}, \varepsilon_{EA,t}, \varepsilon_{G,t}$ are the unexpected components of the equity market returns, which are proxied by the error terms obtained from the regression equation –

$$r_{c,t} = \delta_{0\,c,t} + \delta_{1\,c,t}r_{c,t-1} + \varepsilon_{c,t}$$

where $r_{c,t}$ is the weekly equity returns of each individual economy.

Debt

Unlike Asia's equity markets, its bond markets are more vulnerable to volatility in regional bond markets than global bond market volatility.

Following the same methodology as the variance decomposition of equity markets, the results indicate that variance of Asia's bond market returns, unlike Asia's equity returns, are more subject to regional than global risks (Figures 3.25a, 3.25b). This suggests the rise of Asian local currency bonds as an emerging market asset class. While foreign investors account for a significant share of many Asian local currency bonds, their investment interest for these local currency bonds might be similar across Asian economies. If global investors treat Asian local currency bonds as one emerging market asset class in their global portfolio management, their investment decisions for this asset class will be driven largely by common regional risk factors, making local bond returns most subject to regional market volatility.

Compared with the pre-GFC period, the combined share of variance explained by global and regional shocks also increased, suggesting greater global and regional integration, similar to equity markets. However, the share of regional shocks in local currency bond return variance is generally much greater than the share of global shocks.

Asian local currency bond markets have expanded dramatically since governments took steps to end the currency and maturity mismatches that savaged borrowers in the AFC nearly 20 years ago. Encouraged in part by regional cooperation programs including the Asian Bond Markets Initiative (ABMI), the value of local currency government and corporate bond sales expanded fourfold in the past decade, helping fund much-needed infrastructure development and protect business from global financial shocks (Box 3.2). Growing foreign participation also helped facilitate local currency bond market development—today global investors view Asian local currency bonds as an important asset class. This could have further promoted regional bond market integration post-GFC.

The cross-border dispersion of 10-year local currency government bond yields shows a yield convergence trend in regional bond markets between 2009 and 2014.

The cross-border dispersion of 10-year local currency government bond yields is estimated using σ-convergence of regional local currency government bond yields with 10-year maturity.[34] A noticeable spike was noted during the GFC for Asia and developing Asia, reflecting higher dispersion in Southeast Asia. While the dispersion narrowed after the GFC, Asia's σ-convergence displays a gradual increase between 2014 and 2015 (Figure 3.26a).

Figure 3.25: Share of Variance in Local Bond Returns Explained by Global and Regional Shocks (%)

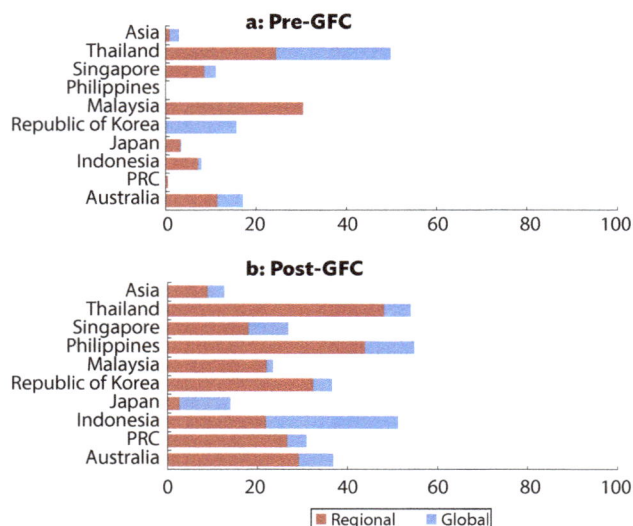

GFC = global financial crisis. PRC = People's Republic of China.
Notes: Pre-GFC = January 1999 to September 2007. Post-GFC = July 2009 to September 2016.
Sources: ADB calculations using data from Bloomberg; World Bank. World Development Indicators http://data.worldbank.org/data-catalog/world-development-indicators (accessed September 2016); and methodology by Lee and Park (2011).

---

34 To compute for the dispersion or **σ-convergence**, each pairwise dispersion of bond yields r between economies i and j was obtained using –

$$\sigma_{ijy} = \left[\frac{1}{n-1} \sum\nolimits_{\forall t}^{n} \left(r_{it} - r_{jt} \right)^2 \right]^{1/2}$$

The formula was applied on a rolling basis, with 52 weekly data points. Each economy's **σ-convergence** is the simple mean of all its pairwise dispersions. The subregional and Asia **σ-convergence** is the unweighted mean of each included economy's **σ-convergence**.

Box 3.2: Asia's Financial Integration Initiatives—Then and Now

In the aftermath of the 1997/98 Asian financial crisis (AFC), the precursors of current financial integration initiatives were formed with financial stability and crisis management as urgent objectives. Once resolved, many became permanent features of the financial integration landscape within the region. Several regional groups are working to increase intraregional financial integration through these evolving initiatives.

The Association of Southeast Asian Nations (ASEAN)

i.   In 1998, the terms of understanding for the ASEAN Surveillance Process (ASP) was endorsed and finalized. In 1999, it began as a mechanism for peer review and exchange of views among senior officials and finance ministers on ASEAN economic developments and policy issues. Since then, the ASP has reviewed global, regional, and individual country developments; and monitored exchange rate and macroeconomic aggregates as well as sectoral and social policies (ADBa, Anas and Atje 2005).

ii.   In 2003, the Roadmap for the Integration (RIA) of ASEAN was endorsed at the 7th Asian Finance Ministers Meeting—and adopted at the 9th ASEAN Summit. A key component of the RIA covers Financial and Monetary Integration (RIA-FIN), which monitors and articulates objectives in four areas: (i) capital market development; (ii) financial services liberalization (FSL); (iii) capital account liberalization; and (iv) ASEAN currency cooperation. The goal was to meet the objectives of the ASEAN Economic Community Blueprint 2015. Several activities are under way (ASEAN 2016).

iii.   In 2004, the ASEAN Capital Markets Forum (ACMF) was established to "develop a deep, liquid, and integrated regional capital market." Initiatives under the ACMF include harmonizing and mutually recognizing frameworks, establishing exchange linkages, building ASEAN as an asset class, strengthening bond markets, and aligning capital market development. The ACMF is focused on achieving its ACMF Vision 2025 (ACMF 2016).

iv.   An ASEAN exchanges website was launched in 2011 to promote members' blue chip companies. This was followed by the creation of the ASEAN trading link (ATL) in September 2012, which electronically connects stock exchanges in Malaysia, Singapore, and Thailand. The ATL aims to promote intra-ASEAN cross-border equity trading by allowing investors to trade across these connected markets. This lowers funding costs for listed companies, trading costs for investors; increases investment flows and harnesses synergies in promoting ASEAN as a single asset class to regional and global investors (ASEAN Exchanges 2012).

v.   The ASEAN Framework for Cross-Border Offering of Collective Investment Schemes (CIS) began operations in Malaysia, Singapore, and Thailand in August 2014 following the signing of a memorandum of understanding (MOU) in October 2013 (ACMF 2014). The framework allows fund managers operating in a member jurisdiction to offer CIS, such as unit trust funds, constituted and authorized in that jurisdiction, to retail investors in other member jurisdictions under a streamlined authorization process. The signatories also signed a separate MOU to provide mutual assistance and exchange of information for cross-border offerings of ASEAN CIS to nonretail investors (Securities Commission of Malaysia 2013). As of 29 February 2016, 13 funds have been authorized as Qualifying CIS Securities (ASEAN 2016).

vi.   In April 2011, ASEAN central bank governors endorsed the ASEAN Financial Integration Framework (AFIF), which is hinged on the FSL objective of RIA-FIN. The AFIF views a semi-financially integrated region by 2020, and entails the harmonization of regulations and further capital flow liberalization (ADB 2013). The ASEAN central bank governors also endorsed the creation of the Task Force on the ASEAN Banking Integration Framework (ABIF), which aims to achieve ASEAN-wide banking sector liberalization by 2020. The Working Committee on Financial Service Liberalization focuses on further liberalization of the banking and insurance sectors (ASEAN 2016).

vii.   In December 2014, ASEAN central bank governors finalized the ABIF, which was implemented by the ASEAN Finance Ministers' Meeting in March 2015. This means qualified ASEAN banks can be treated as local banks in ASEAN member economies if they set up operations, and it will allow small banks to expand activities in other ASEAN economies and for these banks to grow faster (ASEAN 2015a).

ASEAN+3

The Joint Statement on East Asia Cooperation, drafted and approved in November 1999, is the main document that details the establishment of the ASEAN+3 Finance Ministers Process (ASEAN a). The process aims to strengthen policy dialogue, coordination, and collaboration on common financial, monetary, and fiscal issues through its four components: (i) the Economic Review and Policy Dialogue, (ii) the Chiang Mai Initiative (CMI), (III) the Asian Bond Markets Initiative (ABMI), and (iv) the ASEAN+3 Research Group (ASEANb).

Box 3.2 continued

i. Formed in May 2000, the Economic Review and Policy Dialogue (ERPD) established the annual ASEAN+3 Finance Ministers Meeting and semiannual ASEAN+3 deputies meeting, which serve as venues to discuss economic and policy issues, among others. The ERPD contributes to the prevention of financial crises through swift implementation of remedial policies (Kawai and Houser 2007).

ii. The Chiang Mai Initiative (CMI), also formed in May 2000, was the first regional currency swap arrangement. It comprised a network of bilateral swap agreements among ASEAN+3 economies, and the expanded ASEAN swap arrangements to include all ASEAN members. This was replaced on 24 March 2010 by the Chiang Mai Initiative Multilateralization (CMIM), which aims to enhance the effectiveness of the CMI as a form of liquidity support in the region. The initial size of the CMIM Arrangement was $120 billion, which was increased to $240 billion at the 15th ASEAN+3 Finance Ministers and Central Bank Governors Meeting in 2011 (BSP 2016). The CMIM also established an independent regional surveillance mechanism unit, the ASEAN+3 Macroeconomic Research Office (AMRO). Since 2016, this office functions as a formal international organization (AMRO 2016).

iii. Launched in August 2003, the ABMI aims to develop efficient and liquid bond markets to enable the better use of Asian savings for Asian investments. It also aims to contribute to mitigating financial currency and maturity mismatches (Park 2016). Six voluntary working groups were established to focus on crucial areas for bond market development: (i) new securitized debt instruments; (ii) credit guarantee mechanisms; (iii) foreign exchange transactions and settlement issues; (iv) issuance of bonds denominated in local currency by multilateral development banks, foreign government agencies, and Asian multinational corporations; (v) local and regional rating agencies; and (vi) technical assistance coordination (ADB 2005).

ABMI paved way for the creation of the *AsianBondsOnline* (ABO) website in 2004. ABO "is a one-stop clearinghouse of information on sovereign and corporate bonds." It is funded by Japan's Ministry of Finance, through the Investment Climate Facilitation Fund (AsianBondsOnline).

A new ABMI roadmap was signed in May 2008 with four task forces created to (i) promote the issuance of local currency-denominated bonds, co-chaired by the People's Republic of China and Thailand, (ii) facilitate the demand of local currency-denominated bonds, co-chaired by Japan

and Singapore, (iii) improve regulatory frameworks, co-chaired by Japan and Malaysia, and (iv) improve bond market infrastructure to encourage domestic issuance and increase secondary market liquidity, co-chaired by the Republic of Korea and the Philippines (AsianBondsOnline 2008).

Under Task Force I and together with ADB, the Credit Guarantee and Investment Facility (CGIF) was created in November 2010. ADB's Board of Directors approved in April 2010 the establishment of a CGIF trust fund with an initial capital of $700 million (ADB 2010 and ADBb).

Under Task Force III, the ASEAN+3 Bond Market Forum (ABMF)—a working group of experts—was established. Through two subforums, the ABMF proposed the establishment of the ASEAN+3 Multi-currency Banking Integration Framework (AMBIF). One of AMBIF's main goals is to standardize processes in note and bond issuance, as well as investment (ADB 2015a). In September 2015, Japan's Mizuho Bank issued Thai baht-denominated bonds worth THB3 billion, the first under AMBIF (ADB 2015b).

iv. ASEAN+3 finance ministers established a voluntary research group in August 2003 to explore ways to further strengthen regional financial cooperation and support the process. The first ASEAN+3 Research Group meeting was held in March 2004. In May 2005, the ASEAN+3 finance ministers endorsed three research areas for 2005 to 2006: (i) capital flow liberalization and institutional arrangements; (ii) capital market development, including the asset management industry; and (iii) policy coordination (ASEANb).

Executives' Meeting of East Asia Pacific (EMEAP) Central Banks

EMEAP is a forum of central banks and monetary authorities in the East Asia and Pacific region established in 1991. It aims to strengthen cooperation among its 11 members. EMEAP includes central banks from Australia; the PRC; Hong Kong, China; Indonesia; Japan; the Republic of Korea; Malaysia; New Zealand; the Philippines; Singapore; and Thailand (EMEAP).

i. EMEAP launched the first phase of the Asian Bond Fund (ABF1) in June 2003. The initiative facilitates channeling Asian economies' official reserves to investments in domestic bonds. Hence, it serves as an alternative investment for central banks, which allows diversifying investments. With an initial size of about $1 billion, managed passively by the Bank for International Settlements, ABF1 is fully invested in a basket of US dollar-denominated bonds issued by the government from EMEAP economies (except Australia, Japan, and New Zealand) (EMEAP and ADBc).

ii. Building on the success of the ABF1, EMEAP launched the second phase of the Asian Bond Fund (ABF2) initiative in December 2004, 8 months after its announcement in April 2004 (ADBb). In contrast to ABF1, ABF2 invests in local currency government bonds issued by eight EMEAP members. worth $2 billion. Half of the investment is directed to the ABF Pan-Asian-Bond Index Fund, a single bond fund investing in local currency government bonds issued in eight EMEAP markets. The remaining billion is invested in eight single-market funds each investing in local currency government funds, within EMEAP markets. The ABF2 began implementation in May 2005, with the completion of the $2-billion funding, the appointment of fund managers, a master custodian, and index provider for ABF2. The International Index Company constructed the iBoxx ABF index family, the benchmark for ABF2 funds. On 1 July 2006, EMEAP agreed to reinvest in ABF2 (Park 2016 and ADBc).

SAARCFINANCE

SAARCFINANCE is a Network of Central Bank Governors and Finance Secretaries of the South Asian Association for Regional Cooperation (SAARC), comprising Afghanistan, Bangladesh, Bhutan, India, the Maldives, Nepal, Pakistan, and Sri Lanka. It was established on 9 September 1998 as a regional network of the SAARC Central Bank Governors and Finance Secretaries. It is a permanent body, which was formally recognized by SAARC at the 11th SAARC Summit (SAARCFINANCE).

i. The SAARCFINANCE Network objective is to share experiences on macroeconomic policy issues among members. The broad objectives include, among others, regional surveillance, promotion of cooperation among central banks, harmonization of regulations, and working toward a more efficient payment mechanism infrastructure (SAARCFINANCE).

ii. Following the decision of SAARC finance ministers at the SAARC Ministerial Meeting on GFC in 2009, the Reserve Bank of India offered the SAARC swap facility to all SAARC member economies. The SAARC Currency Swap Arrangement is available to all member countries with a floor of $100 million and ceiling of $400 million within an overall limit of $2 billion (RBI 2012). It was initially valid until 14 November 2015, but was extended by Reserve Bank of India to 14 November 2017 to enhance cooperation and strengthen financial stability in the region (RBI 2016).

Figure 3.26: σ-Convergence of 10-Year Government Bond Yields—Asia

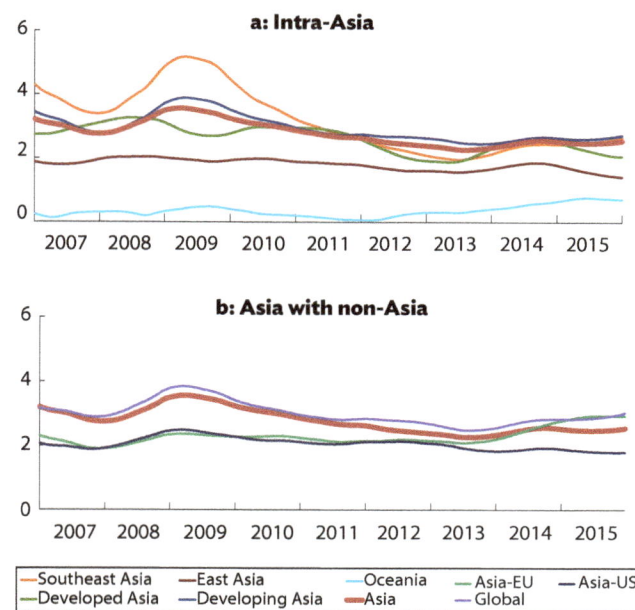

EU = European Union, US = United States.
Notes: Values refer to the unweighted mean of individual economy's σ-convergence, included in the subregion. Each economy's σ-convergence is the simple mean of all its pairwise standard deviation. Data are filtered using Hodrick-Prescott method. East Asia includes People's Republic of China (PRC); Hong Kong, China (HKG); Japan (JPN); the Republic of Korea (KOR); and Taipei,China (TAP). Southeast Asia includes Indonesia, Malaysia, the Philippines, Thailand, and Singapore. Oceania includes Australia and New Zealand. Developed Asia includes JPN, and Oceania. Developing Asia includes Southeast Asia, the PRC, HKG, KOR, and TAP. Asia includes Developed Asia and Developing Asia. Global includes Asia, Colombia, the EU, Mexico, and the US.
Sources: ADB calculations using data from Bloomberg; CEIC; and methodology by Espinoza et al (2010), and Park (2013).

By subregion, East Asia's bond yield dispersion has been declining between mid-2014 and 2015. The decline in the PRC's σ-convergence might have contributed to this. What is driving the increased dispersion in the region is Southeast Asia. In particular, dispersion in Indonesian, Philippine, and Thai bond yields have been rising since end-2013—the latter part of the taper tantrum. Between the taper tantrum and policy normalization, these economies' bond yields have diverged from other Asian yields reflecting their sensitivity to swings in investor sentiment. These emerging market government bond prices fell sharply during the market turmoil due to flight to safety; for example, many investors fled to developed Asia and newly industrialized economy bonds.[35]

---

[35] Newly industrialized economies include Hong Kong, China; the Republic of Korea; Singapore; and Taipei,China.

However, Asia's local currency bond yields remain more linked to US bond yields (Figure 3.26b). While the Asia-US dispersion marginally increased during the taper tantrum, the trend afterward indicates that it has already declined, and remained below Asia's intraregional dispersion. Figure 3.26b also shows the effect of the eurozone crisis on Asia-EU yield convergence. At the onset of the crisis, Asia's bond yields started to diverge from the EU's. The Asia-EU yield dispersion was nearly as narrow as the Asia-US until mid-2014, but by May 2014, it was even higher than Asia's intraregional dispersion.

The AFC highlighted the need for greater regional financial cooperation and integration. Since then, Asian policy makers have enhanced regional financial cooperation and integration through initiatives like the Chiang Mai Initiative Multilateralization (CMIM), the ASEAN+3 Macroeconomic Research Office (AMRO) and the ABMI, among others. Likewise, the current ASEAN Economic Community (AEC) Blueprint 2025 cites financial integration as a strategic objective for the region.

The increasing linkages of Asia with both the region and the world are a result of greater financial openness. Increased regional financial integration yields numerous benefits for the regions' economies, such as more efficient allocation of excess savings toward more productive investment. Baele et al (2004) discuss three interrelated benefits of financial integration: (i) risk sharing, (ii) improved capital allocation, and (iii) economic growth. Lee and Park (2011) echo risk-sharing and more efficient capital allocation as derived benefits from financial integration. At the same time, a higher degree of financial interconnectedness increases the region's potential financial vulnerabilities, for example through financial contagion and spillover. Coupled with the amplification of shock propagation due to the increased synchronicity in financial cycles, greater financial interconnectedness can exacerbate volatility in the region (Ananchotikul et al 2015). As a result, it is also important to monitor the risk of financial contagion and spillovers, while facilitating regional financial integration.

Capital Flow Volatility

Financial inflows have become more stable after the GFC.

Capital flow volatility across all types of financial flows—equity, debt, FDI, and other investment flows—declined after the GFC compared with before the crisis. This general pattern may be the result of various regional various initiatives. FDI remains the least volatile form of financial flows, whereas debt flows represent the most volatile. Following the crisis, volatility in FDI net flows to Asia declined. Surprisingly, portfolio equity flows are less volatile than debt flows.

The composition of sources of funds in the region matters. Financial flows exhibiting unstable patterns can exacerbate uncertainty. Using data from the International Monetary Fund's International Financial Statistics from the first quarter of 1999 to the fourth quarter of 2015, the capital flow volatility has been measured by the standard deviation of net inflows to Asia, normalized by the economy's GDP. The results reveal that FDI is Asia's least volatile form of net flows, with the exception of Oceania, where portfolio flows were less volatile than FDI flows before the GFC (Table 3.13). Between the two types of portfolio flows, equity is surprisingly the more stable one during the sample period. Except in South Asia, where net debt flows are the least volatile asset class among portfolio flows, equity flows are more stable in all other subregions. A comparison of financial net flows to Asia before and after the GFC indicates that FDI net flows have been less volatile since the crisis. For the individual subregions, volatility of FDI net flows declined, except for South Asia.

South Asia's portfolio net inflows became more volatile after the GFC. In particular, the standard deviation of net portfolio debt flows increased to 0.85 (from 0.00 pre-crisis), while the volatility of net portfolio equity flows increased to 1.04 (from 0.90 pre-crisis). Net portfolio flows to East Asia, Southeast Asia, and Oceania have been more stable than in South Asia; the volatility of net debt flows to Central Asia remained unchanged when comparing flows before and after the GFC.

Table 3.13: Capital Flow Volatility—Asia (standard deviation of capital net flow levels as % of GDP)

Region	Portfolio (Debt)			Portfolio (Equity)		
	Pre-GFC Q1 1999–Q3 2007	Post-GFC Q3 2009–Q4 2015	Direction	Pre-GFC Q1 1999–Q3 2007	Post-GFC Q3 2009–Q4 2015	Direction
Central Asia	4.22	4.38	▲	1.97	1.03	▼
East Asia	1.99	1.42	▼	2.04	1.24	▼
South Asia	0.00	0.85	▲	0.90	1.04	▲
Southeast Asia	1.11	0.83	▼	1.05	0.70	▼
Oceania	3.34	2.85	▼	3.54	1.97	▼
Asia	1.46	0.97	▼	1.64	0.95	▼

Region	FDI			Financial Derivatives and Other Investments		
	Pre-GFC Q1 1999–Q3 2007	Post-GFC Q3 2009–Q4 2015	Direction	Pre-GFC Q1 1999–Q3 2007	Post-GFC Q3 2009–Q4 2015	Direction
Central Asia	4.20	2.69	▼	4.25	6.61	▲
East Asia	0.71	0.60	▼	3.51	1.91	▼
South Asia	0.29	0.55	▲	1.65	1.33	▼
Southeast Asia	1.77	1.06	▼	3.02	2.80	▼
Oceania	3.55	1.52	▼	2.89	1.90	▼
Asia	0.68	0.45	▼	2.56	1.43	▼

FDI = foreign direct investment, GDP = gross domestic product, GFC = global financial crisis.
Notes: Central Asia includes Armenia, Azerbaijan, Georgia, Kazakhstan, the Kyrgyz Republic, and Tajikistan. East Asia includes the People's Republic of China; Hong Kong, China; Japan; the Republic of Korea; and Mongolia. South Asia includes India and Sri Lanka. Southeast Asia includes Brunei Darussalam, Indonesia, Malaysia, the Philippines, Singapore, Thailand, and Viet Nam. Oceania includes Australia and New Zealand. Asia includes Central Asia, East Asia, South Asia, Southeast Asia and Oceania.
Sources: ADB calculations using data from CEIC; and International Monetary Fund. Balance of Payments and International Investment Position Statistics. http://www.imf.org/external/np/sta/bop/bop.htm (accessed September 2016).

The drop in volatility may be due to recent policy initiatives, particularly macroprudential and capital flow management measures aimed at strengthening financial stability and deepening the regions' capital markets especially local currency bond markets. Another contributing factor could be strengthened capital and liquidity standards, enhanced supervision, and the improved quality of financial market infrastructure (Box 3.3). In addition, the region's capital market development should be geared toward broadening the investor base and promoting long-term investment to deter speculation. Developing long-term securities could help reduce an economy's vulnerability to sharp swings in investor sentiment and speculative attacks.

Box 3.3: Asia's Financial Market Infrastructure Development and Its Role in Financial Integration

Financial market infrastructure (FMI) plays a pivotal role in developing financial markets and fostering financial integration. An FMI is defined as a multilateral system among participating institutions—including the operator of the system, used for the purposes of clearing, settling, or recording payments, securities, derivatives or other financial transactions.[1] Examples of FMIs include a payment system that provides an efficient and convenient way of sending and receiving payments between economic agents, or a securities settlement system that offers a platform that facilitates the transfer of securities. An illustrative description of an FMI is a "highway for financial transactions." The better the street quality connecting cities A and B, the less it costs to get from A to B, which in turn better links the two cities, leading to more economic and financial integration. While domestic FMIs promote more efficient (financial) resource allocation within an economy, FMIs operating cross-border connect different financial markets. They become the backbone of regional financial integration and the smooth functioning of the financial system as a whole.

The institutional quality of FMIs substantially differs across regions. In Europe, for example, the real-time gross settlement system (RTGS) TARGET2—operated by the Eurosystem—settles large-value payments in central bank money across the European Union (EU). In 2015, the Eurosystem harmonized its post-trading platforms by launching a single pan-European settlement platform TARGET2 Securities (T2S) for all European central security depositories (CSDs). Hence, the Eurosystem provides an FMI-environment that helps achieve a single European financial market. Parallels can be drawn between Europe and the United States (US), where the Federal Reserve System operates both a RTGS system (Fedwire Funds) and a securities settlement system (Fedwire Securities). In the Association of Southeast Asian Nations (ASEAN), however, FMI landscapes differ substantially across members. In some, modern FMIs exist, but others lack even the domestic payments and settlement system prerequisite to establishing regional cross-border linkages.

Regional initiatives work to enhance the FMI environment within ASEAN. Policy makers recognize the importance of improving FMI institutional quality to create an environment conducive to regional financial integration. For example, the ASEAN Economic Community (AEC) prioritizes payment and settlement systems as a cross-cutting area within financial integration, financial inclusion, and financial stability in its *Blueprint 2025* (ASEAN 2015b). The goal is to develop new FMI platforms and improve existing infrastructures for enhancing cross-border trade, remittances, retail payment systems, and capital markets. Standardizing and harmonizing FMIs to international standards

is one priority. The launch of a pilot platform for cross-border clearing and settlement of debt securities in Hong Kong, China and Malaysia is a good example of regional efforts to strengthen post-trading infrastructure and promoting standardization and dissemination of corporate announcements across Asia's emerging markets.

Helping expand local currency bond markets through regional FMI development is a strong element of the Asian Bond Markets Initiative (ABMI) (Park 2016), for example. The 1997/98 Asian financial crisis and the growing need for long-term infrastructure finance underscored the importance of developing Asia's local currency bond markets—leading ASEAN+3 policymakers in 2003 to establish the ABMI, which is supported and facilitated by ADB. It aims to improve the allocation of excess savings within Asia through efficient and liquid local currency bond markets. Well-functioning, deep regional capital markets will attract investment within the region rather than limit investor options to place excess savings abroad.

Numerous ABMI projects and programs are under way that directly and indirectly relate to FMI development in the region. One important milestone was the establishment of the Cross-border Settlement Infrastructure Forum (CSIF) in 2013, which aims to connect regional FMIs by 2020, linking real-time gross settlements and central securities deposits (ADB 2016c).

Lessons learned from Europe show that financial liberalization and integration must be accompanied by macroprudential policies and a region-wide regulatory and supervisory framework (Volz 2016). It is important to take a prudent path toward fully financially integrated markets. In Europe, it took a sovereign debt crisis—amplified by fully integrated financial markets—before a region-wide banking supervision authority was established and for more emphasis to be put on macroprudential policies. Schoenmaker (2011) refers to this as a "financial trilemma"—financial stability, financial integration, and national financial policies are incompatible. The more vulnerable European periphery countries suffered most from capital flow reversals and volatility during the 2008/09 global financial crisis. Prudent policies are needed to mitigate these risks—and important to be kept in mind when further connecting ASEAN members clearly at different stages of financial development.

It is essential to follow an FMI development strategy that is both tailored to the AEC and draws from global best practices. There is no one-size-fits-all approach for regional FMI development. While Europe primarily chose a top-down approach to financial market integration, this is not necessarily right for the AEC. Thus, existing multilateral initiatives should be intensified to provide a policy environment that is both enabling and prudent for the public and private sector to foster a balanced regional FMI development path.

---

[1] Definition according to the Bank for International Settlements (BIS).

References

ADBa. Asia Regional Integration Center. ASEAN Finance Ministers Process. https://aric.adb.org/initiative/asean-finance-ministers-process

ADBb. Credit Guarantee and Investment Facility (CGIF). https://www.adb.org/site/funds/funds/credit-guarantee-and-investment-facility

ADBc. Executives' Meeting of East Asia Pacific Central Banks (EMEAP) Asian Bond Fund (ABF) Initiative. https://aric.adb.org/initiative/executives-meeting-of-east-asia-pacific-central-banks-initiative

_____. 2005. *Technical Assistance for the ASEAN+3 Regional Multicurrency Bond (Financed by the Japan Special Fund)*. Manila.

_____. 2010. ADB to Contribute to ASEAN+3 Credit Guarantee Facility. News release. 14 April.

_____. 2013. *The Road to ASEAN Financial Integration: A Combined Study on Assessing the Financial Landscape and Formulating Milestones for Monetary and Financial Integration in ASEAN*. Manila.

_____. 2015a. *ASEAN+3 Bond Market Forum Sub-forum 1 Phase 3 Report: Implementation of the ASEAN+3 Multi-currency Bond Issuance Framework*. Manila.

_____. 2015b. ADB Welcomes First Cross-Border Bond Under ASEAN+3 Bond Framework. News release. 28 September.

_____. 2015c. *Progress Report on Establishing A Regional Settlement Intermediary and Next Steps: Implementing Central Securities Depository–Real-Time Gross Settlement Linkages in ASEAN+3*. Manila.

T. Anas and R. Atje. 2005. *Economic Surveillance and Policy Dialogue in East Asia: Making the ASEAN Surveillance Process a New*. http://www.asean.org/storage/images/archive/17894.pdf

AsianBondsOnline. About Us. https://asianbondsonline.adb.org/about.php

_____. 2008. ASEAN+3 New ABMI Roadmap. 31 July. https://asianbondsonline.adb.org/publications/adb/2008/abmi_roadmap.pdf

ASEAN+3 Macroeconomic Research Office (AMRO). 2016. Opening Ceremony of AMRO as an International Organization. Press release. 19 February.

ASEAN Capital Markets Forum (ACMF). 2014. ACMF launched framework for the cross-border offering of ASEAN CIS. Press release. 25 August.

_____ (ACMF). 2016. ACMF Action Plan 2016-2020. http://www.theacmf.org/ACMF/upload/acmfactionplan2016-2020.pdf

ASEAN Exchanges. 2012. Launch of ASEAN Trading Link Speech by Dato' Tajuddin Atan, Chief Executive Officer, Bursa Malaysia. http://www.aseanexchanges.org/downloads/DTA_speech_ASEAN_Trading_Link_launch.pdf

Association of Southeast Asian Nations (ASEANa). Joint Statement on East Asia Cooperation. http://asean.org/?static_post=joint-statement-on-east-asia-cooperation-28-november-1999

_____ (ASEANb). Regional Cooperation in Finance. http://asean.org/asean-economic-community/asean-finance-ministers-meeting-afmm/overview/

_____. 2015a. ASEAN Banking Integration: Stronger Regional Banks, More Robust and Inclusive Growth. *Building the ASEAN Community*. http://asean.org/storage/images/2015/October/outreach-document/Edited%20ASEAN%20Banking%20Integration%20Framework-1.pdf

_____. 2015b. ASEAN Economic Community Blueprint 2025. Jakarta.

_____. 2016. Turning Vision into Reality for a Dynamic ASEAN Community. Joint Statement of the 2nd ASEAN Finance Ministers' and Central Bank Governors' Meeting. 4 April.

N. Ananchotikul, S. Piao and E. Zoli. 2015. Drivers of Financial Integration – Implications for Asia. *IMF Working Paper*. No. WP/15/160. Washington, DC: International Monetary Fund.

L. Baele, A. Ferrando, P. Hördahl, E. Krylova, and C. Monnet. 2004. Measuring financial integration in the euro area. *ECB Occasional Paper Series* No 14. Frankfurt: European Central Bank.

Executives' Meeting of Meeting of East Asia Pacific Central Banks (EMEAP). About Us. http://www.emeap.org/index.php/about-emeap/

R. Espinoza, A. Prasad and O. Williams. 2010. Regional Financial Integration in the GCC. *IMF Working Paper.* No. WP/10/90. Washington, DC: International Monetary Fund.

M. Hinojales and C. Y. Park. 2010. Stock Market Integration: Emerging East Asia's Experience. In M. Devereux, P. Lane, C.Y. Park, and S.J. Wei, eds. *The Dynamics of Asian Financial Integration: Facts and Analytics.* Routledge London and New York.

M. Kawai and C. Houser. 2007. Evolving ASEAN+3 ERPD: Towards Peer Reviews or Due Diligence? *ADB Institute Discussion Paper* No. 79. Tokyo: Asian Development Bank Institute.

W. R. Keeton and C.S. Morris. 1987. Why Do Banks' Loan Losses Differ? Economic Review. 72 (3). pp 3–21.

N. Klein. 2013. Non-performing Loans in CESEE: Determinants and Impact on Macroeconomic Performance. *IMF Working Paper.* No. 13/72. Washington, DC: International Monetary Fund.

J. W. Lee and C.Y. Park. 2011. Financial Integration in Emerging Asia: Challenges and Prospects. *Asian Economic Policy Review.* 6 (2). pp. 176-198.

V. Makri, A. Tsagkanos, A. Bellas. 2014. Determinants of Non-performing Loans: The Case of Eurozone. *Panoeconomicus.* 61 (2). pp. 193-206.

C. –Y. Park. 2013. Asian Capital Market Integration: Theory and Evidence. *ADB Economics Working Paper Series.* No. 351. Manila: Asian Development Bank.

_____ 2016. Developing Local Currency Bond Markets in Asia. *ADB Economics Working Paper Series.* No. 495. Manila: Asian Development Bank.

Central Bank of the Republic of the Philippines (BSP). 2016. Chiang Mai Initiative Multilateralization. September. http://www.bsp.gov.ph/downloads/Publications/FAQs/CMIM.pdf

Reserve Bank of India (RBI). 2012. Reserve Bank of India Announces SAARC Swap Arrangement. Press release. 16 May.

_____. 2016. RBI announces the extension of SAARC Swap Arrangement. Press release. 23 February.

SAARCFINANCE. Brief History, Objectives and Activities. http://www.saarcfinance.org/SaarcBriefHistory.html

D. Schoenmaker. 2011. The Financial Trilemma. *Economics Letters.* 111 (2011). pp. 57-59.

Securities Commission of Malaysia. 2013. ACMF announced the framework for the cross-border offering of ASEAN CIS. Media release. 1 October.

U. Volz. 2016. Regional Financial Integration in East Asia against the Backdrop of Recent European Experiences. *International Economic Journal.* 30 (2), 272-293.

4 | Movement of People

Movement of People

Remittances and tourism receipts are an increasingly important and relatively stable source of external financing for Asia and the Pacific. In 2015, however, there was a slowdown in remittances to South Asia and Central Asia due to oil price shocks, the crisis in Ukraine, and the economic slump in the Russian Federation. This trend is expected to have continued in 2016 as weak global growth persists. In the Pacific, the subregion most dependent on tourism, receipts fell slightly in 2014.

Migration from Asia and the Pacific increased between 2010 and 2015—although it is directed more outside than within the region, with significant variations across subregions. The geographical and subregional pattern of inward remittances and outward migration are closely interlinked. Among the host of economic effects of migration, it remains the most important driver of remittances for developing Asia and the Pacific. The region needs to capitalize on the potential for regional migration to reallocate labor from surplus to deficit economies given demographic shifts in the region (Kang and Magoncia 2016). At the same time, the interplay of various economic, demographic, social, political, cultural, and environmental factors shape migration decisions.

Remittances and Tourism Receipts

Remittances and tourism receipts are increasingly important and stable sources of external financing in Asia and the Pacific.

Remittance inflows and tourism receipts to Asia and the Pacific have increased steadily since the 1990s (Figure 4.1). Compared with portfolio equity investment and foreign direct investment (FDI), remittances, and

Figure 4.1: Financial Inflows to Asia
($ billion, by type)

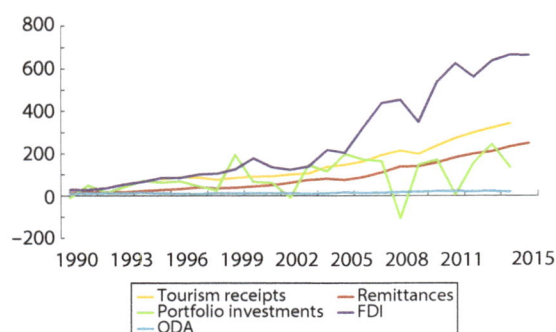

FDI = foreign direct investment; ODA = official development assistance.
Source: ADB calculations using data from World Bank. World Development Indicators. http://databank.worldbank.org/data/reports.aspx?source=world-development-indicators (accessed July 2016).

tourism receipts remained stable even during the 1997/98 Asian financial crisis and 2008/09 global financial crisis. Further, remittances gradually rose to more than 10 times the size of official development assistance in 2014 providing a secure and sustainable economic lifeline for households in developing economies.

For Asia and the Pacific, remittances and tourism receipts are the least volatile types of financial flows (relative to GDP fluctuations).

In assessing volatility by standard deviation, normally stable remittances became even less volatile after the global financial crisis across all subregions except for the Pacific, unsurprisingly given its consumption smoothing nature (Table 4.1). Tourism receipts became more volatile in Southeast Asia after the crisis.

Volatility in both types of financial flows varied across Asian subregions. Before the crisis, remittances were

Table 4.1: Financial Flow Volatility—Asia (by type)

	Pre-GFC				Post-GFC			
Subregions	Tourism Receipts	Remittances	Portfolio Investments	FDI	Tourism Receipts	Remittances	Portfolio Investments	FDI
Asia	0.1	0.1	0.7	0.6	0.1	0.1	0.4	0.2
Central Asia	0.2	0.7	0.6	2.8	0.2	0.1	0.0	1.2
East Asia	0.1	0.1	0.8	0.5	0.0	0.0	0.4	0.2
South Asia	0.1	0.4	0.6	0.6	0.1	0.3	0.6	0.2
Southeast Asia	0.3	0.3	0.9	1.1	0.4	0.2	0.4	0.4
Pacific	0.7	0.7	0.0	1.6	0.6	0.4	0.0	0.7
Oceania	0.2	0.2	1.7	2.5	0.1	0.0	0.4	0.6

FDI = foreign direct investment, GFC = global financial crisis, GDP = gross domestic product.
Notes: Volatility computed as standard deviation of levels as percent of GDP. Pre-GFC period is from 2002 to 2007; post-GFC period is from 2010 up to latest year available.
Sources: ADB calculations using data from International Monetary Fund. World Economic Outlook. http://www.imf.org/external/pubs/ft/weo/2016/02/weodata/index.aspx (accessed July 2016); and World Bank. World Development Indicators. http://databank.worldbank.org/data/reports.aspx?source=world-development-indicators (accessed July 2016).

most volatile in Central Asia, and after the crisis, in the Pacific and South Asia; tourism receipts fluctuated most in the Pacific both before and after the crisis.

Trends in Remittance Inflows

Asia and the Pacific accounts for the largest share of global remittances. In 2015, Asia and the Pacific accounted for 46.6% ($271 billion) of total global remittances ($582 billion) (Figure 4.2). The largest source of remittances to Asia and the Pacific came from within the region itself—$83 billion (31%). North America was the second-largest source at $66 billion (24%). This was followed by remittances from the Middle East at $50 billion (19%) (Figure 4.3).

The largest share of Asia-bound remittances from North America went to East Asia ($26 billion), followed by Southeast Asia ($22 billion) (Table 4.2). Meanwhile, the majority of Asia-bound remittances from the Middle East go to South Asia ($40 billion), followed by Southeast Asia ($11 billion).

East Asia is both the largest source and destination of intraregional remittances. The large intraregional remittance inflows in Asia and the Pacific are mostly sourced from East Asia, accounting for $32 billion (or 39% of total intraregional remittances), followed by South Asia at $20 billion (24%). Southeast Asia follows closely at $18.2 billion (22%), while the Pacific and Oceania sent about $11 billion (13%), and Central Asia about $1 billion (1%).

Figure 4.2: Remittance Inflows—Asia and World

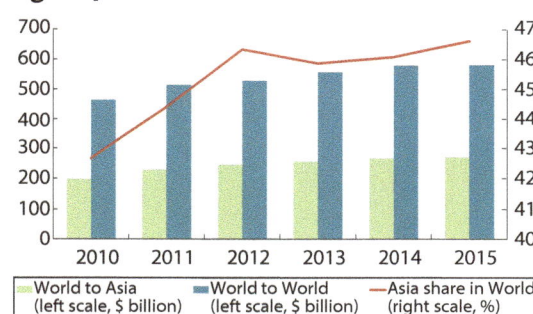

| World to Asia (left scale, $ billion) | World to World (left scale, $ billion) | Asia share in World (right scale, %) |

Note: % share = (remittances inflows from world to Asia / total global remittances inflows) × 100
Source: ADB calculations using data from World Bank. World Bank Migration and Remittances Data. http://www.worldbank.org/en/topic/migrationremittancesdiasporaissues/brief/migration-remittances-data (accessed July 2016).

Figure 4.3: Remittance Inflows to Asia in 2015—by Source, 2015 ($ billion, % share)

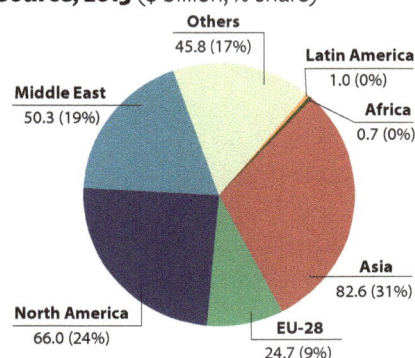

Others 45.8 (17%)
Latin America 1.0 (0%)
Africa 0.7 (0%)
Asia 82.6 (31%)
EU-28 24.7 (9%)
North America 66.0 (24%)
Middle East 50.3 (19%)

EU = European Union.
Source: ADB calculations using data from World Bank. World Bank Migration and Remittances Data. http://www.worldbank.org/en/topic/migrationremittancesdiasporaissues/brief/migration-remittances-data (accessed July 2016).

Table 4.2: Bilateral Remittance Matrix, 2015 ($ million)

From\To	Asia	Central Asia	East Asia	South Asia	Southeast Asia	Pacific	Oceania	European Union	North America	Middle East	World
Asia	82,595	957	38,392	24,292	17489	399	1067	7,426	1,254	1,333	98,649
Central Asia	988	877	104	3	4	0	0	718	1	20	4,843
East Asia	32,196	10	26,832	676	4,480	0	199	695	546	30	34,629
South Asia	20,106	64	1,216	17,908	912	0	6	74	110	6	20,386
Southeast Asia	18,228	0	6,012	2,861	9,118	34	203	739	287	69	19,487
Pacific	155	0	18	21	61	7	48	37	10	0	305
Oceania	10,922	6	4,209	2,822	2,914	358	612	5,163	300	1,209	18,999
European Union	24,712	832	6,716	10,240	5,924	15	985	64,585	1,775	4,015	135,334
North America	65,981	346	25,655	16,966	22,334	204	477	19,239	1,507	4,315	156,990
Middle East	50,582	20	72	39,813	10,674	0	2	214	117	19,207	75,612
World	27,1137	12,220	75,591	117,872	62,080	686	2,687	116,102	8,307	34,727	581,640

Source: ADB calculations using data from World Bank. World Bank Migration and Remittances Data. http://www.worldbank.org/en/topic/migrationremittancesdiasporaissues/brief/migration-remittances-data (accessed July 2016).

The pattern is similar for destinations. East Asia is also the largest recipient of remittances from Asia and the Pacific, receiving $38 billion of the $83 billion total remittance inflows in the region in 2015. South Asia was second, accounting for $24 billion (29%) and followed by Southeast Asia at $17 billion (21%). The Pacific and Oceania received $1.5 billion (1%), while Central Asia accounted for $1 billion (1%) (Table 4.2).

Although there is greater connectivity within Asia and the Pacific, some subregions continue to rely heavily on remittances from outside the region—the Middle East is the main source for South Asia, as the Russian Federation is for Central Asia.

Remittances to subregions in Asia and the Pacific as a share of gross domestic product (GDP) are above the global average.

Among the Asian subregions, South Asia and Central Asia depend most on remittances—peaking in 2012 at 4.7% and 2.9%, respectively. But their shares fell sharply in 2015 to 4.4% and 2.3% because of a steep decline in remittances from the Middle East and the Russian Federation (Figure 4.4). Central Asia relies almost exclusively on the Russian Federation, and was severely affected by the crisis in Ukraine, the recession in the Russian Federation and depreciating ruble.

Figure 4.4: Remittance Inflows (% of GDP)

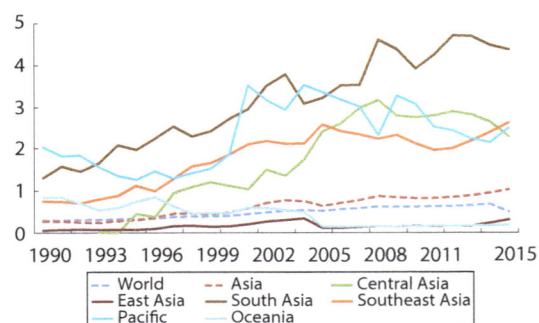

GDP = gross domestic product.
Sources: ADB calculations using data from International Monetary Fund. World Economic Outlook. http://www.imf.org/external/pubs/ft/weo/2016/02/weodata/index.aspx (accessed July 2016); and World Bank. World Development Indicators. http://databank.worldbank.org/data/reports.aspx?source=world-development-indicators (accessed July 2016).

The Middle East is the largest source of remittances for South Asia as host of a sizable expatriate population, accounting for more than a third of the subregion's receipts. The fall in oil prices also affected remittances from the Middle East to South Asia.

Despite these factors, remittance inflows to Asia and the Pacific grew moderately in 2015 as a proportion of the world total (Figure 4.5). As mentioned, the region received the largest share of global remittances in

Figure 4.5: Remittance Inflows (% of world total)

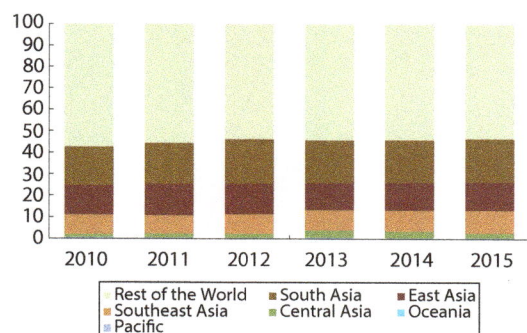

Legend: Rest of the World, South Asia, East Asia, Southeast Asia, Central Asia, Oceania, Pacific

Source: ADB calculations using data from World Bank. World Bank Migration and Remittances Data. http://www.worldbank.org/en/topic/migrationremittancesdiasporaissues/brief/migration-remittances-data (accessed July 2016).

2015—46.6% of the world total, moderately up from 46.1% in 2014.

The intraregional share of global remittance inflows fell between 2010 and 2015 in all subregions of Asia and the Pacific except Southeast Asia.

The intraregional share of global remittance inflows to Asia and the Pacific declined from 33% in 2010 to 31% in 2015—as inflows from outside the region increased at a faster rate of 43% than those sourced from within the region (26%). The decline was sharpest for Oceania.

A comparison of subregional remittance inflows shows the Pacific receiving the largest share of its total remittances from other Asian subregions (57%) and only 1% coming from within the Pacific (Figure 4.6). It is one of two subregions that receive more remittances from within the region. The other is East Asia, which sources 36% from itself and 15% from other subregions.

On the other hand, the major share of Central Asia's remittances is received from economies outside the region, in particular the Russian Federation, with long historical ties as former Soviet republics. In 2015, the subregion received 92% of its total remittances from outside Asia and the Pacific, 7% from within the subregion, and only around 1% from other subregions. Similarly, South Asia has stronger remittance links externally, mostly in the Middle East, receiving almost 80% of its remittances from outside the region, while only 15% are sourced from itself and 5% from other subregions. Southeast Asia's remittance structure is also largely with economies outside Asia and the Pacific (72%), with only 15% of its remittances from within, and 13% from other Asian subregions.

Figure 4.6: Subregional Remittance Share—Asia
(% total global remittances to the subregion)

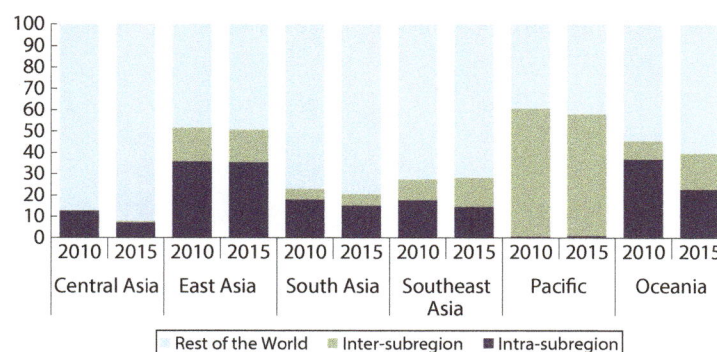

Legend: Rest of the World, Inter-subregion, Intra-subregion

Notes:
(i) % intra-subregional share = (remittance within subregion i / remittance from world to subregion i) × 100
(ii) % inter-subregional share = (remittance from other subregions to subregion i / remittance from world to subregion i) × 100
(iii) % rest of the world = (remittance from rest of the world to subregion i / remittance from world to subregion i) × 100
Source: ADB calculations using data from World Bank. World Bank Migration and Remittances Data. http://www.worldbank.org/en/topic/migrationremittancesdiasporaissues/brief/migration-remittances-data (accessed July 2016).

Figure 4.7: Top 10 Remittance-Recipient Economies—Asia

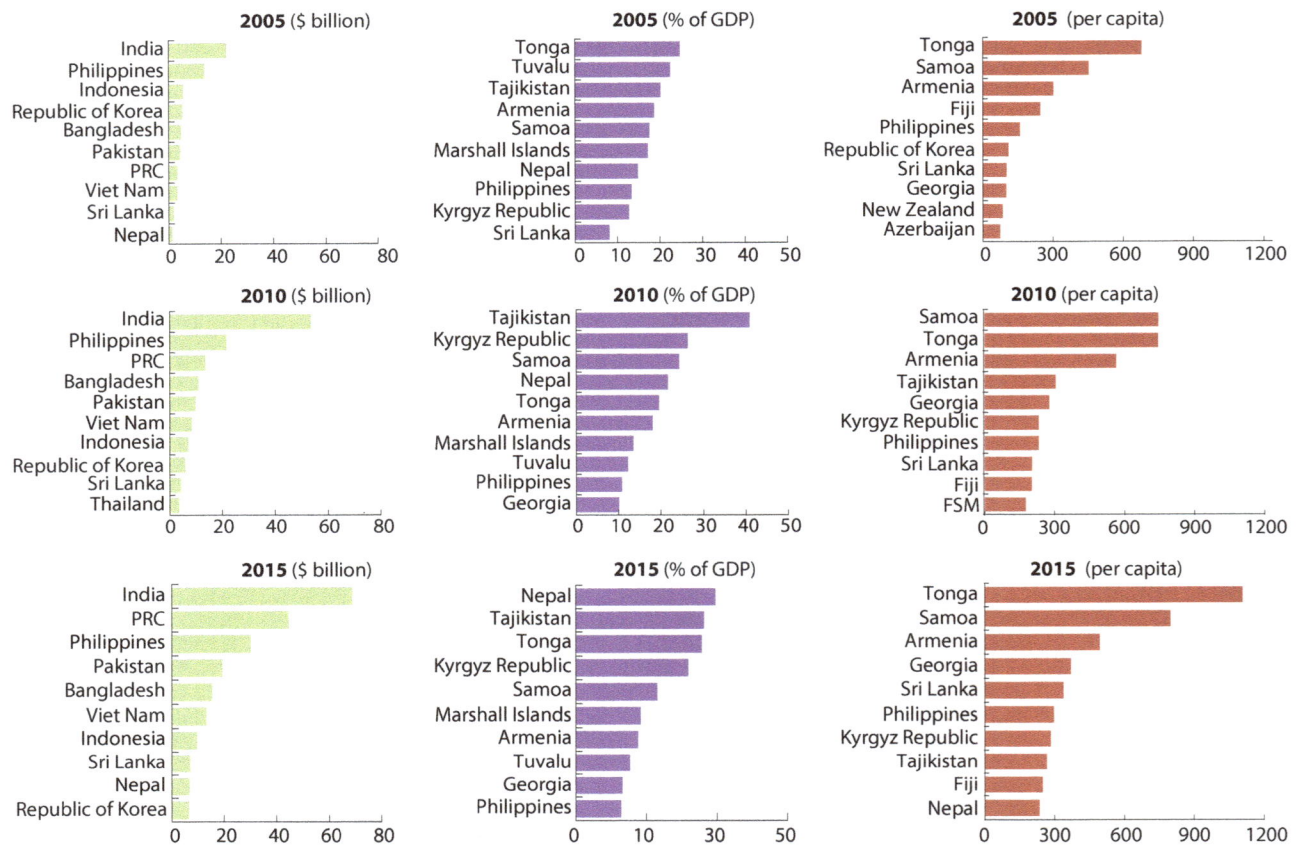

PRC = People's Republic of China, FSM = Federated States of Microneasia, GDP = gross domestic product.
Sources: ADB calculations using data from International Monetary Fund. World Economic Outlook. http://www.imf.org/external/pubs/ft/weo/2016/02/weodata/index.aspx (accessed July 2016); United Nations. Department of Economic and Social Affairs, Population Division. World Population Prospects 2015. https://esa.un.org/unpd/wpp/Download/SpecialAggregates/Ecological/ (accessed April 2016); and World Bank. World Development Indicators. http://databank.worldbank.org/data/reports.aspx?source=world-development-indicators (accessed July 2016).

Figure 4.7 ranks the top 10 inward remittance economies in Asia and the Pacific in 2005, 2010, and 2015. In nominal terms, India was highest in all 3 years. The Philippines ranked second in 2005 and 2010, but fell behind the People's Republic of China (PRC) in 2015 amid low oil prices, which also affected the earnings of Filipino migrants from major oil-exporting economies in the Middle East. As a proportion of GDP, Tajikistan and the Kyrgyz Republic were highest in 2010, but they were overtaken by Nepal in 2015 due to the recession in the Russian Federation and a spike in inflows to Nepal following the 2015 earthquake. In per capita terms, the rankings are dominated by the smaller economies in Central Asia and the Pacific in 2015, with Tonga, Samoa, and Armenia topping the list.

Global remittances dropped 2.7% in 2015 from 2014 and are expected to pick up at a weak pace of 0.8% in 2016 against the continued backdrop of weak economic growth in source economies and low oil prices (World Bank 2016). In addition, structural factors such as tighter bank controls to curb money laundering could make flows through informal remittance channels more attractive. Tighter immigration and work visa policies also pose risks to remittance growth.

Trends in Tourism Receipts

Asia and the Pacific receives the second-largest income from tourism after the European Union (EU). The EU accounts for $470 billion of tourism receipts in 2014

Figure 4.8: Tourism Receipts by Region, 2014
($ billion, % share)

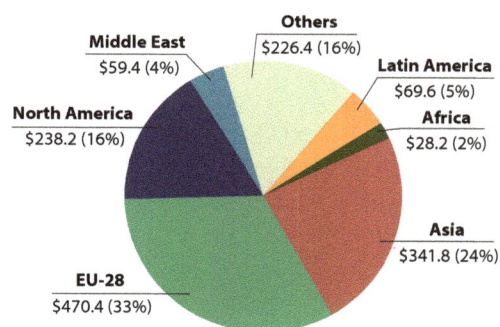

EU = European Union.
Source: ADB calculations using data from World Bank. World Development Indicators. http://databank.worldbank.org/data/reports.aspx?source=world-development-indicators (accessed July 2016).

Figure 4.9: Tourism Receipts (% world total)

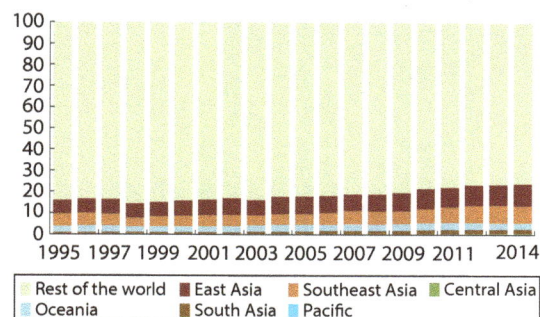

Source: ADB calculations using data from World Bank. World Development Indicators. http://databank.worldbank.org/data/reports.aspx?source=world-development-indicators (accessed July 2016).

Figure 4.10: Tourism Receipts from World—Asia and Asian Subregions (% of GDP)

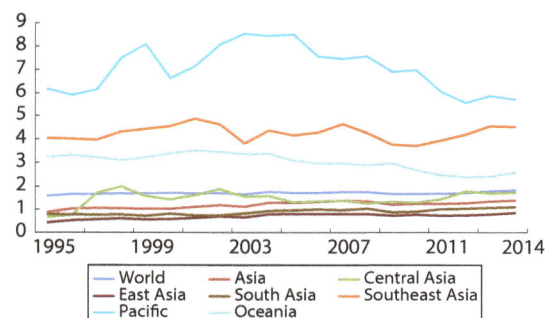

GDP = gross domestic product.
Sources: ADB calculations using data from International Monetary Fund. World Economic Outlook. http://www.imf.org/external/pubs/ft/weo/2016/02/weodata/index.aspx (accessed July 2016); and World Bank. World Development Indicators. http://databank.worldbank.org/data/reports.aspx?source=world-development-indicators (accessed July 2016).

(33% of the global total) (Figure 4.8). Asia and the Pacific came second with $342 billion (24%), and North America followed with $238 billion (16%).

The Asian share of the global total has been increasing since 1995 (16%) to reach 23.8% in 2014, slightly up from 23.4% in 2013 (Figure 4.9). East Asia received the largest amount—$147 billion in 2014, up from $131 billion in 2013. The subregion accounts for 10.2% globally. Southeast Asia came second with $114 billion in both 2013 and 2014, or 8.0% of the world total. Oceania received 3.0% of the world total while South Asia attracted 2.0%—$29 billion in 2014, up from $26 billion in 2013.

Tourism receipts in Asia accounted for 1.4% of GDP; but amounts varied greatly across subregions with the Pacific being most dependent on tourism.

Global tourism receipts as a share of GDP have been generally steady since 1995—1.8% in 2014, unchanged from 2013. Asia and the Pacific showed a similar trend, posting 1.4% of GDP in 2014, unchanged from 2013.

Among subregions, the Pacific's reputation as an idyllic destination makes tourism a prime industry, accounting for almost 6% of GDP (Figure 4.10). However, its share fell slightly—from 5.9% in 2013 to 5.7% in 2014. Next to the Pacific, Southeast Asia and Oceania are the most popular destinations for international tourists, with receipts

accounting for 4.5% and 2.6% of GDP, respectively. East Asia holds the smallest share as a proportion of GDP at less than 1%. While the subregion receives the largest income from tourism in absolute terms, it is the least reliant on tourism receipts as a share of GDP.

Except for South Asia and Central Asia, all other subregions are more dependent on tourism receipts relative to remittances. The share of tourism receipts in GDP compared with remittances is especially low for South Asia (Figure 4.11).

Figure 4.12 ranks the top 10 recipients of tourism receipts in nominal terms and as a share of GDP. Economies in East Asia, Oceania, and Southeast Asia received the

Figure 4.11: Remittances and Tourism Receipts in Asia by Subregions (% of GDP)

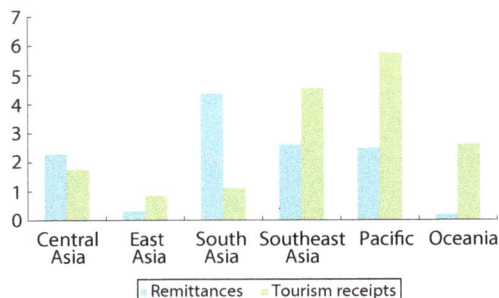

GDP = gross domestic product.
Notes: Remittance data are as of 2015; tourism receipts are as of 2014.
Sources: ADB calculations using data from International Monetary Fund. World Economic Outlook. http://www.imf.org/external/pubs/ft/weo/2016/02/weodata/index.aspx (accessed July 2016); and World Bank. World Development Indicators. http://databank.worldbank.org/data/reports.aspx?source=world-development-indicators (accessed July 2016).

most income from tourism in nominal terms; while as a proportion of GDP, the region's small island economies topped the list.

The PRC remained atop the list in nominal terms in all 3 years—with a large portion of tourist arrivals from neighboring economies such as Hong Kong, China; Taipei,China; and Macau, China. Although the vast majority of tourism in the PRC is for leisure, business travel is also substantial reaching 772 million trips in 2012(EU SME Centre 2014). Australia was second in 2005 and 2010 but fell behind Hong Kong, China and Thailand in 2014.

As a proportion of GDP, the Maldives in the Indian Ocean held the top spot as a tourist destination. Implicitly, the economy relies heavily on tourism, which accounted for 74% of GDP in 2010 and reached 86% in 2014. Palau and

Figure 4.12: Top 10 Tourism Receipts Receiving Economies—Asia

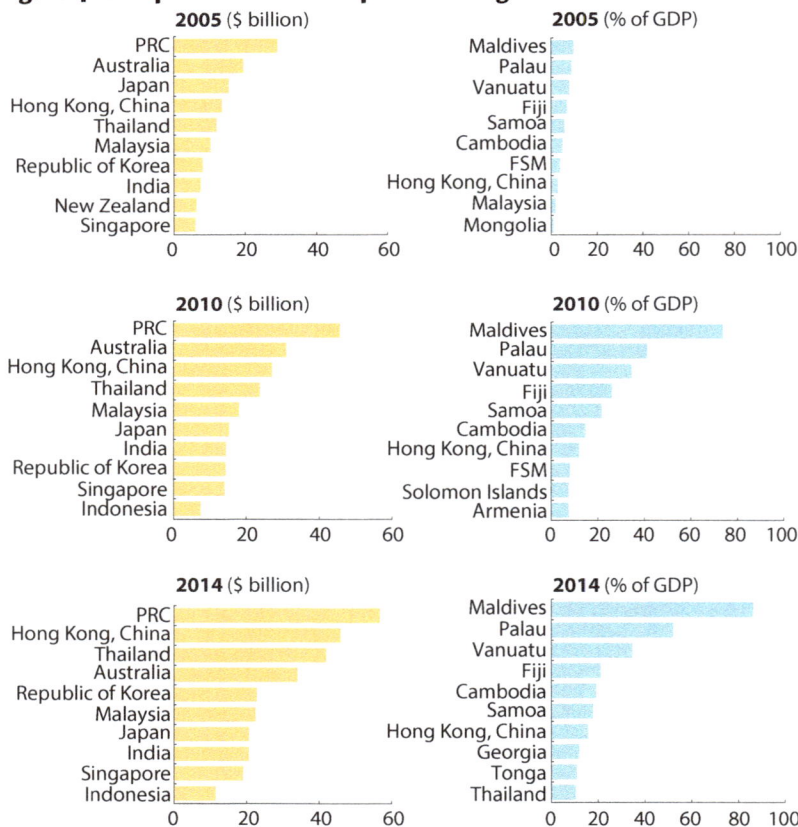

PRC = People's Republic of China, FSM = Federated States of Microneasia, GDP = gross domestic product.
Sources: ADB calculations using data from International Monetary Fund. World Economic Outlook. http://www.imf.org/external/pubs/ft/weo/2016/02/weodata/index.aspx; and World Bank. World Development Indicators. http://databank.worldbank.org/data/reports.aspx?source=world-development-indicators (both accessed July 2016).

Figure 4.13: Subregional Tourism Share—Asia
(% of total tourist arrivals to each subregion)

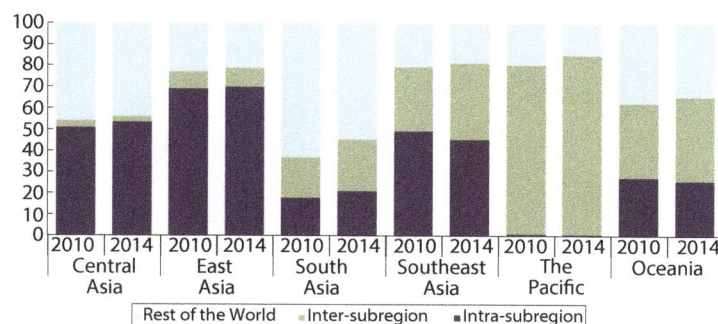

Notes: Due to data unavailability, 2014 tourist arrival for the People's Republic of China are estimated.
(i)   % intra-subregional share = (tourist arrivals within subregion *i* / tourist arrivals from world to subregion *i*) × 100
(ii) % inter-subregional share = (tourist arrivals from subregion *i* to other subregions / tourist arrivals from world to subregion *i*)) × 100
(iii) % rest of the world = (tourist arrivals from subregion *i* to rest of the world / tourist arrivals from world to subregion *i*) × 100
Source: ADB calculations using data from World Tourism Organization. 2016. Tourism Statistics Database.

Vanuatu held the second and third spot, respectively. In 2014, tourism receipts accounted for 52% of GDP in Palau and 35% in Vanuatu. These sea-locked economies need to broaden their economic base outside tourism. Though regarded as a stable source of financing, heavy reliance on tourism receipts may still pose volatility risks.

The intraregional share of tourism within Asia and the Pacific increased from 75% in 2010 to 77% in 2014.

While source data on intraregional tourism receipts is limited, the trend in tourist arrivals between 2010 and 2014 suggests a slight increase in the intraregional share of tourism within the region (Figure 4.13). Between 2010 and 2014, the growth of tourist arrivals from within the region stood at 23%, surpassing that from outside the region (13%). The intraregional share of total tourist arrivals to each subregion increased.

The vast majority of tourists to the Pacific arrive from other Asian subregions—84% of the total. Oceania and Southeast Asia also source a large proportion of tourists from other subregions (40% and 36%, respectively). By contrast, Central Asia is the least connected to other subregions (3%).

In terms of intra-subregional tourism connectivity, East Asians, Central Asians, and Southeast Asians travel most within their subregions (70%, 54%, and 45% of total arrivals, respectively). For East Asia, the substantial share has mainly been driven by a spike in tourism to the PRC from neighboring economies. For Southeast Asia, this can partly be attributed to the Association of Southeast Asian Nations (ASEAN) Framework Agreement on Visa Exemption signed in 2006. The Pacific is the least connected intra-subregionally with only 0.7% of tourists arriving from within.

Tourism continues to show robust growth and a positive outlook.

International tourism was robust in 2014, bolstering economic growth and job creation worldwide. A record $1.43 trillion in tourism receipts were recorded in 2014, up 4.7% from the $1.37 trillion in 2013. The United Nations World Tourism Organization (UNWTO) reported sustained growth of 4.4% in 2015 (UNWTO 2016). Lower fuel costs and greater competition in transport—along with growing online travel options—could also contribute to future tourism growth. In the first half of 2016, global tourist arrivals grew an estimated 4%, showing tourism to be one of the most resilient economic sectors globally (World Bank 2016).

Figure 4.14: International Migration Trend— World and Asia (million, % share)

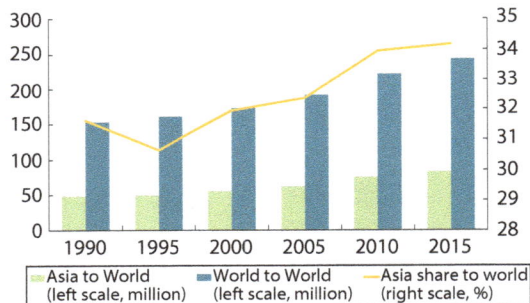

Note: Percent share is computed as (migrants from Asia to World/ total global migrants) × 100.
Source: ADB calculations using data from United Nations. Department of Economic and Social Affairs, Population Division. International Migration Stock 2015. http://www.un.org/en/ development/desa/population/migration/data/estimates2/ estimates15.shtml (accessed July 2016).

Migration Updates

Asia and the Pacific accounts for more than a third of total international migrants.

Global migration continues to rise—driven by economic, demographic, social, political, cultural, and environmental factors—and facilitated by cheaper transportation, ease of communication, and social networking.[36] From 78 million in 1970, the stock of international migrants nearly doubled to 153 million in 1990, reaching a record 244 million in 2015 (Ratha 2016). Asia and the Pacific is the largest source, with international migrants from the

region rising since 1995 to reach 75 million in 2010 and 83 million in 2015 (Figure 4.14).

The EU is the second-largest source of migrants globally, steadily growing to 36 million in 2015 from 33 million in 2010. Third is Latin America, which more than doubled its migrants since 1990 to reach 31 million migrants in 2010 and 32 million in 2015. All other major regions also show increasing trends in migratory movements since 1990s. Most notable is the Middle East, where migration rose from 9 million in 2010 to 13 million in 2015—the highest growth (41%) among all regions (Figures 4.15a, 4.15b). This trend is mainly due to the surge of Syrian refugees estimated at around 4.8 million (Ratha 2016).

South Asia is the largest source of outbound migration from Asia and the Pacific. South Asia has remained the largest source of Asian migrants since the 1990s, accounting for 37 million in 2015 (15% of all international migrants) — larger than the number of migrants from the EU. Southeast Asia is second with 20 million migrants in 2015 (8%), up from 18 million migrants in 2010. East Asia remained relatively steady with a 6% share—14 million migrants in 2015 from 13 million in 2010.

Intra-Asian migration accounts for 72% of total inbound migration to Asia and the Pacific.

Migration to Asia and the Pacific has been growing since 1990. From 34 million in 1990, it increased to 40 million in 2010 and 42 million in 2015. Intraregional migration accounted for 31 million in 2015 or 72% of total international migrants bound for the region, up from 29 million in 2010 (Table 4.3 and Figures 4.16a, 4.16b). South Asia is the largest source of intra-Asian migration, consistent with the global trend—with close to a third of the total—reaching close to 12 million in 2015. Southeast Asia is the second-largest source with almost 10 million. South Asia is also the largest host of intra-Asian migration receiving 10.7 million in 2015, with the vast majority (9.7 million) sourced from within the subregion. Southeast Asia follows with 9 million Asian migrants with almost 7 million from within the subregion. Between subregions, most migration flows are from South Asia to Southeast Asia (1.2 million), and from Southeast Asia to East Asia (1.1 million).

---

[36]   This subsection estimates international migrants using stock data from the United Nations Population Division, which "equates international migrants with the foreign-born population whenever this information is available, which is the case in most countries or areas. In most countries lacking data on place of birth, information on the country of citizenship of those enumerated was available, and was used as the basis for the identification of international migrants, thus effectively equating, in these cases, international migrants with foreign citizens. In countries where citizenship is conferred on the basis of jus sanguinis, people who were born in the country of residence may be included in the number of international migrants even though they may have never lived abroad. Conversely, persons who were born abroad and who naturalized in their country of residence are excluded from the stock of international migrants when using citizenship as the criterion to define international migrants" (UN 2015), p. 7.

Figure 4.15: Total International Outbound Migrants to the World by Region
(million)

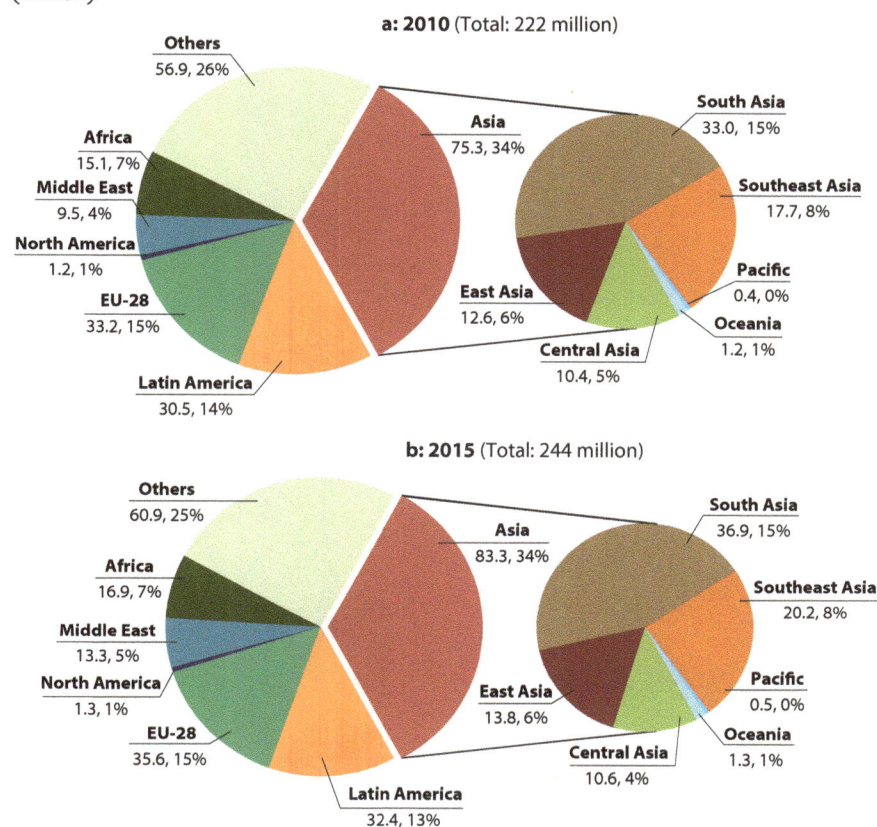

a: 2010 (Total: 222 million)

Others 56.9, 26%
Africa 15.1, 7%
Middle East 9.5, 4%
North America 1.2, 1%
EU-28 33.2, 15%
Latin America 30.5, 14%
Asia 75.3, 34%
East Asia 12.6, 6%
South Asia 33.0, 15%
Southeast Asia 17.7, 8%
Pacific 0.4, 0%
Oceania 1.2, 1%
Central Asia 10.4, 5%

b: 2015 (Total: 244 million)

Others 60.9, 25%
Africa 16.9, 7%
Middle East 13.3, 5%
North America 1.3, 1%
EU-28 35.6, 15%
Latin America 32.4, 13%
Asia 83.3, 34%
East Asia 13.8, 6%
South Asia 36.9, 15%
Southeast Asia 20.2, 8%
Pacific 0.5, 0%
Oceania 1.3, 1%
Central Asia 10.6, 4%

EU = European Union.
Source: ADB calculations using data from United Nations. Department of Economic and Social Affairs, Population Division. International Migration Stock 2015. http://www.un.org/en/development/desa/population/migration/data/estimates2/estimates15.shtml (accessed July 2016).

Table 4.3: Bilateral Migration Matrix, 2015 (thousand)

From\To	Asia	Central Asia	East Asia	South Asia	Southeast Asia	Pacific	Oceania	European Union	North America	Middle East	World
Asia	**30,578**	**1,027**	**6,134**	**10,748**	**9,036**	**64**	**3,570**	**8,032**	**3,126**	**13,560**	**83,281**
Central Asia	1,062	983	55	18	0	0	6	1,602	28	20	10,583
East Asia	6,745	35	4,770	225	873	5	837	1,322	1,121	15	13,790
South Asia	11,810	9	183	9,654	1,213	5	746	3,156	1,053	10,961	36,873
Southeast Asia	9,838	0	1,092	849	6,887	21	989	1,604	855	2,563	20,215
Pacific	318	0	0	0	22	13	283	16	28	0	490
Oceania	804	0	35	1	40	21	707	332	40	1	1,329
European Union	**3,220**	**298**	**84**	**51**	**76**	**3**	**2,709**	**19,884**	**2,101**	**57**	**35,620**
North America	**127**	**0**	**47**	**2**	**14**	**0**	**64**	**226**	**0**	**1**	**1,286**
Middle East	**429**	**19**	**6**	**65**	**22**	**0**	**318**	**1,797**	**444**	**5,662**	**13,340**
World	**42,350**	**6,018**	**7,206**	**11,377**	**9,857**	**89**	**7,803**	**54,071**	**7,836**	**25,001**	**243,700**

Source: ADB calculations using data from United Nations. Department of Economic and Social Affairs, Population Division. International Migration Stock 2015. http://www.un.org/en/development/desa/population/migration/data/estimates2/estimates15.shtml (accessed July 2016).

Figure 4.16: International Inbound Migrants from World to Asia by Region (million)

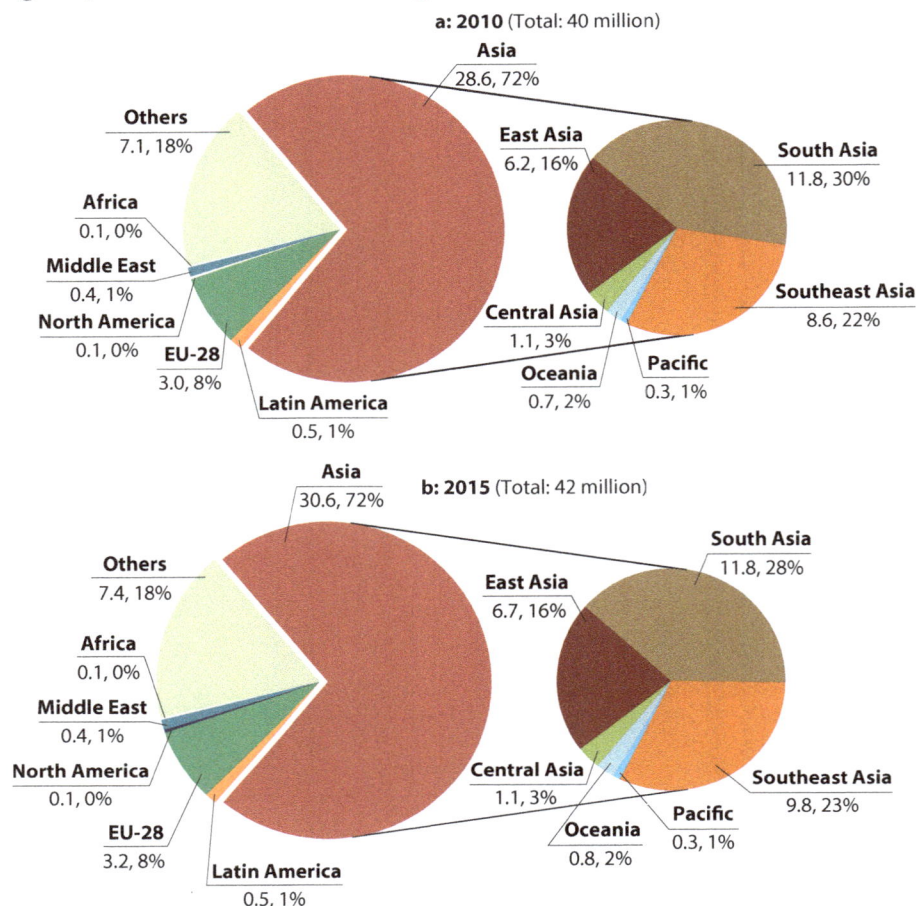

a: 2010 (Total: 40 million)

Asia
28.6, 72%

Others
7.1, 18%

Africa
0.1, 0%

Middle East
0.4, 1%

North America
0.1, 0%

EU-28
3.0, 8%

Latin America
0.5, 1%

East Asia
6.2, 16%

South Asia
11.8, 30%

Southeast Asia
8.6, 22%

Central Asia
1.1, 3%

Oceania
0.7, 2%

Pacific
0.3, 1%

b: 2015 (Total: 42 million)

Asia
30.6, 72%

Others
7.4, 18%

Africa
0.1, 0%

Middle East
0.4, 1%

North America
0.1, 0%

EU-28
3.2, 8%

Latin America
0.5, 1%

East Asia
6.7, 16%

South Asia
11.8, 28%

Southeast Asia
9.8, 23%

Central Asia
1.1, 3%

Oceania
0.8, 2%

Pacific
0.3, 1%

EU = European Union.
Source: ADB calculations using data from United Nations. Department of Economic and Social Affairs, Population Division. International Migration Stock 2015. http://www.un.org/en/development/desa/population/migration/data/estimates2/estimates15.shtml (accessed July 2016).

Intra-Asian migration slightly declined as a share of total Asian outbound migration during 2010–2015.

The share of Asia's intraregional migration fell marginally from 38.0% in 2010 to 36.7% in 2015; intraregional migration grew at a lower rate of 6.8%, compared with the 10.6% growth of overall migration from Asia and the Pacific to the world (Figure 4.17). In fact, the share of intra-Asian migration has been declining since 1990 (46.8%), as migrants move in greater numbers outside the region than within. This trend has mainly been driven by South Asia.

The share of intraregional migrants from South Asia declined from 29% in 1990 to 14% in 2015 (Figure 4.18).

Figure 4.17: Intraregional Migration in Asia

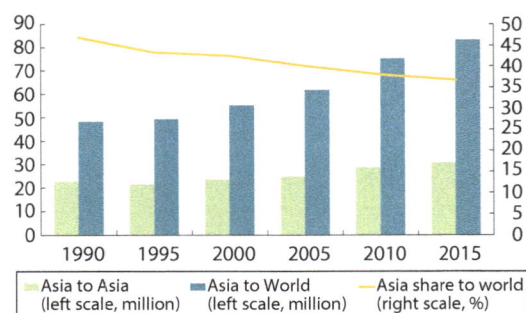

| Asia to Asia (left scale, million) | Asia to World (left scale, million) | Asia share to world (right scale, %) |

Note: Percent share is estimated as (migrants from Asia to Asia / migrants from Asia to worls) × 100.
Source: ADB calculations using data from United Nations. Department of Economic and Social Affairs, Population Division. International Migration Stock 2015. http://www.un.org/en/development/desa/population/migration/data/estimates2/estimates15.shtml (accessed July 2016).

Central Asia displayed a similar trend—falling from 3.0% in 1990 to 1.3% in 2015. In contrast, Southeast Asia's share increased from 5.5% in 1990 to 11.8% in 2015, and is expected to grow further, especially intra-subregionally—the ASEAN Economic Community, launched in 2015, significantly promotes labor mobility.

Figure 4.18: Intraregional Migration by Subregions
(% of total outbound migration from Asia)

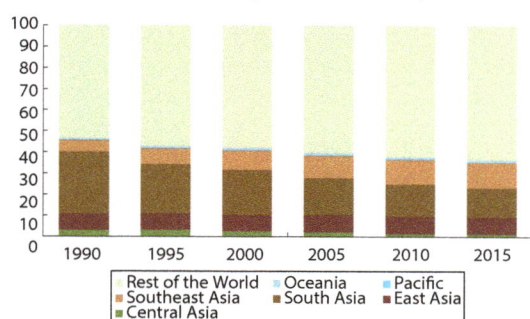

Source: ADB calculations using data from United Nations. Department of Economic and Social Affairs, Population Division. International Migration Stock 2015. http://www.un.org/en/development/desa/population/migration/data/estimates2/estimates15.shtml (accessed July 2016).

The patterns of geographical distribution of outward migration and inward remittances in Asia and the Pacific are closely related.

The Pacific sends the vast majority of its outbound migrants to other Asian subregions (62.3% of total migrants from the subregion in 2015), followed by Southeast Asia (14.6 %), and Central Asia the least (0.8%) (Figure 4.19). In contrast, the majority of migrants from Oceania come from within the subregion (53%). East Asia (34.6%) and Southeast Asia (34.1%) also have high intra-subregional shares.

Subregional trends and patterns of migration and remittances closely track one another (Figure 4.19, as compared with Figure 4.6 and Box 4.1). Central Asia, for example, sends most of its migrants outside Asia and the Pacific (90%), and also receives the largest share of remittances from the rest of the world (92%). That the highest share of migrants from the Pacific is bound for other Asian subregions is reflected in the dominant share of inter-subregional remittances (57%). However, Oceania and Southeast Asia receive a disproportionately

Figure 4.19: Subregional Migration Share—Asia
(% of total migration)

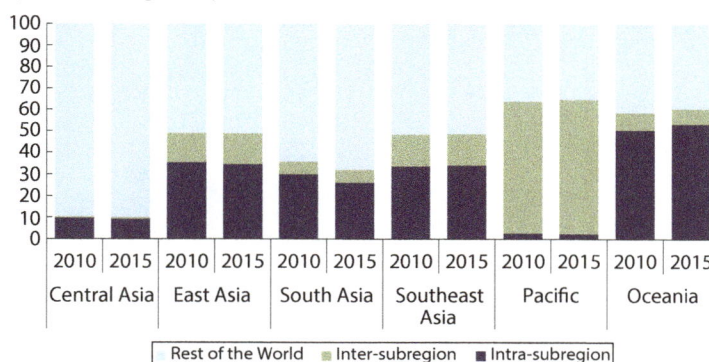

Notes:
(i) % intra-subregional share = (migrants within subregion i / migrants from subregion i to world) × 100
(ii) % inter-subregional share = (migrants from subregion i to other subregions / migrants from subregion i to world) × 100
(iii) % rest of the world = (migrants from subregion i to rest of the world / migrants from subregion i to world) × 100
Source: ADB calculations using data from United Nations. Department of Economic and Social Affairs, Population Division. International Migration Stock 2015. http://www.un.org/en/development/desa/population/migration/data/estimates2/estimates15.shtml (accessed July 2016).

Box 4.1: Impact of Migration on Remittances

The drivers of remittances can be empirically investigated using two broad approaches—at the micro level using household survey data and data aggregated at the economy level. For the latter, research, through country or comparative economy study designs, has tended to examine the macroeconomic push (host economy) and pull (source economy) factors that drive remittances (Gupta 2005, Hasan 2008, and Coulibaly 2014). But cross-economy investigations are rare.

Despite the importance of macroeconomic and institutional factors in both sending and receiving economies, the stock of outbound migration should, theoretically, be the most significant driver of inward remittances. Using aggregate economy-level data, and employing a simple regression analysis, the analysis here shows that the stock of migrants as a proportion of the population is the most economically and statistically significant predictor of inward remittances in a cross-economy Asian context.

The equation includes real GDP per capita in 2010 prices to control for the level of development. Also included is the percentage of population living in urban areas as a measure of demographic factors. Unreported regressions include a host of other macroeconomic variables, such as the real effective exchange rate, real interest rate, foreign direct investment, and the unemployment rate, but none of these is found to be significant in explaining remittances.

Regression Analysis: Impact of Migration on Remittances in Asia and the Pacific

Dependent Variable: Remittances (% of GDP)	Pooled OLS			Random Effects		
	(1)	(2)	(3)	(4)	(5)	(6)
Migrant Stock (% of population)	0.32*** (0.04)	0.38*** (0.06)	0.33*** (0.04)	0.23*** (0.07)	0.30*** (0.08)	0.23*** (0.07)
Log(real GDP per capita)	-1.20* (0.64)	-1.16* (0.65)	-1.56** (0.67)	-0.07 (0.92)	0.12 (0.93)	-0.31 (0.94)
Urban population (% of total)	-0.04 (0.03)	-0.04 (0.03)	-0.03 (0.03)	-0.09** (0.04)	-0.11** (0.04)	-0.08** (0.04)
Post-GFC		2.39 (1.89)			2.34 (1.66)	
Post-GFC*Migrant stock		-0.14** (0.07)			-0.11** (0.05)	
ASEAN			0.76 (0.92)			-0.53 (1.89)
ASEAN*Migrant stock			-0.61*** (0.08)			-0.45*** (0.17)
Number of observations	188	188	188	188	188	188
Countries	41	41	41	41	41	41
R-squared	0.37	0.38	0.41	0.66	0.66	0.70
LM test p-value				0.00	0.00	0.00
Hausman test p-value				0.24	0.30	0.28

ASEAN = Association of Southeast Asian Nations, GDP = gross domestic product, GFC = global financial crisis, LM = Lagrange multiplier, OLS = ordinary least squares.
***significant at 1%, **significant at 5%, *significant at 10%.
Notes:
(i) Robust standard errors clustered by economies reported in parenthesis. Observations at 5-year intervals from 1990–2015. All specifications, except (2) and (5) include time fixed effects.
(ii) Post-GFC takes a value of 1 following the global financial crisis, and 0 otherwise.
(iii) ASEAN takes a value of 1 for ASEAN countries and 0 otherwise.
(iv) Under the null of Breusch-Pagan LM test, there is no panel effect and pooled OLS is consistent and efficient.
(v) Under the null of Hausman test, random effects is consistent and efficient (and preferred over fixed effects).
Sources: ADB calculations using data from International Monetary Fund. World Economic Outlook. http://www.imf.org/external/pubs/ft/weo/2016/02/weodata/index.aspx (accessed July 2016); United Nations. Department of Economic and Social Affairs, Population Division. International Migration Stock 2015. http://www.un.org/en/development/desa/population/migration/data/estimates2/estimates15.shtml (accessed July 2016); United Nations. Department of Economic and Social Affairs, Population Division. World Population Prospects 2015. https://esa.un.org/unpd/wpp/Download/SpecialAggregates/Ecological/ (accessed April 2016); and World Bank. World Development Indicators. http://databank.worldbank.org/data/reports.aspx?source=world-development-indicators (accessed July 2016).

Additionally, some of the empirical specifications include economy-level fixed effects to control for unobserved economy characteristics to mitigate omitted variable bias. These fixed effects capture time-invariant factors, such as culture, geography, historical experience, colonial origin, and slow-moving institutions, which may simultaneously determine both remittances and migration. Finally, our model includes time effects to capture time-varying common shocks that simultaneously impact all countries in the sample. The equation is estimated for a sample of 41 economies in Asia and the Pacific for 1990–2015 at 5-year intervals. Based on the diagnostics, our preferred estimation methodology is random effects.

The regression results suggest that the stock of migrants is the most statistically significant determinant of remittances: an increase in an economy's migrant stock (as a percentage of total population) by 1 percentage point leads to an increase of almost 0.3 percentage points in remittances as a proportion of GDP (box table). In other words, if the worldwide migrant stock of Azerbaijan (12%), for example, increased to the level of Kazakhstan (23%) all else being equal, remittances received as a proportion of GDP would increase from 2.7% to 6.3%.

The level of development is negatively correlated with remittances, but unsurprisingly loses significance once economy-level fixed effects are incorporated. The association of remittances with the level of urbanization is negative, indicating that most remittances go to rural areas. We also investigate whether the link between migration and remittances has changed over time, and find that the association has become weaker since the global financial crisis. Finally, we examine if the link between migration and remittances varies across subregions, and find it to be weaker for Southeast Asian economies compared with the rest of Asia and the Pacific.

lower remittance share from within their respective subregions (15% and 23%, respectively) relative to the share of intra-subregional migrants (53% and 34%, respectively).

Drivers of Migration

Economic factors—such as better living conditions and job opportunities—are often behind the attraction of voluntary international migration.

The complex and growing movement of people is playing a critical social and economic role in economies across the Asia and Pacific region (Box 4.2). At the same time, the interplay of various factors—economic, demographic, social, political, cultural, and environmental—shapes the conditions, circumstances, and environment in which people decide whether to migrate. Among economic drivers of migration, temporary contractual labor dominates in Asia and the Pacific. Migration flow is predominantly outward for economies with a per capita GDP less than $20,000, while migration is mostly inward for economies with a GDP per capita higher than $20,000 (Table 4.4).

Economies in Asia and the Pacific vary considerably in size and level of development, and the differences are in many cases very significant, creating economic imbalances that induce people to move in search of better living standards. Migrants look for better income opportunities, education, and health services. In Cambodia, for example, 19% of the respondents to a 2010 National Institute of Statistics Socio Economic Survey cited employment search as one of the main reasons for migration (Table 4.5).

In migration from subregions to the rest of the world, Sugiyarto (2015) shows that in Southeast Asia, the large difference in average wage rates in origin and destination economies is the main driver of international migration. In 2012, the difference was more than 12 times the rate from origin to destination economy. In fact, the average wage rate of a lower skilled professional in the destination economy is even higher than that of higher skilled professional in the source economy (Figure 4.20).

Box 4.2: Impact of Migration

Growing numbers of migrants have large-scale impact not only in destination economies, but also in their economies of origin. As well as outward migration being a significant driver of inward remittances for developing Asia and the Pacific (see Box 4.1), it also affects GDP and labor markets of source and destination economies, as documented in the United Nations Economic and Social Commission for Asia and the Pacific (UNESCAP) 2015 migration report (UNESCAP 2015).

Impact on Source Economies

Views on the impact of international migration on source economies are varied and have evolved. The issue has shifted from extremely negative—focused on the "brain drain"—to extremely positive. Beine, Docquier, and Rapoport (2001) found two types of impact on human capital formation and growth in the source economy of migrants. The first impact, potentially beneficial, is that migration opportunities foster investment in education because source economies get a higher expected return—the "brain effect". The second impact, undoubtedly detrimental, is the departure of some, if not all, educated agents—"drain effect".

Meanwhile, Chen (2006) found interesting policy implications for migration restrictions. In his simulation results, a source economy whose goal is to increase economic growth should

aim to place some restrictions on the emigration of high-skilled workers. On the other hand, allowing more low-skilled workers to emigrate will increase economic growth in the source economy if the probability of migration of low-skilled workers is higher than a certain critical value ($p^L > p^*$), and it will reduce growth if the probability of migration of low-skilled workers is lower than the critical value ($p^L < p^*$).

Impact on Destination Economies

Immigration increases the size of the host economy's labor force and, by doing this, increases its productive capacity. Some studies show that the standard analysis of the economic impact of migrant workers on destination economies assumes that employment and economic output increases after immigration and wages fall over the medium term (UNESCAP 2015). Other studies argue that there is no negative effect from immigration on host-economy growth and employment. Migrant labor induces job creation in some low-wage sectors, including agriculture and domestic work. For example, if migrants were not available, or if wages were not so low, some households might decide not to employ a domestic helper or to employ one rather than two. Highly skilled migrants are generally found to contribute to innovation and rising productivity. Migrant entrepreneurs may spot opportunities because of their different frame of reference and start businesses that employ both migrant and local workers.

Philippine doctors are a case in point: they move abroad as nurses or paramedics because the standard salaries of medical doctors at home are much lower than those of lower-skilled medical personnel in the destination economy. Further, the demand for workers in the Middle East drives much of the migration from South Asia and Southeast Asia.

Demographic factors are also a significant driver of migration flows in Asia and the Pacific, especially young workers.

In 2013, some 28.2 million international migrants were aged 15 to 24— only 12% of the 232 million international migrants worldwide (UN 2016). This suggests that economies with declining young workforces could attract migrants in the future, whereas economies with increasing numbers of young workers would see net outward migration.

In Asia and the Pacific, many economies could expand their role as the source or host economy for migrant workers. Labor supply is still growing in developing economies—such as Cambodia, Indonesia, the Lao People's Democratic Republic, Mongolia, Myanmar, India, Pakistan, and the Philippines—and they could export labor across the region. In contrast, developed but aging economies such as Hong Kong, China; the Republic of Korea; Japan; and Singapore are unable to meet labor demand with their dwindling workforce. Hence, these economies would benefit from immigrant labor. Kang and Magoncia (2016) further discuss the potential for migration to reallocate labor from surplus to deficit economies and offer a glimpse of how the demographic shift will frame Asia's future population structure, particularly the future working age population. Among the issues explored is the magnitude of labor force surpluses and deficits within different economies in Asia (Box 4.3).

Table 4.4: Net Migration versus GDP per Capita in Selected Asian Economies

Economies	1995 GDP per capita[a]	1995 Net Migration[b]	2005 GDP per capita[a]	2005 Net Migration[b]	2015 GDP per capita[a]	2015 Net Migration[b]
Japan	38,945	−0.7	42,302	−1.3	44,657	−1.2
Australia	38,038	−3.8	48,656	−4.4	54,718	−6.2
Brunei Darussalam	34,279	−0.1	33,079	−0.1	29,138	−0.1
Singapore	29,008	−0.8	40,020	−1.5	51,855	−2.2
New Zealand	26,965	−0.2	33,658	−0.3	36,464	−0.2
Hong Kong, China	21,894	−1.9	27,689	−1.9	36,117	−1.8
Republic of Korea	12,224	1.7	18,586	1.5	25,023	1.0
Malaysia	6,206	−0.2	7,942	−0.3	10,877	−0.7
Thailand	3,544	−0.4	4,308	−1.5	5,775	−3.1
Indonesia	2,223	1.6	2,525	2.4	3,834	3.5
Philippines	1,507	2.3	1,821	3.4	2,635	5.1
India	649	0.3	1,012	3.7	1,806	10.4
Pakistan	817	−0.3	978	0.7	1,152	2.3
Viet Nam	607	1.5	1,036	2.0	1,685	2.5
Bangladesh	447	4.5	601	4.6	973	5.8
Nepal	403	0.2	505	0.4	690	1.1
Cambodia	342	0.3	611	0.6	1,021	1.1

GDP = gross domestic product.
[a] GDP per capita (constant 2010 US dollars).
[b] Net migration (in millions) is difference between outbound and inbound migration. Thus, a (-) net migration denotes higher inbound migration while a (+) sign denotes higher outbound migration.
Sources: ADB calculations using data from United Nations. Department of Economic and Social Affairs, Population Division. International Migration Stock 2015. http://www.un.org/en/development/desa/population/migration/data/estimates2/estimates15.shtml (accessed July 2016); and United Nations. Department of Economic and Social Affairs, Population Division. World Population Prospects 2015. https://esa.un.org/unpd/wpp/Download/SpecialAggregates/Ecological/ (accessed April 2016).

Table 4.5: Reasons for Outbound Migration in Cambodia

Reason for Migration	External 2009 Persons	External 2009 %	External 2010 Persons	External 2010 %
Transfer to work place	1,922	1.8	2,398	2.8
Search of employment	14,884	14.0	16,143	19.0
Education	1,164	1.1	–	–
Marriage	6,835	6.4	2,209	2.6
Family moved	25,160	23.6	25,326	29.8
Lost land or lost home	499	0.5	–	–
National calamities	–	–	–	–
Insecurity	3,980	3.7	547	0.6
Repatriation or return after displacement	50,806	47.7	38,407	45.2
Orphaned	–	–	–	–
Visiting only	742	0.7	–	–
Other reason	475	0.4	–	–
Total	106,467		85,030	

– = not available
Source: ADB. 2015. *Cambodia: Addressing the Skills Gap Employment Diagnostic Study.* Manila.

Box 4.3: Can Migration Help Solve Population Aging in Asia and Pacific?

World populations are aging—with the speed and extent of the demographic shift varying across developed and developing economies. Asia and the Pacific is at the heart of this demographic shift with the world's largest share of people aged 60 or over—estimated to reach 62% by 2050. With the high and growing share of economically inactive retirees and declining fertility rates, labor supply will suffer, ultimately undermining the region's economic output.

How will the demographic shift frame Asia's future population structure, particularly working-age population? Using population accounting methodology, Kang and Magoncia (2016) show how effective certain policies could address the challenges associated with the demographic change of population aging. One of the policies explored is the increase in regional migration to augment labor force deficits in aging economies in the region.

Box figure 1 illustrates the deficits and surpluses across age categories and aging stages using 2010 as the baseline scenario. The transition toward an older population given the huge deficits in young populations (from ages 0–14 to 15–29) is apparent, while the older working population (ages 30–44 and 45–64), and the elderly (age 65 and above) continue to post surpluses until 2050.

Box figure 2 shows the overall breakdown in surplus and deficit in population based on aging stage. Economies at the advanced aging stage hold overall deficits from 2015 up to 2050 for populations aged 0–14, 15–29, and 30–44, but posts total surpluses for the population aged 65 and above. In contrast, economies in the middle-aging stage—including the People's Republic of China—hold huge overall deficits from 2015 to 2050 for the populations aged 0–14, 15–29, and 30–44 years. The results show the working age group remains dominant across the region. However, we clearly see declining fertility and the accumulation of the elderly population from 2015 to 2050.

1: Change in Population by Age Group—Asia (base year = 2010, million)

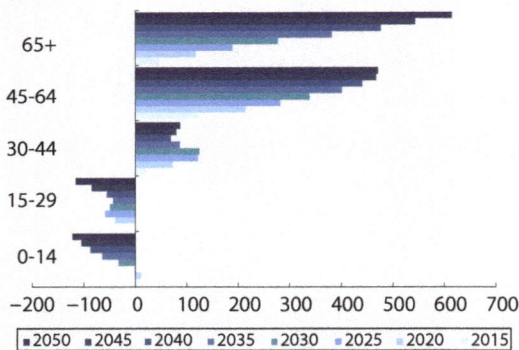

Source: Kang and Magoncia (2016).

2: Change in Population by Age Categories and Aging Stage (base year = 2010, million)

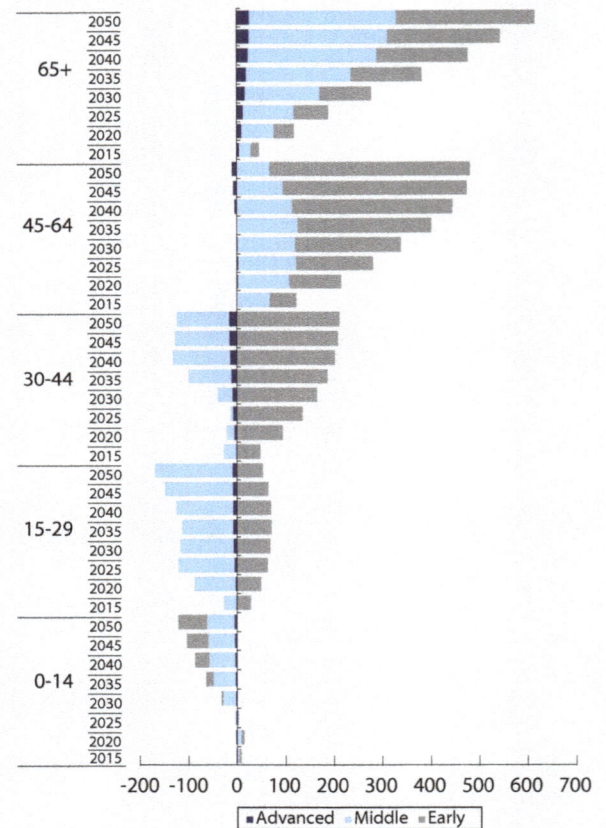

Source: Kang and Magoncia (2016).

3: Augmenting Labor Force through Increased Migration (base year = 2010, million)

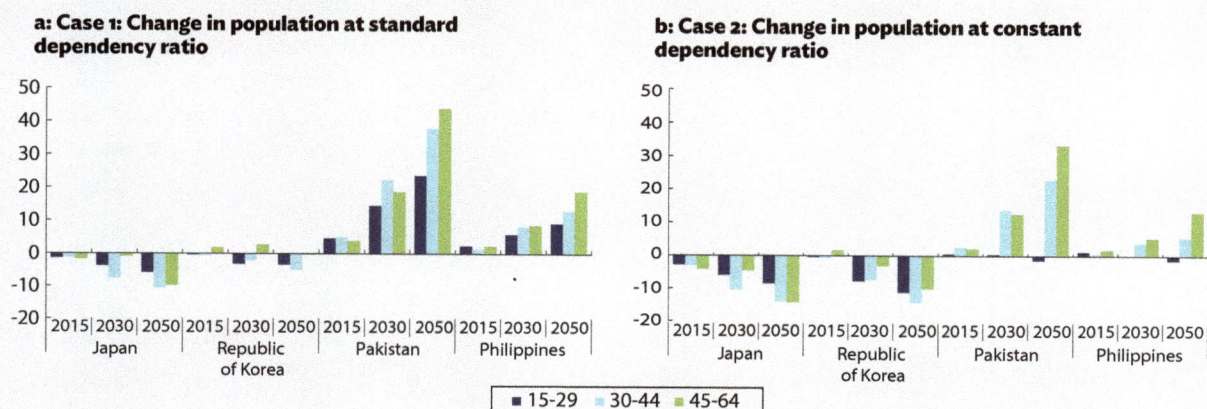

a: Case 1: Change in population at standard dependency ratio

b: Case 2: Change in population at constant dependency ratio

■ 15-29   ■ 30-44   ■ 45-64

Source: ADB calculations using estimates from Kang and Magoncia (2016).

In estimating the required migration demands from source to host economies within the region, two scenarios were compared using 2010 as base year: (i) deficit or surplus based on the projected population and dependency ratio (Case 1); and (ii) deficit or surplus based on the projected population, using a constant 2010 total dependency ratio (0–14 and 65 plus years) (Case 2), and comparing this to United Nations population projections as the baseline scenario.

Case 1 results show that potential host economies (such as Japan and the Republic of Korea) and potential source economies (such as Pakistan and the Philippines) could benefit from labor migration (box figure 3). The two aging economies post large deficits across all age groups under the working age bracket from 2015 up to 2050. In contrast, potential source economies show surpluses across age groups in the workforce population over the same period.

Case 2 results show that to maintain the United Nations baseline scenario in 2050, Japan needs to augment its labor force by 37 million people, and the Republic of Korea needs to import labor to address a worker shortfall of 36 million (box figure 3.b). For the source economies, Pakistan and the Philippines, the working populations show surpluses from 2015 to 2050. These estimates are expected as the two economies have relatively younger populations.

This accounting exercise shows that many economies in Asia and the Pacific could expand their role as source or host economy for migrant workers. Developing economies such as Cambodia, Indonesia, the Lao People's Democratic Republic, Mongolia, Myanmar, India, Pakistan, and the Philippines still have a growing supply of labor and could export labor across the region. In contrast, developed but aging economies like Hong Kong, China; the Republic of Korea; Japan; and Singapore are unable to meet labor demand with their dwindling workforces. Hence, these economies would benefit from immigrant labor. However, increasing migration flows will require proactive efforts in host and source economies. The magnitude of these changes critically depends on policy decisions, especially in the areas of healthcare and pension provision, and business opportunities. Authorities are exploring ways to ease constraints on immigration. Recently, the Japanese government embarked on new policies to ease foreign worker entry, easing delivery of permanent residency cards for skilled migrants. As shown in our simulation, the gaps filled by sending workers to host economies are substantial in addressing labor shortages.

Source: Kang and Magoncia (2016).

Figure 4.20: Wage Disparities Across Selected Economies: Average Monthly Wage ($)

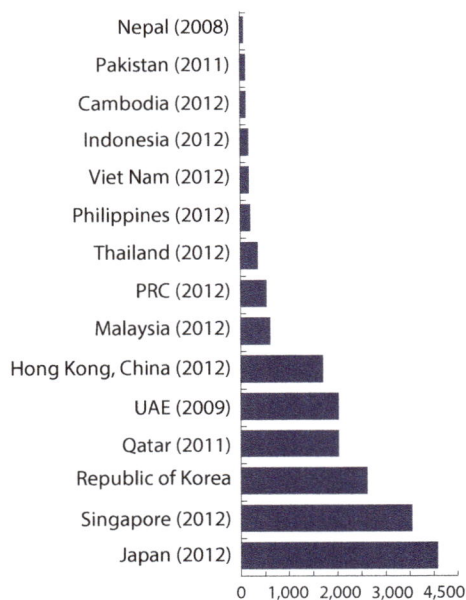

Nepal (2008)
Pakistan (2011)
Cambodia (2012)
Indonesia (2012)
Viet Nam (2012)
Philippines (2012)
Thailand (2012)
PRC (2012)
Malaysia (2012)
Hong Kong, China (2012)
UAE (2009)
Qatar (2011)
Republic of Korea
Singapore (2012)
Japan (2012)

0   1,000 2,000 3,000 4,500

PRC= People's Republic of China, UAE = United Arab Emirates.
Source: G. Sugiyarto. 2015. Internal and International Migration in South East Asia. In I. Coxhead. ed. *Handbook of Southeast Asian Economics.* London: Routledge Taylor and Francis Group.

International migration in Asia and the Pacific is affected by multiple political drivers as well.

People are forced to move because of conflict, political persecution, or statelessness. This is the case in Afghanistan and Myanmar, for example, which have over 3 million refugees hosted by neighboring economies, including Iran, Pakistan, and Thailand. In addition, climate change may emerge as a factor in displacing people, although most migration in Asia and the Pacific attributable to environmental causes has been internal. However, one can expect increased cross-border migration as the natural environment becomes more stressed.

A combination of factors is behind intraregional migration—including immigration and migrant labor policies, and migration costs. Further, migrants' preferences should also be accounted for: these include traditions and culture of migration and, in some cases,

shared language—which reduces barriers to crossing borders (even for those with low education or skills). There is also the "natural" migration of some ethnic groups—historically and politically separated by national boundaries into different economies. Intra-ASEAN migration will likely continue to increase as part of ASEAN's commitment to make the region an economic community with greater mobility of skilled workers.

References

Asian Development Bank. 2015. *Cambodia: Addressing the Skills Gaps, Employment Diagnostic Study.* Manila.

M. Beine, F. Docquier, and H. Rapoport. 2001. Brain Drain and Economic Growth: Theory and Evidence. *Journal of Development Economics.* 61 (1). pp. 275–289. http://ac.els-cdn.com/S0304387800001334/1-s2.0-S0304387800001334-main.pdf?_tid=243ec11a-84a5-11e6-9e7a-00000aacb362&acdnat=1474975729_25c8c29 5532f9fcb3155353eb37de375

H.J. Chen. 2006. Migration and Economic Growth: A Source Country Perspective. *Journal of Population Economics.* 19 (4). pp. 725–748. http://www.jstor.org/stable/pdf/20008042.pdf

D. Coulibaly. 2009. Macroeconomic Determinants of Migrants' Remittances: New Evidence from a Panel VAR. *Documents de Travail du Centre d'Economie de la Sorbonne.* Paris.

EU SME Centre. 2014. *Tourism Market in China.* Beijing. http://www.ccilc.pt/sites/default/files/eu_sme_centre_report_tourism_market_in_china_july_2014.pdf

P. Gupta. 2005. Macroeconomic Determinants of Remittances: Evidence from India. *IMF Working Paper.* 5 (224). India.

M.M. Hasan. 2008. The Macroeconomic Determinants of Remittances in Bangladesh. *Munich Personal RePEc Archive Paper.* No. 27744. Munich.

J. Kang and G. Magoncia. 2016. How to Fill the Working-Age Population Gap in Asia: A Population Accounting Approach. *ADB Economics Working Paper Series.* No. 499. Manila.

E.M. Mouhoud, J. Oudinet and E. Unan. 2008. Macroeconomic Determinants of Migrants' Remittances in the Southern and Eastern Mediterranean Countries. *CEPN Working Paper.* No 4. Paris: Centre d'Économie de l'Université Paris-Nord.

D. Ratha, et al. 2016. Migration and Remittances Recent Developments and Outlook. *Migration and Development Brief.* No. 26. Washington DC: World Bank.

G. Sugiyarto. 2015. Internal and International Migration in South East Asia. In I. Coxhead. ed. *Handbook of Southeast Asian Economics.* London: Routledge Taylor and Francis Group. http://samples.sainsburysebooks.co.uk/9781317586050_sample_867814.pdf

United Nations Economic and Social Commission for Asia and the Pacific (UNESCAP). 2015. *Asia-Pacific Migration Report 2015 Migrants' Contributions to Development.* Bangkok. http://www.unescap.org/sites/default/files/SDD%20AP%20Migration%20Report%20report%20v6-1-E.pdf

United Nations Department of Economic and Social Affairs. 2016. Youth Issue Briefs. http://www.un.org/esa/socdev/documents/youth/fact-sheets/youth-migration.pdf

World Bank. 2016. Remittances to Developing Countries Expected to Grow at Weak Pace in 2016 and Beyond. Oct 6.

World Tourism Organization. 2016. International tourist arrivals up 4% reach a record 1.2 billion in 2015. 18 Jan.

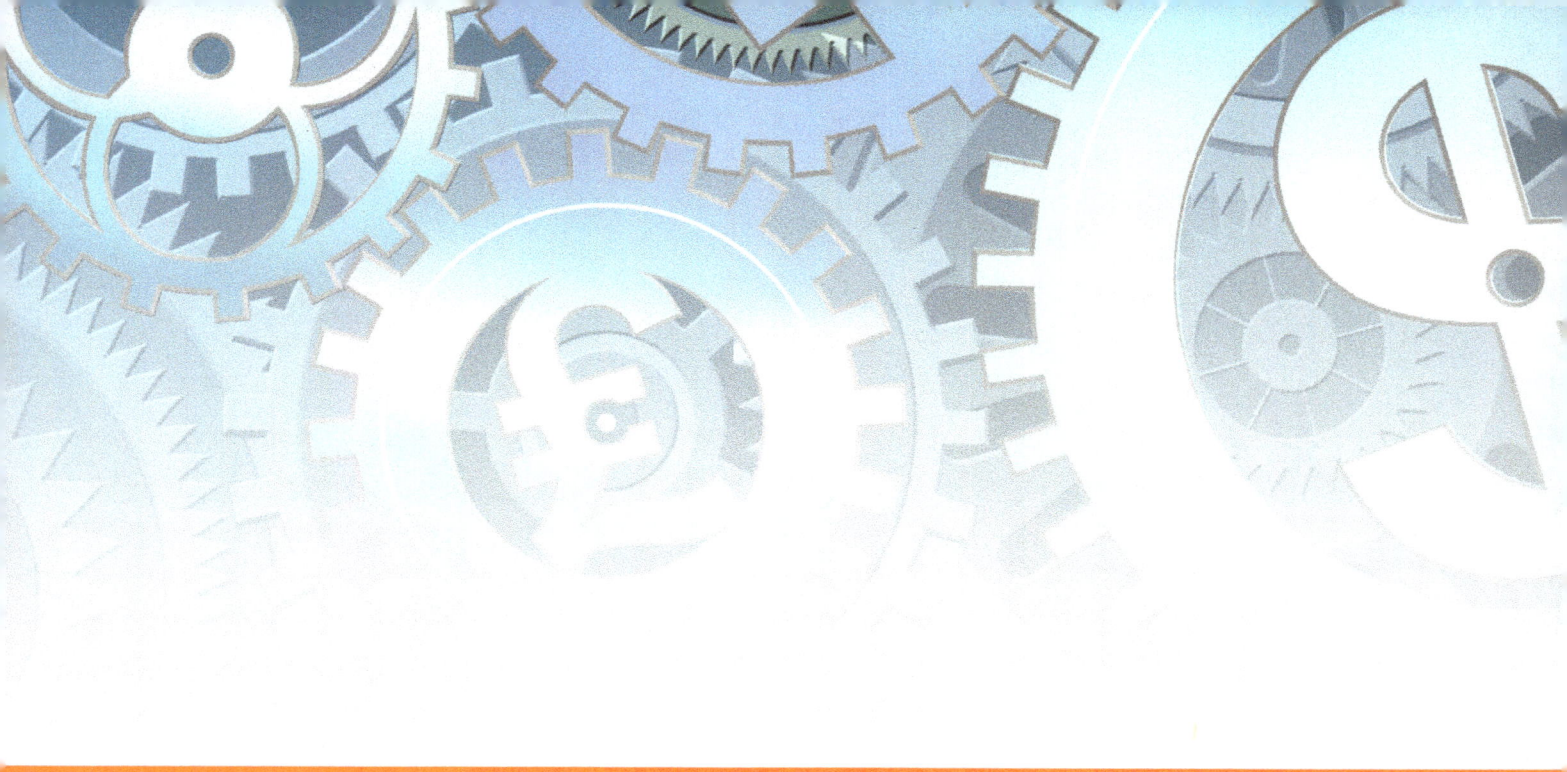

5 | Subregional Cooperation Initiatives

Subregional Cooperation Initiatives

Central and West Asia: Central Asia Regional Economic Cooperation Program

The Central Asia Regional Economic Cooperation (CAREC) program plays a pivotal role in promoting regional economic cooperation through common infrastructure development and policy dialogue. Intraregional trade and investment shares have started to rise, as CAREC was particularly instrumental in creating a network of multimodal transport corridors that open up economic opportunities by lowering trade costs, enhancing the flow of trade and people, and linking Central Asian countries to each other and with the rest of the world. CAREC members are expected to set new targets for a 2025 strategy reflecting the region's emerging new challenges and opportunities.

Overview

Established in 2001, the CAREC program today covers 11 countries: Afghanistan, Azerbaijan, the People's Republic of China (PRC), Georgia, Kazakhstan, the Kyrgyz Republic, Mongolia, Pakistan, Tajikistan, Turkmenistan, and Uzbekistan. The program focuses on regional infrastructure development and trade issues prioritizing the following areas of cooperation (i) energy, (ii) transport, (iii) trade facilitation, and (iv) trade policy.[37]

CAREC members vary significantly in population, basic economic structure, and development patterns, as well as trade links among themselves and externally (Table 5.1). From a geographical perspective, the group is centered on five Central Asian economies (Kazakhstan, the Kyrgyz Republic, Tajikistan, Turkmenistan, and Uzbekistan), stretches eastward to the PRC and Mongolia, south to Afghanistan and Pakistan, and to Azerbaijan and Georgia west of the Caspian Sea.

CAREC's institutional framework is informal and project-oriented. In the initial years, its programs focused on building confidence and improving communications among members. The first Senior Officials Meeting was held in 2001 and Ministerial Conference in 2002. Now in its second decade, CAREC is guided by the ADB Strategy 2020, which has the primary goal of enhancing participating economies' trade and competitiveness (ADB 2012). The program's overall portfolio has grown to 166 projects, a total of $27.7 billion by the end of 2015, from its initial six projects of $247 million.

Six multilateral institutions support CAREC: the ADB, European Bank for Reconstruction and Development, International Monetary Fund, Islamic Development Bank, United Nations Development Programme, and the World Bank. Out of the program's total investment as of 2015, ADB financed 35.5%, CAREC governments 25.1%, World Bank 21.5%, Islamic Development Bank 5.8%, European Bank for Reconstruction and Development 5.1%, and other development partners 7.0%.

---

[37] More information about CAREC is available from the program's website: http://carecprogram.org/

Table 5.1: Selected Economic Indicators—CAREC, 2015

	Population (million)	Nominal GDP ($ billion)	GDP Growth (%, 2011–15 average)	GDP Per Capita (current prices, $)	Trade Openness (total trade % as of GDP)
Afghanistan	32.5	19.2	4.7	591	44.7
Azerbaijan	9.7	53.0	2.8	5,492	79.3
People's Republic of China	1,370.0	10,900.0	7.4	7,956	48.7
Kazakhstan	17.5	184.0	3.9	10,514	71.2
Kyrgyz Republic	6.0	6.6	4.5	1,102	139.5
Mongolia	3.0	11.8	8.5	3,986	109.6
Pakistan	189.0	270.0	4.6	1,429	32.7
Tajikistan	8.5	7.8	6.4	926	90.6
Turkmenistan	5.4	37.3	9.5	6,946	117.6
Uzbekistan	31.3	66.7	8.1	2,131	60.5
CAREC	1,672.7	11,556.4	7.2	6,909	49.6

CAREC = Central Asia Regional Economic Cooperation, GDP = gross domestic product.
Note: Total trade is equal to exports plus imports. Georgia only became a CAREC member in October 2016.
Source: ADB calculations using data from World Bank. World Development Indicators. http://databank.worldbank.org/data/reports.aspx?source=world-development-indicators (accessed November 2016).

Priority Areas

The CAREC Program's priority areas of cooperation include transport and trade facilitation, energy, and trade policy; with investment projects concentrated mostly in transport.

Transport and trade facilitation. CAREC aims to develop sustainable, user-friendly transport infrastructure and trade networks to enhance competitiveness and ensure safe and efficient movement of goods and people across the region. The CAREC Transport and Trade Facilitation Strategy 2020 seeks to accomplish three main tasks: (i) develop a multimodal corridor network comprising roads, railways, logistics hubs, and border crossings; (ii) improve trade and border crossing services—through customs reforms and modernization, coordinated border management, development of national single windows, and integrated trade facilitation; and (iii) strengthen institutions, policies, and operational effectiveness to better support road maintenance, road safety, and seamless rail connections (ADB 2014a).

ADB has provided technical support for trade facilitation under the CAREC program. Thirteen technical assistance

projects have been delivered regionally and in the PRC and Mongolia from the start of the CAREC program in 2001 through 2015, cumulatively amounting to $21.2 million. Three investment projects totaling $60 million have been delivered in the PRC and Mongolia.[38] Investment projects in the Kyrgyz Republic, Pakistan, and Tajikistan complement these efforts. Delivery of this technical support is guided by the CAREC Transport and Trade Facilitation Strategy 2020 (ADB 2014). The strategy targets three sector outcomes: (i) establish competitive corridors across the CAREC region; (ii) facilitate the efficient movement of goods and people through the CAREC corridors and across borders; and (iii) develop sustainable, safe, user-friendly transport and trade networks. CAREC trade facilitation has two components:

(i) Customs cooperation entails customs reform and modernization in five priority areas: simplification

---

[38] In addition to contributions under the CAREC program, $24 million for an investment project supporting the development of cold chain logistics facilities at Tianjin port, in the PRC, was approved in 2012. Tianjin, at the south end of the CAREC transport corridor 4b linking Mongolia and the PRC, has since the 1990s served as a key seaport for Mongolia's international trade (based on a bilateral agreement signed in 1991). The project thus also supports the improvement of services to Mongolia's export of agricultural produce.

Figure 5.1: CAREC Approved Investment Projects by Sector (cumulative since 2001)

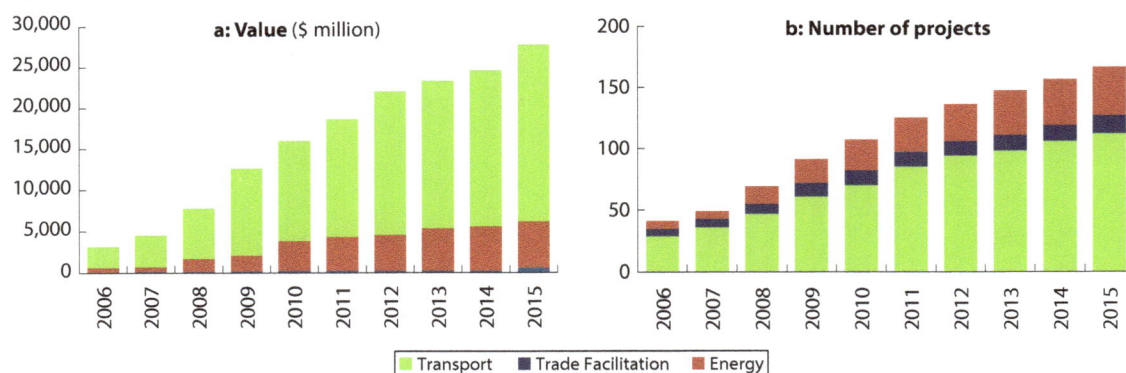

CAREC = Central Asia Regional Economic Cooperation Program.
Source: ADB. CAREC Program Portfolio.

and harmonization of customs procedures, information and communication technology for customs modernization and data exchange, risk management, joint customs control, and regional transit development.

(ii) Integrated trade facilitation promotes efficient regional trade logistics development and supports the development of priority trade corridors, single-window facilities, enhanced interagency cooperation and private sector participation, improved sanitary and phytosnitary (SPS) measures, and capacity building.

The trade facilitation program is coordinated through (i) the Customs Cooperation Committee, which comprises heads of customs administrations of all CAREC economies and provides a regional forum for discussing issues of common interest; and (ii) the CAREC Federation of Carrier and Forwarder Associations.[39] The association's major objectives are to facilitate transport, trade, and logistics development in the region and to advance the interests of road carrier, freight forwarder, and logistics service provider member associations.

In addition, ADB worked with CAREC economies to launch a regional initiative on SPS cooperation, and the CAREC Ministerial Conference in September 2015 endorsed a CAREC Common Agenda for Modernization of SPS Measures.

ADB supports trade facilitation initiatives through regional technical assistance and investment projects. This support has encouraged progress in customs modernization and trade facilitation in CAREC economies. Particularly important are the CAREC Regional Improvement of Border Services projects in the Kyrgyz Republic, Mongolia, Pakistan, and Tajikistan. The projects aim to streamline transport, customs, and other border control operations along CAREC corridors and thereby increase trade in Central Asia. ADB is also supporting a project to modernize SPS inspections of import and exports of agricultural-food products in Mongolia to rehabilitate laboratories and inspection and quarantine facilities at the border.

Energy. The long-term aim for strengthening the energy sector is to achieve regional energy security, integrated markets, and energy trade-driven economic growth. The CAREC Energy Strategy and Work Plan (2016–2020) includes thematic priorities to (i) invest in strategic projects, (ii) develop sustainable energy resources, (iii) enhance technological knowledge and capacity, (iv) establish robust legal and regulatory frameworks to support private investment, and (v) support cross-border energy trade (ADB 2015a). These priorities translate into six work areas: (i) develop the East-Central Asia-South Asia regional energy market, (ii) promote regional electricity trade and harmonization, (iii) manage energy-water linkages, (iv) prioritize clean energy technologies, (v) mobilize financing for priority projects, and (vi) promote capacity building and knowledge management.

---

[39]   The organization was established in 2009 under ADB financing as a nongovernment and nonprofit organization, and incorporated as a limited company in 2012.

Trade policy. CAREC also supports national trade policies aimed at promoting growth in an open-economy environment. The CAREC 2013–2017 Trade Policy Strategic Action Plan aims for (i) accession to the World Trade Organization (WTO) by all members, (ii) greater trade openness with simplified trade taxes and elimination of quantitative restrictions, (iii) reduction of the negative impact of technical regulations and SPS measures on trade, (iv) expansion of service trade, and (v) enhancement of members' capacity building and knowledge sharing on trade issues (CAREC 2013).

CAREC investment projects focus on transport, which in 2015 reached $21.6 billion (or 78% of the total), followed by energy ($5.6 billion invested, or 20.2%) (Figure 5.1). Resources allocated to trade facilitation and trade policy projects were $584 million in 2015 (or 1.8% of the total). In addition, CAREC received 253 technical assistance projects worth $440 million from 2001 to 2015. CAREC countries financed 23%, ADB 32%, CAREC multilateral partners 8%, and other development partners 37%.

Development Results

CAREC annually reviews progress toward the goals of the Comprehensive Action Plan through a "development effectiveness review". The assessment uses quantitative indicators and qualitative information to describe the challenges faced by the program and highlight opportunities for complementary work between sectors. It aims to help members take corrective action when targets are not met.

Transport and Trade Facilitation. CAREC members have agreed to create six multimodal transport corridors in the region. By 2015, substantial progress was made toward corridor implementation with the development of two ports, two logistics centers, three border crossings, and six civil aviation centers. As a result, CAREC projects contributed to building (or improving) 809 kilometers (km) of expressways or national highways, bringing cumulative progress to 7,229 km, or 93% of the target under the Transport and Trade Facilitation Strategy 2020. Moreover, 2015 CAREC operations included project implementation in road safety, road asset management, transport facilitation, and the improvement of a total of 40 km of railways. In October 2016, the CAREC

Ministerial Conference endorsed the CAREC Road Safety Strategy 2017–2030 and the CAREC Railway Strategy 2017-2030.

Trade facilitation also helped achieve positive results. ADB estimates that average time taken to clear a border-crossing point along CAREC transport corridors—by rail and road—was reduced to 13.1 hours in 2015 from 14.1 in 2014 (ADB 2015b). The drop in travel time by rail was also high—from 32.6 hours to 27.4 hours in 2015; while average train travel speed increased 20%. Cross-border time by road was reduced to 9.3 hours in 2015 from 9.9 hours in 2014. Similarly, costs decline: average border-crossing cost dropped to $161 in 2015 from $172 in 2014 as road transport costs declined from $177 to $149. Average border crossing costs, by contrast, rose from $148 to $208, as fees associated with the transfer of goods increased. A Regional Food Safety Initiative was launched at the 15th CAREC Ministerial Conference to help institutionalize international food safety standards in participating countries and contribute to CAREC's Common Agenda for Modernization of Sanitary and Phytosanitary Measures.

Energy. In 2015, CAREC energy strategies were aligned with major global trends, accounting for the reduction in renewable energy prices and international commitments on climate change. The program has embraced a new strategy aimed at promoting energy efficiency and diversification to reduce members' dependence on fossil fuels. In addition, it is building human resources from CAREC economies and increasing their capacity to discuss climate change and related technology through specific training on regulation, forecasting, off-grid solar systems, and storage. Preparations for the Turkmenistan–Afghanistan–Pakistan (TAP) Transmission Line for export of power from Turkmenistan to Pakistan through the southern Afghan corridor have started. A 500kV transmission line of the Turkmenistan-Uzbekistan-Tajikistan-Afghanistan–Pakistan (TUTAP) Interconnection Project for the Turkmen section has been completed and construction of the other sections has begun. ADB is providing transaction advisory services for the Turkmenistan–Afghanistan–Pakistan–India (TAPI) gas pipeline. It also helped establish the project company with Turkmenistan Gas as the consortium leader and supported the TAPI stakeholders finalize and sign a Shareholder Agreement in December 2015 and an Investment Agreement in April 2016. The project is now moving to the detailed design stage. An Energy Investment Forum was successfully held in October 2016 in Islamabad, which provided a platform for government officials, potential investors, energy companies, financing institutions and development partners to deliberate on policy environment and investment opportunities in the energy sector.

The completion of ADB projects in Azerbaijan, Mongolia, and Uzbekistan helped achieve long-term regional energy targets. In 2015, 923 km of transmission lines were installed or upgraded, over 201 megawatts (MW) of generation capacity added or rehabilitated, and almost 785 mega volt amps installed or upgraded in substations. CAREC also made progress in the development of the Central Asia-South Asia Regional Electricity Market, and pipes are being laid for the natural gas pipeline that will connect Turkmenistan, Afghanistan, Pakistan and India. Activities are under way to complete the Turkmenistan-Afghanistan interconnection under the broader TUTAP project.

Trade Policy. The progress in trade policy has been mixed due to the changing macroeconomic environment and government policy responses to mitigate the negative impact of external shocks on their national economies. During 2015, at least eight CAREC economies were able to (i) eliminate all import taxes and fees—or incorporate them into tariffs, (ii) reduce average tariff rates to 10% or less, (iii) cap tariffs at 20%, (iv) eliminate or convert quantitative import restrictions into tariffs, and (v) acknowledge the importance of the WTO SPS and technical barriers to trade agreements. In addition, five countries eliminated all remaining discrepancies between taxes applied to domestic production and imports. Kazakhstan became a member of the WTO in November 2015, while the Kyrgyz Republic joined the Eurasian Economic Union in August 2015. Moreover, Afghanistan's WTO membership terms were approved at a special ceremony in December 2015, while the PRC ratified its WTO Trade Facilitation Agreement. Recognizing the post-accession challenges, CAREC has been deepening its collaboration with international development partners to help newly acceded members in meeting their WTO commitments especially in the areas of SPS measures, technical barriers to trade and expansion of services trade, through knowledge sharing and capacity building.

Economic Corridor Development. In 2014, CAREC started the Almaty–Bishkek Corridor Initiative (ABCI) between Kazakhstan and the Kyrgyz Republic, aiming to increase economic activity for creating jobs, diversifying the economy, and promoting sustainable development through an economic corridor linking the two cities.[40] Technical and economic analyses have been completed and priority areas have been identified in education, heath, agriculture, agribusiness, tourism, disaster risk management, and information and communications technology. The ABCI Investment Framework was adopted at the 15th CAREC Ministerial Conference. The investment framework details the conceptual development plan for economic corridor in the region, comprising investments, policy reforms and institutional development. The two participating countries, Kazakhstan and the Kyrgyz Republic, are working to institutionalize Almaty-Bishkek economic corridor development by establishing a Corridor Development Authority with coordination at higher government levels.

CAREC Institute. The virtual CAREC Institute, created in 2007, established its physical base in March 2015 in Urumqi, PRC, and established a management team a few months later. The intergovernmental agreement for the CAREC Institute was signed in the sidelines of the 15th Ministerial Conference in Islamabad. The institute, which aims to generate world-class knowledge resources in CAREC's priority areas, conducts research and capacity building activities for CAREC members and trains government officials and other country experts on regional economic cooperation issues.

Opportunities and Challenges

Slowing growth. In 2015, economic growth dropped sharply in seven CAREC members (including the five Central Asian economies plus Azerbaijan and Mongolia), hit by external macroeconomic shocks including the fall of oil, gas, and other commodity prices; the recession in the Russian Federation; and slower economic growth in the PRC. These economies face the challenges of accelerating structural transformation and economic diversification; improving the local business environment

---

[40]   Almaty and Bishkek city administrations signed a memorandum of understanding in November 2014.

to facilitate private initiative, entrepreneurship, and job creation; and enhancing human capital development, especially through educational reform. Afghanistan and Pakistan, meanwhile, are struggling with internal security issues, with considerable impact on economic development prospects.

New multilateral initiatives. Nonetheless, the recent progress of initiatives strengthening economic cooperation in Central Asia offers new growth opportunities for members. Examples include the PRC's Belt and Road initiative, the New Silk Road pioneered by the United States, the Eurasia Initiative promoted by the Republic of Korea, Quality Infrastructure sponsored by Japan, and the Silk Road Fund set up by the PRC. The entry of Kazakhstan and the Kyrgyz Republic into the Eurasian Economic Union is also expected to reduce internal trade and investment barriers to the free flow of goods, services, and people, and promote economic growth—providing further impetus to the development of the ABCI economic corridor between Almaty and Bishkek. At the same time, the recent establishment of the Asian Infrastructure Investment Bank and the New Development Bank expands multilateral development financing options in the region.

New development strategy. At the 15th Ministerial Conference in October 2016, CAREC members decided to start working on a new development strategy following an extensive Mid-Term Review, bringing the group to the year 2025. Some institutional mechanisms may need strengthening and some sector focus may need recalibration, while the program's overall coverage may be expanded to include areas beyond transport, energy, and trade.

Southeast Asia: Greater Mekong Subregion Program

Since its establishment in 1992, the Greater Mekong Subregion (GMS) Program has gained strong ownership and active participation from the GMS economies using an activity-based and results-oriented approach. And better cross-border connectivity within the subregion has helped improve members' socioeconomic conditions. GMS economies nonetheless face unprecedented changes creating both serious challenges and widespread opportunities.

Overview

Cambodia, the PRC (Yunnan Province and Guangxi Zhuang Autonomous Region), the Lao People's Democratic Republic (Lao PDR), Myanmar, Thailand, and Viet Nam make up the GMS. The subregion's aggregate GDP expanded from $796 billion in 2010 to $1.2 trillion in 2015 (Table 5.2). GMS economies have averaged 6.9% gross domestic product (GDP) growth annually in the last 5 years, led by double-digit growth in Guangxi Province (10.1%) and Yunnan Province (11.1%).

GMS members are also more integrated with each other. Intra-GMS trade shares increased from 2% in 1992 ($5 billion) to 9.3% in 2015 ($444 billion). Aggregate intra-GMS foreign direct investment (FDI) increased from $8.3 billion in 2001–2006 to $29.2 billion in 2010–2015. And physical connectivity among members improved. The PRC's liner shipping bilateral connectivity index reached its highest with Viet Nam (0.59), followed by Thailand (0.58) in 2015. Viet Nam's connectivity with Cambodia (0.29) and Myanmar (0.22) were more modest in 2015.

Robust GDP per capita growth has lifted GMS incomes. Guangxi and Yunnan per capita income (current international dollars, purchasing power parity) rose 13.1% and 12.4%, respectively, (2010- 2014 average annual growth), the highest rates in the subregion. Incidence of poverty also dropped for all GMS economies, as per data from the early to mid-1990s and the early 2000s.

Table 5.2: Selected Economic Indicators—Greater Mekong Subregion, 2015

	Population (million)	Nominal GDP ($ billion)	GDP Growth (%, 2011-15, average)	GDP Per Capita (current prices, $)	Trade Openness (total trade as % of GDP)
Cambodia	16	18.0	7.4	1,128.1	146.0
Guangxi, PRC	48	269.3	10.1	5,610.0	17.1
Yunnan, PRC	47	219.8	11.1	4,677.4	10.6
Lao People's Democratic Republic	7	12.3	7.7	1,761.1	64.9
Myanmar	54	56.3	7.5	1,042.3	51.8
Thailand	68	395.2	2.9	5,811.3	101.6
Viet Nam	92	193.2	5.9	2,100.4	169.5
GMS	332	1,164.2	6.9	3,506.6	74.0

PRC = People's Republic of China, GMS = Greater Mekong Subregion, GDP = gross domestic product.
Note: Weighted average for GMS GDP average growth rate using the economies' nominal GDP.
Source: ADB calculations using data from CEIC.

Strategic Areas of Cooperation

The latest GMS strategic framework is anchored on a corridor-development approach that focuses on widening and deepening GMS economic corridors along several important routes by developing areas along and contiguous to these corridors (ADB 2011).[41] This requires close intersectoral coordination; involvement of all key stakeholders, particularly provincial and local authorities and the private sector; and a clear concentration on making a manageable number of effective interventions work. It also requires coordinated and resolute action on transport and trade facilitation, promotion of cross-border economic linkages, and logistics development along GMS corridors. This can contribute to increased demand for trade, boosting trade benefits for the less-developed economies and reducing poverty.

The GMS Program continues to focus on a broad range of sector and multisector strategic priorities:

- developing the major GMS corridors as economic corridors;
- strengthening transport links, particularly roads and railways;
- developing an integrated approach to deliver sustainable, secure, and competitive energy;
- developing and promoting tourism using the Mekong as a single destination;
- promoting competitive, climate-friendly, and sustainable agriculture;
- enhancing environmental performance; and
- supporting human resource development initiatives that facilitate GMS integration while addressing any negative consequences of greater integration.

To implement its strategic framework, the GMS endorsed a regional project pipeline for 2013–2022 of 200 projects estimated at $52 billion.[42] During the 21st GMS Ministerial Conference in December 2016, GMS Ministers endorsed the Regional Investment Framework Implemention Plan 2020, which provides a shortlist of 107 investment

---

[41] At the 4th GMS Summit in December 2011 in Nay Pyi Taw, Myanmar, leaders endorsed a new GMS Strategic Framework for 2012–2022. It builds on the success and progress of the GMS Program, and the continuing commitment of the member economies to increased regional integration and action-oriented approach to cooperation that adheres to the principles of country ownership, equal consultation, mutual benefit, steady progress, focus on results, and recognition of the varying levels of members' development.

[42] The regional project pipeline is referred to as the GMS Regional Investment Framework 2013–2022 (GMS RIF) (ADB 2013). The projects in the GMS RIF are being financed and will be financed by GMS governments; ADB, together with other development partners; and the private sector.

and technical assistance projects estimated to cost $32.7 billion.

The program's institutional arrangements have also contributed to its success thus far. They include (i) a GMS leaders' summit at the political level, (ii) a ministerial conference supported by meetings of senior officials, (iii) ministerial level meetings on key sectors, and (iv) sector forums and working groups at the program and operational levels. A national secretariat coordinates GMS activities in each economy. The GMS Secretariat at ADB headquarters provides overall secretariat support to the GMS Program in coordination with the national secretariats. Private sector and development partners are also invited to join many of the meetings. The GMS Business Council and the GMS Freight Transportation Association facilitate GMS cooperation with the private sector. GMS institutional arrangements have proved flexible, simple, and generally effective in supporting the pragmatic, activity-driven, and results-oriented approach.

Development Results

The GMS Program has made important contributions to greater economic integration and prosperity of the region.

Since its launch in 1992, it has enhanced economic relations among the GMS members by focusing on high-priority subregional projects in transport (hardware and software), energy, urban development, tourism, agriculture, the environment, and human resource development.

Cross-border physical connectivity. Cross-border infrastructure development has been the core of the program, with the near completion of the transport component of its three main corridors—the East-West, North-South, and Southern Economic Corridors (Table 5.3). The reach of these corridors is also being widened through several bridges and linked secondary roads. Since 1992, almost 7,000 kms of road have been built and rehabilitated. The program is also preparing a new GMS Multimodal Transport Strategy to broaden its focus on the transport sector to include railways. A broad long-term strategy for connecting railways is

Table 5.3: Status of Greater Mekong Subregion Economic Corridors

Description	Status
North–South Economic Corridor	
• The North–South Economic Corridor involves three routes along the north-to-south axis of the GMS: • The Western Subcorridor: Kunming (People's Republic of China [PRC]) – Chiang Rai (Thailand) – Bangkok (Thailand) via Lao People's Democratic Republic (Lao PDR) or Myanmar • The Central Subcorridor: Kunming (PRC) – Ha Noi (Viet Nam) – Hai Phong (Viet Nam) which connects to the existing Highway No. 1 running from the northern to the southern part of Viet Nam • The Eastern Subcorridor: Nanning (PRC) – Ha Noi (Viet Nam) via the Youyi Pass or Fangchenggang (PRC) – Dongxing (PRC) – Mong Cai (Viet Nam) route.	The construction and rehabilitation of corridor roads have substantially been completed, with funding assistance from the ADB and countries' internal budgets, as well as support from other development partners, the PRC, and Thailand. The last key missing link, the Fourth International Mekong Bridge between Chiang Khong (Thailand) and Houayxay (Lao PDR) was opened to traffic in December 2013.
East–West Economic Corridor (EWEC)	
Runs from Da Nang Port in Viet Nam, through the Lao PDR, Thailand, and to the Mawlamyine Port in Myanmar.	The key sections of the road corridor have been completed, with the ADB and Japan helping finance key sections in the Lao PDR and Viet Nam, including Route 9, the Hai Van Tunnel, and the Da Nang port. Thailand is helping finance connections between Thailand and Myanmar at the Myawaddy-Mae Sot border by upgrading the existing section of the East–West Economic Corridor road in Kayin State, while ADB is financing the section from Eindu to Kawkareik in Myanmar.
Southern Economic Corridor	
• The Central Subcorridor: Bangkok–Phnom Penh–Ho Chi Minh City–Vung Tau; • The Northern Subcorridor: Bangkok–Siem Reap–Stung Treng–Rattanakiri–O Yadov–Pleiku–Quy Nhon; • The Southern Coastal Subcorridor: Bangkok–Trat–Koh Kong–Kampot–Ha Tien–Ca Mau City–Nam Can; and • The Intercorridor Link: Sihanoukville–Phnom Penh–Kratie–Stung Treng–Dong Kralor (Tra Pang Kriel)–Pakse–Savannakhet, which links the three Southern Economic Corridor subcorridors with the East-West Economic Corridor.	The key sections of the Southern Economic Corridor are also mostly completed, with the key missing link (the Mekong Bridge at Neak Loueng along the Phnom Penh-Ho Chi Minh City Highway) having opened to traffic in 2015 with financing assistance from Japan.

Source: ADB.

in place, together with a plan for coordinating GMS railway development.

Transport and trade facilitation. Initiated in 1999, the landmark GMS Cross Border Transport Facilitation Agreement uses a single legal instrument for key, nonphysical measures for efficient cross-border land transport. With the ratification of Thailand and Myanmar in 2015, the agreement is now fully ratified by all GMS members. The Single Stop Inspection between the Lao PDR and Viet Nam at Lao Bao–Dansavanh in February 2015 is among its major achievements. New Single Stop Inspection sites are being developed at other border crossing points along the East-West and Southern economic corridors. Development impact of both hardware and software was significant at key border crossing points: travel time between Bavet (Cambodia) and Moc Bai (Viet Nam) was reduced from 9–10 hours in 1999 to 5–6 hours in 2013. Cross-border trade increased from $10 million in 1999 to $708 million in 2013. In Moc Bai border economic zone, 41 projects totaling $270 million were implemented and nearly 3,000 jobs created. The GMS National Transport Facilitation Committee Retreat in July 2016 reached a historic agreement to launch the GMS Road Transport Permit by January 2017, a significant step toward opening the GMS transport market.

Energy. GMS power projects are preparing grid interconnections in the GMS, while major hydropower projects have been developed with private sector participation, as Nam Theun 2 Hydroelectric Project. Before 1992, the only significant GMS cross-border power transmission existed to export hydropower from the Lao PDR to Thailand through two 200 MW hydropower plants. Some low voltage lines also connected certain areas in the Lao PDR to Thailand and separately to Cambodia, distributing power to remote border regions. Moreover, remote border regions of Cambodia, the Lao PDR, and Viet Nam have benefitted from accessing cross-border power supply based in neighboring countries. Recently, the GMS economies agreed to establish the Regional Power Coordination Center, a permanent institution to enhance regional power trade and implement regional power interconnection initiatives in the GMS. The selection of the center's host country is under way.

Agriculture. The Core Agriculture Support Program (CASP) Phase I, 2011–2015 focused on issues involving cross-border trade in food and agricultural products, and climate change adaptation. The CASP II 2011–2020 is focusing more on issues of expanding cross-border trade in agricultural-food products, climate change adaptation, and food and bioenergy security. A Strategy and Action Plan for Promoting Safe and Environment-Friendly Agro-Food Value Chain Investments in the GMS is being developed.

Environment. The GMS countries recognize the importance of addressing environmental concerns.[43] Achievements include (i) capacity development for a range of environmental and social planning and safeguard methods and tools, (ii) integration of strategic environmental assessment results into national socioeconomic development plans, and (iii) replication of Biodiversity Conservation Corridor approaches in Cambodia, the Lao PDR, and Viet Nam. The Fourth Environment Ministers' Meeting in Myanmar in January 2015 reaffirmed support for implementing priority environment projects in the GMS Regional Investment Framework Implementation Plan, emphasized the importance of investing in the subregion's natural capital as well as its physical, human, and social capital to secure more inclusive and sustainable GMS development.

Tourism. A series of promotional campaigns and other subregional cooperation initiatives have helped place the GMS firmly on the world tourism itinerary. Tourist arrivals in the GMS reached 57.9 million in 2015 and tourism receipts $65 billion, from $15.6 billion in 2007. A new GMS Tourism Marketing Strategy and Action Plan for 2015–2020 was endorsed by the GMS Tourism Working Group in 2015 (ADB 2015c). Preparation of the 2016-2025 GMS Tourism Sector Strategy is also under

---

[43]   In 2005, the GMS Environment Ministers endorsed the Core Environment Program and Biodiversity Conservation Corridors Initiative (2005–2011), which consolidated environmental initiatives under a single integrated program with the aim of achieving a poverty-free and ecologically rich GMS. The second phase for 2012–2016 is part of an ongoing, concerted effort by multiple development and implementing partners to strengthen the means to address environmental issues in a regional development context. It also addresses current and emerging environmental pressures within the GMS Economic Cooperation Program and the economic corridors, alignment with GMS economies' and ADB's economic development and investment strategies and frameworks.

Figure 5.2: Sectoral Distribution of GMS Investment Projects Financed by ADB, 1994–2015

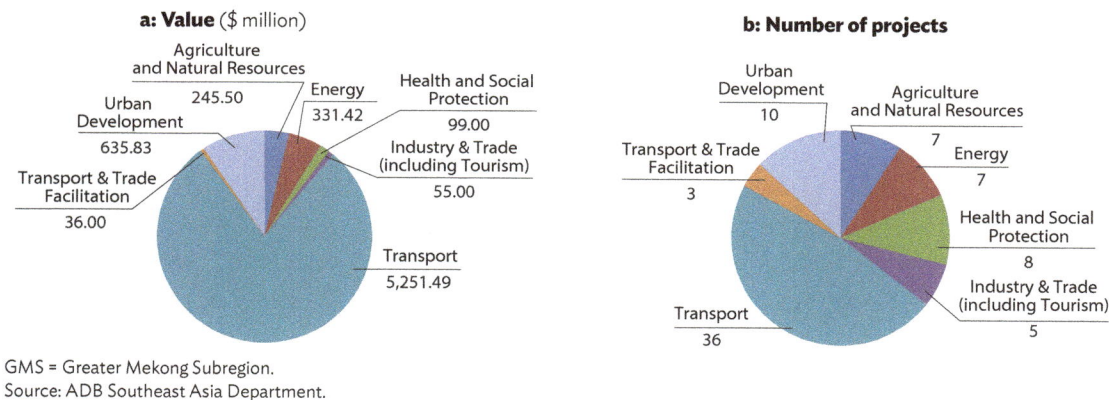

a: Value ($ million)

Agriculture and Natural Resources 245.50
Energy 331.42
Health and Social Protection 99.00
Urban Development 635.83
Industry & Trade (including Tourism) 55.00
Transport & Trade Facilitation 36.00
Transport 5,251.49

b: Number of projects

Urban Development 10
Agriculture and Natural Resources 7
Transport & Trade Facilitation 3
Energy 7
Health and Social Protection 8
Industry & Trade (including Tourism) 5
Transport 36

GMS = Greater Mekong Subregion.
Source: ADB Southeast Asia Department.

way. An award-winning Mekong tourism digital platform features visitor information, an e-magazine, and social media. Efforts are also progressing toward establishment of the Mekong Tourism Coordinating Office in Bangkok, Thailand as an intergovernmental organization.

Human resource development. Major accomplishments including the implementation of projects focused on preventing and controlling communicable diseases, including HIV/AIDS. The GMS led a successful pilot project implementing a framework for the mutual recognition of skills and qualifications to address skill shortages and enhance subregional competitiveness. It also extended efforts to support safe labor migration and address human trafficking. Frameworks are being developed for the mutual recognition of skills and qualifications in selected skill areas, new training standards for technical and vocational education and training, and an Academic Credit Transfer System Framework and university networking system.

The GMS impact and success across this broad range of areas would not have been possible without the mobilization of substantial financial resources. As of December 2015, ADB had extended loans totaling $6.6 billion for 76 investment projects costing about $17.8 billion in total (Figures 5.2a and 5.2b). These have involved subregional roads, railway improvements, hydropower projects, corridor town development, tourism infrastructure development, communicable disease control, trade facilitation, and biodiversity conservation. GMS governments and development partners provided $4.7 billion and $6.5 billion, respectively, for these projects.

From 1993 to 2015, ADB also provided about $124.9 million for 205 technical assistance projects with a total cost of $368.95 million for project preparation, capacity development, economic, thematic, and sector work, and coordination and secretariat assistance. GMS governments contributed $20 million, while development partners provided $224.02 million in cofinancing. ADB has also played the role of honest broker for the GMS Program, facilitating subregional dialogue and promoted agreements on key issues among GMS economies.

Opportunities and Challenges

Rising Mekong Regionalism. Despite major downside risks to the global and regional economy, regional cooperation and integration in the GMS, continues to deepen and intensify. First, the establishment of the Association of Southeast Asian Nations (ASEAN) Economic Community in 2015 creates major opportunities to accelerate and deepen regional economic integration.

Second, various subregional programs are emerging in the GMS subregion. Starting with the GMS Program in 1992, 11 additional regional arrangements involving one or all Mekong countries were established during 1992–2015.

Third, bilateralism has become more prominent. In some sectors, bilateral and trilateral agreements offer more practical and speedier solutions than regional arrangements that often take time for negotiation and ratification. Within this context, bilateral arrangements are emerging and becoming part of the Mekong regionalism process. If GMS economies can capitalize on these trends, they can be better placed for better income growth and poverty reduction.

Structural changes. Major structural changes are likely within Asia in coming years. And it will be important for GMS governments and firms to be fully aware of their implications, preparing to adapt and take advantage of new opportunities. Economies are rebalancing toward domestic markets throughout Asia, which will likely continue as an emerging middle class boosts consumption. Higher unit labor costs (and possibly appreciating currencies) in the PRC as well as other Asian economies will lead to shifts in corporate strategies. Meanwhile, for exports, the most rapidly growing markets will be in Asia, with the PRC and India likely to be particularly important for the GMS because of their size, growth, and proximity. To benefit, the GMS must ensure it retains competitive advantage through appropriate macro and other policies fostering a positive business climate, combined with enhanced transport and service connectivity.

Missing infrastructure links. The bulk of the missing links is in Myanmar, which has only joined corridor development since its political opening in 2012. While most major roads along the corridors have been completed, the feeder road network connecting production and trade hubs within the corridor is not yet fully developed, and interoperability among different modes of transport remains inefficient.

Development assistance. As noted in the previous section (see "Central and West Asia: CAREC Program"), new financing sources are emerging such as the Asian Infrastructure Investment Bank and Silk Road Fund. GMS economies can capitalize on these new development sources to help meet infrastructure needs.

Urban investments. Strategically targeted, economically sound, and environmentally sustainable urban investments are crucial to widening and deepening GMS corridors. Spatial concentration of development and growing urbanization are likely to continue. Both are important features of efficient and speedy development, but they can also lead to growing inequality within economies and across countries. In this context, the GMS focus on agriculture, infrastructure, and human resources

can help produce more equitable growth within and between GMS members.

Migration. Migration within and across countries will almost certainly be a powerful force in enhancing GMS living standards. While some economies are aging faster, which can cause labor shortages and sap competitiveness, working-age populations are increasing in others and will need good job opportunities. Imbalances in labor availability alongside economic disparities driven by spatial concentration of economic development will create push and pull forces for migration. This calls for stronger human capital development and better mechanisms to promote safe migration and to connect migrants with their homes, such as good transport links and financial services that support remittance transfers.

Climate change. Two aspects are important to the GMS—in addition to implications for food security. First, the push to mitigate climate change, including controlling greenhouse gas emissions, is raising the value of still-ample GMS forest resources. It also creates additional incentives for investment in new green growth technologies. Second, the increasingly likely need to adapt to climate change will raise the value of commodities used intensively in scarce factors such as water. GMS countries need to unlock the potential value-added of their natural resource supply through appropriate agriculture, human resource, and infrastructure development. Development of low-carbon cities and low-carbon power generation are equally important.

East Asia: Support to CAREC and GMS Programs

Emerging government-led multilateral cooperation initiatives are opening new opportunities to engage inter-subregionally and offering strong potential to enhance the impact of existing support through the two programs.[44]

---

44   The ADB's East Asia department has also provided technical assistance to formalize and deepen the Association of Southeast Asian Nations (ASEAN)-PRC, Pan-Beibu Gulf Economic Cooperation, and exchanges information with the Greater Tumen Initiative in which Mongolia and the PRC, as well as the Republic of Korea and the Russian Federation, participate. The Greater Tumen Initiative was established in 1991 with United Nations Development Program support to promote regional development in northeast Asia.

Nonetheless, regional integration in East Asia, inherently connected to the CAREC and GMS programs, faces crucial constraints—some practical obstacles, others more policy- or capacity-related—such as long delays at border crossings. Research, monitoring, and reporting mechanisms can identify the causes of bottlenecks. Given the PRC's position as principal trading partner to both ASEAN and Central Asian countries, it is critical to address these constraints to improve cross-border infrastructure connectivity in both CAREC and GMS.

Overview

Mongolia and the PRC are active participants in ADB's CAREC Program (Mongolia and the PRC) and the GMS Economic Cooperation Program (the PRC). ADB country partnership strategies for both the PRC and Mongolia highlight regional cooperation as a cross-cutting theme and thrust of ADB assistance.

In addition, trade and investment relations between the PRC and Mongolia have flourished in recent years. The PRC has become Mongolia's largest trading partner and principal source of foreign direct investment. ADB supports the development of an enhanced economic partnership between the two.

Progress on Regional Cooperation

Mongolia. Regional cooperation and trade are critical for promoting economic growth in landlocked Mongolia. International trade has always been important for the economy given its abundance of natural resources and agriculture. Regional cooperation offers an opportunity to strengthen physical and economic links with the country's neighbors to access broader markets and realize growth potential.

The strategic priorities for Mongolia under CAREC are physical connectivity and trade facilitation. ADB has provided financial support for the construction of regional roads and railways, regional logistics development and infrastructure, and urban services in border towns. Support has also been provided for the modernization of customs services and improvement of SPS measures to increase trade in agricultural and food products.

Mongolia is implementing transport projects along the Trans-Mongolian CAREC corridor and the Western Regional Road Development to the PRC border. Also in progress are the construction of the access road from Ulaanbaatar to the new international airport, the Western Regional Road Development Phase 2 connecting Ulaanbayshint (border point to the Russian Federation) and Yarant (border point to the PRC), and the Undurkhaan-Baruun-Urt-Bichigt-Huludao/Chifeng-Jinzhou road.

People's Republic of China. ADB works closely with the government to support regional cooperation and integration through country programs and regional technical assistance, with a focus on transport connectivity, development of corridor cities, and trade facilitation to promote economic corridors. The PRC has upgraded road and rail routes to its northern, western, and southern borders in Yunnan province ("Yunnan"), Inner Mongolia, Xinjiang Uyghur, and Guangxi Zhuang ("Guangxi") Autonomous Regions, mostly internally financed through significant ADB contributions under CAREC and the GMS (Box 5.1).

The PRC has also contributed substantially to regional cooperation and integration, both financially and through sharing its rich development experience. To strengthen the partnership with ADB, the PRC established a Poverty Reduction and Regional Cooperation Fund. Alongside ADB, it is also sponsoring, training programs under GMS and CAREC, setting up a Regional Knowledge Sharing Initiative, and taking the lead in establishing the CAREC Institute.

New initiatives. Following the global financial crisis, new government-led, sub-regional, and inter-subregional cooperation initiatives have emerged to promote regional integration as part of an overall effort to diversify export markets toward Asia. These provide new layers of engagement, complementing existing regional platforms such as GMS and CAREC.

The most notable is the PRC's initiative developing the Silk Road Economic Belt and the 21st Century Maritime Silk Road, jointly called the Belt and Road Initiative (Box 5.2). The "belt" on land aims to promote greater connectivity between the PRC and the central and western parts of Eurasia. The "road" at sea seeks to

Box 5.1: PRC Involvement in Greater Mekong Subregion Economic Cooperation

The Greater Mekong Subregion (GMS) North–South Economic Corridor connects the province of Yunnan and Guangxi Zhuang Autonomous Region of the People's Republic of China (PRC) with Thailand, and is a direct conduit between southern PRC and northern Viet Nam, as well as with Myanmar and the Lao People's Democratic Republic. Yunnan and Guangxi share the PRC's only two borders with Association of Southeast Asian Nations (ASEAN), making the corridor a clear gateway for ASEAN–PRC trade. This is expected to expand rapidly with the implementation of the free trade agreement between the PRC and ASEAN.

ADB is facilitating implementation of the memorandum of understanding (MOU) between the PRC and Viet Nam on jointly developing border economic zones, and a new regional technical assistance project is being prepared to provide support for border economic zone development. Implementing the MOU is expected to boost trade and investment, contributing to the development of the North–South Economic Corridor. Work is also under way to design a regional cooperation and integration loan for Guangxi Zhuang Autonomous Region to enhance the PRC participation in the GMS program, with expected positive spillovers for Viet Nam.

Source: ADB East Asia Department.

establish closer links with economies in South and Southeast Asia, as well as Africa. As outlined in the 13th Five Year Plan 2016–2020, the Belt and Road Initiative serves to implement the government's foreign policy. It will also help develop the PRC's more remote regions by enhancing connectivity to national and international markets as part of the government's strategy for rebalancing growth.[45]

Box 5.2: Belt and Road Initiative

The Belt and Road Initiative aims to strengthen infrastructure on the westward land route through Central Asia and Europe and the southern maritime route through Southeast Asia, on to South Asia, Africa, and Europe.

The initiative has two components: (i) the Silk Road Economic Belt; and (ii) the 21st Century Maritime Silk Road. The belt links the People's Republic of China (PRC) by land to Central Asia and Europe, while the Maritime Silk Road would connect the PRC's east coast to Europe. The two-pronged initiative would connect Asia and the Pacific, Europe, and Africa across five routes:

The Silk Road Economic Belt will focus on three economic corridors linking the PRC to:

(i) Europe through Central Asia and the Russian Federation;
(ii) the Middle East through Central Asia; and
(iii) Southeast Asia, South Asia, and ports in the Indian Ocean.

The Maritime Silk Road will focus on linking the PRC coastal ports to:

(i) Europe and
(ii) the southern Pacific Ocean.

The Belt and Road Initiative's networks connecting Asia, Europe, Africa, and the Middle East will pass through more than 60 countries in five regions that are home to 3.2 billion people (about 45% of the world total) and a combined gross domestic product (GDP) of $13 trillion in 2014 (box table). Trade in Belt and Road Initiative nations with the PRC reached around $1 trillion in 2014.

The economic and infrastructure conditions vary considerably across countries along the initiative route. At present, there are 9 low-income economies; 16 lower-middle-income economies; 14 upper-middle-income economies; and 7 high-income economies. Alleviating poverty therefore remains a major challenge. The economies are also diverse in land area, population density, road density, paved roads, and rail density, and so on. Many economies along the route have poorly developed transport infrastructure networks relative to population density (box figure). Paved to total roads ratio is relatively low and rail access or movement for some is limited. These gaps in transport infrastructure hamper trade and investment flows.

Thus, the Belt and Road Initiative—if supported by adequate resources and well-designed sequencing—could help the region

---

[45]   For instance, the Belt and Road Initiative starts in the central PRC Xian, opening trade routes to inland provinces.

address some of these challenges by drawing investments in infrastructure and enhancing connectivity to facilitate trade flows.

Economies Covered in the Belt and Road Initiative

Region	Economies
Central and West Asia	Afghanistan, Armenia, Azerbaijan, Georgia, Kazakhstan, the Kyrgyz Republic, Pakistan, Tajikistan, Uzbekistan, Turkmenistan
Southeast Asia	Brunei Darussalam, Cambodia, Indonesia, the Lao People's Democratic Republic, Malaysia, Myanmar, the Philippines, Singapore, Thailand, Viet Nam
South Asia	Bangladesh, Bhutan, India, the Maldives, Nepal, Sri Lanka
Other Asia	Mongolia, Timor-Leste
European Union	Bulgaria, Croatia, Czech Republic, Estonia, Hungary, Latvia, Lithuania, Poland, Romania, Slovak Republic, Slovenia
Middle East	Bahrain, Egypt, Iran, Iraq, Israel, Jordan, Kuwait, Lebanon, Oman, Qatar, Saudi Arabia, Syria, the United Arab Emirates, Yemen
Others	Albania, Belarus, Bosnia and Herzegovina, Macedonia, Moldova, Montenegro, the Russian Federation, Serbia, Ukraine, Turkey

Note: Economies in Asia grouped based on ADB definition.
Source: HKTDC Research. http://china-trade-research.hktbc.com

Population Density, 2014 Versus Road Density, 2011

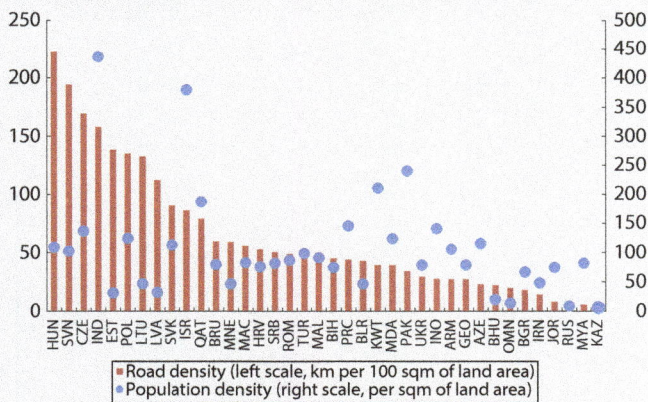

ARM = Armenia, AZE = Azerbaijan, BGR = Bulgaria, BHR = Bahrain, BIH = Bosnia and Herzegovina, BLR = Belarus, BRU = Brunei Darussalam, BHU = Bhutan, PRC = People's Republic of China, CZE = Czech Republic, EST = Estonia, GEO = Georgia, HRV = Croatia, HUN = Hungary, IND = India, INO = Indonesia, IRN = Iran, ISR = Israel, JOR = Jordan, KAZ = Kazakstan, km = kilometer, KWT = Kuwait, LTU = Lithuania, LVA = Latvia, MAC = Macedonia, MAL = Malaysia, MDA = Moldova, MNE = Montenegro, MYA = Myanmar, OMN = Oman, PAK = Pakistan, POL = Poland, QAT = Qatar, ROM = Romania, RUS = Russian Federation, SRB = Serbia, sqm = square meter, SVK = Slovak Republic, SVN = Slovenia, TUR = Turkey, UKR = Ukraine.
Source: ADB calculations using data from World Bank. World Development Indicators. http://databank.worldbank.org/data/reports.aspx?source=world-development-indicators (accessed June 2016).

The PRC National Development and Reform Commission explained its vision and action plan for Belt and Road Initiative on 3 March 2015 (NDRC et al. 2015). It aims to institute a new era of "open regionalism" that creates greater momentum for regional cooperation and integration across and beyond Asia and the Pacific and on a geographic scale far exceeding past efforts. Investments coordinated under the initiative will help align development plans of economies connected across the initiatives corridors, expand markets, and promote investment while boosting employment growth and enhancing cross-cultural exchange and knowledge. It is formulated as a strategic framework for PRC financial institutions (Asian Infrastructure Investment Bank, Silk Road Fund, and dedicated financial arm to be established under the Shanghai Cooperation Organization, among others); and bilateral and multilateral partners. However, the success of the Belt and Road Initiative relies on strong cooperation networks.

Targeted government-led initiatives could strengthen these commitments, such as the trilateral cooperation of the PRC, Mongolia, and the Russian Federation promoting the development of a Eurasian land bridge as an economic corridor connecting the three economies and prioritized by the Belt and Road Initiative. The economies launched a joint development plan in June 2016. Mongolia's Steppe Road Program, which will focus on construction and rehabilitation of trans-border transport infrastructure, will also be anchored to the Belt and Road initiative.

Opportunities and Challenges

New multilateral cooperation mechanisms, particularly recent ones from the PRC, move regional cooperation and integration beyond the conventional subregional approach toward more inter-subregional cooperation.

This has implications for ADB-supported subregional programs—particularly CAREC and the GMS. There is a need to strengthen coordination and synergy between the existing regional cooperation and integration programs and the Belt and Road Initiative Program and other new government-led initiatives. Providing effective coordination and objective intermediation is a hallmark of

ADB's approach to regional cooperation and integration. ADB's long experience and outreach can help build coherence on regional issues and programs, along with country-level implementation.

South Asia: South Asia Subregional Economic Cooperation Program

Since 2001, the South Asia Subregional Economic Cooperation (SASEC) program has been helping members improve cross-border connectivity and increase trade through a pragmatic, results-oriented initiative focused on transport, trade facilitation, and energy. Priority areas have included (i) improving international corridors to expand trade and commerce; (ii) modernizing customs operations, improving border facilities, and facilitating trade through transport; and (iii) improving cross-border power transmission connectivity to boost energy security and reliability in the subregion. Changing global economic and trade landscapes have prompted SASEC economies to develop a new vision to achieve the subregion's collective growth and development objectives.

Overview

SASEC was formed in 2001 when four South Asian Growth Quadrangle countries (Bangladesh, Bhutan, India, and Nepal) requested for ADB assistance in advancing their economic cooperation initiative. The initiative stemmed from the belief that regional cooperation can help address constraints of size, geography, and institutional capacity that hinder the subregion's development (Table 5.4). The SASEC economies lack the factors that typically drive faster integration, while facing high costs to trade, inadequate infrastructure, and landlocked status—especially in smaller Bhutan and Nepal. ADB functions as lead financier, Secretariat, and development partner, with support covering (i) capacity building and institutional strengthening, (ii) various regional initiatives, and (iii) financing for projects and technical assistance. In 2014, the Maldives and Sri Lanka joined the program, expanding opportunities for enhancing economic links in the subregion.

The SASEC program is institution light but project heavy.

SASEC institutional arrangements are simple. SASEC Nodal Officials meet once a year on the sidelines of ADB's Annual General Meetings to discuss the program's strategic issues, and again during the yearly meeting of SASEC working groups, which reviews progress of

Table 5.4: Selected Economic Indicators—SASEC Members, 2015

	Population (million)	Nominal GDP ($ billion)	GDP Growth (%, 2011-15, average)	GDP Per Capita (current prices, $)	Trade Openness (total trade as % of GDP)
Bangladesh	161.0	195.1	6.3	1,212	42.1
Bhutan	0.8	2.0	5.9	2,532	116.0
India	1,311.1	2,116.2	6.7	1,614	30.4
Maldives	0.4	3.1	4.8	7,681	200.7
Nepal	28.5	20.9	4.1	732	53.2
Sri Lanka	21.0	82.3	6.1	3,926	48.5

GDP = gross domestic product, SASEC = South Asia Subregional Economic Cooperation Program.
Sources: ADB calculations using data ADB (2016); CEIC; World Bank. World Development Indicators. http://databank.worldbank.org/data/reports.aspx?source=world-development-indicators (accessed November 2016).

projects and plan future activities.[46] SASEC has also taken a flexible, multi-track, multi-speed, and building-block approach that has enabled economies to process projects at their own pace and build on success at each step. This approach has benefited the program by improving cross-border connectivity, facilitating faster and less costly trade and generally reducing various cross-border constraints. Since 2001, 43 SASEC projects worth more than $8.8 billion have been completed or are under way.

Strategic Areas of Cooperation

Transport, trade facilitation, and energy. Since 2011, SASEC has focused on three sectors—transport, trade facilitation, and energy. Cooperation in transport seeks to promote connectivity among national transport systems to facilitate the seamless movement of goods and people across the subregion. This is complemented by trade facilitation to reduce or eliminate bottlenecks at the border as well as along the supply chain to lower trade costs. Cooperation in energy seeks to enhance electricity trade to expand and diversify energy supply to secure power reliability.

Other subregional initiatives. SASEC working groups in these three sectors meet regularly to plan and monitor implementation of regional projects and resolve project-related issues. SASEC also complements the South Asian Association for Regional Cooperation (SAARC) and the Bay of Bengal Initiative for Multi-Sectoral Technical and Economic Cooperation (BIMSTEC) by implementing some key SAARC projects. ADB has provided technical assistance to assist SAARC and BIMSTEC carry out analytical studies, such as the SAARC Regional Multimodal Transport Study and the BIMSTEC Transport Infrastructure and Logistics Study—transport master plans for the two programs. Through technical assistance to SAARC and BIMSTEC, and constructive dialogue with their secretariats, ADB helps advance economic cooperation of the two organizations and SASEC to broaden benefits to the region's constituents.

---

[46] The SASEC working groups include the Trade Facilitation and Transport Working Group and Energy Working Group. Subgroups (such as the SASEC Customs Subgroup and SASEC Electricity Transmission Utility Forum) meet at least yearly to discuss detailed activities under the working group's work plans.

Development Results

SASEC cooperation has improved access to key markets in smaller economies, reduced real trade costs and behind-the-border barriers to stimulate investment; and enabled cross-border power exchanges to ensure power supply affordability, reliability, and overall grid stability.

Transport. The SASEC program is developing sections of two high-priority SAARC Corridors—Corridor 4 covering Kakarbhitta (Nepal)- Panitanki/Phulbari (India)–Banglabandha (Bangladesh); and Corridor 8 covering Phuentsholing (Bhutan)–Jaigaon/Changrabandha (India)–Burimari (Bangladesh). Various SASEC road connectivity projects in Bangladesh, Bhutan, Nepal, and India's northeastern regions are improving parts of the Asian Highway Network, constructing alternate routes and developing access roads while improving land customs stations and customs systems. ADB-supported railway enhancement projects in Bangladesh are improving the international connectivity of the rail system. Improvements in border-crossing facilities such as land customs stations and dry ports in Bhutan, and land customs stations and integrated check posts in India are speeding border processing and increasing efficiency. When completed, the SASEC-Myanmar Corridor will promote South Asia-Southeast Asia connectivity. SASEC also plans for comprehensive port development in Bangladesh and India to better handle subregional maritime trade. SASEC transport projects have all emphasized "last-mile" connectivity, improving border facilities and promoting multi- and inter-modality (road-rail-water transport)—when combined with enhanced transit facilities and trade facilitation measures, will help maximize trade and commerce expansion.

Trade Facilitation. SASEC's Trade Facilitation Strategic Framework 2014–2018 is undertaking several national and subregional projects in five priority areas: (i) customs modernization and harmonization, (ii) standards and conformity assessments focusing on SPS measures, (iii) improvement of cross-border facilities, (iv) through transport facilitation, and (v) institutional capacity building. It has provided support to Bangladesh, Bhutan, the Maldives, and Nepal to undertake policy-based and regulatory reforms and streamlining processes and procedures, as well as planning the institutional arrangements toward the establishment of national single windows (ADB 2014).

The Trade Facilitation Strategic Framework, the SASEC Customs Subgroup, is overseeing subregional and national projects including exchange of documents at major border crossings and automation of transit processes.

Protocols to implement the Bangladesh-Bhutan-India-Nepal Motor Vehicles Agreement are being finalized. This landmark framework agreement aims to facilitate passenger, personal, and cargo vehicular traffic between these countries to reduce costly and time-consuming transshipment of people and goods at border crossings. A similar Motor Vehicles Agreement among India-Myanmar-Thailand will be finalized soon to ensure efficient transport between South Asia and Southeast Asia. Key training programs have been implemented in the areas of customs core competencies (such as customs valuation, risk assessment, national single window) and standards and conformity assessment. This trade facilitation will help create a more closely integrated subregional market that can enhance scale economies of local firms, increase competition and efficiency, and reduce real trade costs and behind-the-border barriers to attract more investment into SASEC members.

Energy. SASEC economies are forging bilateral and regional arrangements for energy trade, recognizing the multiple benefits of integrated energy markets, and enabling sharing of generation investments and improving energy security.

Bhutan has developed hydropower projects for export. The first Bangladesh-India 500 MW interconnection started in October 2013, and an additional 500 MW transmission capacity will be in place by December 2017. Approvals in 2015 included technical assistance in Bhutan to prepare hydropower for export from the eastern region, and a second interconnection project to increase capacity of imports from India to Bangladesh.

An ongoing project preparatory facility for energy in Nepal has been helping prepare energy export projects

using public–private partnerships for hydropower and power transmission projects. An energy reform program in Nepal for ADB assistance in 2017–2019 is also being prepared under the facility.

The SASEC Electricity Transmission Utility Forum is overseeing the conduct of the SASEC Transmission Master Plan Study, which is looking at the most economical cross-border transmission options and generation plants for 2020–2030.

All these efforts at improving cross-border interconnections for power trade are already bringing concrete benefits. The first interconnection project enabling export of up to 500 MW of power from India to Bangladesh, which commenced in 2013, is helping reduce power shortages in Bangladesh, providing alternative markets for Indian power suppliers, and improving grid stability in the subregion. Rising exports of Bhutan's hydropower to India boosts environment-friendly and sustainable power sources in the overall energy mix of the subregion.

Opportunities and Challenges

South Asia faces numerous challenges as it works to regain and sustain the pre-crisis high economic growth momentum. SASEC economies are formulating a SASEC Vision to provide the overarching framework to achieve members' collective growth and development objectives.

The SASEC Operational Plan's focus will involve (i) reinforcing existing value chains and developing new value chain linkages between in-country corridors, (ii) upgrading key transport and trade facilitation infrastructure, and (iii) designing institutional mechanisms for coordination and collaboration among the government and various stakeholders in economic corridor development.

Challenges include (i) increasing productivity and investment, (ii) creating jobs for the growing labor force, and (iii) mitigating macroeconomic and structural vulnerabilities. To do this, a SASEC Vision document provides the overarching framework and long-term strategy for sustained and inclusive growth.

For the next decade, SASEC's agenda will be framed within wider integration processes taking place in Asia. This implies enhancing economic linkages with East and Southeast Asia and harnessing the full potential of Asian integration. SASEC's connectivity agenda should be better aligned with the frameworks of SAARC and BIMSTEC to generate greater synergy with these regional initiatives. The SASEC Operational Plan for 2016–2025 reflects these priorities, with SASEC's current pipeline of projects reflecting priority projects identified by SAARC and BIMSTEC studies—supplemented with projects that will meet the subregion's emerging needs. Myanmar is considering full membership in SASEC—a step that will help realize SASEC's strategic role in building connectivity between South Asia and Southeast Asia (SASEC Secretariat 2016).

Transport. The challenge is to address capacity constraints and increased demand for service quality and safety given continued economic growth, rising incomes, and greater demand for travel. Transport infrastructure will help realize seamless movement along intermodal transport systems in key trade routes by removing physical and nonphysical constraints, thus increasing trade. Promoting "multimodality" for transport will involve developing land and maritime transport, improving access to and reducing congestion at border crossings, and improving logistics infrastructure.

Trade facilitation. Trade facilitation bottlenecks are the leading nontariff barriers constraining intraregional trade within SASEC—long travel times and high costs to trade in South Asia. For the next decade, cross-border transport and trade facilitation will involve extending the Trade Facilitation Strategic Framework 2014–2018 and expanding its thrusts to cover multimodal transport, including both land- and sea-based transport focusing on logistics chains. A key component of the trade facilitation strategy is to elevate the practices and processes of border clearance to international best practices.

The operational priorities for trade facilitation for 2016–2025 will focus on simplifying border-crossing procedures and optimizing the use of automated systems; promoting inter-agency collaboration to develop national single windows; strengthening national conformity boards; developing SPS-related facilities and exploring mutual recognition agreements; implementing through-

transport motor vehicle agreements; developing trade-related infrastructure and logistics facilities in SASEC ports, as well as land borders; and building institutional mechanisms to enhance trade information and regional cooperation among trade-related stakeholders in the SASEC region.

Energy. The main challenge is to meet the growing demand from strong economic growth and rising per capita incomes. Other challenges include reducing coal as fuel for power generation and import dependence, lack of capacity and diversification of energy sources to meet energy needs, inadequate infrastructure and policy frameworks that limit power trade potential, and lack of funds for capital-intensive energy investment.

Improving energy trade infrastructure and developing regional power markets should be complemented by developing low-carbon alternatives along with energy efficiency and conservation measures. The operational priorities for energy for 2016–2025 are (i) improving interconnections to access large-scale electricity and natural gas resources, (ii) harnessing unused regional hydropower potential, (iii) developing low carbon energy (wind and solar), and (iv) facilitating bilateral and regional coordination mechanisms and knowledge sharing.

Economic corridor development. The SASEC Operational Plan 2016–2025 includes economic corridor development as a new priority area, focusing on transport connectivity and trade facilitation to be complemented by multi-sector investments in special economic and industrial zones and logistics centers, backed by coordinated plans for raising domestic competitiveness (SASEC Secretariat 2016). The economic corridor development approach aims to extend the positive effects of simple transport routes by spreading benefits to the hinterlands for more inclusive growth, and by synchronizing and integrating urbanization and sustainable industrialization to boost productivity and living standards.

The Pacific: Framework for Pacific Regionalism

A new Framework for Pacific Regionalism developed by and for Pacific island countries underpins a more focused push toward greater regional cooperation among the small and remote economies of the Pacific.

Priorities include fisheries, climate change and disaster risk reduction, and information and communications. Progress has been most evident in oceanic fisheries, where regional action has resulted in substantially higher revenues from fishing licenses sold to foreign fleets. As with previous attempts at promoting broader regionalism in the Pacific, effectively translating regional strategies and policies into workable national actions is a key challenge.

Overview

Endorsed by Pacific Islands Forum Leaders at their 46th forum in July 2014, the Framework for Pacific Regionalism is the subregion's current master strategy for strengthening cooperation and integration between the states and territories of the broader Pacific subregion (Pacific Islands Forum Secretariat 2014a). It includes 13 of the 14 Pacific developing member countries (DMCs) of ADB (Timor-Leste being the exception).

The framework replaced the 2005 Pacific Plan for Strengthening Regional Cooperation and Integration under which progress was stalled by excessive "priorities" and issues surrounding sovereignty and a lack of regional ownership (ADB and ADBI 2015).

The new framework supports "focused political conversations and settlements that address key strategic issues, including shared sovereignty, pooling resources and delegating decision-making" (Pacific Islands Forum Secretariat 2014a). Instead of a list of priorities, the framework outlines a clear process through which Pacific priorities will be identified and implemented.

Strategic Areas of Cooperation

A Specialist Sub-Committee on Regionalism was subsequently established to consider proposed priorities from stakeholders including Pacific governments, regional and international organizations, civil society organizations, and citizens. The first 68 submissions received were considered against the test for regionalism consistent with the new framework. Five regional issues were passed on to the Pacific Island Leaders. These were then discussed during the Pacific Islands Forum in Port Moresby, Papua New Guinea in September 2015 (Pacific Islands Forum Secretariat 2015). A further 47 submissions were considered and four regional issues passed to the leaders for discussion ahead of the September 2016 meeting in Pohnpei, Federated States of Micronesia. The 2016 Forum Communique highlighted regional issues including oceans, climate change and disaster risk management, cervical cancer, harmonization of business practices, and fisheries (Pacific Islands Forum Secretariat 2016).

Oceanic fisheries. After successfully raising fishing license revenues with the establishment of a regional vessel day scheme, Pacific governments are now considering further regional cooperation initiatives to increase economic returns from fisheries while ensuring sustainable resource management.

The Parties to the Nauru Agreement's vessel day scheme involves a subgroup of Pacific economies—including Kiribati, the Marshall Islands, the Federated States of Micronesia, Nauru, Palau, Papua New Guinea, Solomon Islands, and Tuvalu. The vessel day scheme is one of the most successful examples of regional cooperation in the Pacific. It aims to safeguard sustainability and maximize revenues from the sale of fishing licenses to foreign fleets that work the vast exclusive economic zones of Pacific DMCs (Table 5.5). It establishes a maximum number of total days for fishing in the waters of agreement members, allocated to each country based on historical fishing in their economic zones. Countries can either sell their vessel days to fishing fleets, subject to a minimum benchmark fee, or trade days with other members. Since full implementation in 2012, the scheme has generated a substantial increase in incomes from the extensive fisheries resources of its members (Figure 5.3).

Table 5.5: Land Area and Exclusive Economic Zones of Pacific Developing Member Countries

Pacific DMC	Land Area		EEZ		EEZ to Land Area
	km²	% of total	km²	% of total	
Cook Islands	240	0.0	1,830,000	9.7	7,625.0
Fiji	18,274	3.4	1,281,122	6.8	70.1
Kiribati	811	0.1	3,437,345	18.2	4,238.4
Marshall Islands	181	0.0	1,992,232	10.5	11,006.8
Federated States of Micronesia	702	0.1	2,992,597	15.8	4,263.0
Nauru	20	0.0	308,506	1.6	15,425.3
Palau	459	0.1	604,289	3.2	1,316.5
Papua New Guinea	462,840	85.2	2,396,575	12.7	5.2
Samoa	2,840	0.5	131,812	0.7	46.4
Solomon Islands	28,900	5.3	1,597,492	8.5	55.3
Timor-Leste	14,870	2.7	77,051	0.4	5.2
Tonga	750	0.1	664,853	3.5	886.5
Tuvalu	26	0.0	751,797	4.0	28,915.3
Vanuatu	12,189	2.2	827,891	4.4	67.9
Total	543,102	100.0	18,893,562	100.0	34.8

DMC = developing member country, EEZ = exclusive economic zone, km = kilometer.
Sources: ADB 2016. ADB Basic Statistics 2016 Manila; and University of British Columbia. Global Fisheries Cluster Sea Around Us Project. www.seaaroundus.org

During the Pacific Islands Forum in September 2015, leaders endorsed the Regional Roadmap for Sustainable Pacific Fisheries, setting a 5-year window for further increasing economic returns from fisheries through regional cooperation. A joint taskforce composed of

Figure 5.3: Fishing License Revenues—Select Parties to The Nauru Agreement Members
($ million)

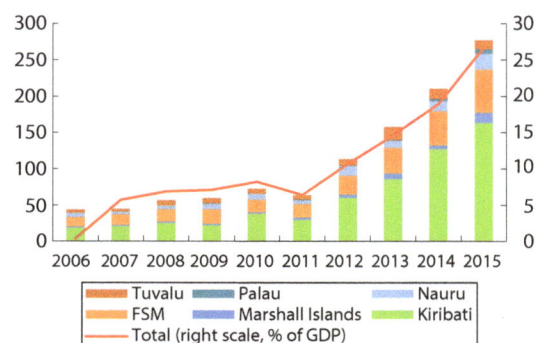

FSM = Federated States of Micronesia.
Source: ADB. 2016. *Pacific Economic Monitor* (July). Manila.

Parties to the Nauru Agreement, the Forum Fisheries Agency, and the Forum Secretariat was created to develop a work program for achieving this objective. During the subsequent Forum held in September 2016, Pacific Leaders endorsed the taskforce's work program and report, covering four key areas: reform management of longline fisheries, increasing employment and ensuring effective labor standards, facilitating investment and trade, and value chain participation.

Climate change. Recognizing climate change as the single greatest threat to security, livelihood, and well-being across the subregion, Pacific governments are working together to keep the focus on the subregion's vulnerabilities prominent in global discourse.

The Pacific Islands Forum is the subregion's primary vehicle for maintaining a strong, unified voice calling for urgent action to address looming and potentially existential climate change threats. Pacific governments welcome the Paris Agreement and fully support its goal of limiting global temperature rises to 1.5 degrees celsius above pre-industrialized levels.

The 47th Pacific Islands Forum (September 2016) recognized and endorsed the Framework for Resilient Development in the Pacific for its potential to support coordinated action on climate change and disaster risk management. As a voluntary and nonpolitical framework, the framework supplements rather than replaces existing regional statements or declarations, and is seen to be fully operationalized upon entry into force of the Paris Agreement. As of September 2016, eight Pacific economies had already ratified the Paris Agreement, and the Pacific Islands Forum is encouraging all members to sign and ratify it by the end of 2016.

ADB has continuously supported Pacific DMCs through a series of regional climate change initiatives, including the Pacific Climate Change Program. This program is envisioned to be a "one-stop-climate change service" responding to climate change-related technical and financing needs across the Pacific. ADB has mobilized about $80 million in new and additional financing from the Climate Investment Funds and Green Energy Fund and is working closely with Pacific countries, especially Fiji, to access Green Climate Fund resources. More broadly, ADB is looking to work with Pacific governments and regional agencies to explore options to strengthen disaster risk financing.

Information and communication technology (ICT). ICT remains grossly underutilized across the Pacific, and governments are turning to subregional cooperation to help unlock massive potential benefits from better digital connectivity.

Pacific governments recognize the wide range of economic opportunities ICT solutions present, including greater access to global knowledge and world markets. However, challenges to full connectivity in the subregion are significant. In the remote island countries of the Pacific, as little as 1% of the population has access to the internet, and costs are largely prohibitive—amounting to as much as $650 per month. The Forum Secretariat and the University of the South Pacific—a regional university supported by 12 Pacific island countries—are considering the creation of a regional ICT Advisory Council that could help facilitate greater digital connectivity in the subregion.

ADB's ICT operations in the Pacific focus on funding ICT infrastructure through submarine cable projects, developing regulatory capacity, and supporting applications for social services, including e-Health and e-Learning initiatives. For example, the cost of internet access in Tonga fell by 60% in 2013 after completion of the submarine cable system linking Tonga to Fiji—a component of the Pacific Regional Connectivity Project— cofinanced by ADB and the World Bank. While there have been clear gains in ICT access, for example, setting up an online company registration system that reduced the number of days to start a business from 14 to 1, challenges with uptake remain, with still under 10% of Tongan firms with their own websites (compared with a 40% average for Asia and the Pacific) (ADB 2015).

Support for Regional Institutions

Some of the most significant regional services today are offered through the Pacific Aviation Safety Office, Pacific Financial Technical Assistance Centre, the Pacific Association of Supreme Audit Institutions, and more recently, the Private Sector Development Initiative, the Pacific Regional Infrastructure Facility, and the Pacific Islands Financial Managers' Association (ADB 2009). These regional institutions are predominantly development-partner funded. They help achieve economies of scale in delivering services.

Development Results

Fishing license revenues. In the Pacific, fisheries have perhaps achieved the most dramatic progress in regional cooperation with tangible economic gains. In 2010, fishing license revenues collected by Parties to the Nauru Agreement members amounted to only about 2.9% of the estimated $2.0 billion value of the total tuna catch. By 2014, this increased to 10.4% ($2.6 billion). Available data from Kiribati, the Marshall Islands, the Federated States of Micronesia, Nauru, Palau, and Tuvalu show a twofold increase in fishing license revenues since full implementation of the vessel day scheme in 2012. Collections climbed from the equivalent of 7.1% of GDP in 2008–2011 to 17.7% in 2012–2015. In per capita terms, average fishing license revenues amounted to $704 per year in 2012–2015, 136% higher than in 2008–2011, across these six island countries (Figure 5.4).

At the country level, Kiribati saw the most dramatic rise in fishing license revenue collections. Collections in 2015 reached $164 million, a staggering 99% of GDP. Strong fishing license collections have helped reverse Kiribati's fiscal position from previous deficits to rising surpluses equivalent to 10% (2013), 23% (2014), and 48% (2015) of GDP. These surpluses allowed the government to deposit increasing amounts into the Revenue Equalization Reserve Fund (RERF). Building up the RERF is central to Kiribati's long-term fiscal sustainability, and increased collections and prudent use of fishing license revenues have so far contributed to this significantly.

In general, other Parties to the Nauru Agreement members have also benefited, with sharp increases in fishing license revenues enabling island countries to (i) improve fiscal positions, (ii) increase savings in public trust funds, and (iii) fund sensible increases in government expenditures. As revenue increases are derived from a structural shift to a new licensing regime underpinned by the vessel day scheme, annual collections can be sustained at current high levels provided regional cooperation and conservation agreements remain effective. Given the high importance of the public sector in Pacific economic prospects, improved fiscal outcomes through greater regional cooperation in oceanic fisheries management can help fuel more inclusive and sustainable growth.

Figure 5.4: Relative Importance of Fishing License Revenues, 2008–2011 versus 2012–2015

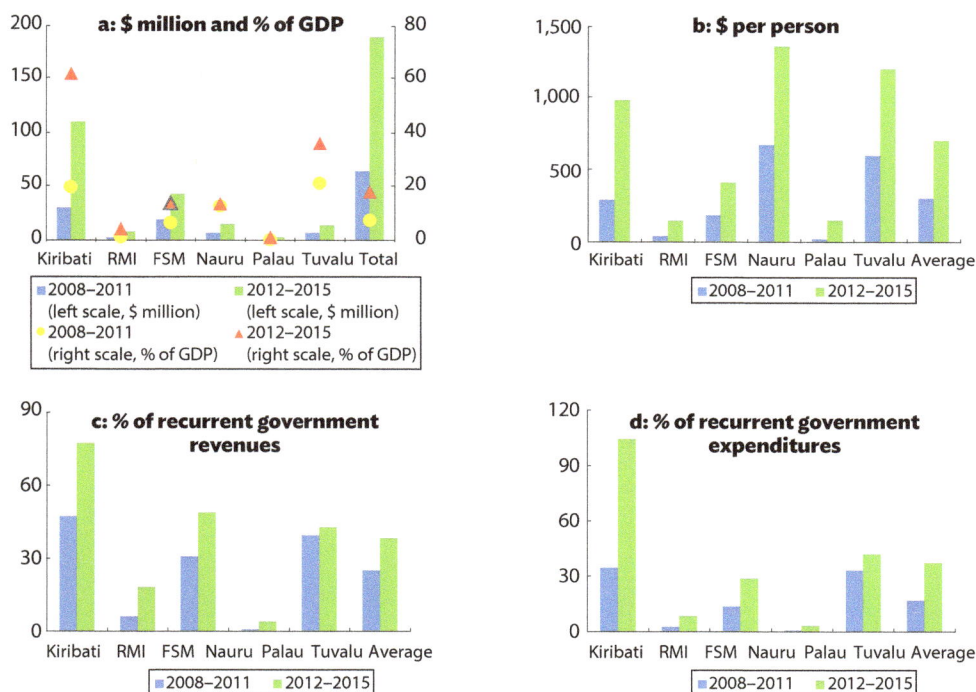

FSM = Federated States of Micronesia, GDP = gross domestic product, RMI = Marshall Islands.
Source: ADB. 2016. *Pacific Economic Monitor* (July). Manila.

Opportunities and Challenges

The Framework for Pacific Regionalism ultimately aims for a more focused and streamlined regional agenda that is determined and driven by the Pacific's own leadership. Learning lessons from previous, less successful attempts at advancing a regional agenda is an appropriate first step. Challenges remain, however, particularly in ensuring that agreed upon regional policies and priorities are effectively operationalized.

References

ADB. 2009. *Technical Assistance for Private Sector Development Initiative, Phase 2.* Manila (TA 7430-REG).

_____. 2011. *The Greater Mekong Subregion Economic Cooperation Program Strategic Framework 2012–2022.* Manila.

_____. 2012. *CAREC 2020: A Strategic Framework for the Central Asia Regional Economic Cooperation Program 2011–2020.* Manila: Asian Development Bank.

_____. 2013. *GMS Regional Investment Framework 2013–2022.* Manila.

_____. 2014a. *CAREC Transport and Trade Facilitation Strategy 2020.* Manila.

_____. 2014b. *SASEC Trade Facilitation Strategic Framework 2014–2018.* Manila.

_____. 2015a. *CAREC Corridor Performance Measurement and Monitoring Annual Report 2015.* Manila: Central Asia Regional Economic Cooperation.

_____. 2015b. Energy Strategy and Work Plan (2016–2020) for Regional Cooperation in the Energy Sector of CAREC Countries. Background paper for the CAREC Senior Officials' Meeting. Ulaanbaatar. 23–25 September 2015.

_____. 2015c. *Greater Mekong Subregion Tourism Marketing Strategy and Action Plan 2015–2020.* Manila

ADB and ADB Institute. 2015. *Pacific Opportunities: Leveraging Asia's Growth.* Manila.

Central Asia Regional Economic Cooperation Program. 2013. Trade Policy Strategic Action Plan for 2013–2017. Background paper for the CAREC Senior Officials' Meeting. Astana. 23–24 October 2013.

_____. http://www.carecprogram.org/

National Development and Reform Commission, Ministry of Foreign Affairs, and Ministry of Commerce of the People's Republic of China, with State Council authorization. 28 March 2015. *Vision and Actions on Jointly Building Silk Road Economic Belt and 21st-Century Maritime Silk Road.* Beijing.

Pacific Islands Forum Secretariat. 2014a. *The Framework for Pacific Regionalism.* Suva.

_____. 2014b. Pacific Islands Forum Leaders Special Retreat on the Pacific Plan Review (Forum Outcomes Document). Rarotonga.

_____. 2015. *Forty-Sixth Pacific Islands Forum Communique.* Port Moresby.

_____. 2016. *Forty-Seventh Pacific Islands Forum Communique.* Port Pohnpei.

South Asia Subregional Economic Cooperation (SASEC) Secretariat. 2016. *SASEC Program: Operational Plan 2016–2025.* Manila.

South Asia Subregional Economic Cooperation (SASEC) Program. http://sasec.asia/

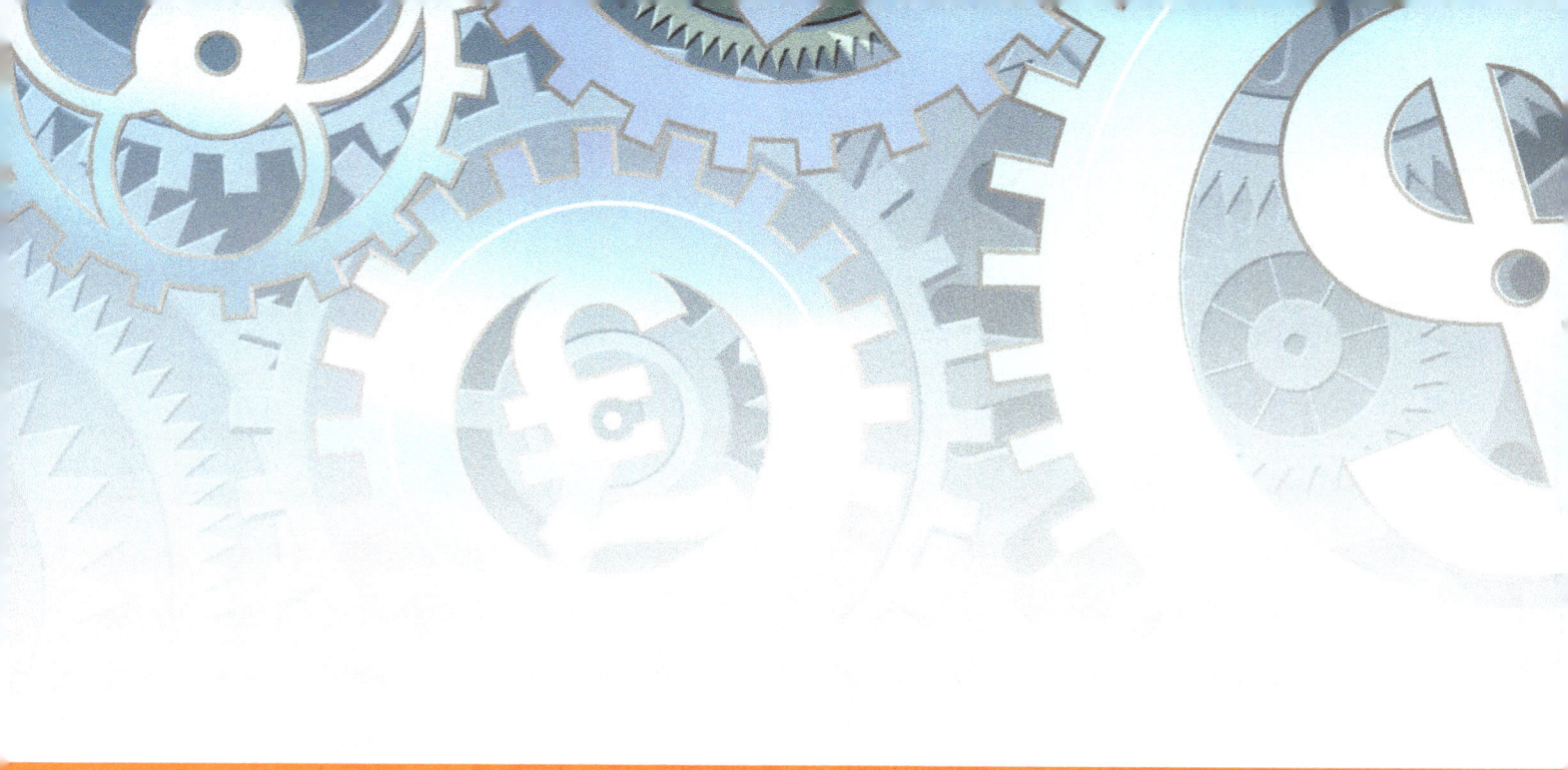

6 | Special Theme: What Drives Foreign Direct Investment in Asia and the Pacific?

Special Theme: What Drives Foreign Direct Investment in Asia and the Pacific?

Introduction

Foreign direct investment can help achieve inclusive economic growth and regional integration.

Foreign direct investment (FDI) worldwide has grown markedly since the 1970s, reaching $1.76 trillion in 2015. Developing Asia is now the largest recipient and accounts for almost one-third of total FDI inflows (UNCTAD 2016). FDI helps inclusive economic growth and integration. It contributes directly to economic growth through physical and human capital accumulation, as well as enhancing total factor productivity through technological and knowledge spillovers—thereby facilitating economic development for capital-starved and technologically backwards developing countries.[47] Moreover, FDI potentially facilitates regional integration by allowing economies to link to global and regional value chains—an export-oriented development strategy that many in Asia have followed successfully. In the process, recipient economies achieve industrial and export upgradation.[48] Finally, FDI can foster inclusiveness through job creation, increased wages, gender empowerment, and improvements in working conditions.[49]

As the main organizers of trade and FDI, multinational corporations enter a foreign market either through building new assets (greenfield FDI) or acquiring existing ones (merger and acquisitions), either to serve the domestic market (horizontal FDI) or to serve the international market (vertical or export platform FDI).

Multinationals' central role in trade and FDI has been one of the main features of economic globalization over the past few decades. Multinationals are motivated by two main, and possibly overlapping, market considerations. They can set up affiliates in a foreign country to serve the domestic market as a substitute for exports (horizontal or market-seeking FDI), replicating the production process in another country to avoid trade costs. Alternatively, a multinational relocates parts of its production process in search of lower production costs for re-exporting intermediate and/or final goods either to their home country (vertical FDI) or a third country (export-platform FDI). The offshored production process may be kept within the firm or outsourced, which results in increasingly complex international production networks.[50] Because vertical and export-platform FDI underpins the emergence of an extensive network of global value chains (GVCs), in which intermediate goods cross borders multiple times during the production process before final assembly (GVC–trade), this kind of efficiency-seeking FDI is referred to as GVC–FDI throughout the remainder of this chapter.

---

[47] Excellent surveys of the literature can be found in Moran (2001), Navaretti and Venables (2005), Caves (2007), Dunning and Lundan (2008), or Moran (2011).

[48] See, for example, Antras and Foley (2009), Harding and Javorcik (2011), and Athukorala (2013), among others.

[49] Several studies point out that multinational corporations provide higher wages, exercise greater corporate social responsibility, and are more gender sensitive in providing employment opportunities. See, for example, Aitken et al. (1996), Morrisey and Te Velde (2003), Lipsey and Sjoholm (2004), Harrison and Scorce (2005), among others.

[50] It is no longer whether to integrate an input used for production of a final good at headquarters, but about how to integrate and where to locate a multidimensional global value chain with final goods directed to global markets.

The decision over whether a multinational invests in greenfield FDI or uses the merger and acquisition (M&A) route depends not only on traditional considerations of comparative advantage and integration, but also to a great extent on the investment policy regime and domestic regulations of the host economy. In developing Asia, for example, domestic regulations in many economies— including the People's Republic of China (PRC), India, and the Philippines—limit foreign ownership in various industries to joint ventures, therefore erecting high barriers for greenfield FDI. At the same time, restrictions on foreign investors are generally relaxed in special economic zones (SEZs) designed in part to encourage greenfield investments.

The benefits of FDI are not automatic: they depend on the type of FDI and the absorptive capacity of the recipient economy—and policy makers may wish to attract the type of FDI most suited to their overall development strategy.

What drives the location decision of a multinational, in terms of motivation and the mode of entry? What factors determine the sectoral and industry composition of the FDI? And given the recent phenomena of emerging economies becoming important sources of FDI outflows, do the pull factors for emerging economy multinationals differ from those of multinationals based in advanced economies? These are important questions. because empirical evidence on the impact of aggregate FDI on the recipient economy is mixed.

The extent of any benefit depends on the "type" of FDI and the country context. While contributions of FDI to the host economy are generally recognized as positive and well documented in various studies, not all FDIs bring the same benefits, especially if the host economy lacks proper absorptive capacity and institutional quality. As an example, many studies point out that in order to benefit from FDI extractive industries, particularly natural resources, it is important to supplement the policy regime with an institutional framework that minimizes the potential for rent-seeking and corruption typically inherent in natural resource exploitation.[51] In the Asian context, this is particularly relevant for

resource-rich economies, including those in Central Asia: projects dealing with extraction, and to a lesser extent processing of natural resources, account for more than 50% of total foreign investments in the region (ADBI 2014). Other than vulnerability to volatility in global commodity markets, the positive impacts of these investments have been confined by sector, geography, and political considerations.

Thus, policy makers may wish to attract the type of FDI most suited to the overall development strategy and that matches the stage of development and absorptive capacity of the host economy. For instance, considering the mode of entry, countries lacking the absorptive capacity to take advantage from M&As tend to benefit more from greenfield investments.[52] Labor-abundant economies which may be following an export-oriented development strategy would benefit more from GVC–FDI.

Sectoral composition matters too. FDI literature has traditionally attributed greater technological spillovers to FDI that flows into manufacturing, due to the presence of more extensive vertical linkages.[53] However, given the increasing tradability of services in an age of e-commerce, and its importance as an input to production, developing economies also want to attract services FDI. Services account for more than 60% of global FDI stock (UNCTAD 2016). Finally, economies with poor institutional quality and business environment may find it easier to attract multinationals from other emerging countries with a smaller cultural, institutional, and structural distance.[54]

What are the drivers—comparative advantage, institutions, integration, and policy— of different types of FDI?

The focus of the research in this chapter is to provide an understanding of the country-specific and bilateral policy drivers that help to attract not only aggregate FDI, but differentiating FDI by both the market-serving motivation of the multinational and mode of entry—as has not

---

[51]   See, for example, Coolidge and Rose-Ackerman (1997), Alfaro (2003).

[52]   See, for example, Wang and Wong (2009) and Harms and Méon (2014).
[53]   See, for example, Alfaro et al. (2003) Aykut and Sayek (2007), and Golub (2009)
[54]   See, for example, Alesynska and Havrylchyk (20011), Lipsey and Sjoholm (2011), and Darby et al. (2013).

been done in previous literature. The analysis is done by sector and provides some insight into the relatively recent phenomenon of the internationalization of emerging country multinationals. Furthermore, it is not clear from either theory or empirical evidence whether the market-serving motivation of a multinational and its mode of entry are linked. While encouragement of one particular mode of entry over another can be directly affected through changes in domestic regulations and investment policy, the policy influence over domestic market-seeking or efficiency-seeking FDI is more limited. For instance, in a developing Asian economy seeking to attract GVC–FDI—so it can link a given sector to a regional value chain—it is unclear whether greenfield investments or M&As would be more helpful. This chapter seeks to fill this gap.

The drivers of the FDI considered in the analysis can be grouped broadly into factors capturing comparative advantage (for example, per capita GDP, market size, capital–labor ratio, share of skilled workforce); institutions (quality of governance, financial development); policy (FDI incentives and restrictions, more general policy regimes); and integration (logistics and infrastructure, trade and investment agreements).

In addition to investigating a broad set of determinants, this chapter focuses more specifically on international investment policies as important drivers of FDI. International investment agreements (IIAs) and regional trade agreements have proliferated in recent decades. Despite the increasing use of IIAs by developed and developing economies alike, there is no consensus in the empirical literature about their impact on FDI. The lack of empirical evidence can be attributed to existing studies not accounting for the wide heterogeneity in the design of IIAs in relation to their underlying provisions and the interrelationships between these provisions. This chapter attempts to cover this ground, adopting a granular approach by unbundling IIAs into their various provisions to investigate the impact, not only on aggregate FDI, but on FDI when differentiating by mode of entry.

The next section highlights recent trends in Asia's FDI and presents some stylized facts, both in aggregate as well as by motivation and mode of entry. The third section examines the determinants of FDI distinguished by market-serving motivation of the multinational and

explores the link between GVC–FDI, GVC–trade, and the fragmentation of production. The fourth examines the drivers of FDI by the multinational's mode of entry. The fifth presents an analysis of the relation between the motivation and mode of entry, and provides policy prescriptions for economies eyeing GVC–FDI. The sixth section distills relevant policy implications from the empirical analysis, and summarises the key findings. The special section of this chapter investigates the role of IIAs and includes a trend analysis, empirical analysis, and policy implications.

Trends and Patterns of FDI in Asia and the Pacific

Aggregate FDI

After having fallen since 2012, global FDI inflows surged to nearly $1.8 trillion in 2015, the highest since the global financial crisis.

Since 2012, global GDP growth has fallen below its long-term average. This global anemic growth has pushed FDI into the limelight, reinforcing its role as an integral catalyst for development. Global FDI inflows in 2015 increased 38% from $1.3 trillion in 2014 (Figure 6.1). That jump is considerable when set against a backdrop of 3

Figure 6.1: Total FDI Inflows ($ billion)

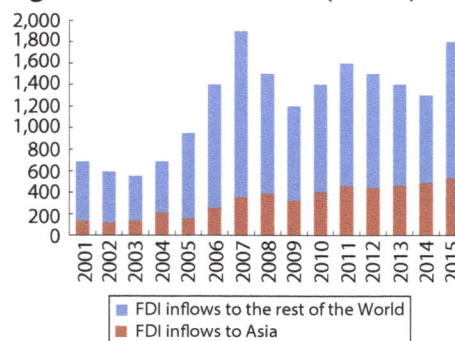

FDI = foreign direct investment.
Sources: ADB calculations using data from Association of Southeast Asian Nations Secretariat; CEIC; Eurostat. Balance of Payments. http://ec.europa.eu/eurostat/web/balance-of-payments/data/database (accessed August 2016); and United Nations Conference on Trade and Development. Bilateral FDI Statistics. http://unctad.org/en/Pages/DIAE/FDI%20Statistics/FDI-Statistics-Bilateral.aspx (accessed August 2016).

Table 6.1: Top Asian FDI Recipients from the World
($ billion)

Source	2010	2015	Growth (%)	Change
Hong Kong, China	72.3	174.9	141.8	102.6
People's Republic of China	114.7	135.6	18.2	20.9
Singapore	55.1	65.3	18.5	10.2
India	27.4	44.2	61.2	16.8
Australia	36.4	22.3	-38.9	-14.2
Indonesia	13.8	15.5	12.6	1.7
Viet Nam	8.0	11.8	47.5	3.8
Malaysia	9.1	11.1	22.8	2.1
Thailand	14.6	10.8	-25.6	-3.7
Philippines	1.3	5.2	303.2	3.9

Sources: ADB calculations using data from Association of Southeast Asian Nations Secretariat; CEIC; Eurostat. Balance of Payments. http://ec.europa.eu/eurostat/web/balance-of-payments/data/database (accessed August 2016); and United Nations Conference on Trade and Development. Bilateral FDI Statistics. http://unctad.org/en/Pages/DIAE/FDI%20Statistics/FDI-Statistics-Bilateral.aspx (accessed August 2016).

Figure 6.2: Global FDI Inflows to Asia by Subregion

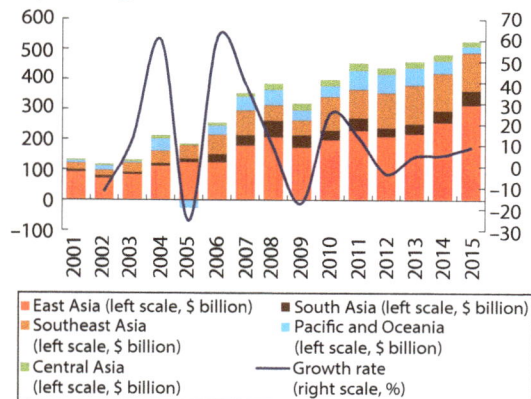

FDI = foreign direct investment.
Sources: ADB calculations using data from Association of Southeast Asian Nations Secretariat; CEIC; Eurostat. Balance of Payments. http://ec.europa.eu/eurostat/web/balance-of-payments/data/database (accessed August 2016); and United Nations Conference on Trade and Development. Bilateral FDI Statistics. http://unctad.org/en/Pages/DIAE/FDI%20Statistics/FDI-Statistics-Bilateral.aspx (accessed August 2016).

Figure 6.3: Global FDI Inflows to Asia by Subregion, 2015 (%)

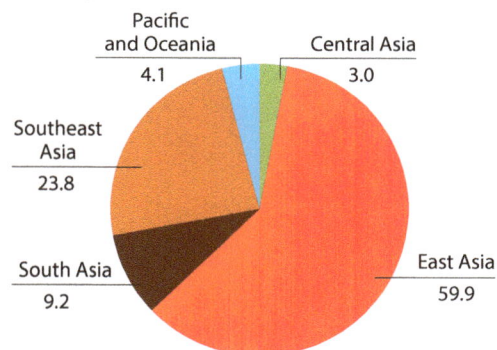

FDI = foreign direct investment.
Sources: ADB calculations using data from Association of Southeast Asian Nations Secretariat; CEIC; Eurostat. Balance of Payments. http://ec.europa.eu/eurostat/web/balance-of-payments/data/database (accessed August 2016); and United Nations Conference on Trade and Development. Bilateral FDI Statistics. http://unctad.org/en/Pages/DIAE/FDI%20Statistics/FDI-Statistics-Bilateral.aspx (accessed August 2016).

consecutive years of negative growth after 2012, falling commodity prices, and rising geopolitical uncertainty.

The surge was driven largely by a buoyant market for M&As, which topped $272 billion, nearly 1.6 times the value in 2014. Most flows originated from the United States (US); the United Kingdom (UK); the Netherlands; Luxembourg; and Hong Kong, China. The Asia and the Pacific region remained the prime recipient, attracting $527 billion in FDI, a 9% increase from $484 billion in 2014. With almost a third of global FDI flowing into the region, Hong Kong, China received $175 billion and replaced the PRC, which received $136 billion, as the largest host economy, with Singapore and India following (Table 6.1). Large FDI volumes into Hong Kong, China underscore its importance as a hub for financial investment (Nylander 2015). This also explains the large FDI flows between the PRC and Hong Kong, China.

East Asia accounts for the largest share of Asia-bound global FDI (60%); Central Asia draws the least (3%).

By subregion, East Asia continues to be the primary destination, accounting for 60% of all Asia-bound global FDI and driven primarily by the PRC and Hong Kong, China (Figures 6.2 and 6.3). The subregion received

$59 billion more in 2015 compared with 2014, part of which was due to the merger and restructuring of Li Ka-shing's Cheung Kong Holdings and subsidiary Hutchison Whampoa (UNCTAD 2016). Southeast Asia and South Asia also posted a slight increase, with 24% and 9%, respectively, of the total inflows to the region. Within these two subregions Singapore ($65.3 billion) and India ($44 billion) dominate. About half of FDI to Singapore, an established center for multinational investments, went to financial services. An improved business climate in India lifted FDI—flows from North America and Pacific and Oceania regions doubled, while flows from Southeast Asia rose 85%. There remains ample room to improve intraregional ties for both Central Asia and the Pacific subregions. Sharing best practices to accelerate financial development and enhance the FDI environment in these economies could help attract more FDI. In 2015, the FDI shares of Central Asia (3%) and the Pacific and Oceania subregions (4.1%) remained small. FDI to Central Asia contracted 23% to $15.6 billion, from $20.3 billion in 2014. Higher investment flows ($174 million) into the Pacific countries were overshadowed by FDI flows to Oceania—lower by $20.8 billion. Total inflows into the 14-member Pacific subregion are less than 1% of world inflows into Asia and the Pacific in 2015, while Oceania's share fell to 4.0% from 8.0% in 2014.

In 2015, intraregional FDI inflows in Asia grew 8.6% to $277 billion from $255 billion in 2014.

Within the region, outflows rose 9% to $22 billion, with East Asia accounting for $20 billion (Figure 6.4). Most of the intraregional outflows from East Asia are sourced

Table 6.2: Top Asian Sources of FDI ($ billion)

Source	2010	2015	Growth (%)	Change
Japan	56.3	128.7	128.7	72.4
PRC	68.8	127.6	85.4	58.7
Hong Kong, China	88.0	55.1	–37.4	–32.9
Singapore	35.4	35.5	0.2	0.1
Republic of Korea	28.3	27.6	–2.3	–0.6
Taipei,China	11.6	14.8	27.6	3.2
Malaysia	13.4	9.9	–26.1	–3.5
Thailand	8.2	7.8	–4.7	–0.4
India	15.9	7.5	–53.0	–8.4
Indonesia	2.7	6.2	134.6	3.6

FDI = foreign direct investment, PRC = People's Republic of China.
Source: ADB calculations using data from United Nations Conference on Trade and Development. Bilateral FDI Statistics. http://unctad.org/en/Pages/DIAE/FDI%20Statistics/FDI-Statistics-Bilateral.aspx (accessed August 2016)

from Hong Kong, China; the PRC; and Japan (Table 6.2). The pattern of intraregional FDI inflows as a share of total flows suggests that Asia is becoming marginally more integrated with Asia than with non-Asian regions. Asia's intraregional FDI share rose from 36% in 2006–2009 to an average share of 52% since 2010. Intraregional FDI inflows are also primarily driven and dominated by East Asia and, to a lesser extent, Southeast Asia. These two regions accounted for 60% and 24%, respectively, of intraregional FDI inflows in 2015. For Central and South Asia subregions, intraregional FDI ties remain weak. In 2015, the two subregions received 12% of global FDI inflows to Asia; but its intraregional share was only 8%. The Pacific and Oceania region, which drew an average 11% of global inflows in 2011–2015, accounted for a 4% intraregional share.

Outward FDI from the Asia and Pacific region dropped 9% in 2015 after rising to a historically high level in 2014.

The drop in FDI flows tracked a $20 billion decline in investments from Oceania and a $12 billion fall in investments from Southeast Asia, due to a slowdown in aggregate demand, falling commodity prices, depreciating national currencies, and geopolitical concerns (Figure 6.5). In 2015, total FDI outflows from Asia amounted to $417.7 billion, 15% of global outflows. Despite the sharp fall, Asia remains the second largest source of global investments after the European Union

Figure 6.4: Intraregional FDI Inflows—Asia

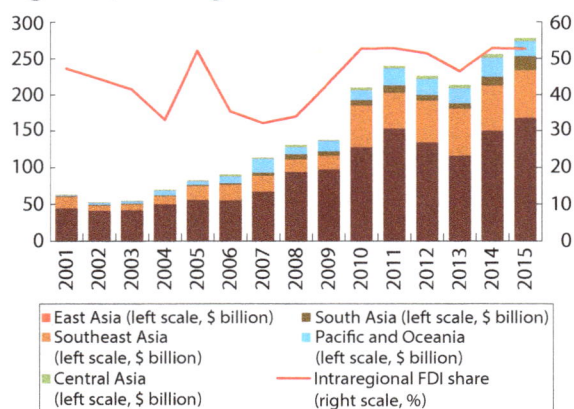

FDI = foreign direct investment.
Sources: ADB calculations using data from Association of Southeast Asian Nations Secretariat; CEIC; Eurostat. Balance of Payments. http://ec.europa.eu/eurostat/web/balance-of-payments/data/database (accessed August 2016); and United Nations Conference on Trade and Development. Bilateral FDI Statistics. http://unctad.org/en/Pages/DIAE/FDI%20Statistics/FDI-Statistics-Bilateral.aspx (accessed August 2016).

Figure 6.5: Total FDI flows—Asia ($ billion)

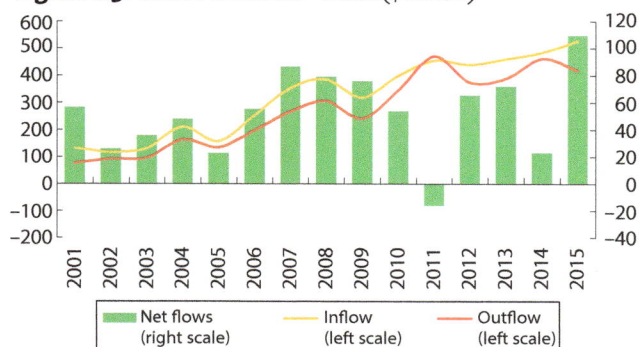

FDI = foreign direct investment.
Sources: ADB calculations using data from Association of Southeast Asian Nations Secretariat; CEIC; Eurostat. Balance of Payments. http://ec.europa.eu/eurostat/web/balance-of-payments/data/database (accessed August 2016); and United Nations Conference on Trade and Development. Bilateral FDI Statistics. http://unctad.org/en/Pages/DIAE/FDI%20Statistics/FDI-Statistics-Bilateral.aspx (accessed August 2016).

Table 6.3: Major Destinations of FDI Flows from Emerging Asian Investors, 2015

Source	Major Destinations	$ million	% of Total Investor's Outbound FDI
PRC	Luxembourg	5,943	8.3
	Nigeria	4,860	6.8
	Netherlands	2,640	3.7
	Asia	50,625	70.8
Malaysia	United States	1,062	14.6
	Turkey	429	5.9
	France	164	2.3
	Asia	5,503	75.8
India	Netherlands	575	13.3
	United States	435	10.1
	United Kingdom	409	9.5
	Asia	1,669	38.6

PRC = People's Republic of China, FDI = foreign direct investment.
Sources: ADB calculations using data from Association of Southeast Asian Nations Secretariat; CEIC; Eurostat. Balance of Payments. http://ec.europa.eu/eurostat/web/balance-of-payments/data/database (accessed August 2016); and United Nations Conference on Trade and Development. Bilateral FDI Statistics. http://unctad.org/en/Pages/DIAE/FDI%20Statistics/FDI-Statistics-Bilateral.aspx (accessed August 2016).

(EU)—also with a 15% share. East Asian economies such as the PRC, Japan and the Republic of Korea were among the top 10 Asian sources of global FDI (Table 6.2). In Southeast Asia, Singapore and Malaysia also figured in the list, as well as Australia.

Emerging Asian economies such as the PRC, India, and Malaysia mainly invest in Asia (Table 6.3). Despite the slowdown in its economy, the PRC's investments abroad continued and stood at $71.5 billion in 2015—making it the second largest investor from Asia and the sixth largest globally. In contrast, FDI outflows from India fell to $4.3 billion in 2015, just half of the $8.6 billion outflow in 2014. The destination of India's overseas investments changed perceptibly in the past 6 years. In 2010, at least 50% of outflows were destined for Asia, with the EU and the US at less than 5% each. By 2015, the EU and the US shares of total FDI from India were 29% and 10%, respectively. Outward FDI from Malaysia has been slowing since 2012. In 2015, investment outflows from Malaysia were $7.3 billion, 40% below 2014, and 48% lower than the 2012 peak of $14.2 billion. Most of Malaysia's overseas investments have been to North America, with Asia's share falling from 42% to 20% in 2012–2014, but this trend reversed in 2015, when Malaysia's investments to Asia rose to $5.5 billion in 2015, from $2.3 billion the previous year.

Patterns in global value chains and foreign direct investment

Japan is the dominant source of GVC–FDI in Asia, while the PRC is the most popular host.

Multinationals play an especially critical role in investment flows. Not only are they the main organizers and coordinators of GVCs, but they also serve foreign markets by relocating the production process as an alternative to trade. The great trade expansion in developing Asia—before being disrupted by the global financial crisis—was propelled in large part by the regional and global value chains spawned by Japanese multinationals across developing Asia. Using data on global ultimate headquarters (GUH) of multinationals and their overseas subsidiaries and/or affiliates that both import and export (Box 6.1), the PRC is the largest host for multinationals engaged in GVC–FDI, whereas Japan is the dominant source (Table 6.4). The PRC hosts the most GVC–FDI, not only for multinationals from Organisation for Economic Co-operation and Development (OECD) economies such as Japan, the US, and Germany, but also

Box 6.1: Identifying Global Value Chain–FDI in the Data

The main challenge in analyzing the global value chain FDI (GVC–FDI) is the dearth of data linking the parent or headquarters of the multinational with its affiliates or subcontractors. Moreover, information on the destination of sales of an affiliate is required to distinguish between GVC–FDI and horizontal (market-seeking) FDI. The data used are from the Worldbase registry compiled by Dun and Bradstreet, which provides detailed information on the global ultimate headquarters (GUH) of multinationals and affiliated subsidiaries, together with their industry codes (at the 4-digit level of the Standard Industrial Classification). Data also link subsidiaries that belong to the same GUH within and across borders. Crucially, the data record whether a plant is engaged in international trade activities or not, allowing the distinction to be made between plants that are exclusively dedicated to servicing host markets and those that produce for the international market. GUHs owning overseas subsidiaries that trade (through both imports and exports) can be identified as being engaged in GVC–FDI.

Data are from 2015, and the country coverage for host economies (identified as the location of the subsidiary/affiliate)

includes 27 Asian economies. For origin economies (identified as the location of the GUH parent), the data includes 36 economies from the Organisation for Economic Co-operation and Development (OECD) and selected emerging economies. Those from Asia include Australia; the People's Republic of China; Hong Kong, China; India; Indonesia; Japan; the Republic of Korea; Malaysia; New Zealand; Singapore; Taipei,China; and Thailand. All manufacturing industries, mining, and business services—services integral to the performance of GVCs—are covered.

The data supports three stylized facts that are well known in the literature about multinational production (box figure): (i) exporters are larger than firms that serve domestic markets in line with models of trade involving heterogeneous firms (Melitz et al. 2003); (ii) foreign plants are larger than domestic plants, as has been documented extensively using industrial census data from the United States (US) and Europe (Helpman, Melitz, and Yeaple 2004); and (iii) foreign affiliates that export are larger than foreign affiliates that do not export. The third fact has not been confirmed before, except for multinationals based in the US, and this analysis is one of the first attempts to do so across a large cross-section of economies.

Exporters and Foreign Affiliates in Worldbase

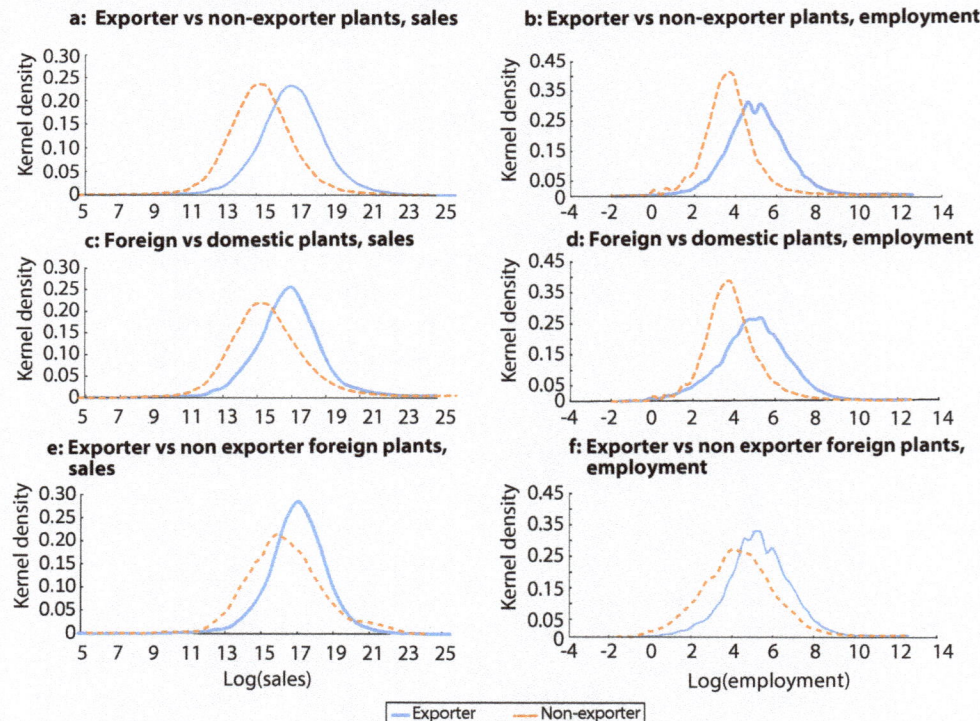

a: Exporter vs non-exporter plants, sales

b: Exporter vs non-exporter plants, employment

c: Foreign vs domestic plants, sales

d: Foreign vs domestic plants, employment

e: Exporter vs non exporter foreign plants, sales

f: Exporter vs non exporter foreign plants, employment

Source: ADB calculations using data from Dun & Bradstreet. D&B Worldbase.

Table 6.4: GVC–FDI—Most Common Bilateral Pairs

Destination	Origin	Number of Affiliates that Import and Export	% of Affiliates that Import and Export
PRC	Japan	2,260	81
PRC	Hong Kong, China	1,314	76
PRC	United States	646	74
PRC	Germany	625	76
PRC	Taipei,China	401	79
PRC	Republic of Korea	358	86
PRC	Singapore	337	71
Viet Nam	Japan	306	72
Thailand	Japan	258	64
Indonesia	Japan	214	53
Taipei,China	Japan	212	74
PRC	France	177	77
Malaysia	Japan	175	78
Philippines	Japan	171	69
Singapore	Japan	164	54

FDI = foreign direct investment, GVC = global value chain, PRC = People's Republic of China.
Note: GVC–FDI refers to foreign affiliates engaged in both exports and imports.
Source: ADB calculations using data from Dun & Bradstreet. D&B Worldbase.

Table 6.5: Number of Trade-Oriented Firms as Share of Total Foreign Firms—Selected Asian Economies

	Exporters	Importers	Exporters and Importers
Australia	0.225	0.216	0.151
PRC	0.815	0.878	0.789
Hong Kong, China	0.480	0.292	0.237
India	0.469	0.392	0.350
Indonesia	0.521	0.524	0.415
Japan	0.202	0.310	0.183
Republic of Korea	0.438	0.447	0.356
Malaysia	0.711	0.694	0.648
New Zealand	0.000	0.200	0.000
Singapore	0.518	0.446	0.403
Taipei,China	0.766	0.835	0.740
Thailand	0.722	0.784	0.661

PRC = People's Republic of China.
Source: ADB calculations using data from Dun & Bradstreet. D&B Worldbase.

from Hong Kong, China; Singapore; and Taipei,China. Almost 80% of foreign-owned plants in the PRC are engaged in exporting and importing, followed by 74% in Taipei,China; Viet Nam (70%); Thailand (66%); and Malaysia (65%) (Table 6.5).

Comparison of FDI flows from Japanese multinationals with those of the PRC and India digs deeper into the destinations of FDI (overall and GVC) in Asia from OECD versus other emerging Asian economies. For overall FDI, Japan's main destination in Asia is the PRC, a large and relatively cheap market (Figure 6.6a). Less developed economies, such as Indonesia, Thailand, and Viet Nam, are the next most popular Asian destinations for Japanese multinationals. The PRC concentrates almost 30% of its foreign affiliates in Australia—the richest economy in the area (Figure 6.6c). That Hong Kong, China is the second most popular destination for PRC multinationals is not surprising: United Nations Conference on Trade and Development (UNCTAD) points to a high flow of back-and-forth FDI between the PRC and Hong Kong, China. The less developed economies in Asia account for more than 15% of outward FDI from the PRC. Indian multinationals choose Singapore, an economy

specializing in services, as their most popular destination, followed by Australia and the Philippines (Figure 6.6d).

The distribution of affiliates engaged in GVC–FDI is much the same across these source countries: the favorite location for Japanese affiliates engaged in international trade remains the PRC, and Singapore tops Indian choices. However, Viet Nam is the favorite economy for the PRC multinationals to locate GVC–FDI, rather than Australia or Hong Kong, China. Almost 76% of the PRC-owned affiliates in Viet Nam are engaged in trade-oriented activities. This indicates that the PRC multinationals may be using Viet Nam as a production base to take advantage of its lower production costs.

Manufacturing attracts multinationals most engaged in GVCs in Asia, and business services draws in the least.

By sector, manufacturing attracts multinationals most engaged in GVCs in Asia, and business services draws in the least: almost 70% of affiliates belonging to foreign manufacturer parents are engaged in international trade, but only 14% of foreign-owned affiliates in business services import or export. Industries that attract the most GVC–FDI in Asia are motor vehicle components, electronics, machinery, and chemicals (Table 6.6).

Figure 6.6: GVC–FDI to Asia—Selected Source Economies

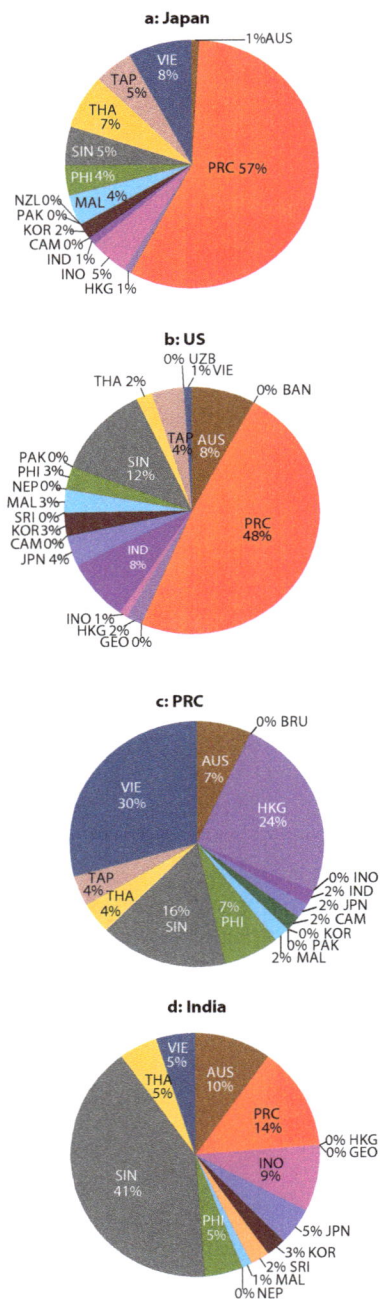

a: Japan

AUS 1%
VIE 8%
TAP 5%
THA 7%
SIN 5%
PHI 4%
NZL 0%
PAK 0%
MAL 4%
KOR 2%
CAM 0%
IND 1%
INO 5%
HKG 1%
PRC 57%

b: US

UZB 0%
VIE 1%
THA 2%
BAN 0%
TAP 4%
AUS 8%
SIN 12%
PAK 0%
PHI 3%
NEP 0%
MAL 3%
SRI 0%
KOR 3%
CAM 0%
JPN 4%
IND 8%
INO 1%
HKG 2%
GEO 0%
PRC 48%

c: PRC

BRU 0%
AUS 7%
HKG 24%
VIE 30%
TAP 4%
THA 4%
SIN 16%
PHI 7%
INO 0%
IND 2%
JPN 2%
CAM 2%
KOR 0%
PAK 0%
MAL 2%

d: India

VIE 5%
THA 5%
AUS 10%
PRC 14%
HKG 0%
GEO 0%
INO 9%
SIN 41%
PHI 5%
JPN 5%
KOR 3%
SRI 2%
MAL 1%
NEP 0%

AUS = Australia; BAN = Bangladesh; BRU = Brunei Darussalam;
CAM = Cambodia; GEO = Georgia; HKG = Hong Kong, China; IND = India;
INO = Indonesia; JPN = Japan; KOR = Republic of Korea; MAL = Malaysia;
NEP = Nepal; PAK = Pakistan; PHI = Philippines; PRC = People's Republic of
China; SIN = Singapore; SRI = Sri Lanka; TAP = Taipei,China; THA = Thailand;
US = United States; UZB = Uzbekistan; VIE = Viet Nam; GVC = global value chain;
FDI = foreign direct investment.
Notes: Number of affiliates, in each country, as a share of the total number of
affiliates belonging to global ultimate headquarters from each of the selected
countries.
Source: ADB calculations using data from Dun & Bradstreet. D&B Worldbase.

Table 6.6: Most Common Industries

Affiliate Industry	Number of Affiliates that Import and Export
Motor vehicle brake system	1,925
Other electronic component	1,358
Plastics pipe and pipe fitting	980
Pharmaceutical preparation	859
Paint and coating	710
Semiconductor and related device	694
Custom computer programming services	542
Telemarketing bureaus	532
Farm machinery and equipment	490
Ethyl alcohol	477
Plastics material and resin	465
All other petroleum and coal products	434
All other miscellaneous general purpose machinery	433
Other engine equipment	395
Computer systems design services	391

Source: ADB calculations using data from Dun & Bradstreet. D&B Worldbase.

Interestingly, a business services industry—telemarketing bureaus—shows up in eighth place.

A breakdown of outward and inward FDI and GVC–FDI from selected economies by sector (Tables 6.7, 6.8, 6.9, 6.10) shows 16% of all the PRC-owned affiliates in other countries are engaged in mining, second only to South Africa. The share of foreign-owned affiliates in manufacturing is highest for developing Asian economies including Taipei,China; Hong Kong, China; and the Republic of Korea, followed by Japan. Indian multinationals own the largest share of affiliates in business services (56%), even higher than US multinationals (39%), which have traditionally been dominant in this sector. For inward FDI, Australia (8%) plays host to the biggest share of foreign-owned affiliates in mining, while the PRC attracts the greatest share of foreign-owned affiliates in manufacturing (93%), followed by Viet Nam (92%). Hong Kong, China and Singapore

Table 6.7: Selected Source Economies— Outward FDI, by Sector

| | Share of Foreign Plants | | | |
	Mining	Manufacturing	Business Services	Other
PRC	0.163	0.465	0.298	0.074
India	0.036	0.378	0.562	0.024
Thailand	0.029	0.619	0.105	0.248
Malaysia	0.041	0.589	0.342	0.027
Indonesia	0.100	0.500	0.400	0.000
Japan	0.012	0.885	0.096	0.007
Republic of Korea	0.010	0.913	0.069	0.008
Hong Kong, China	0.007	0.919	0.070	0.003
Taipei,China	0.003	0.935	0.054	0.008
Singapore	0.018	0.783	0.174	0.025
Australia	0.058	0.527	0.397	0.018
United States	0.016	0.590	0.388	0.006
Brazil	0.094	0.406	N/A	0.500
South Africa	0.167	0.444	0.333	0.056

FDI = foreign direct investment, PRC = People's Republic of China.
Notes: Each row shows the fraction of affiliates from economy n abroad in each sector. Each row should sum up to one.
Source: ADB calculations using data from Dun & Bradstreet. D&B Worldbase.

Table 6.9: Selected Host Economies—Inward FDI, by Sector

| | Share of Foreign Plants | | | |
	Mining	Manufacturing	Business Services	Other
PRC	0.006	0.924	0.069	0.001
India	0.012	0.587	0.399	0.002
Viet Nam	0.010	0.921	0.069	0.000
Malaysia	0.027	0.821	0.139	0.013
Singapore	0.022	0.460	0.494	0.025
Taipei,China	0.030	0.835	0.134	0.000
Hong Kong, China	0.007	0.172	0.817	0.004
Indonesia	0.044	0.831	0.091	0.034
Thailand	0.024	0.916	0.060	0.000
Republic of Korea	0.020	0.815	0.158	0.007
Japan	0.012	0.551	0.437	0.000
Australia	0.076	0.474	0.377	0.073

FDI = foreign direct investment, PRC = People's Republic of China.
Notes: Each row shows the fraction of trade-oriented affiliates from economy n abroad in each sector.
Source: ADB calculations using data from Dun & Bradstreet. D&B Worldbase.

Table 6.8: Selected Source Economies—Outward GVC-FDI, by Sector

| | Share of Foreign Plants | | | |
	Mining	Manufacturing	Business Services	Other
PRC	0.022	0.800	0.178	0.000
India	0.013	0.625	0.363	0.000
Thailand	0.000	0.974	0.026	0.000
Malaysia	0.000	0.909	0.091	0.000
Indonesia[a]	0.500	0.500	0.000	0.000
Hong Kong, China	0.001	0.984	0.014	0.001
Taipei,China	0.002	0.988	0.004	0.006
Singapore	0.004	0.956	0.040	0.000
Australia	0.000	0.865	0.124	0.011
Republic of Korea	0.007	0.972	0.021	0.000
Japan	0.009	0.969	0.022	0.000
United States	0.015	0.856	0.125	0.004
Brazil	0.167	0.667	0.000	0.167
South Africa	0.000	0.833	0.167	0.000

FDI = foreign direct investment, GVC = global value chain, PRC = People's Republic of China.
[a]The data on Indonesia only includes two affiliates.
Notes: Each row shows the fraction of affiliates from economy n abroad in each sector. Each row should sum up to one.
Source: ADB calculations using data from Dun & Bradstreet. D&B Worldbase.

Table 6.10: Selected Host Economies—Inward GVC-FDI, by Sector

| | Share of Foreign Plants | | | |
	Mining	Manufacturing	Business Services	Other
PRC	0.005	0.980	0.014	0.001
Indonesia	0.005	0.796	0.200	0.000
Viet Nam	0.005	0.989	0.006	0.000
Malaysia	0.020	0.955	0.022	0.002
Indonesia	0.023	0.971	0.005	0.000
Hong Kong, China	0.008	0.311	0.674	0.008
Taipei,China	0.027	0.918	0.055	0.000
Singapore	0.019	0.682	0.276	0.022
Republic of Korea	0.035	0.930	0.030	0.005
Thailand	0.031	0.958	0.010	0.000
Japan	0.014	0.784	0.201	0.000
Australia	0.053	0.828	0.114	0.005

FDI = foreign direct investment, GVC = global value chain, PRC = People's Republic of China.
Notes: Each row shows the fraction of trade-oriented affiliates from economy n abroad in each sector.
Source: ADB calculations using data from Dun & Bradstreet. D&B Worldbase.

Table 6.11: Number of FDI Firms by Origin of Global Ultimate Headquarters

	Asia	Outside Asia	Selected Emerging Asia Economies	Rest of the World	PRC	India
All plants	203,132	26,998	86,094	144,036	31,297	52,008
Foreign plants (share of total)	0.05	0.37	0.01	0.14	0.007	0.005
Fraction that exports	0.73	0.52	0.43	0.63	0.35	0.48
Fraction that imports	0.76	0.53	0.37	0.66	0.27	0.37
Fraction that imports and exports	0.67	0.45	0.29	0.58	0.21	0.32

FDI = foreign direct investment, PRC = People's Republic of China.
Note: The selected emerging Asian economies in this list include the PRC, India, Indonesia, Malaysia, and Thailand.
Source: ADB calculations using data from Dun & Bradstreet. D&B Worldbase.

host the greatest share of FDI in business services—82% and 50% of all foreign-owned affiliates, respectively.

Affiliates belonging to Asian multinationals are more extensively engaged in GVCs in Asia than non-Asian owned: this is driven primarily by affiliates owned by Japan and the Republic of Korea.

Finally, some interesting patterns relate to intra-Asian GVC–FDI and to the activities of multinationals from some selected emerging Asian economies, especially the PRC and India (Table 6.11).[55] Subsidiaries belonging to Asian GUHs are more extensively engaged in GVCs than non-Asian (67% versus 45%). However, Asian multinationals' higher participation in GVC–FDI is driven by affiliates of multinationals owned by Japan and the Republic of Korea. Considering the subset of other emerging Asian economies, only 29% of subsidiaries owned by these multinationals are engaged in GVC activities. Also, despite the increasing internalization of multinationals from the PRC, the fraction of PRC-owned affiliates engaged in GVC–FDI remains substantially smaller than India (21% versus 32%).

Trends in greenfield investment and merger and acquisitions

Information on FDI's mode of entry is obtained by tracing the investment activity of firms and, unlike standard balance of payments data, traces the global ultimate ownership of the investment.

Multinationals decide either to take over production facilities and assets through M&A or to build new ones through greenfield investments. The main data challenge in measuring the size of specific investment projects by these different modes of entry is that the nominal value is often not reported due for reasons of confidentiality, especially in the case of M&As. Therefore, most analyses of FDI by mode of entry in the literature rely on a single input at the extensive margin: the number of investment projects.

Information on FDI mode of entry is obtained by tracing the investment activity of firms. Unlike standard balance of payments data, this dataset provides information on the global ultimate ownership of the investment, and is therefore not distorted by phenomena such as "round-tripping" and "transshipping".[56] Data is aggregated at the sectoral and bilateral level, covers 2003–2005 and

---

[55] The list of selected emerging Asian economies comprises the PRC, India, Indonesia, Malaysia, and Thailand.

[56] The International Monetary Fund (2004) defines round-tripping as "the channeling by direct investors of local funds to special purpose entities abroad and the subsequent return of the funds to the local economy in the form of direct investment." Transshipping takes place when funds channeled to special purpose entities in offshore financial centers are not routed back to the originating economy but to other economies instead.

comes from two sources. The fDi Markets database maintained by The Financial Times provides information on greenfield investments, while M&A deals are reported by the Zephyr database, maintained by Bureau Van Dijk.[57] Both sources estimate the nominal value of investments where they are not actually reported due to confidentiality reasons. Therefore information provided based on the number of projects is considered more reliable, and is the one reported mostly in this chapter.

Traditionally, economies in Asia and the Pacific region have received more greenfield investments, but the number of M&As have been steadily increasing.

After the global financial crisis, M&As steadily increased and the number of deals exceeded the number of greenfield projects for the first time in 2015 (Figure 6.7). This trend has been driven mainly by M&As from the rest of the world (ROW) to Asia. The number of greenfield projects has remained stagnant after a sharp fall at the beginning of the global financial crisis in 2007. However, in nominal terms greenfield investments remain significantly higher (Figure 6.8). The largest recipient economy for both greenfield FDI and M&As is the PRC (Table 6.12). Emerging Asian economies tend to receive more greenfield investments, while the richer economies in the region including Japan, Australia, and New Zealand rank higher in M&As.

Figure 6.7: Number of FDI Projects (thousands)

FDI = foreign direct investment, M&A = merger and acquisition.
Note: Asia refers to the 48 regional members of ADB.
Sources: ADB calculations using data from Financial Times. fDi Markets; and Bureau van Dijk. Zephyr M&A Database.

Figure 6.8: Value of FDI in Asia ($ billion)

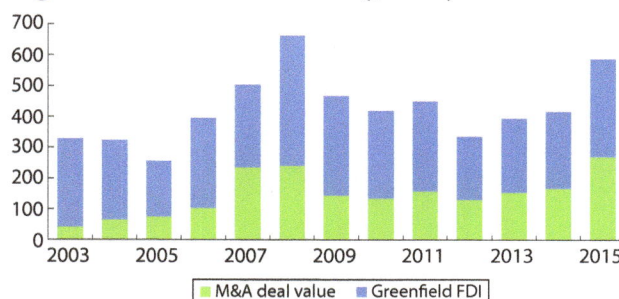

FDI = foreign direct investment, M&A = merger and acquisition.
Notes: The nominal value for many deals is not available due to confidentiality, especially for M&A. Asia refers to the 48 regional members of the Asian Development Bank.
Sources: ADB calculations using data from Financial Times. fDi Markets; and Bureau van Dijk. Zephyr M&A Database.

Greenfield FDI is more common in manufacturing, with M&As in services.

By sector, greenfield FDI is the more common mode of entry in manufacturing and M&As in services (Figures 6.9a, 6.9b). In fact, most of the increase in the number of M&As since the global financial crisis has been driven by services, particularly for intra-Asian investments (Figures 6.10a, 6.10b). The number of investments in services exceeded manufacturing after 2011. In this period, business services were the top recipient industry for investments within the region. On the other hand, both greenfield FDI and M&As in manufacturing declined in 2011–2015, mainly driven by a fall in investment from outside Asia in the years after the global financial crisis. A similar trend is observed for natural resources, where investments from within and outside Asia decreased both at extensive and intensive margins, and for both modes of entry. This is consistent with the commodity price shock that followed the crisis and dampened investment demand.

The number of outward Asian M&As has been increasing.

Even though balance of payments data shows an increasing trend in Asian outward FDI, the number of Asian investments shows a more mixed picture, particularly for greenfield FDI (Figures 6.11a, 6.11b). The number of Asian M&As, however, has been clearly increasing, both within and outside Asia, despite a slight drop in 2015. Almost 50% of Asian investment projects

Table 6.12: Top 10 Recipients of FDI in Asia (number of projects)

Rank	Greenfield FDI			Merger and Acquisitions		
	Host Economy	**2003–2015**	**2011–2015**	**Host Economy**	**2003–2015**	**2011–2015**
1	PRC	15,371	5,166	PRC	8,468	3,176
2	India	9,109	3,514	Australia	6,997	3,376
3	Singapore	3,797	1,909	India	5,832	2,988
4	Australia	3,155	1,642	Japan	3,546	1,729
5	Viet Nam	2,594	960	Republic of Korea	2,248	1,210
6	Hong Kong, China	2,169	910	Hong Kong, China	2,176	957
7	Thailand	2,141	733	Singapore	1,947	979
8	Malaysia	1,997	843	Indonesia	1,190	842
9	Japan	1,910	773	Malaysia	1,090	606
10	Indonesia	1,555	858	New Zealand	1,020	534

FDI = foreign direct investment, PRC = People's Republic of China.
Sources: ADB calculations using data from Financial Times. fDi Markets; and Bureau van Dijk. Zephyr M&A Database.

Figure 6.9: Number of FDI Projects by Sector (thousand)

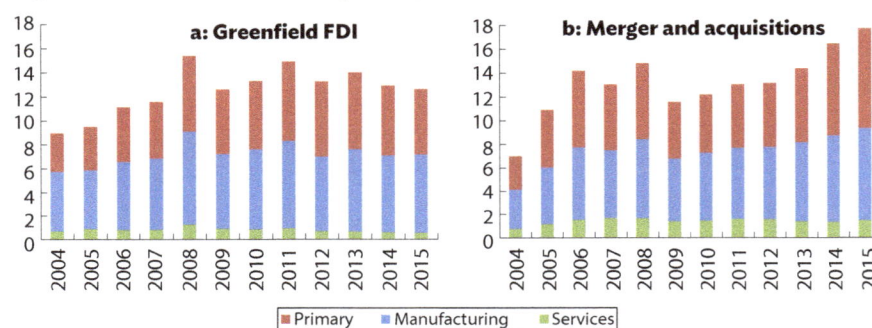

FDI = foreign direct investment.
Sources: ADB calculations using data from Financial Times. fDi Markets; and Bureau van Dijk. Zephyr M&A Database.

Figure 6.10: Intra-Asia FDI Projects, by Sector (number of projects)

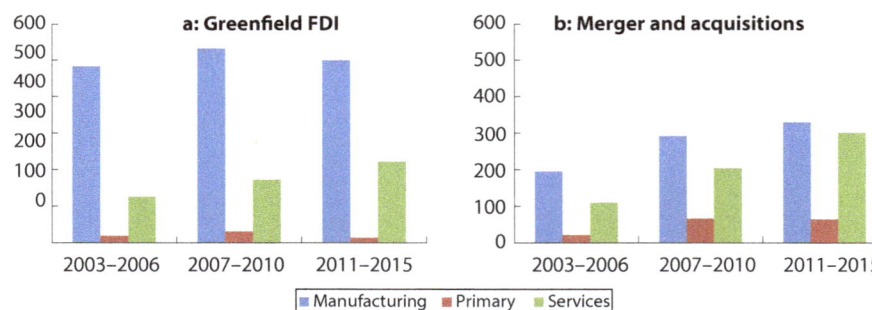

FDI = foreign direct investment.
Notes: Asia refers to the 48 regional members of ADB. The trend is reported at the extensive margin—number of projects and deals. The nominal value for many deals is not available due to of confidentiality, especially for merger and acquisitions. The number of projects and deals is averaged for 2003-2006, 2007-2010, and 2011-2015 for the purpose of comparison across the three periods.
Sources: ADB calculations using data from Financial Times. fDi Markets; and Bureau van Dijk. Zephyr M&A Database.

Figure 6.11: Asia Outward FDI, by Destination (number of projects, thousand)

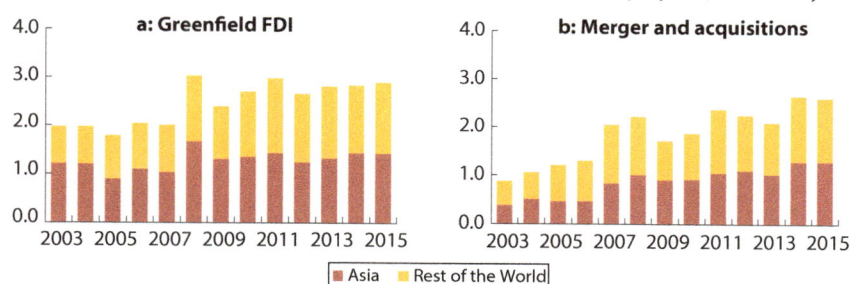

FDI = foreign direct investment.
Notes: The trend is reported at the extensive margin i.e. number of projects and deals. Asia refers to the 48 regional members of Asian Development Bank.
Sources: ADB calculations using data from Financial Times. fDi Markets; and Bureau van Dijk. Zephyr M&A Database.

Table 6.13: Top 10 Asian Sources of FDI in the World (number of projects)

Rank	Greenfield			Cross-border M&A		
	Source Economies	2003–2015	2011–2015	Source Economies	2003–2015	2011–2015
1	Japan	11,777	4,867	Japan	6,036	2,982
2	PRC	3,752	2,144	Australia	3,444	1,499
3	India	3,603	1,591	Singapore	3,393	1,998
4	Australia	2,228	1,050	Hong Kong, China	2,295	1,059
5	Republic of Korea	2,695	1,021	Taipei,China	1,965	1,022
6	Singapore	1,666	787	PRC	1,964	1,089
7	Taipei,China	1,810	726	India	1,577	581
8	Hong Kong, China	1,526	662	Malaysia	1,285	609
9	Malaysia	973	329	Republic of Korea	824	406
10	Thailand	537	292	New Zealand	490	209

PRC = People's Republic of China, FDI = foreign direct investment, M&A = merger and acquisition.
Sources: ADB calculations using data from Financial Times. fDi Markets; and Bureau van Dijk. Zephyr M&A Database.

(aggregating both greenfield FDI and M&As) have been directed within Asia since 2011 (Figure 6.12), followed by the EU (20%) and North America (16%). Table 6.13 shows that the largest Asian investing economy is Japan for both modes of entry. The PRC and India are the next largest source economies for greenfield FDI, while Australia and Singapore are the largest sources for M&As.

Figure 6.12: Asia Outward FDI, by Destination Region, 2011–2015 (% of total FDI projects)

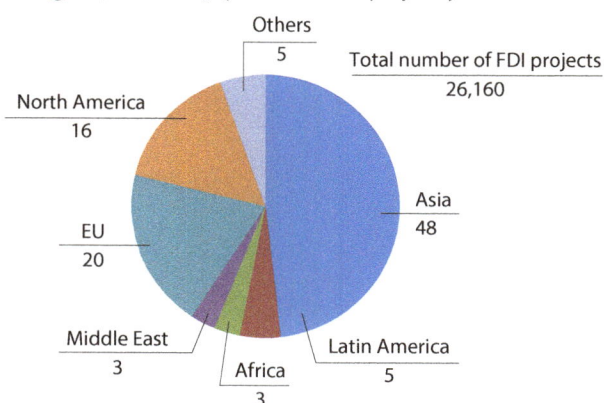

EU = European Union, FDI = foreign direct investment.
Notes: The trend is reported at the extensive margin i.e. number of projects and deals. Total FDI projects is the sum of greenfield FDI projects and merger and acquisitions. Asia refers to the 48 regional members of the Asian Development Bank. Other regional groupings follow ADB classification.
Sources: ADB calculations using data from Financial Times. fDi Markets; and Bureau van Dijk. Zephyr M&A Database.

Asia's Investment Patterns in the Age of Global Value Chains

Participating in GVCs matters for growth in GDP growth and increased international trade—so understanding what drives GVC–FDI is important.

Understanding the factors that lead multinationals to set up operations in a certain location and engage in trade-oriented activities is important for many reasons. Economies with the fastest growing GVC participation have seen GDP per capita growth rates two percentage points above the global average from 1990–2010 (UNCTAD 2013). Within the Asian sample, economies with GDP per capita growth above the median had higher GVC participation, both in trade and FDI, than those with growth rates below the median (Table 6.14).

GVCs are also an important channel through which shocks are transmitted across economies. The increasing interdependence of economies through supplier linkages has created more synchronized business cycles. GVCs also impact the political economy of trade policy by creating different incentives for lobbying by producers at different stages in the production process, as well as clear differential effects on policy within an industry. Two producers at different stages of the production

Table 6.14: Participation in the GVC and GDP per Capita Growth

	Low (%)	High (%)	Observations
GVC–Trade	2.1	3.3	8
GVC–FDI	2.8	3.6	27
FDI Intensity	2.5	3.4	12

FDI = foreign direct investment, GVC = global value chain.
Notes: The numbers in first two columns refer to average growth rate of real GDP per capita for 2000-2010. Low (High) FDI intensity refers to countries with sales of foreign plants (as a share of total sales), below (above) the median share across countries. Low (High) GVC-FDI refers to countries with a fraction of trade-oriented foreign plants that export below (above) the median share across countries. Low (high) GVC-trade refers to countries with DVA shares above (below) the median across countries.
Sources: ADB calculations using data from ADB Multiregional Input-Output Tables and methodology by Wang, Wei, and Zhu (2014); Dun & Bradstreet. D&B Worldbase.

process (for example, input production and assembly) often conflict over which goods should be protected from imports.

Finally, GVC expansion drove the largest growth in world trade relative to GDP, starting from the middle of 1980s until the global financial crisis. However, just as GVC–trade was the driving force during rapid trade expansion, the collapse of trade in intermediate goods was one reason for the global trade growth slowdown that followed the financial crisis. Demand shocks hurt trade in intermediate goods harder than trade in final goods (the so-called "bullwhip effect"), as multinationals postpone investment decisions and draw down inventories in times of uncertainty.

Participation in GVCs has enabled export-led growth and industrial upgradation in many developing Asian economies (Box 6.2). Until the global financial crisis, integration with international production networks among developing Asian economies increased, especially those in East Asia and Southeast Asia. This happened for three main reasons: (i) they eased restrictions to let foreign firms in; (ii) communication technologies became far more sophisticated and widespread; and (iii) trade costs—both shipping costs and trade barriers—decreased dramatically.

This section describes an investigation into the factors that influence a multinational's decision to concentrate on the domestic market instead of trade-oriented activities. The traditional determinants of that decision—within an economy and industry—can be grouped broadly into comparative advantage, integration, institutions, and responses to policy. The analysis also includes indicators of production fragmentation (input–output links) and measures of engagement in GVC–trade to investigate how linkages within the domestic economy and international production networks affect GVC–FDI.

A descriptive analysis below explores the relationship between host economy characteristics and GVC–FDI. A more formal regression analysis then examines the country and industry determinants of GVC–FDI. The main analysis relating to an economy's characteristics employs both data for firms and a standard gravity model framework for bilateral pairs. In the case of an economy's characteristics, the GVC–FDI is proxied by a

Box 6.2: GVC–Trade in Asia

Features of participation in value chains in Asia can be highlighted through an accounting framework developed by Wang, Wei, and Zhu (2014). The framework decomposes gross export into four value added components based on where the value added is absorbed: domestic value added that is ultimately absorbed abroad (DVA); foreign value added used in the production for exports (FVA); returned domestic value, or the portion of domestic value added that is initially exported and returned home embedded in imports (RDV); and pure double counted terms due to the back and forth nature of intermediate goods trade (PDC). The export value added decompositions are carried out using the ADB Multiregional Input-Output Tables, which are a substantial extension of country and time coverage in the World Input-Output Database (WIOD).

Measures of DVA and RDV, as a share of gross exports, are available for 35 industries, including services, and 46 economies. A lower DVA share and higher RDV share reflects increased engagement in global value chains (GVCs) in the "Factory Asia" context, where most developing countries remain a hub for final assembly of products destined for markets throughout the world.

Box table 1 indicates that, based on the DVA share, the ADB Asian members on average show lower engagement with GVCs than both the global average and that of non-Asian ADB members. However, two of the largest developing Asian economies, the People's Republic of China and India, not only increased participation in international production networks between 2000 and 2014, they moved into higher value added activities. This is particularly true for India, which has seen an increase in the share of RDV in its value added exports alongside a simultaneous increase in DVA.

The link between the level of engagement in GVCs and how upstream an economy's export components are can also

be investigated. Export "upstreamness" is a measure of the position an economy occupies in the production process, with natural resource extraction being the most upstream (and final assembly of export products most downstream). The degree of engagement in GVCs is proxied through the DVA share in exports: the lower the DVA share, the greater the GVC participation. The measure adopted here aggregates a measure of export upstreamness in each industry using the export shares as weights, and is constructed by Antras et al. (2012). In the sample of Asian economies, the measure ranges from 1.3 (for the ready-made garment center Bangladesh) to 3.36 for Kazakhstan (a prominent producer of minerals) with higher values indicating the more upstream one is in the production process.

1: Summary Statistics—GVC–Trade

	All	Asia	Others	PRC	India
Domestic Value Added					
2000	0.771	0.804	0.754	0.860	0.860
2015	0.782	0.810	0.768	0.851	0.876
Foreign Value Added					
2000	0.166	0.142	0.181	0.102	0.103
2015	0.164	0.143	0.177	0.109	0.095
Returned Domestic Value Added					
2000	0.0043	0.0031	0.0015	0.0050	0.0013
2015	0.0037	0.0030	0.0018	0.0073	0.0027

GVC = global value chain, PRC = People's Republic of China.
Note: Domestic value added, foreign value added, and returned domestic value of exports are expressed as shares of gross exports, an average across sectors and bilateral-pairs.
Sources: ADB calculations using data from ADB Multiregional Input-Output Tables and methodology by Wang, Wei, and Zhu (2014).

binary variable that takes a value of 1 when the foreign-owned affiliate both imports and exports, and a value of 0 otherwise. The gravity model measures GVC–FDI by the fraction of foreign-owned affiliates that both import and export. All empirical specifications are estimated using the ordinary least squares (OLS) methodology and a host of an economy's and industry fixed effects are controlled for depending on the level of aggregation at which the estimation is carried out.[58]

---

[58]   While estimating the specification with country-level determinants.

Box 6.2 continued

Regression analysis using ordinary least squares (OLS) methodology finds that export upstreamness is negatively correlated with GVC–trade in the global sample, with the relationship even more pronounced for Asian economies (box table 2). This holds across all sectors. The estimated coefficient of export upstreamness is significant at the 1% level in all alternative specifications. The capital–labor ratio is negatively

associated with GVC–trade in manufacturing and positively related in mining, even more so in Asian economies. Both these relations reaffirm the Factory Asia phenomenon—on average Asian economies linked to international production networks are more labor abundant, specializing in more downstream parts of production such as final assembly.

2: Determinants of GVC-Trade—Country Characteristics

Dependent variable: DVA as share of gross exports	(1)	(2)	(3)	(4)	(5)	(6)
Log(real GDP per capita)	0.023*** (0.008)	0.019* (0.009)	0.135*** (0.011)	−0.069*** (0.018)	−0.101*** (0.024)	0.138+ (0.072)
Log(real GDP)	0.031*** (0.001)	0.038*** (0.001)	0.013*** (0.002)	0.063*** (0.001)	0.089*** (0.002)	0.011*** (0.004)
Log(capital–labor ratio)	0.014** (0.006)	0.027*** (0.007)	−0.099*** (0.009)	0.019* (0.010)	0.033** (0.014)	−0.146*** (0.046)
Years of schooling	−0.013*** (0.001)	−0.015*** (0.001)	−0.021*** (0.001)	0.001 (0.002)	0.007*** (0.003)	−0.017* (0.009)
Rule of law	−0.021*** (0.004)	−0.019*** (0.005)	−0.048*** (0.005)	0.043*** (0.004)	0.045*** (0.005)	−0.019* (0.010)
Export upstreamness	0.052*** (0.005)	0.081*** (0.007)	0.099*** (0.008)	0.164*** (0.005)	0.242*** (0.008)	0.216*** (0.008)
Private credit	−0.011** (0.005)	−0.014** (0.007)	0.020*** (0.006)			
Number of observations	183,068	79,597	5,362	42,195	20,539	1,249
R–squared	0.670	0.577	0.420	0.690	0.675	0.647
Sample industries	all	mfg	mining	all	mfg	mining
Sample countries	all	all	all	Asia	Asia	Asia

*** = significant at 1%, ** = significant at 5%, * = significant at 10%.
DVA = domestic value added, GDP = gross domestic product, GVC = global value chain, mfg = manufacturing.
Notes: Observations are at the bilateral economy–sector level for different years. Controls refer to the exporter economy. All specifications with importer and industry-year fixed effects. Robust standard errors, clustered by importer–exporter, in parentheses.
Sources: ADB calculations using data from ADB Multiregional Input-Output Tables and methodology by Wang, Wei, and Zhu (2014); Antras, et al. (2012); Barro and Lee (2013); Beck, et al. (2009); Penn World Tables (8.0 and 8.1) http://www.wiod.org/database/seas13 (accessed July 2016); and World Bank. Worldwide Governance Indicators. http://data.worldbank.org/data-catalog/worldwide-governance-indicators (accessed July 2016).

Value-chain investments and an economy's characteristics

Overall, GVC–FDI in Asia is concentrated in economies with exports more downstream— sectors closer to final assembly—with weak rule of law, lower costs to export and import, lower capital–labor ratios, and lower incomes.

The relationship between selected host economy characteristics and GVC–FDI is investigated overall

and across sectors. Table 6.15 shows the share of foreign-owned affiliates that are trade-oriented (have exports and imports) as a proportion of all foreign-owned affiliates. The shares are shown separately for two groups of economies: those with a value of a given characteristic below the median or above the median, across economies. The table reveals that overall, GVC–FDI is concentrated where there are more downstream exports, weak rule of law, lower costs to export and import, lower capital–labor ratios, and lower incomes. This pattern repeats by sector—with business services being the least pronounced. The last three variables in the

Table 6.15: GVC–FDI and Economy Characteristics

Economy Charateristic	All Sectors		Mining		Manufacturing		Business Services	
	Below	Above	Below	Above	Below	Above	Below	Above
Export upstreamness	0.71	0.39	0.67	0.30	0.75	0.42	0.47	0.33
Rule of Law	0.69	0.24	0.57	0.19	0.70	0.24	0.58	0.25
Cost to export (and import)	0.64	0.27	0.54	0.20	0.68	0.31	0.46	0.24
Capital-labor ratio (K/L)	0.61	0.32	0.37	0.34	0.66	0.32	0.43	0.31
Real GDP per capita (rgdpl)	0.66	0.30	0.55	0.23	0.68	0.33	0.51	0.28
FVA share	0.16	0.64	0.15	0.54	0.16	0.68	0.16	0.48
KLd/KLo	0.64	0.29	0.44	0.23	0.67	0.30	0.46	0.29
rgdpld/rgdplo	0.63	0.32	0.48	0.22	0.67	0.35	0.44	0.30

FDI = foreign direct investment, FVA = foreign value added, GDP = gross domestic product, GVC = global value chain.
Notes: Below (above) refers to group of economies with the value of the given economy's characteristic variable below (above) the median across all economies in the sample. The numbers shown in the columns refer to the average fraction of foreign affiliates that export and import in each group of economies, for all and each sector separately. The variables KLd/KLo and rgdpld/rgdplo refers to the capital-labor ratio and real GDP per capita, respectively, between the destination and origin economy. The variable FVA share is the bilateral foreign value added in exports from the host to source economy, as a share of gross bilateral exports.
Sources: ADB calculations using data from Antras, et al. (2012); Dun & Bradstreet. D&B Worldbase; Penn World Tables (8.0 and 8.1) http://www.wiod.org/database/seas13 (accessed July 2016); Wang, et al. (2014); World Bank. World Development Indicators. http://data.worldbank.org/data-catalog/world-development-indicators (accessed July 2016); and World Bank. Worldwide Governance Indicators. http://data.worldbank.org/data-catalog/worldwide-governance-indicators (accessed July 2016).

table are bilateral variables: an economy will have much more GVC–FDI if the foreign value added in their exports to the source economy—in which the parent company is located—is high, and their capital–labor ratios and real GDP per capita are lower than in the source economy.

Table 6.16 is an exhaustive list of averaged characteristics for two groups of foreign-owned affiliates: those engaged in international trade and those that exclusively serve local markets. Characteristics can be grouped into variables related to an economy's integration, comparative advantage, institutional environment (governance), and policy (business environment). In addition, given the interest in exploring the link between GVC–FDI and GVC–trade, characteristics are considered as relating to engagement and position in the value chain.

Several differences are striking. First, foreign-owned affiliates engaged in international trade are located in economies with substantially lower costs to export and import, as measured by a range of metrics from the World Bank's World Development Indicators and Ease of Doing Business indicators. Tariffs, at least in aggregate, do not seem to play a major role in attracting GVC–FDI.

Second, on comparative advantage, plants engaged in international trade are located in relatively poorer economies with abundant unskilled labor. This is in line with the findings of the literature on horizontal versus vertical FDI. Moreover, these host economies are at a substantially lower development stage, and have less capital than the economies where the multinational is headquartered. Figure 6.13a shows in more detail the relationship between the difference in real GDP per capita between host and source economy and the fraction of foreign affiliates engaged in international trade. On average, a source economy with double the income of the host economy has a 17% larger fraction of GVC–FDI as a share of the total number of affiliates from the same source that exports and imports. Additionally, Figure 6.13b shows that the distance between host and source markets, decrease the amount of GVC–FDI—economies twice as far apart have 12% fewer affiliates engaged in GVC–FDI. This has important implications on the role greater integration and trade facilitation measures play in promoting GVC–FDI, and enabling economies to link to international production networks.

Broadly, the region's economies have worked to lower trade barriers and facilitate trade—as reflected by generally improving scores of the ease of "trading across borders" component of Ease of Doing Business indicators (World Bank 2016). In Central Asia for example, Azerbaijan introduced an electronic system

Table 6.16: GVC–FDI and Average Country Characteristics

	Imports and Exports	Only Domestic Sale
Integration variables		
Trade restrictiveness index	0.05	0.05
Burden of custom process	4.43	4.77
Cost to export ($ per container)	577	752
Cost to import ($ per container)	622	804
Number of documents to export	6.74	5.24
Number of documents to import	5.35	5.83
Logistics performance index	3.48	3.57
Quality of port infrastructure	4.55	4.93
Applied tariff rate	3.53	2.48
RTAs	0.34	0.36
BITs	0.55	0.38
BITs, investor-state dispute mechanism	1.9	1.7
DTTs	0.91	0.78
Comparative advantage variables		
Real GDP per capita (rgdpl)	13,006	24,227
Capital-labor ratio	76,379	156,101
Average years schooling	7.61	8.73
Log rgdpl, host relative to source	–1.32	–0.75
Log capital-labor ratio, host relative to source	–1.51	–0.78
Institutional variables		
Rule of law	–0.09	0.68
Regulatory quality	0.05	0.76
Government effectiveness	0.27	0.87
Control of corruption	–0.05	0.69
Political stability	–0.29	0.23
Voice and accountability	–0.95	0.12
Policy Variables		
Days required to enforce a contract	390	353
Nuber of processes to register a business start-up	6.6	4.45
Cost of business start-up procedure (% of GNI)	8.6	4.7
Days to get electricity	57.9	58.9
Days required to register property	27.1	16.4
Days required to start business	17.1	8.2
Time spent dealing with regulations	0.9	0.9
Hours required to prepare and pay taxes	304	168
Private credit (% of GDP)	0.46	0.91
GVC-trade variables		
DVA share	0.72	0.79
FVA share	0.21	0.16
Export upstreamness (overall)	1.97	2.2

BIT = bilateral investment agreement, DTT = double taxation treaty, DVA = domestic value added, GDP = gross domestic product, GNI = gross national income, GVC = global value chain, RTA = regional trade agreement.
Notes: "Time spent dealing with regulations" is the time spent dealing with government regulations measured in percentage of senior management time. DVA share and FVA shares refer to the domestic and foreign value added, respectively, as a share of gross exports, at the bilateral level.
Source: ADB calculations using data from ADB Multi-Regional Input-Output Tables and methodology by Wang, Wei, and Zhu (2014); ADB. Asia Regional Integration Center FTA Database. https://aric.adb.org/fta (accessed September 2016); Antras, et al. (2012); Barro and Lee (2013); Beck, et al. (2009); Chaisse and Bellak (2015); Kee, et al. (2009); Dun & Bradstreet. D&B Worldbase; Penn World Tables (8.0 and 8.1) http://www.wiod.org/database/seas13 (accessed July 2016); World Bank. Ease of Doing Business Indicators http://www.doingbusiness.org/rankings (accessed July 2016); World Bank. World Development Indicators. http://data.worldbank.org/data-catalog/world-development-indicators (accessed July 2016); and World Bank. Worldwide Governance Indicators. http:// data.worldbank.org/data-catalog/worldwide-governance-indicators (accessed July 2016).

Figure 6.13: Comparative Advantage, Geography, and GVC-FDI

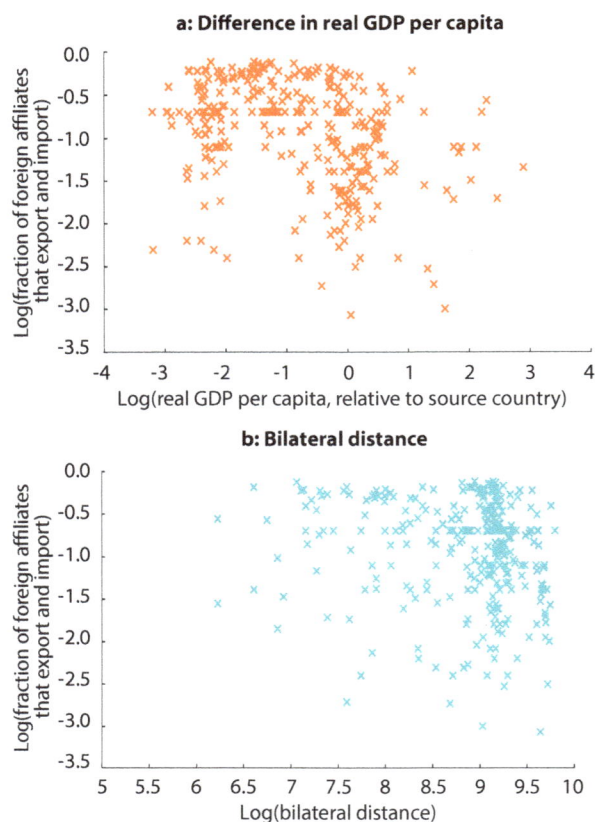

FDI = foreign direct investment, GDP = gross domestic product, GVC = global value chain.
Notes: The y-axis variable i is the number of affiliates in "country" c belonging to parents in n that export, as a share of total affiliates in country c belonging to parents in n. The x-axis variable is the log(real GDP per capita) and log(bilateral distance) for panels a and b, respectively, of the host relative to the source economy. In all cases origin and destination countries are different (c ≠ n). The OLS coefficient for a fitted line is -0.17 (standard error: 0.03) for the top chart and -0.12 (standard error: 0.05) for the bottom panel chart.
Sources: ADB calculations using data from ADB Multiregional Input-Output Tables; and methodology by Wang, Wei, and Zhu (2014); Institute for Research on the International Economy. http://www.cepii.fr/ CEPII/en/cepii/cepii.asp (accessed July 2016); Penn World Tables 8.1 http://www.wiod.org/database/seas13 (accessed July 2016); and World Bank. World Development Indicators. http://data.worldbank.org/data-catalog/world-development-indicators (accessed July 2016).

for submitting export and import declarations, while Georgia improved its electronic document processing. Kazakhstan reduced documentary requirements for customs clearance. The Kyrgyz Republic's accession to the Eurasian Economic Union must have contributed to reducing the time and cost of regional trade. In South Asia, India simplified border and documentary procedures and launched its ICEGATE portal. Nepal implemented an electronic data interchange system, while Pakistan enhanced its electronic customs platform. Similarly, in Southeast Asia, Viet Nam implemented an electronic customs clearance system.

Third, the institutional variables capturing governance of the host economy are on average, lower where foreign affiliates that trade are located. The relationship with variables on "doing business" is similar. This is intuitive, as firms care more about the "rule of law" when their activities are directly linked to the domestic market. If their main activity is to export, the institutional environment may matter less—particularly as affiliates may be "shielded" from the regulatory and business

environment of the host economy through special legislation and SEZs. On the flip side, multinationals may wish to avoid stringent domestic regulations, creating a "race to the bottom" among economies competing to attract GVC–FDI. Greater regional cooperation in harmonizing the tax and regulatory environment, for example, would help.

SEZs have been widely used in developing Asia as valuable tool of trade and investment policy. They have enabled many of the region's economies integrate with GVCs, especially in labor-intensive manufacturing (Box 6.3). Even with a relatively low number of observations, more

Box 6.3: Special Economic Zones as Instruments for Attracting FDI—Case Study from Thailand

Foreign direct investment (FDI) has been a catalyst of Thailand's industrial development since the 1980s. FDI brings in capital and jobs, but also new technology, along with managerial and organizational know-how. These flow into domestic industries through backward and forward linkages. The strategy succeeded in positioning Thailand as a regional FDI host, with low production costs and a rich source of relatively skilled workers.

However, Thailand's competitiveness in attracting FDI has deteriorated markedly since the 2008/09 global financial crisis. Several factors account for the decline—most notably escalating labor costs, political uncertainty, and the rise of the People's Republic of China (PRC) and India as competing FDI destinations. Thailand's share of inward FDI in gross fixed capital formation in Asia was 11.0% in 2015, noticeably lower than its 13.7% average during 2005–2007 (box table). The economic downturn of major investors such as the European Union, Japan, and the United States also contributed to the slowdown. These challenges have pressured the country to revive its FDI competitiveness. In 2015, Thailand planned to develop 10 special economic zones (SEZs) in Tak, Sa Kaeo, Trat, Mukdahan, Songkhla, Chiang Rai, Kanchanaburi, Narathiwat, Nakhon Phanom, and Nong Khai. The SEZs are located at border areas and offer investors generous financial incentives, comprehensive trade facilitation measures, and government efforts to ramp up physical and institutional infrastructure.

The SEZs provide firms with incentives that include a reduction in the corporate tax rate for up to 8 years (with the possibility of extension), machinery and raw material import duty exemptions, export duty exemptions, double deductions from the costs of transportation, electricity, and water supply for 10 years, and

Inward FDI (% of gross fixed capital formation)

Economy	2005–2007 (Pre-GFC annual average)	2013	2014	2015
Thailand	13.7	15.6	3.5	11.0
Indonesia	6.1	6.4	7.5	5.4
Malaysia	16.4	14.1	12.4	14.3
Southeast Asia	21.1	18.6	18.1	18.6
Developing Asia	11.0	6.2	6.3	7.4
Developing Economies	11.8	7.6	7.6	8.7
World	11.6	7.8	6.7	9.9

FDI = foreign direct investment, GFC = global financial crisis.
Source: UNCTAD (2016).

other non-tax incentives such as exclusive rights to employ foreign workers from neighboring countries, low interest rate loans, and rights to rent land. The ability to employ foreign labor is a key incentive for firms to set up plants within these border SEZs.

The Thailand case shows clearly how the provision of adequate infrastructure and related services is a prerequisite to attracting FDI into the SEZs. Investors can benefit from the cost-effective and reliable industrial facilities in the zones. The government supports firms by improving infrastructure and has set aside over $200 million to improve physical transportation infrastructure, check points, and other public utilities. For example, the second Thailand-Myanmar Friendship Bridge, scheduled to be completed in 2017, will help reduce traffic congestion and

Box 6.3 continued

speed up border-crossing at the Tak SEZ. The transportation budget for building roads, bridges, railways, ports, and airports has reached $137 million, while budgeted expenditures for improving customs checkpoints is about $53 million. The SEZs also use the one-stop service center approach to work permits, investment applications, and other issuance procedures in each SEZ. Permits for foreign workers can be granted within 1 working day and investment application approvals must be made before a maximum 40 working days.

The SEZs' strategic border locations allow firms to leverage complementary features of neighboring economies. Specifically, border SEZs allow firms to combine sources of comparative advantage present on both sides of the border, such as low-cost labor from Myanmar and the quality facilities in Thailand. In addition to labor inputs, firms can use the abundant agricultural and fishery products in Myanmar and process these using Thailand's more efficient factories and improved transportation facilities. The ongoing agenda of cross-border collaboration to reduce cross-border trade costs and improve transportation will also help firms benefit from the complementarities in these locations.

Thailand's SEZs also heighten the overall attractiveness of Association of Southeast Asian Nations (ASEAN) as an inclusive production hub. Thailand's SEZs could complement production chains and enhance regional integration, given that current SEZs in Cambodia, the Lao People's Democratic Republic, and Myanmar face constraints—a lack of skilled labor, unreliable and costly logistics and utilities, and weak institutional transparency.

The availability of relatively skilled labor and facilities also make the entire region more viable for manufacturing. Most investors in these neighboring SEZs are from the PRC, Thailand, and Viet Nam.

While these SEZs hold great potential to rejuvenate FDI inflows to Thailand, their optimal economic gains can be limited due to a lack of training, preferential policies given to large firms, and land grabbing issues. Many large investments are from high value-added sectors, which require high-quality labor. The government could partner with the private sector to coordinate training and match fields in technical vocational education and training with accurate market information. Certain rules for operating in the SEZs are restrictive, such as Board of Investment applications that require detailed tax documents and strict business plans, and timelines that tend to favor large over smaller enterprises. Small and medium-size enterprises, both foreign and local, require more flexibility, especially given their importance in amplifying economic gains through backward and forward linkages.

When the location for an SEZ is announced, land speculation leads to price escalation, which can weaken its attractiveness. The Industrial Estate Authority of Thailand, for instance, could play a bigger role in limiting these effects, by providing knowledge and tools in price control and land allocation. With the right policy tools, the SEZs could successfully revive FDI inflows to Thailand and to the ASEAN more generally, most importantly supporting strong business development at home and within the region.

SEZs are associated with more GVC–FDI (Table 6.17). In contrast, bilateral regional trade agreements do not seem to play a major role in attracting GVC–FDI. But bilateral investment treaties (BITs)—particularly with dispute settlement provisions—and double taxation treaties (DTT) do attract more.

Finally, trade-oriented foreign affiliates are mostly located in economies where exports are concentrated in more downstream activities with less domestic and more foreign value added.

Figure 6.14 explore in more detail the relationship between GVC–trade and GVC–FDI. GVC–trade

Table 6.17: Special Economic Zones and GVC-FDI

	Number of SEZ	SEZ per km²	GVC-FDI (%)
Bangladesh	8	0.00006	10
Cambodia	14	0.00008	41
India	199	0.00007	47
Kazakhstan	10	0.000004	100
PRC	1,475	0.00016	82
Philippines	312	0.001041	66
Sri Lanka	12	0.00019	36

PRC = People's Republic of China, FDI = foreign direct investment, GVC = global value chain, km² = square kilometer, SEZ = special economic zones.
Notes: The number of SEZs is for 2014. GVC–FDI refers to the fraction of foreign affiliates in the economy that exports.
Sources: ADB calculations using data from Dun & Bradstreet. D&B Worldbase; and ADB (2015).

is measured in four ways: (i) bilateral DVA share; (ii) bilateral FVA share; (iii) differences in export upstreamness between host and source economies; and (iv) differences in the average DVA share (with all trading partners) between host and source economies.

Figures 6.14a and 6.14b show two sides of the same coin. The DVA content of exports in the host economy is negatively correlated with the fraction of trade-oriented foreign plants at the bilateral level, whereas the opposite is true for FVA. When an economy is part of a twice as fragmented a GVC, manifested in a lower DVA (and higher FVA), it attracts three times larger share of affiliates engaged in GVC–FDI; if FVA shares are considered instead, the magnitude of the effect is 55% higher.

Moreover, Figure 6.14c shows that the less upstream exports of the host are to the affiliates' source economy, the greater the GVC–FDI activity of those affiliates in the host economy. Conversely, those with a small share of GVC–FDI have exports in more upstream sectors than the source economy. The effects are large—increasing the difference in export upstreamness from the median to the 99th percentile implies a 30% increase in the fraction of trade-oriented foreign affiliates. Finally, if one looks at the differences in DVA shares between exports of the host relative to the source economy of the affiliates, the results are similar—the lower the share of domestic value added embedded in exports of the affiliates in the host economy, the higher the fraction of affiliates engaged in GVC–FDI. All this evidence is extremely suggestive of trade-oriented affiliates of multinationals being part of the GVC.

Figure 6.14: GVC–Trade and GVC–FDI, Bilateral Level

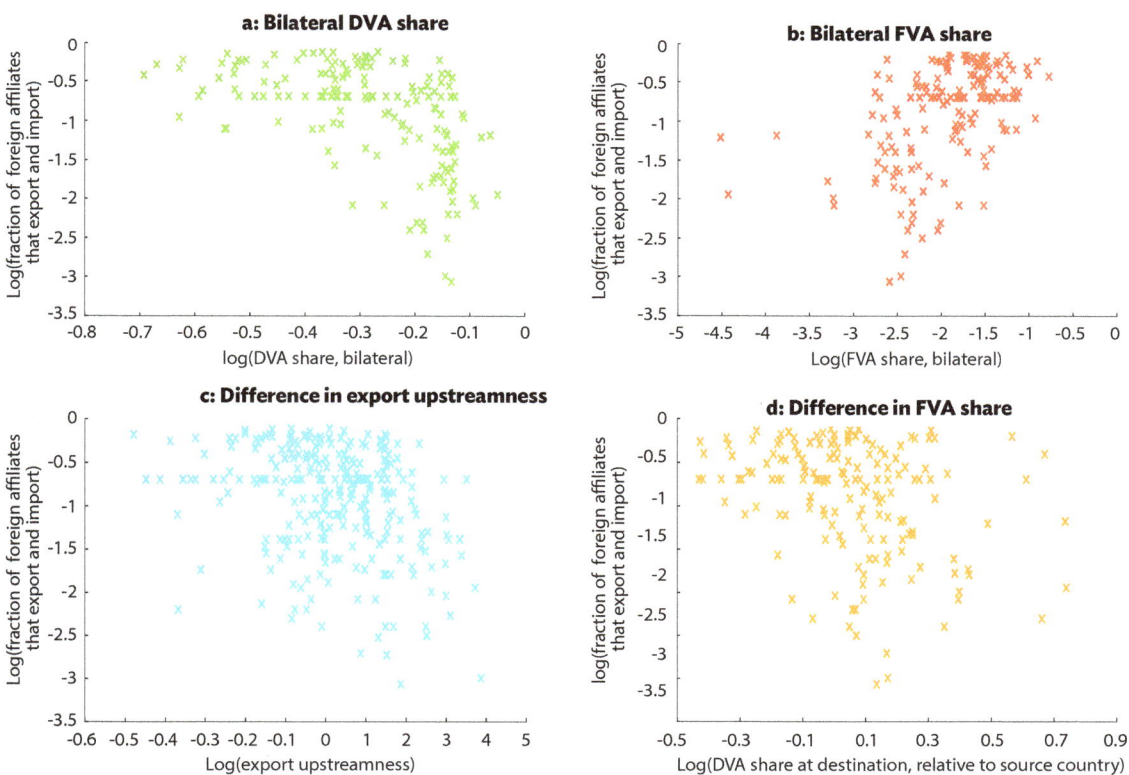

DVA = domestic value added, FDI = foreign direct investment, FVA = foreign value added, GDP = gross domestic product, GVC = global value chain, OLS = ordinary least square, .

Notes: The y-axis variable i is the number of affiliates in "country" c belonging to parents in n that export, as a share of total affiliates in country c belonging to parents in n. The x-axis variable is the domestic value added (DVA)—foreign value added (FVA)—of exports from c to n, as a share of gross exports from c to n in Figure 6.14a (Figure 6.14b, resp.), the ratio of export upstreamness of host to source country in Figure 6.14c, and the ratio of DVA shares of host relative to source country in Figure 6.14d. In all cases origin and destination countries are different (c z n). The OLS coefficient for a fitted line is -0.17 (standard error 0.03) for the left panel chart and -0.12 (standard error 0.05) for the right panel chart. In all cases origin and destination countries are different (c ≠ n). The OLS coefficient for a fitted line is -0.17 (standard error 0.03) for the left panel chart and -0.12 (standard error 0.05) for the right panel chart.

Sources: ADB calculations using data from ADB Multiregional Input-Output Tables and methodology by Wang, Wei, and Zhu (2014); Antras, et al. (2012); Dun & Bradstreet. D&B Worldbase; and World Bank. World Development Indicators. http://data.worldbank.org/data-catalog/world-development-indicators (accessed July 2016).

Regression analysis by economy and industry characteristics

Regression analysis of the determinants of GVC–FDI by Asian economy starts by using a dummy variable that indicates whether exports and imports are present (1) or not (0). Most establishments have both sides of international trade flows; only a few observations export or import only. This regression (Table 6.18) captures domestic versus trade-oriented activities at the affiliate level and informs the salient features on the literature on horizontal versus vertical FDI.

Controls in this regression include variables for affiliates, different economies, and bilateral pairs, while industry factors are absorbed by industry effects. Among the economy's variables included are those related to integration, institutional, and comparative advantage, and variables related to GVC–trade—the level of upstreamness of exports, and the share of domestic value added in exports.

The results indicate that foreign-owned affiliates engaged in international trade activities are consistently larger than those devoted exclusively to serve their market of operations: a plant with 10% more sales than

Table 6.18: Determinants of GVC–FDI—Economy Characteristics

Dependent Variable: D(exports>0 and imports >0)	(1)	(2)	(3)	(4)	(5)
Log(affiliate) sales	0.038***	0.036***	0.037***	0.044***	0.038***
Log(real GDP)	−0.030***	−0.092***	0.013***	−0.059***	0.032***
Log(real GDP per capita)	0.714***	0.095	0.671***	0.940***	0.150**
Log(KL)	−0.495***	−0.173*	−0.777***	−1.056***	−0.525***
Log(years of schooling)	−0.010*	−0.029***	0.021***	0.053***	0.118***
Rule of law	−0.296***				
Private credit		0.227***			
TRI			−3.446***		
Export upstreamness				−0.548***	
× KL				0.009*	
Exporter DVA share					−1.034***
D(Asian GUH)	0.118	−0.009	0.032	−0.190**	0.124
× Rule of law	0.012				
× Log(real GDP per capita)	−0.012				
× Private credit		0.003			
× TRI			−0.097		
× Export upstreamness				0.108***	
× Exporter DVA share					−0.151
Number of observations	17,126	8,581	15,458	12,256	14,344
R-squared	0.351	0.283	0.355	0.200	0.375
Sample	foreign	foreign	foreign	foreign	foreign

*** = significant at 1%, ** = significant at 5%, * = significant at 10%.
DVA = domestic value added, FDI = foreign direct investment, GDP = gross domestic product, GUH = global ultimate headquarters, GVC = global value chain, KL = capital-labor ratio, TRI = trade restrictiveness index.
Notes: The dependent variable is a dummy variable equal to 1 if the plant reports export and import activity. The economy-level variables are for the economy where the plant is located. The variable "private credit" refers to private credit as share of GDP. The variable "export upstreamness" refers to the level of export upstreamness of the host economy. DVA is calculated as a share of gross exports of the destination economy, at the economy level, an average across years, for all sectors. The dummy D(Asian GUH) equal to 1 if the plant belongs to a GUH in Asia. KL indicates the log(capital intensity), with respect to labor, of the industry of the affiliate. Domestic plants which are also GUHs are excluded. All specifications with affiliate industry fixed effects.
Sources: ADB calculations using data from ADB Multiregional Input-Output Tables and methodology by Wang, Wei, and Zhu (2014); Antras, et al. (2012); Barro and Lee (2013); Beck et al. (2009); Dun & Bradstreet. D&B Worldbase; Kee, et al. (2009); Penn World Tables (8.0 and 8.1) http://www.wiod.org/database/seas13 (accessed July 2016); World Bank. World Development Indicators. http://data.worldbank.org/data-catalog/world-developmentindicators (accessed July 2016); and World Bank. Worldwide Governance Indicators. http://data.worldbank.org/data-catalog/ worldwide-governance-indicators (accessed July 2016).

another is 30% more likely to be engaged in international trade activities.

A higher capital–labor ratio at host economy is associated with less trade-engaged plants. This suggests that in Asia, GVC–FDI seeks labor-abundant economies. The quality of institutions, captured by the rule of law index, is an important factor in creating plants oriented to serving the domestic market. The availability of private credit in an economy also seems to matter in attracting GVC–FDI. As expected, the degree of trade restrictiveness deters the creation of trade-oriented plants.

Turning to the factors related to GVC trade, the estimates suggest that economies with exports in more upstream sectors are less likely to have trade-oriented plants. For instance, when export upstreamness goes from the 50th percentile to the 95th percentile (this is like giving Japan the levels of export upstreamness of a commodity dependent economy such as Australia), the probability of observing a trade-oriented foreign plant decreases by more than 35%. Similarly, the DVA share of an economy's exports is associated negatively with the presence of GVC–FDI: an increase in the DVA bilateral share from the median (0.74) to the 95th percentile (0.88)—this is like increasing the DVA share in bilateral exports from India to the PRC to the DVA the share in bilateral exports from India to Japan—is associated with a decrease in GVC–FDI of 16%.

The last rows of Table 6.18 explore more systematically the differences in the impact of an economy's variables covering the origin of the affiliates' GUHs. Once the host-market characteristics are controlled in the analysis, the coefficient on the dummy indicating Asian and non-Asian affiliates is either negative or insignificant. That contrasts with the descriptive analysis showing that Asian multinationals are more likely to engage in GVC–FDI. The result, most likely, points to a selection effect: Asian GUHs choose to locate their affiliates in markets that are friendlier to trade; once those characteristics are controlled, there is nothing advantageous about being an affiliate of an Asian corporation in terms of engagement in GVC–FDI.

The variable that presents a significant difference between Asian-owned affiliates and other affiliates is the

level of export upstreamness of a receiving economy: the negative effect on GVC–FDI is significantly dampened for affiliates of Asian GUHs. That is, an economy with exports in more upstream sectors is not as likely to attract GVC–FDI, but this is less pronounced for affiliates belonging to an Asia GUH. Moreover, Asian-owned multinationals are also less likely to be attracted by differences in factor endowments while engaging in GVC–FDI (Table 6.18). These two facts suggest that Asian multinationals tend not to use other Asian economies as hubs for final assembly.

The investigation now turns to a standard relationship in the trade and multinational literature: the gravity equation. This equation states that the flow of FDI (or goods) between two economies should be inversely proportional to bilateral resistance factors, such as geographical distance. Following state-of-the-art procedures in estimating the gravity model, the host and source economy factors are subsumed in two sets of an economy's fixed effects.

The regressions are meant to establish "gravity" facts for Asian economies, using direct measures of bilateral affiliates' activity, such as sales, and measures of bilateral GVC–FDI (Table 6.19). Specifications in all columns of the table are aggregated at the bilateral level; for example, the dependent variable in columns 1–3 is sales of affiliates in economy n belonging to GUHs in economy i. Moreover, the standard gravity specification is augmented by a variable related to GVC–trade: the bilateral DVA, embedded in gross exports from the host to the source economy of foreign affiliates (columns 3 and 6 in Table 6.19).

The effects of distance are negative and with a coefficient closer to 1, as found in the literature. However, the effect of distance loses significance in the case of GVC–FDI (columns 4–6 in Table 6.19), most likely because distance refers to proximity between the economy of the affiliate and the economy of its GUH, but exports (imports) can be to (from) any other economy. Sharing a language has a positive effect on the bilateral activity of affiliates of multinationals, as well as belonging to the same regional trade agreement, and having signed a DTT. The presence of a regional trade agreement or DTT between economies does not affect the fraction of

Table 6.19: Determinants of Bilateral FDI and GVC–FDI—Gravity Model

	Affiliate Sales			Fraction of Affiliates with Exports and Imports		
	(1)	**(2)**	**(3)**	**(4)**	**(5)**	**(6)**
Log(distance)	–1.360**	–1.360**	–1.093*	0.069	0.069	0.131
	(0.284)	(0.284)	(0.461)	(0.085)	(0.085)	(0.173)
D(shared language)	0.801**	0.801**	1.209*	0.071	0.071	0.039
	(0.296)	(0.296)	(0.548)	(0.099)	(0.099)	(0.162)
D(shared colonial past)	0.349	0.349	–0.211	–0.047	–0.047	–0.096
	(0.400)	(0.400)	(0.510)	(0.113)	(0.113)	(0.147)
D(RTA)	1.724**	1.724**	1.347**	0.013	0.013	–0.005
	(0.276)	(0.276)	(0.452)	(0.108)	(0.108)	(0.168)
D(DTT)	0.621*	0.621*	0.389	0.115	0.115	0.009
	(0.282)	(0.282)	(0.403)	(0.092)	(0.092)	(0.123)
D(BIT)	–0.296	–0.296	0.527	–0.228**	–0.228**	–0.301*
	(0.246)	(0.246)	(0.350)	(0.078)	(0.078)	(0.119)
Log($rgdpld/rgdplo$)	–7.398**			–0.675**		
	(1.633)			(0.068)		
KLd/KLo		–7.237**			–0.667**	
		(1.597)			(0.067)	
Log(DVA share)			3.347			–0.415
			(2.428)			(0.679)
Number of observations	409	409	205	331	331	1821
R-squared	0.735	0.735	0.753	0.592	0.592	0.634

** = significant at 5%, * = significant at 10%.
BIT = bilateral investment treaty, DVA = domestic value added, FDI = foreign direct investment, GVC = global value chain, RTA = regional trade agreement.
Notes: The dependent variable is a measure of the activity of affiliate of multinational firms, affiliate sales, as well as the number of foreign affiliates that export and import, as a share of the total number of foreign affiliates, from source economy i in host economy n. The variables KL_d/KL_o and $rgdpl_d/rgdpl_o$ refer respectively to the ratio of capital-labor ratio and real GDP per capita between the host and source country. The variable (log) DVA share refers to the DVA share in exports from the host economy of the affiliate to the source country, an average across years, for all sectors. All specifications with source and host fixed effects. Robust standard errors are in parentheses.
Sources: ADB calculations using data from ADB Multiregional Input-Output Tables and methodology by Wang, Wei, and Zhu (2014); ADB. Asia Regional Integration Center FTA Database. https://aric.adb.org/fta (accessed September 2016); Dun & Bradstreet. D&B Worldbase; Institute for Research on the International Economy. http://www.cepii.fr/CEPII/en/cepii/cepii.asp (accessed July 2016); Penn World Tables 8.0 http://www.wiod.org/database/seas13 (accessed July 2016); United Nations Conference on Trade and Development. Investment Policy Hub. http://investmentpolicyhub. unctad.org/IIA (accessed August 2016); World Bank. World Development Indicators. http://data.worldbank.org/data-catalog/ world-development-indicators (accessed July 2016); and World Bank. Worldwide Governance Indicators. http://data.worldbank.org/ data-catalog/worldwide-governance-indicators (accessed July 2016).

affiliates that are trade-oriented, and the presence of a BIT between two economies discourages trade-related affiliates' activities, favoring horizontal FDI instead.[59]

Income differences between source and host economies significantly encourage multinational activity when the host is the poorer economy and, as shown above, also encourage the trade-related activities of affiliates. Similarly, bilateral GVC–FDI increases with the labor abundance of the host economy relative to the source economy.

Industry factors affecting GVC–FDI are shown in Table 6.20. In these regressions, economy-level factors are subsumed in fixed effects. Similar to the economy-level analysis, GVC–FDI is attracted by less capital

---

[59]   This does not contradict findings in the descriptive analysis that show trade-oriented affiliates are located in economes that, on average, signed more BITs; the regression results, apart from including several other controls and being at the country-pair level, are about the intensive margin of GVC–FDI—i.e., BITs affect the fraction of trade-engaged affiliates.

Table 6.20: Determinants of GVC–FDI—Industry Variables

Dependent Variable: D(export>0 and import>0)	(1)	(2)	(3)
Log(affiliate sales)	0.049*** (0.003)	0.050*** (0.003)	0.050*** (0.003)
Log(KL)	-0.177** (0.083)	-0.056** (0.022)	-0.047** (0.022)
× Export upstreamness	0.060* (0.035)		
Log(SL)	-0.009 (0.024)	-0.008 (0.025)	-0.020 (0.026)
R&D	0.351 (0.330)	0.335 (0.351)	0.483 (0.344)
$D(dr_{ap} > 0 \ \& \ dr_{pa} > 0)$	0.026* (0.015)		
Average dr_{ap}		0.343 (0.340)	
Average dr_{pa}			0.807 (0.645)
D(Asian GUH)	-0.484*** (0.120)	-0.472*** (0.117)	-0.444*** (0.125)
× Log(KL)	0.055** (0.023)	0.053** (0.022)	0.047** (0.023)
× Average dr_{ap}		-0.224 (0.368)	
× Average dr_{pa}			-0.047 (0.755)
Number of observations	6,393	6,393	6,393
R-squared	0.220	0.219	0.220
Sample	foreign	foreign	foreign

*** = significant at 1%, ** = significant at 5%, * = significant at 10%.
FDI = foreign direct investment, GUH = global ultimate headquarters, GVC = global value chain, KL = capital–labor ratio, R&D = research and development, SL = skill intensity.
Notes: Estimated by ordinary least squares. The dependent variable is a dummy variable equal to 1 if the establishment reports export and import activity. The variable "KL" refers to the log of capital intensity of the industry, relative to labor, while SL refers to the log of skill intensity of the industry, relative to (unskilled) labor. The dummy $D(dr_{ap} > 0 \ \& \ dr_{pa} > 0)$ is equal to one when both direct requirement coefficients (i.e. when the affiliate is upstream and downstream of the parent) are higher than zero. Average dr_{ap} (dr_{pa}) refers to the average direct requirement coefficient of the industry of the affiliate, with respect to downstream (upstream) industries. The dummy D(Asian GUH) is 1 if the plant has an Asian GUH and includes only plants that are not GUH and in the manufacturing sector. All specifications with source and host fixed effects. Standard errors, clustered at the parent level, are in parentheses.
Sources: ADB calculations using data from ADB Multiregional Input-Output Tables and methodology by Wang, Wei, and Zhu (2014); Antras, et al. (2012); Bureau of Economic Analysis; Dun & Bradstreet. D&B Worldbase; National Bureau of Economic Research; Penn World Tables 8.0 http://www.wiod.org/database/seas13 (accessed July 2016).

intensive industries. Neither the skill-intensity of an industry nor the intensity of research and development seem to affect GVC–FDI. Meanwhile, industry input–output links between the affiliate and the parent are somewhat positively related to GVC–FDI. Distinguishing between Asian and non-Asian GUH does not affect the impact of input–output links on GVC–FDI, but there is a difference in the impact of capital intensity. Like the previous set of results on the impact of the characteristics of an economy, Asian GUHs are less attracted to labor-intensive industries. The coefficient on the dummy indicating the Asian origin of the GUH is significantly negative: while the descriptive analysis suggests otherwise, once the industry characteristics of the affiliate are controlled for in the analysis, being Asian decreases the likelihood that the affiliate is engaged in GVC–FDI. As in the previous set of regression results, the explanation can be based on selection: Asian multinationals choose to open affiliates in industries for which it is easier to engage in GVC–FDI; once the industry features are controlled, affiliates of Asian GUHs are more likely to be horizontal (which may be due to a better knowledge of the local Asian markets).

In sum, the regression anaysis indicates that GVC–FDI in Asia is concentrated in relatively larger plants compared with horizontal FDI. This is in line with the finding in the trade literature about exporters and importers. Relatively poorer, smaller, and labor-abundant economies are favored as hosts for foreign affiliates engaged in international trade. Those with less impediments to international trade are naturally more attractive locations for GVC–FDI, while economies with exports concentrated in more downstream sectors are also more attractive, particularly so for affiliates of non-Asian multinationals.

The rule of law does not seem to be a particularly important factor for attracting proportionally more plants engaged in GVC–FDI; the fact that trade-oriented plants are "shielded" from the institutional environment of the host economy—through special legislation and instruments such as SEZs—may be a key reason as discussed earlier. Still, good governance indicators are vital to attracting affiliates oriented to serve the host market of operations (horizontal FDI).

Industries and economies with a larger share of vertically linked domestic plants attract greater FDI in general, and GVC–FDI in particular.

Finally, we also find that the extent of production fragmentation among domestic manufacturing industries, as measured by the strength of input–output linkages between the industry of operation of the parents and affiliates, leads to greater GVC–FDI (Box 6.4). This analysis included both foreign-owned and domestically owned affiliates, and found in particular that industries and economies with a larger share of vertically linked domestic plants have a larger share of both foreign-owned affiliates and trade-oriented foreign-owned affiliates.

Box 6.4: Product Fragmentation and GVC–FDI: Regression Results

The relationship between engagement in global value chain–foreign direct investment (GVC–FDI) and the degree of production fragmentation within a corporation can be measured by the industry input–output links between the parent and the affiliate. The novel feature in this analysis is that the data allow to go a step beyond previous analysis, associating the production fragmentation observed between the parent and its affiliate directly with the trade activities of the affiliate. Analysis is restricted to manufacturing plants belonging to parents also operating in manufacturing. Plants with global ultimate headquarters (GUHs) in the same and different economy are included, but (domestic) plants that operate as their own GUH are excluded.

This part of the study provides a deeper exploration of an important characteristic of industries and industry-pairs—the strength of their links with other industries. The presence of stronger input-output links between two industries can allow more scope for production fragmentation and therefore offers greater potential to be part of the GVC.

The analysis presented in the box table below shows that first, domestic and foreign corporations concentrate activities in industries that are strongly related by input-output relationships; second, plants are larger when operating in industries that are important providers (recipients) of inputs to (outputs) from the industry of the headquarters, regardless of whether domestic and foreign; and third, at the industry-economy level, having more plants with strong input-output links with their parent (both domestic and foreign) is related to the presence of more plants engaged in international trade; and finally, industry and economies with a larger share of domestic plants with strong input-output links with their headquarters have a larger share of foreign plants (both trade and host-market oriented).

All in all, these results suggest that the larger the scope of industries (and economies) for production fragmentation, the larger their plants will be, and the more they are oriented toward international trade. The results also suggest that stronger GVCs among domestic firms in the host industry attracts more FDI, regardless whether it is horizontal or GVC–FDI.

Product Fragmentation and GVC–FDI: Regression Results

	Log(affiliate sales) (1)		Number of Affiliates that import and export (2)	Log (share of foreign affiliates) (3)	Log(share of trade-oriented foreign affiliates) (4)
dr_{ap}	0.221*** (0.087)				
dr_{pa}		0.286*** (0.098)			
Number of affiliates with $dr_{ap}>0$ & $dr_{pa}>0$			0.547*** (0.057)		
Log(share of domestic affiliates with $dr_{ap}>0$ & $dr_{pa}>0$)				0.279*** (0.066)	0.065* (0.057)
Number of observations	6787	6787	8741	451	407
R-squared	0.039	0.056	0.634	0.866	0.588
Sample	Foreign	Foreign	Foreign		

*** = significant at 1%, ** = significant at 5%, * = significant at 10%.
FDI = foreign direct investment, GVC = global value chain.
Notes: In columns (1) the dependent variable is at the firm level. In column (2), the dependent variable is the number of plants in operation in industry k_a and "country" c_a belonging to parents in industry k_p and country c_p. In column (3) and (4), the dependent variable refers to the share of affiliates operating in industry k and economy n. Average dr_{ap} (dr_{pa}) refers to the average direct requirement coefficient of the industry of the affiliate, with respect to downstream (upstream) industries. Only affiliate-parents in the manufacturing sector and only plants that are not their own parent companies are included. All specifications with source and host fixed effects. Estimated by ordinary least squares. Standard errors, clustered at the parent level, in parentheses.
Sources: ADB calculations using data from ADB Multiregional Input-Output Tables and methodology by Wang, Wei, and Zhu (2014); Bureau of Economic Analysis; Dun & Bradstreet. D&B Worldbase.

FDI Drivers by Mode of Entry

The two FDI modes of entry may have different welfare effects in host economies because of their distinctive characteristics.

The question is then to understand how policy and institutional factors affect the mode of entry so that policy makers can properly design frameworks to attract the type of FDI that is more appropriate to their economy, and particularly orient multinationals to choose one mode of entry over the other (Byun et al. 2012).[60] Moreover, it is particularly interesting from a policy perspective to investigate how these factors impact the multinationals' decision to invest through a certain entry mode depending on the sector, as well as how they depend on the developmental distance between the source and host.

In this discussion, institutional quality is measured through the Worldwide Governance Indicators, and the policy environment through World Bank's Ease of Doing Business indicators (see Annex 6a for the list of economies with available data). For integration, a separate regression analysis tests for the impact of regional trade agreements and bilateral investment treaties.

Governance is the most important factor for attracting FDI, particularly M&As, and especially when the source is a high-income economy.

The analysis based on gravity modelling (Annex 6b) offers some new findings. Firstly, the quality of local governance exerts a highly significant positive effect on FDI, irrespective of mode (greenfield versus M&A) and regardless of the relative income of source or host economy. The effect on M&As is more pronounced

than that of greenfield, which is not surprising given that M&As are the more common mode of entry for market-seeking multinationals as discussed in the next section. The impact is especially pronounced for multinationals from high income economies investing in developing economies (Table 6.21).

Exploring in further detail, multinationals from high-income economies are demonstrably more responsive to the quality of governance in developing economies than multinationals from emerging economies. This is in line with similar findings in the literature, based on individual or comparative studies, that multinationals from emerging economies are less constrained by poor institutional environments. The empirical analysis in this chapter is the first to confirm this in a cross-economy context. However, this distinction between high-income and emerging-economy sources does not hold for Asian host economies, indicating that governance matters in the Asian context regardless of the developmental distance with the source economy. Based on this analysis, an example would be that if governance in the Philippines improved to the level of Malaysia, all else being equal, it would have received 80% more greenfield FDI and 120% more M&As from high-income economies over 2003–2015.

When governance is disaggregated into various dimensions (sub-indicators), it is found across all sub-indicators that governance is less of a factor in attracting multinationals from emerging economies. The most critical governance sub-indicators for FDI attraction from high-income economies to developing ones are "regulatory quality" and "government effectiveness" for both greenfield investments and M&As, and especially for Asian hosts (Table 6.22).

Trends in FDI and governance indicators may bear this out. Among the five Asian subregions, economies in East Asia on average rank the highest in WGI's measures of "government effectiveness" and "regulatory quality", the two governance subcomponents that the regression analysis found most important for FDI attraction. Economies in Southeast Asia, on average, also perform well in terms of scores for "government effectiveness" and "regulatory quality". In addition, since 1998 both the subregions have improved significantly in most of the six governance dimensions, especially the two

---

60 Wang and Wong (2009) find that greenfield FDI promotes economic growth while M&As promote growth only when the host country has adequate human capital. Harms and Méon (2011) also find that while greenfield investment substantially enhances growth, M&As have no effect, at best. But Ashraf et al. (2015) find that greenfield FDI has no statistically significant effect on total factor productivity (TFP), while M&As have a positive effect on TFP in the sample of both developed and developing host economies of FDI.

Table 6.21: The effect of Governance and Business Environment on FDI

	Greenfield investment						Cross-border M&A					
	High-income Economies (Source)			Emerging Economies (Source)			High-income Economies (Source)			Emerging Economies (Source)		
	Host			Host			Host			Host		
	High-income (1)	Developing (2)	Asia (3)	High-income (4)	Developing (5)	Asia (6)	High-income (7)	Developing (8)	Asia (9)	High-income (10)	Developing (11)	Asia (12)
Overall Ease of Doing Business Index - host (expected sign = plus)	0.005	0.022***	0.044***	-0.002	-0.001	-0.004	0.001	0.009	-0.000	-0.008	-0.023	-0.028
	(0.011)	(0.007)	(0.012)	(0.014)	(0.010)	(0.010)	(0.011)	(0.006)	(0.015)	(0.013)	(0.016)	(0.018)
Overall World Governance Index - host (expected sign = plus)	0.026***	0.043***	0.033***	0.031*	0.021***	0.035***	0.051***	0.074***	0.071***	0.053***	0.049***	0.082***
	(0.010)	(0.005)	(0.010)	(0.018)	(0.007)	(0.009)	(0.012)	(0.008)	(0.009)	(0.013)	(0.010)	(0.017)
RTA between source and host (= 1 if yes)	0.393**	0.081	0.347***	-0.193	0.676***	0.956***	0.746***	-0.322**	0.317	0.244	0.619***	0.365
	(0.157)	(0.110)	(0.119)	(0.275)	(0.143)	(0.166)	(0.161)	(0.131)	(0.202)	(0.209)	(0.175)	(0.283)
BIT between source and host (= 1 if yes)	0.319**	-0.118	0.051	0.012	0.797***	0.814***	-0.341**	-0.292**	-0.152	0.057	1.132***	0.706**
	(0.160)	(0.103)	(0.148)	(0.245)	(0.163)	(0.178)	(0.165)	(0.123)	(0.199)	(0.189)	(0.188)	(0.275)
log(Population-host)	0.758***	0.924***	0.693***	0.804***	0.467***	0.317***	0.760***	1.020***	0.809***	0.692***	0.516***	0.314***
	(0.048)	(0.021)	(0.031)	(0.078)	(0.033)	(0.038)	(0.042)	(0.040)	(0.058)	(0.061)	(0.044)	(0.059)
log(PCGDP-host)	0.248	0.413***	-0.062	0.646***	0.313***	0.002	-0.052	0.459***	0.275*	0.307	0.324***	0.237
	(0.178)	(0.061)	(0.087)	(0.195)	(0.085)	(0.104)	(0.192)	(0.085)	(0.151)	(0.193)	(0.110)	(0.197)
Growth Rate-host	0.087***	0.021*	0.236***	0.125***	0.005	0.083***	-0.077***	-0.048**	0.109***	0.002	-0.114***	0.088**
	(0.020)	(0.011)	(0.026)	(0.026)	(0.020)	(0.025)	(0.027)	(0.019)	(0.033)	(0.043)	(0.037)	(0.044)
Inflation Rate-host	0.167***	-0.024**	-0.037*	0.224***	0.002	-0.016	0.143***	-0.010	0.033	0.162***	-0.006	0.063*
	(0.027)	(0.009)	(0.022)	(0.033)	(0.010)	(0.024)	(0.039)	(0.011)	(0.022)	(0.045)	(0.013)	(0.034)
log(Distance between source and host)	0.094	-0.651***	0.177	-0.566**	-0.471***	-0.299**	0.066	-1.177***	0.085	-0.493***	-0.633***	-0.311**
	(0.118)	(0.078)	(0.147)	(0.247)	(0.102)	(0.145)	(0.124)	(0.091)	(0.191)	(0.150)	(0.100)	(0.153)
Common language (=1 if yes)	0.754***	0.609***	0.705***	0.565***	0.927***	0.601***	0.749***	0.972***	0.365*	1.529***	1.081***	0.768**
	(0.200)	(0.115)	(0.154)	(0.255)	(0.183)	(0.165)	(0.201)	(0.171)	(0.211)	(0.298)	(0.213)	(0.299)
Contiguity (=1 if yes)	0.474*	-0.250	1.342***	0.500	0.655***	0.578***	0.301	-1.182***	2.556***	0.440	0.979***	0.859**
	(0.244)	(0.180)	(0.414)	(0.350)	(0.158)	(0.185)	(0.222)	(0.371)	(0.521)	(0.290)	(0.211)	(0.337)
Constant	-14.535***	-13.506***	-18.538***	-17.457***	-7.450***	-6.173***	-17.414***	-17.460***	-21.755***	-14.333***	-8.206***	-10.351***
	(1.762)	(0.661)	(1.722)	(2.412)	(1.256)	(1.512)	(2.045)	(1.106)	(2.503)	(2.439)	(1.470)	(2.297)
Number of observation	3096	6792	1992	1290	2830	830	3096	6792	1880	1290	2830	830
R-squared	0.641	0.841	0.892	0.610	0.543	0.628	0.696	0.798	0.868	0.636	0.527	0.687

*** = significant at 1%, ** = significant at 5%, * = significant at 10%.

BIT = bilateral investment treaty, FDI = foreign direct investment, M&A = merger and acquisition, PCGDP = GDP per capita, RTA = regional trade agreement.

Notes: Estimates are obtained with Poisson Pseudo-Maximum Likelihood (PPML) estimator. Source country-period fixed effects and period fixed effects are included but not shown for brevity. Standard errors are in parenthesis are based on clustering by country-pair.

Sources: ADB calculations using data from Bureau van Dijk. Zephyr M&A Database; Financial Times. fDi Markets; Institute for Research on the International Economy. http://www.cepii.fr/CEPII/en/cepii/cepii.asp (accessed July 2016); World Bank. Ease of Doing Business Indicators http://www.doingbusiness.org/rankings (accessed July 2016); World Bank. World Development Indicators. http://data.worldbank.org/data-catalog/world-developmentindicators (accessed July 2016); and World Bank. Worldwide Governance Indicators. http://data.worldbank.org/data-catalog/worldwide-governance-indicators (accessed July 2016).

subcomponents most important for attracting FDI. In contrast, most economies in Central Asia and Pacific lag significantly behind the rest of developing Asia across most dimensions of governance, including "government effectiveness" and "regulatory quality". Given these empirical results, which show the importance of governance, for any reforms aimed at attracting FDI as a development strategy these economies would need to work toward improving governance.

Comparison across sectors shows that, irrespective of entry mode, multinationals from high-income economies and emerging economies are less responsive to local governance quality when they invest in natural resources than when they invest in services or manufacturing. This too is in line with expectations, given the extractive nature of investments in natural resources (Table 6.23).

Table 6.22: Effects of "Sub-indicators of Governance" on FDI

	Source	Host	(1) Average WGI	(2) Voice and Accountability	(3) Political Stability	(4) Government Effectiveness	(5) Regulatory Quality	(6) Rule of Law	(7) Control Corruption
Greenfield investment	High-income	High-income	0.032*** (0.006)	0.002 (0.005)	0.013*** (0.005)	0.031*** (0.005)	0.042*** (0.007)	0.032*** (0.007)	0.026*** (0.004)
		Developing	0.048*** (0.004)	0.017*** (0.003)	0.025*** (0.004)	0.039*** (0.004)	0.046*** (0.004)	0.030*** (0.003)	0.027*** (0.004)
	Emerging	High-income	0.028** (0.012)	-0.007 (0.007)	0.014* (0.008)	0.029*** (0.007)	0.039*** (0.013)	0.032** (0.015)	0.032*** (0.007)
		Developing	0.020*** (0.006)	0.011*** (0.004)	0.015*** (0.005)	0.005 (0.006)	0.020*** (0.005)	0.004 (0.005)	0.008* (0.005)
Cross-border M&A	High-income	High-income	0.050*** (0.007)	0.043*** (0.006)	-0.002 (0.005)	0.037*** (0.006)	0.060*** (0.008)	0.045*** (0.007)	0.037*** (0.006)
		Developing	0.074*** (0.007)	0.036*** (0.005)	0.035*** (0.004)	0.051*** (0.007)	0.068*** (0.007)	0.047*** (0.006)	0.041*** (0.007)
	Emerging	High-income	0.046*** (0.011)	0.026*** (0.007)	-0.004 (0.007)	0.035*** (0.008)	0.061*** (0.012)	0.047*** (0.011)	0.031*** (0.008)
		Developing	0.040*** (0.008)	0.030*** (0.005)	0.016*** (0.006)	0.018** (0.008)	0.040*** (0.008)	0.016** (0.007)	0.015** (0.007)

*** = significant at 1%, ** = significant at 5%, significant at 10%.
FDI = foreign direct investment, M&A = merger and acquisition, WGI = World Governance Index.
Notes: Estimates are obtained with Poisson Pseudo-Maximum Likelihood (PPML) estimator, using the components of World Governance Index. Equations include host country-specific and pair-specific control variables as well as source country-period fixed effects and period fixed effects but not shown for brevity. Source country-period fixed effects as well as period fixed effects are included but not shown for brevity. Standard errors are in parenthesis are based on clustering by country-pair.
Sources: ADB calculations using data from Bureau van Dijk. Zephyr M&A Database; Financial Times. fDi Markets; Institute for Research on the International Economy. http://www.cepii.fr/CEPII/en/cepii/cepii.asp (accessed July 2016); United Nations Conference on Trade and Development. Investment Policy Hub. http://investmentpolicyhub. unctad.org/IIA (accessed August 2016); World Bank. World Development Indicators. http://data.worldbank.org/data-catalog/worlddevelopment-indicators (accessed July 2016); and World Bank. Worldwide Governance Indicators. http://data.worldbank.org/data-catalog/worldwide-governanceindicators (accessed July 2016).

Table 6.23: Effects of Governance on FDI in Different Sectors

		Greenfield Investment				Cross-border M&A			
Source	Host	All (1)	Primary Sector (2)	Service Sector (3)	Other (4)	All (5)	Primary Sector (6)	Service Sector (7)	Other (8)
High-income	High-income	0.032*** (0.006)	0.038*** (0.007)	0.023*** (0.007)	0.039*** (0.005)	0.050*** (0.007)	0.093*** (0.014)	0.047*** (0.009)	0.045*** (0.007)
	Developing	0.048*** (0.004)	0.032*** (0.005)	0.051*** (0.005)	0.048*** (0.004)	0.074*** (0.007)	0.039*** (0.008)	0.080*** (0.008)	0.075*** (0.007)
Emerging	High-income	0.028** (0.012)	0.022* (0.013)	0.014 (0.011)	0.045*** (0.017)	0.046*** (0.011)	0.180*** (0.053)	0.028** (0.011)	0.034*** (0.010)
	Developing	0.020*** (0.006)	0.011 (0.008)	0.022*** (0.007)	0.020*** (0.007)	0.040*** (0.008)	0.021* (0.011)	0.045*** (0.012)	0.042*** (0.008)

*** = significant at 1%, ** = significant at 5%, * = significant at 10%, FDI = foreign direct investment, M&A = merger and acquisition.
Notes: Estimates are obtained with Poisson Pseudo-Maximum Likelihood (PPML) using overall World Governance Index (WGI). Equations include host country-specific and pair-specific control variables as well as source country-period fixed effects and period fixed effects but not shown for brevity. Source country-period fixed effects as well as period fixed effects are included but not shown for brevity. Standard errors are in parenthesis are based on clustering by country-pair.
Sources: ADB calculations using data from Bureau van Dijk. Zephyr M&A Database; Financial Times. fDi Markets; Institute for Research on the International Economy. http://www.cepii.fr/CEPII/en/cepii/cepii.asp (accessed July 2016); United Nations Conference on Trade and Development. Investment Policy Hub. http://investmentpolicyhub. unctad.org/IIA (accessed August 2016); World Bank. World Development Indicators. http://data.worldbank.org/data-catalog/worlddevelopment-indicators (accessed July 2016); and World Bank. Worldwide Governance Indicators. http://data.worldbank.org/data-catalog/worldwide-governanceindicators (accessed July 2016).

The policy regime as reflected by the business environment appears to help attract FDI, particularly greenfield investments, especially for economies with low scores for governance.

Multinationals from high-income economies are in general more responsive to the local business environment of developing hosts than they are to high-income hosts. In fact, for Asian hosts, multinationals from high-income economies are especially sensitive to the quality of the policy regime. In contrast, multinationals from emerging economies appear to be relatively less sensitive to local business environments (see Table 6.21). The quality of the business environment appears to complement governance: for economies with high quality governance, the local business environment does not have as discernable an effect on FDI as it does for those with lower governance indicator scores, particularly for greenfield investments. This finding suggests that a favorable local business environment may compensate for poor governance (Table 6.24). In terms of attracting multinationals from high-income economies, the most important sub-indicators of the business environment for M&A are the ease of "getting credit", while the ease of being able to "register property" matters most for greenfield investments.

In general, economies in the region have been improving their business environments in various ways. Some recent reforms are documented in ADB's Asian Development Outlook 2016 (ADB 2016). For instance,

India's parliament recently introduced an updated bankruptcy law to streamline debt restructuring. From September 2015 to February 2016, Indonesia introduced 10 reform packages to attract investment, particularly in manufacturing, by opening 35 more sectors to foreign ownership. Additionally, regulations were simplified, procedures for land title registration and business licensing accelerated, formula for minimum wages made more predictable, and new tax incentives provided for labor-intensive industries. In terms of infastructure development, port logistics services are to be reformed and SEZs further developed.

Similarly, in Myanmar, the government's newly developed National Transport Master Plan aims for substantial upgrade to the existing transport infrastructure, including urban-rural links as well as links with neighboring economies across all modes of transport, especially through enhancement of intermodal transport and networks. In Fiji, reformed tax policies aim to stimulate private investment and consumption, and to enhance transparency and compliance. In Georgia, specialized agencies now facilitate exports and upgrade entrepreneurial skills, and work to enhance productive capacity in partnership with the private sector.

More specifically, based on the World Bank's Doing Business 2017 report, economies across the region have improved the business environment as shown by a wide range of "ease of doing business" indicators (World Bank 2016). Of the 10 economies highlighted by

Table 6.24: Interaction Effects of EoDB and WGI on Greenfield FDI Flows from High-income to Developing Countries

	(1) Average EoDB	(2) Starting Business	(3) Dealing with Business Construction	(4) Registering Property	(5) Getting Credit	(6) Protecting Minority Investors	(7) Paying Taxes	(8) Trading Across Borders	(9) Enforcing Contracts	(10) Resolving Insolvency
EoDB	0.096***	0.012	0.026**	0.065***	0.012	0.008	0.048***	0.017*	0.069***	0.008
	(0.022)	(0.012)	(0.013)	(0.011)	(0.008)	(0.015)	(0.008)	(0.009)	(0.013)	(0.009)
EoDB*WGI_ave	-0.002***	-0.000	-0.000*	-0.001***	-0.000	-0.000	-0.001***	-0.000	-0.001***	-0.000
	(0.000)	(0.000)	(0.000)	(0.000)	(0.000)	(0.000)	(0.000)	(0.000)	(0.000)	(0.000)
WGI_ave	0.140***	0.059***	0.076***	0.130***	0.041***	0.053***	0.118***	0.050***	0.134***	0.053***
	(0.025)	(0.019)	(0.018)	(0.015)	(0.011)	(0.014)	(0.011)	(0.013)	(0.017)	(0.007)

*** = significant at 1%, ** = significant at 5%, * = significant at 10%.
EoDB = Ease of Doing Business Index, FDI = foreign direct investment, WGI = World Governance Index.
Notes: Estimates are obtained with Poisson Pseudo-Maximum Likelihood (PPML) estimator. Source country-period fixed effects and period fixed effects are included but not shown for brevity. Standard errors are in parenthesis are based on clustering by country-pair.
Sources: ADB calculations using data from Bureau van Dijk. Zephyr M&A Database; Financial Times. fDi Markets; Institute for Research on the International Economy. http://www.cepii.fr/CEPII/en/cepii/cepii.asp (accessed July 2016); World Bank. Ease of Doing Business Indicators http://www.doingbusiness.org/rankings (accessed July 2016); World Bank. World Development Indicators. http://data.worldbank.org/data-catalog/worlddevelopment-indicators (accessed July 2016); and World Bank. Worldwide Governance Indicators. http://data.worldbank.org/data-catalog/worldwide-governance-indicators (accessed July 2016).

the report as having made the biggest improvements in business regulations, five are in Asia and the Pacific—Brunei Darussalam, Georgia, Indonesia, Kazakhstan, and Pakistan. Moreover, many economies in the region undertook reforms specifically to ease "getting credit," which our empirical analysis identifies as most important for attracting M&As through improved legislation and procedures, as well as streamlined functioning of credit bureaus. The economies which introduced significant reforms in this regard include Brunei Darussalam, Cambodia, the PRC, and Papua New Guinea. Indonesia and Singapore simplified procedures to register and transfer property, which is important to attract greenfield FDI. At the same time—without attributing any causal inferences as FDI performance depends on a whole host of factors—developing Asia has witnessed an increasing number of M&As (Figure 6.10), particularly in the economies cited. Other economies in the region may benefit by instituting similar reforms to ease credit restrictions and property registrations procedures.

While RTAs increase north-south greenfield FDI, the effect on south-south FDI and north-north FDI is not as clear cut.

The impact of regional trade agreements on FDI could theoretically work through opposing channels, and is an empirical question. If FDI is market-seeking or tariff-jumping—and therefore a substitute for trade—an RTA could clearly reduce FDI. Even in the case of vertical or GVC–FDI, if economies are at a similar stage of development and have similar factor endowments, multinationals have little scope to slice up the production process. The impact of RTAs also depends on the strength of investment provisions.

While RTAs intensify greenfield FDI when a high-income economy is the source and a developing economy is host (North-South FDI), these agreements have negative impact on FDI for greenfield investments in manufacturing and services from emerging to developing economies (South-South FDI). This suggests that South-South (SS) FDI may be motivated by tariff-jumping and market-seeking considerations. This finding does not necessarily imply that RTAs always reduce SS FDI: as trade linkages deepen and trade barriers fall due to greater integration, widening the scope for efficiency seeking, GVC investments may increase even among

economies at a similar level of development. Therefore, over a longer time horizon, RTAs may well increase SS FDI. No impact of RTAs on North-North (NN) FDI was found in the empirical analysis, but again the potential for greater NN FDI could be unlocked with the progress of greater integration resulting from RTAs (Tables 6.25, 6.26).

GVC–FDI: More Greenfield Investments or M&As?

Multinationals engaging in GVC–FDI in Asia are more likely to use the greenfield mode of entry, while M&As are more probable when domestic markets are the target.

The theoretical literature on FDI mode of entry amounts to only a small part of the many studies dedicated to the behavior of multinational corporations. One notable exception is Nocke and Yeaple (2007), who developed a model of FDI entry in which firms choose to enter a market either through M&As or by establishing completely new entities (greenfield investments). The model provides some guidance: (i) more greenfield FDI than M&As may be expected among firms that are productive, and (ii) relative to M&As, greenfield FDI goes to lower-income markets than the source. More generally, some research has documented that multinational expansion is dominated by M&As in the developed world and by greenfield investments in the developing world, even though M&A FDI is becoming more commonly used to access developing economies as well.[61]

By combining the international trade orientation of foreign-owned affiliates with the mode of entry, the mode of FDI entry can be linked to the market-serving activities that multinationals do most in any given host market. The question is whether the choice of a particular mode of entry into a market (and industry) is linked to the role of the affiliate in either serving the domestic market or being engaged in international trade-oriented activities.

Empirical findings suggest that multinationals prefer greenfield FDI for affiliates engaged in trade-oriented

---

[61] See Nocke and Yeaple (2007), Head and Ries (2008), and UNCTAD (2000).

Table 6.25: Effects of RTA and BIT on FDI

Source	Greenfield Investment				Cross-border M&A			
	High-income Economies		Emerging Economies		High-income Economies		Emerging Economies	
	(1)	(2)	(3)	(4)	(5)	(6)	(7)	(8)
RTA between source and host (= 1 if yes)	0.099** (0.044)		-0.279*** (0.094)		0.073 (0.000)		-0.065 (0.148)	
BIT between source and host (= 1 if yes)	0.050 (0.050)		0.214** (0.089)		-0.308 (0.000)		-0.114 (0.209)	
RTA * high-income host		-0.015 (0.066)		0.155 (0.120)		-0.037 (0.000)		-0.217 (0.197)
RTA * Developing host		0.157** (0.062)		-0.412*** (0.105)		0.226 .		0.090 (0.202)
BIT * high-income host		0.033 (0.087)		0.157 (0.168)		-0.464 (0.000)		-0.271 (0.265)
BIT * Developing host		0.050 (0.056)		0.227** (0.103)		-0.264 (0.000)		0.148 (0.304)
Number of observations	9302	9302	3202	3202	6978	6978		2118
R-squared	0.990	0.990	0.966	0.967	0.987	0.987		0.958

*** = significant at 1%, ** = significant at 5%, * = significant at 10%.
BIT = bilateral investment treaty, FDI = foreign direct investment, M&A = merger and acquisition, RTA = regional trade agreement.
Notes: Estimates are obtained with Poisson Pseudo-Maximum Likelihood (PPML) using overall World Governance Index (WGI). Equations include host country-specific and pair-specific control variables as well as source country-period fixed effects and period fixed effects but not shown for brevity. Source country-period fixed effects as well as period fixed effects are included but not shown for brevity. Standard errors are in parenthesis are based on clustering by country-pair.
Sources: ADB calculations using data from ADB. Asia Regional Integration Center FTA Database. https://aric.adb.org/fta (accessed September 2016); Bureau van Dijk. Zephyr M&A Database; Financial Times. fDi Markets; Institute for Research on the International Economy. http:// www.cepii.fr/CEPII/en/cepii/cepii.asp (accessed July 2016); United Nations Conference on Trade and Development. Investment Policy Hub. http://investmentpolicyhub. unctad.org/IIA (accessed August 2016); World Bank. World Development Indicators. http://data.worldbank.org/data-catalog/world-development-indicators (accessed July 2016); and World Bank. Worldwide Governance Indicators. http://data.worldbank.org/data-catalog/worldwide-governance-indicators (accessed July 2016).

Table 6.26: Effects of RTA and BIT on Greenfield FDI in Different Sectors

	High-income Economies				Emerging Economies			
	All (1)	Primary Sector (2)	Service Sector (3)	Other (4)	All (5)	Primary Sector (6)	Service Sector (7)	Other (8)
RTA * high-income host	-0.015 (0.066)	0.267 (0.213)	0.103 (0.091)	-0.115 (0.092)	0.155 (0.120)	0.042 (0.397)	0.463*** (0.159)	-0.059 (0.191)
RTA * Developing host	0.157** (0.062)	0.223* (0.135)	0.171* (0.088)	0.176*** (0.067)	-0.412*** (0.105)	-0.293 (0.282)	-0.474** (0.202)	-0.460*** (0.133)
BIT * high-income host	0.033 (0.087)	0.904* (0.481)	-0.174 (0.142)	0.069 (0.111)	0.157 (0.168)	0.064 (0.693)	0.161 (0.233)	0.140 (0.207)
BIT * Developing host	0.050 (0.056)	-0.068 (0.143)	0.071 (0.067)	0.059 (0.065)	0.227** (0.103)	0.575* (0.312)	0.111 (0.187)	0.158 (0.156)
Number of observations	9302	4375	7088	7569	3202	1246	2140	2324
R-squared	0.990	0.900	0.991	0.986	0.967	0.821	0.952	0.964

*** = significant at 1%, ** = significant at 5%, * = significant at 10%.
BIT = bilateral investment treaty, FDI = foreign direct investment, M&A = merger and acquisition, RTA = regional trade agreement.
Notes: Estimates are obtained with Poisson Pseudo-Maximum Likelihood (PPML) using overall World Governance Index (WGI). Equations include host country-specific and pair-specific control variables as well as source country-period fixed effects and period fixed effects but not shown for brevity. Source country-period fixed effects as well as period fixed effects are included but not shown for brevity. Standard errors are in parenthesis are based on clustering by country-pair.
Sources: ADB calculations using data from Bureau van Dijk. Zephyr M&A Database; Financial Times. fDi Markets; Institute for Research on the International Economy. http://www.cepii.fr/CEPII/en/cepii/cepii.asp (accessed July 2016); United Nations Conference on Trade and Development. Investment Policy Hub. http://investmentpolicyhub.unctad.org/IIA (accessed August 2016); World Bank. World Development Indicators. http://data.worldbank.org/data-catalog/world-development-indicators (accessed July 2016); and World Bank. Worldwide Governance Indicators. http://data.worldbank.org/data-catalog/worldwide-governance-indicators (accessed July 2016).

Box 6.5: Analyzing the Link between GVC–FDI and Mode of Entry

The two variables of interest are first, the ratio of the number of foreign direct investment (FDI) transactions of merger and acquisition (M&A) to greenfield FDI transactions. Second, the number of foreign affiliates that export and import (global value chain (GVC)–FDI) as a proportion of the total number of foreign affiliates. The average ratio of M&A to greenfield FDI across host economies is 0.63, and the median value is 0.35 (box table 1). Bangladesh has the lowest (non-zero) ratio of M&As entry relative to greenfield in Asia, while the region's richest economies (Australia, Japan, the Republic of Korea, and New Zealand) have ratios of well above 1. The average ratio of GVC–FDI affiliates is of 0.30 (and a median of 0.29), reaching a (non-zero) minimum in Australia (0.16) and a maximum in the PRC (0.79), followed by Taipei,China and Viet Nam.

The relationship between FDI entry mode and affiliate activity as a function of some characteristics of the host economy is interesting. In box table 2 the dependent variable represents GVC–FDI while the control variable is the ratio of M&A to greenfield FDI (counts), both expressed in logs. Clearly, the negative relationship between the two variables survives when other economy controls and sector fixed effects are added to the equation. Moreover, the relation is significant for all sectors pooled together and also for manufacturing. Column (1) indicates that doubling the number of multilaterals choosing M&A entry above greenfield entry, at the bilateral-sector—an increase equivalent to moving from the 90th to the 95th percentile—decreases the share of affiliates exposed to trade by almost 10%. We also tested the share of GVC–FDI as an explanatory variable and the share of M&A FDI entry as a dependent variable, relative to greenfield FDI entry. Results show a similar negative correlation, but quantitatively, the relationship is much larger: doubling the share of GVC–FDI decreases the ratio of M&A to greenfield FDI entry by almost 40%.

1: GVC–FDI and FDI Entry, by Economy

Host Economy	Rank GVC–FDI	Rank M&A–GF Ratio	M&A–GF Ratio	GVC–FDI
PRC	1	9	0.44	0.79
Taipei,China	2	13	0.30	0.74
Viet Nam	3	17	0.23	0.70
Malaysia	4	10	0.41	0.65
Thailand	5	22	0.15	0.65
Philippines	6	16	0.26	0.59
Brunei Darussalam	7	23	0.00	0.50
Indonesia	8	7	0.61	0.42
Kazakhstan	9	20	0.16	0.41
Singapore	10	14	0.29	0.40
Republic of Korea	11	5	1.23	0.35
India	12	11	0.41	0.35
Georgia	13	6	0.77	0.33
Sri Lanka	14	19	0.20	0.28
Hong Kong, China	15	8	0.46	0.23
Bangladesh	16	15	0.27	0.20
Japan	17	4	1.25	0.18
Australia	18	2	1.41	0.16
New Zealand	19	1	3.74	0.00
Uzbekistan	20	3	1.29	0.00
Armenia	21	12	0.33	0.00
Pakistan	22	21	0.16	0.00
Kyrgyz Republic	23	26	n/a	0.00
Afghanistan	24	25	0.00	0.00
Nepal	25	18	0.20	0.00
Azerbaijan	26	24	0.00	0.00

PRC = People's Republic of China, FDI = foreign direct investment, GF = greenfield, GVC = global value chain, M&A = merger and acquisition.
Notes: M&A–GF ratio refers to the ratio of the number of M&As to the number of greenfield projects in an economy. GVC-FDI refers to the share of foreign affiliates in an economy that both export and import. The rank variables just rank the economy with respect to each variable.
Sources: ADB calculations using data from Bureau van Dijk. Zephyr M&A Database; Dun & Bradstreet. D&B Worldbase and Financial Times. fDi Markets.

2: Determinants of GVC–FDI (ordinary least squares) Dependent variable: log of GVC–FDI, bilateral sector level

	(1)	(2)	(3)
log M&A to GF (counts)	-0.095***	-0.076***	-0.049
	(0.026)	(0.025)	(0.076)
log(distance)	-0.067	-0.028	0.034
	(0.044)	(0.039)	(0.137)
D(sharing language)	-0.086	-0.061	-0.158
	(0.077)	(0.073)	(0.257)
D(sharing colonial past)	-0.240**	-0.128	0.018
	(0.118)	(0.081)	(0.451)
D(RTA)	-0.118	-0.078	-0.444
	(0.079)	(0.068)	(0.295)
D(DTT)	0.087	0.032	0.589**
	(0.103)	(0.077)	(0.281)
D(BIT)	-0.050	-0.073	-0.095
	(0.058)	(0.054)	(0.186)
log(rgdpl)	0.921***	0.734***	2.014*
	(0.215)	(0.197)	(1.044)
log(KL)	-0.537***	-0.284	-1.387
	(0.206)	(0.198)	(1.100)
log(rgdp)	-0.069***	-0.063***	-0.249
	(0.026)	(0.022)	(0.150)
Rule of law	-0.604***	-0.705***	-0.958**
	(0.109)	(0.102)	(0.442)
Number of observations	416	266	38
R-squared	0.548	0.387	0.609
Sample	all	manufacturing	mining

*** = significant at 1%, ** = significant at 5%, * = significant at 10%.
BIT = bilateral investment treaty, DTT = double taxation treaty, FDI = foreign direct investment, GVC = global value chain, GF =greenfield, M&A = merger and acquisition, RTA = regional trade agreement.
Notes: The dependent variable is the number of affiliates with export and import activities, as a share of total affiliates, at the bilateral-sector level, in logs. The control variable of interest is the number of M&A to the number of greenfield FDI, in logs, at the bilateral- sector level. Specification in column a with sector fixed effects. Standard errors, clustered at the host-source level, in parentheses.
Sources: ADB calculations using data from Bureau van Dijk. Zephyr M&A Database; Dun & Bradstreet. D&B Worldbase; Financial Times. fDi Markets; Institute for Research on the International Economy. http://www.cepii.fr/CEPII/en/cepii/cepii.asp (accessed July 2016); Penn World Tables 8.0 http://www.wiod.org/database/seas13 (accessed July 2016); United Nations Conference on Trade and Development. Investment Policy Hub. http://investmentpolicyhub.unctad.org/IIA (accessed August 2016); Worldwide Governance Indicators. http://data.worldbank.org/data-catalog/worldwide-governance-indicators (accessed July 2016).

activities (Box 6.5). Although theoretical grounds have yet to be established, one can think of multinationals wanting to acquire domestic firms when their goal is to penetrate a domestic market; the domestic firms would provide strategic assets in the form of local knowledge on institutions, suppliers, the customer base, the labor force, and perhaps conditions for obtaining funding through local capital markets. On the other hand, should the multinational want to use the particular market as an export platform, greenfield FDI may offer more control and thus be a better option.

Policy Implications

Policy makers need to take into account the nuances involved in attracting different types of FDI in devising policies, to fit the economy's development stage, comparative advantage, and industrial policy perspective.

Attitudes about FDI have shifted significantly in recent decades, with economies moving toward greater liberalization and casting off restrictions to foreign ownership. However, FDI regimes in Asia still vary widely and policy makers need to account for the nuances involved in attracting different types of FDI when forming policies, in line with the economy's development stage, comparative advantage, and industrial policy perspective. Economies like Bangladesh, Cambodia, and the Lao People's Democratic Republic attract more labor-intensive FDI, while the India, the Republic of Korea, Malaysia, and Thailand, for example, encourage capital and technology-intensive FDI.

Good governance and quality of institutions in the host economy could signal its government's commitment to honoring the interests of foreign investors and their investments.

Without these conditions, significant increases in FDI are not likely. Based on perception surveys, the quality of institutions varies widely across the region. For example, World Bank Enterprise Surveys note that about 33% of firms globally and 18% of firms in East Asia, Southeast Asia, and the Pacific identify corruption as a major constraint to doing business, compared with about 40%

in South Asia and 22% in Central Asia. Moreover, in South Asia, 17% of firms indicate that the judicial system is a major constraint, compared with 8% in East Asia and Southeast Asia and about 5% in Central Asia (World Bank Enterprise Surveys 2005-2016).

Developing economies with relatively poor governance can still foster FDI inflows by improving the business environment.

A good investment climate attracts the productive domestic and foreign private investment that helps fuel growth and reduces poverty. Improving the business environment is particularly important for economies still working to develop quality institutions, where reform takes time to implement fully. Firms cite tax rates and tax administration as prominent constraints, with surveys across subregions reporting these as concerns for firms in South Asia (26% for tax rates and 19% for tax administration), in Central Asia (24% and 15%), and in East Asia and Southeast Asia (16% and 7%).

The determinants of FDI are diverse and span different modes of entry, motivation, sector, and source economies.

Multinationals' choice of entering a foreign market through acquiring a local firm or by building a new facility also has welfare implications for the host economy, depending on absorptive capacity. It was found that the quality of governance was the most important driver of FDI, more so for M&As than for greenfield FDI, and in particular for multinationals from high-income economies investing in manufacturing and services. The policy regime that helps define the business environment is a major factor in attracting greenfield FDI in economies that lack strong institutions.

The analysis also shows that in terms of market serving motivation, the major factors for attracting trade-promoting or GVC–FDI (as opposed to domestic market-seeking FDI) were labor abundance, low trade barriers (expedited trading procedures and low costs of exporting and importing), as well as an already existing network of domestic firms linked by input–output relations. Less developed economies were more likely to host these type of trade-oriented affiliates, due not only to low labor costs, but also the prevalence of SEZs that can act as "shields" from a more difficult domestic environment.

Linking to GVCs enables industrial upgrading, and is a successful export-oriented development strategy followed by many economies in the region, particularly in East and Southeast Asia. While seemingly disadvantageous, a low development stage can be leveraged to attract FDI, which can help link a host economy to GVCs. Labor abundance can also draw in GVC–FDI, further supported by lowering trade barriers. Developing countries can also attract more GVC–FDI by fostering richer linkages between domestic industries. The Penang export hub in Malaysia is an example of an area that first attracted multinationals into labor-intensive industries, and subsequently moved into higher value-added segments of the value chain through a successful investment promotion strategy and a rich network of domestic vendors (Athukorala 2014). This could hold particular relevance to those economies that have yet to adequately connect their domestic industries to international production networks.

For instance, most economies in Central Asia draw more than 50% of FDI into natural resources, with another large portion going to sectors serving domestic markets—including real estate development, trade, finance, construction, and communications. There is little evidence of investment projects linking into regional or global value chains. The strong appreciation of regional currencies in 2000–2012 and widespread migration of workers from the Kyrgyz Republic, Tajikistan, and Uzbekistan to Kazakhstan, the Russian Federation, and some other countries keeps wages in the region relatively high—therefore discouraging investment in labor-intensive sectors (ADBI 2014).

This chapter also shows that trade-promoting GVC–FDI is relatively more commonly linked to greenfield projects than to M&As. Hence, help for multinationals to build from the ground up seems important in enabling economies to effectively join GVCs. Firms in less developed economies may not have much to offer as M&A targets, but support for greenfield-GVC–FDI may help create a network of local firms which, through growing interaction with multinationals, can climb the technology ladder and acquire knowledge to operate in the global market. A good example is Wal-Mart in the

PRC, as documented by Head et al. (2014). Even though Wal-Mart eventually decided not to tap the PRC market (horizontal FDI), it kept its "global procurement centers", buying local products to export to its stores around the world. In this way, local firms built access to the international market, and PRC suppliers (whose products were exported through Wal-Mart) started exporting their own products as their brands gained international recognition.

Special Section: The Role of International Investment Policy

The number of bilateral investment treaties (BITs) and other treaties with investment provisions has risen rapidly in recent years. The United Nations Conference on Trade and Development (UNCTAD) lists 2,954 BITs and 362 other treaties with investment provisions, of which 2,319 BITs and 294 treaties with investment provisions are currently in force.

While BITs and other international investment agreements are increasingly important, empirical evidence on the impact of BITs is mixed and inconclusive.[62] Bellak (2015) argues in a meta-analysis to investigate the effect of BITs on FDI that much of the empirical evidence suffers from a publication selection bias, with misleading implications for policy makers. The results of the meta-analysis reveal BITs have no statistically and practically significant effect on FDI after correcting for the bias. Chaisse and Bellak (2015) conduct a descriptive analysis, which shows a wide range of estimated semi-elasticities of FDI on BITs across various measures, with only some statistically significant. The inconclusiveness of existing empirical evidence can be attributed to large differences in research design. Empirical studies differ widely in many aspects, including by dependent variable (FDI flow or FDI stock) and the dataset used (cross-section or longitudinal), and also

---

[62]   See Hallward-Driemeir (2003), Egger and Pfaffermayr (2004), Lesher and Miroudot (2006), and Berger et al. (2010).

in the time periods, control variables, and econometric models employed.

Against this background, the research in this section starts by asking whether bilateral and regional trade and investment agreements in Asia differ much from others—by being more heterogeneous. For this stylized facts on Asia's BITs and the investment chapters of Regional Trade and Investment Agreements (RTIAs) are examined.

Moreover, instead of using a simple BIT dummy variable, the "BITSel Index" created by Chaisse and Bellak (2015) is used. This index helps quantitatively assess the various BIT provisions and international investment agreements. Isolating the effects of each provision allows us to investigate the precise nature of links between investment treaties and FDI. This approach helps understand the links between heterogeneous BIT provisions and their effect on FDI projects, a question that has interested Asian policy makers over the past few decades.

Use of a Poisson Quasi-Maximum Likelihood approach and granular FDI distinguishing by mode of entry—yields interesting insights on the importance of common provisions in BIT and/or RTIAs in boosting FDI recently. Empirical analyses show that BITs which specifically provide foreign investors access to international arbitration mechanisms, and RTIA provisions that protect foreign investors from discrimination, have a large and statistically significant positive effect on FDI. In particular, a "pro-FDI" BIT tends to increase the number of FDI projects by 35.3%, or by 58.4% for a "pro-FDI" RTIA.

BIT Trend Analysis: Data and Heterogeneity of BIT Provisions

Data for BIT trend analysis for Asia consists of 195,840 observations, representing annual observations covering 2000–2016 for each of the 11,520 pairs of economies. Table 6.27 summarizes the data and statistics. It shows the number of Asian BITs enforced within the Asian region (intra-Asia BITs) and other major economic regions. Asian economies enforced 1,075 BITs globally over 2000–2015, according to the UNCTAD database. This is a significant proportion of the BITs enforced worldwide (Figure 6.15).

Table 6.27: Asian BIT Statistics

Regional Pair	UNCTAD BIT[a]		BITSel BIT[a]	
	Number	Percent	Number	Percent
Asia-Asia[b]	306	28.5	142	29.3
Asia-PRC	27	2.5	8	1.6
Asia-Japan	13	1.2	8	1.6
Asia-Republic of Korea	21	2.0	11	2.3
Asia-US	8	0.7	7	1.4
Asia-EU[c]	367	34.1	177	36.5
Asia-Rest-of-World[d]	333	31.0	132	27.2
Total	**1,075**	**100.0**	**485**	**100.0**

BIT = bilateral investment treaty, PRC = People's Republic of China, EU = European Union, UNCTAD = United Nations Conference on Trade and Development, US = United States.
Notes:
[a] Number of UNCTAD BITs refers to the cumulative number of BITs in 2000–2016, according to the UNCTAD database, while the number of BITSel BITs refers to the accumulated number of BITs in the BITSel database by Chaisse and Bellak (2015).
[b] Asia refers to the 48 regional members of the Asian Development Bank.
[c] EU refers to the 28 member economes of the European Union.
[d] Rest-of-world includes all the countries excluding Asia, the People's Republic of China, the European Union Japan, the Republic of Korea, and the United States.
Sources: ADB calculations using data from United Nations Conference on Trade and Development. Investment Policy Hub. http://investmentpolicyhub.unctad.org/IIA (accessed August 2016) and Chaisse and Bellak (2015).

Figure 6.15: World BITs (number)

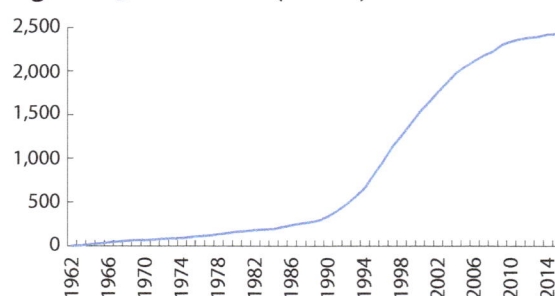

BIT = bilateral investment treaty.
Source: ADB calculations using data from United Nations Conference on Trade and Development. Investment Policy Hub. http://investmentpolicyhub.unctad.org/IIA (accessed August 2016).

The region has maintained the strongest link in BITs with the European Union (EU), which comprises 34.1% of Asian BITs over 2000-2015. This is followed by the rest of the world, with a 31.0% share. Intraregional BITs comprise 28.5%. Notwithstanding, intraregional BITs have become increasingly important in recent years (Figure 6.16). It is also interesting that Asian economies have maintained the most BIT links with the People's Republic of China (PRC), then the Republic of Korea, followed by Japan. A smaller number of BITs have been enforced with

Figure 6.16: Asian Intraregional BITs, 2000–2015 (number)

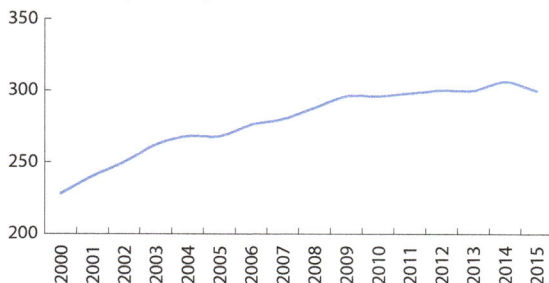

BIT = bilateral investment treaty.
Note: This figure corresponds to Asia–Asia BITs (intra-regional BITs).
Source: ADB calculations using data from United Nations Conference on Trade and Development. Investment Policy Hub. http://investmentpolicyhub.unctad.org/IIA (accessed August 2016).

advanced economies outside Asia, such as the United States (US).

Analyzing the heterogeneity of Asian BITs and RTIAs

The analysis was based on the BITSel Index created by Chaisse and Bellak (2015), which codes the 11 most important provisions included in BITs and RTIAs. The database assigns a value to each of the 11 components of the BITSel index, ranging from 1 (least favorable to FDI) to 2 (most favorable to FDI).[63] We group each component into one of five broad categories:

- ENTRY: average of (i) entry rules (admission versus establishment), (ii) non-economic standards (yes versus no), and (iii) free transfer of investment-related funds (no versus yes);
- TREAT: average of (i) national treatment (no versus yes) and (ii) most-favored nation status (no versus yes);
- SCOPE: average of (i) definition of investment (narrow versus broad), (ii) umbrella clause (no versus yes), and (iii) temporal scope of application (short versus long);
- PROTEC: average of (i) fair and equitable treatment (no versus yes) and (ii) direct and indirect expropriation covered (no versus yes); and
- ISDM: investor-related dispute mechanism (no versus yes).

The sample period is 2000–2016. Figure 6.17 presents the average scores of the provisions in the BITs and RTIAs of Asia with the world and major economic regions. The provisions in Asian BITs with the world seem generally favorable for FDI, with average scores above 0.5 across all five categories. By comparison, Asian RTIAs are less favorable to FDI, especially in provisions for treatment and access to international arbitration. This indicates that Asian bilateral treaties grant foreign investors more substantive rights than regional treaties.

A similar story holds when decomposing Asia's BITs and RTIAs with other major economic regions. For instance, of ADB's 48 Asian regional members, 32 have enforced at least one BIT with another Asian regional member during 2000–2016, while only 13 have enforced at least one RTIA with another Asian regional member(s) over that time. On average, Asian BITs receive above average scores for all five categories, with access to fair and equitable treatment and coverage of direct and indirect expropriation the highest, at an index score of 0.95. Depending on partner economy, the scores for investor-state dispute mechanisms (ISDM) vary widely. Usually, Asia-Asia BITs have lower scores in ISDM than those in Asia-advanced economies BITs such as Asia-US BITs. On the other hand, Asian RTIAs receive less favorable scores—averages of 0.18 for treatment, 0.43 for scope, and 0.16 for access to international arbitration.

Asia BIT provisions also strengthened during 1975–2012 to attract more FDI. Over that period, the ISDM, TREAT, and PROTEC measures have featured more prominently in Asian BITs (Figure 6.18).

For FDI, the Financial Times' fDi Markets database was used, which tracks cross-border greenfield FDI across all sectors and economies worldwide.[64] The database provides novel FDI data that offer important advantages over traditional balance of payments FDI data. For one, it covers a very large number of economies and sectors and provides entry mode classification for FDI projects.

The empirical analysis is based on an ADB research paper contributed by Desbordes (2016), the original dataset contains 983,280 observations of FDI, representing annual observations for 2000–2016 for each of the

---

[63]   For notational convenience, we recode this to 0 (least favorable to FDI) and 1 (most favorable to FDI).

[64]   See the fDi Markets website at http://www.fdimarkets.com.

Figure 6.17: Average Scores of Provisions in BITs and RTIAs

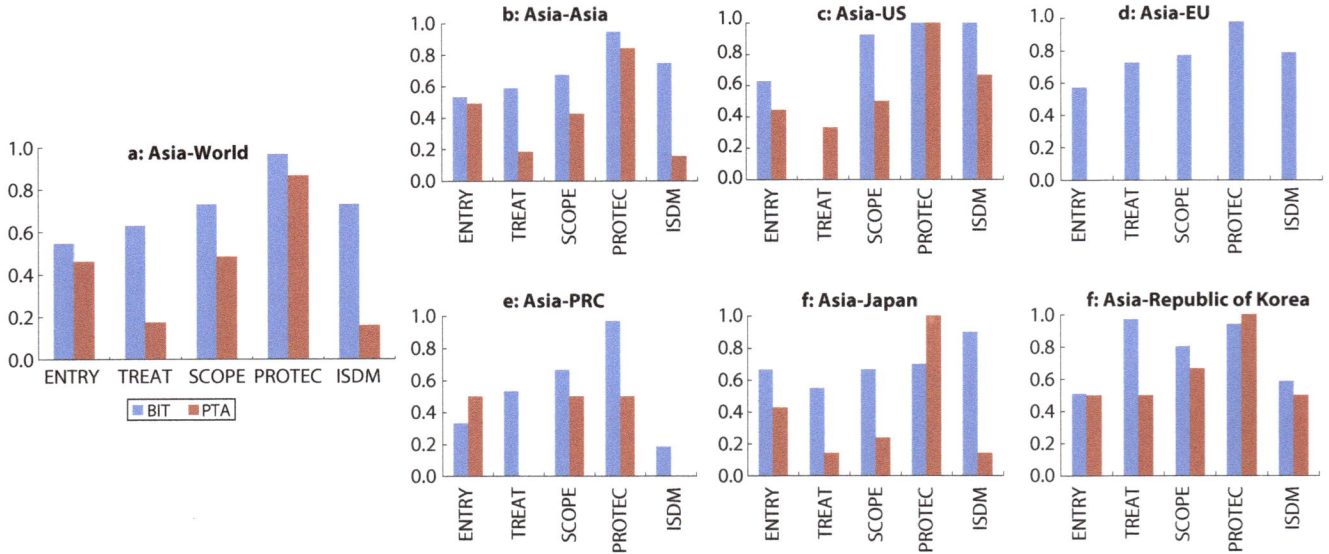

BIT = bilateral investment treaties, PRC = People's Republic of China, EU = European Union, ISDM = investor-state dispute mechanism, RTIA = regional trade investment agreement, US = United States.
Note: See definition of ENTRY, TREAT, SCOPE, PROTEC, and ISDM on page 161.
Source: ADB calculations using data from Chaisse and Bellak (2015).

Figure 6.18: Asian Regional BIT Provisions Over the Past Decades

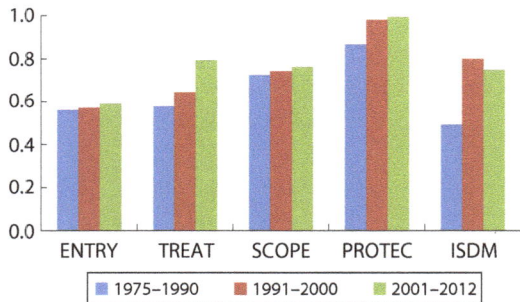

BIT = bilateral investment treaty.
Note: See definition of ENTRY, TREAT, SCOPE, PROTEC, and ISDM on page 161.
Source: ADB calculations using data from Chaisse and Bellak (2015).

57,840 pairs of economies. Then, we construct a cross-sectional data set by getting the average of the variables over the 2004–2010 sample period. We use the cumulated number of FDI projects over 2004–2010 and control for a large number of observed and unobserved variables. We estimate the following cross-sectional exponential model:

$$FDI0410_{ij} = \exp\left(\delta_1 \overline{BIT}_{ij} + \overline{CONT}_{ij}\beta + \theta FDI03_{ij} + \alpha_i + \alpha_j\right)\epsilon_{ij}$$

where $FDI0410_{ij}$ is the cumulated number of FDI projects of firms headquartered in source economy in host economy over 2004–2010, $\overline{BIT}_{ij}$ corresponds to the average of BIT_{ij} which is a dummy indicating the existence, for at least 2 years, of an enforced BIT or of various BIT-related investment provisions, $\overline{CONT}_{ij}$ is the average of the vector of dyadic control variables, $FDI03_{ij}$ is the (log+1) value of the number of bilateral projects in 2003, αi and αj are country fixed effects, and ϵij the multiplicative error term.[65] The vector of dyadic control variables includes geographic distance, time zone difference, and the presence of a common border, language, religion, legal origin, and colonial past. The model also controls for when an RTA or a currency union is in place.

Heterogeneous Impacts of the Provisions of BITs and RTIA

Table 6.28 presents the overall impact of BIT and that of each BIT provision on FDI with other control variables. In all columns, the model controls for country fixed effects, dyadic control variables, double taxation treaties (DTT),

---

[65]   Hence, $FDI03_{ij} = \ln(FDI03_{ij}) + 1$.

Table 6.28: World to World Country Pairs—Specific BIT Provisions

	Cumulated Number of FDI Projects					
	BIT (1)	**ENTRY** (2)	**TREAT** (3)	**SCOPE** (4)	**PROTEC** (5)	**ISDM** (6)
BIT Provision	0.264*** (0.064)	0.402*** (0.106)	0.196*** (0.071)	0.276*** (0.072)	0.275*** (0.063)	0.302*** (0.063)
Number of observations	26,093	26,093	26,093	26,093	26,093	26,093

*** = significant at 1%, ** = significant at 5%, * = significant at 10%.
BIT = bilateral investment treaty, DTT = double taxation treaty, FDI = foreign direct investment, ISDM = investor-state dispute mechanism.
Notes: Cluster-robust standard errors are in parentheses. Country fixed effects, the dyadic control variables, DTT, and RTA are included in all columns. See definition of ENTRY, TREAT, SCOPE, PROTEC, and ISDM on page 161.
Sources: ADB calculations using data from Chaisse and Bellak (2015) and Financial Times. fDi Markets.

and RTAs. Column (1) reveals that BITs tend to increase the cumulated number of FDI projects by approximately 26.4% and this is statistically significant at the 1% level. Columns (2) to (6) indicate that all the BIT provisions have a large, statistically significant, positive effect on FDI, with favorable ENTRY conditions having increased the number of FDI projects by about 40.2%.

Table 6.29 assesses the relative importance of each BIT provision to determine which of the five categories matters most from the perspective of foreign investors. In column (1), the marginal effects of each provision on FDI are presented. Results show that ISDM s the only provision statistically significant among the five categories. To perform robustness checks, we examine the overall effect of BIT in columns (2) to (6) and the individual effects of the four BIT provisions while controlling for ISDM.

The exercise confirms the robustness of the result in column (1): BIT and the four BIT provisions do not matter marginally once the presence of an ISDM is controlled. These results indicate the BITs specifically granting access to an ISDM have large, positive, and statistically significant effects on FDI. Hence, the most important provision in BITs is access to international arbitration—a finding in line with the sentiment of many legal scholars, suggesting that access to ISDM is the principal advantage of a BIT.[66]

Table 6.30 shows the effects of RTIAs on FDI, controlling for the presence of BIT and DTT along with the fixed

effects and dyadic control variables. Although RTIAs have no statistically significant effect on FDI, the presence of most RTIA provisions has a large, statistically significant, positive effect on FDI, with the largest being TREAT, at approximately 46.0%, and ENTRY, at about 42.5%.[67] ISDM, on the other hand, does not appear to matter in RTIAs, perhaps because it is absent from most RTIAs in our sample.

In Table 6.31, the relative importance of each RTIA provision is assessed to determine which among the five categories matter most to foreign investors. Column (1) shows the marginal effects of each provision on FDI. Results show that TREAT is the only statistically significant provision. To perform robustness checks, in columns (2) to (6) the overall effect of RTIA and the marginal effects of the four other RTIA provisions are examined while controlling for TREAT. The exercise confirms the result in column (1) that RTIA and the four RTIA provisions do not matter additionally once controlling for the presence of favorable treatment conditions. RTIAs granting the basic principles of national treatment and most-favored nation status have large, positive, and statistically significant effects on FDI. Hence, the most importance provision in an RTIA is the protection from discrimination that it offers foreign investors.

66   See Walde (2005) and Allee and Peinhardt (2010), for instance.

67   These findings support the "multilateral" findings of Buthe and Milner (2014).

Table 6.29: Relative Importance of BIT Provisions—World to World Country Pairs

	Cumulated Number of FDI Projects					
	(1)	(2)	(3)	(4)	(5)	(6)
ISDM	0.282*	0.287**	0.297**	0.308***	0.327**	0.265*
	(0.153)	(0.145)	(0.123)	(0.076)	(0.128)	(0.145)
BIT		0.016				
		(0.145)				
ENTRY	-0.019		0.009			
	(0.216)		(0.202)			
TREAT	-0.024			-0.012		
	(0.082)			(0.083)		
SCOPE	-0.129				-0.035	
	(0.192)				(0.143)	
PROTEC	0.159					0.042
	(0.199)					(0.144)
Number of observations	26,093	26,093	26,093	26,093	26,093	26,093

*** = significant at 1%, ** = significant at 5%, * = significant at 10%.
BIT = bilateral investment treaty, DTT = double taxation treaty, FDI = foreign direct investment, ISDM = investor-state dispute mechanism.
Notes: Cluster-robust standard errors are in parentheses. Country fixed effects, the dyadic control variables, DTT, and RTA are included in all columns. See definition of ENTRY, TREAT, SCOPE, PROTEC, and ISDM on page 161.
Sources: ADB calculations using data from Chaisse and Bellak (2015) and Financial Times. fDi Markets.

Table 6.30: Specific RTIA Provisions—World to World Country Pairs

	Cumulated Number of FDI Projects					
	RTIA	ENTRY	TREAT	SCOPE	PROTEC	ISDM
	(1)	(2)	(3)	(4)	(5)	(6)
RTIA Provision	0.012	0.425**	0.460***	0.339**	0.254**	0.138
	(0.136)	(0.186)	(0.165)	(0.171)	(0.112)	(0.171)
BIT	0.216***	0.252***	0.247***	0.215***	0.203***	0.220***
	(0.076)	(0.077)	(0.074)	(0.076)	(0.076)	(0.076)
DTT	0.183**	0.192***	0.173**	0.188***	0.192***	0.186***
	(0.073)	(0.072)	(0.073)	(0.072)	(0.071)	(0.072)
Number of observations	22,585	22,585	22,585	22,585	22,585	22,585

*** = significant at 1%, ** = significant at 5%, * = significant at 10%.
BIT = bilateral investment treaty, DTT = double taxation treaty, FDI = foreign direct investment, ISDM = investor-state dispute mechanism, RTIA = regional trade and investment agreement.
Notes: Cluster-robust standard errors are in parentheses. Country fixed effects and dyadic control variables are included in all columns. See definition of ENTRY, TREAT, SCOPE, PROTEC, and ISDM on page 161.
Sources: ADB calculations using data from ADB. Asia Regional Integration Center FTA Database. https://aric.adb.org/fta (accessed September 2016); Chaisse and Bellak (2015); Financial Times. fDi Markets; and United Nations Conference on Trade and Development. Investment Policy Hub. http://investmentpolicyhub. unctad.org/IIA (accessed August 2016).

Impact of BITs and RTIAs on Greenfield FDI in Emerging Asia: A Robustness Check

Panel regressions are conducted for robustness checks on the empirical results of the World-World BIT "country" pairs, using data on Asia-World BIT country pairs and on the impact of BITs on greenfield FDI projects into developing Asia from the World. Data for Asia-World BIT country pairs were taken from the same data source used for the World-World BIT analysis.

The baseline econometric model is given by the following:

$$FDI_{ijt} = \exp(\gamma_1 BIT_{ijt} + \beta X_{ijt} + a_{ij})u_{ijt}$$

where FDI_{ijt} is the cumulated number of FDI projects of firms with headquarters in source country j, in host country i at year t, BIT_{ijt} is a dummy variable equal to 1 if a BIT has been enforced for at least 2 years or BIT-related

Table 6.31: Relative Importance of RTIA Provisions —World to World Country Pairs

	Cumulated Number of FDI Projects					
	(1)	**(2)**	**(3)**	**(4)**	**(5)**	**(6)**
TREAT	0.679** (0.301)	0.460*** (0.165)	0.390* (0.213)	0.436*** (0.163)	0.349 (0.220)	0.722** (0.281)
RTIA		0.007 (0.134)				
ENTRY	0.033 (0.259)		0.119 (0.235)			
SCOPE	0.256 (0.242)			0.287 (0.169)		
PROTEC	0.128 (0.213)				0.119 (0.148)	
ISDM	-0.432 (0.273)					-0.294 (0.256)
BIT	0.240*** (0.077)	0.247*** (0.074)	0.253*** (0.076)	0.244*** (0.074)	0.234*** (0.074)	0.252*** (0.073)
Number of observations	22,585	22,585	22,585	22,585	22,585	22,585

*** = significant at 1%, ** = significant at 5%, * = significant at 10%.
BIT = bilateral investment treaty, DTT = double taxation treaty, FDI = foreign direct investment, ISDM = investor-state dispute mechanism, RTIA = regional trade and investment agreement.
Notes: Cluster-robust standard errors in parentheses. Country fixed effects, the dyadic control variables, and DTT are included in all columns. See definition of ENTRY, TREAT, SCOPE, PROTEC, and ISDM on page 161.
Sources: ADB calculations using data from Chaisse and Bellak (2015) and Financial Times. fDi Markets.

investment provisions are in place between economies i and j at year t, and equal to zero otherwise, while X_{ijt} is a vector of dyadic control variables, α_{ijt} are country pair fixed effects, and u_{ijt} is the multiplicative error term.[68]

The baseline model is extended to analyze the effects of RTIAs on FDI:

$$FDI_{ijt} = \exp(\gamma_1 BIT_{ijt} + \gamma_2 RTIA_{ijt} + \beta X_{ijt} + a_{ij})u_{ijt}$$

where $RTIA_{ijt}$ is a dummy variable equal to 1 if an enforced RTIA has been in existence for 2 years or various RTIA-related investment provisions are in place between economies i and j at year t, and zero otherwise. The effects of BIT and RTIA on FDI are analyzed, controlling for the existence of double taxation treaties:

$$FDI_{ijt} = \exp(\gamma_1 BIT_{ijt} + \gamma_2 RTIA_{ijt} + \gamma_3 DTT_{ijt} + \beta X_{ijt} + a_{ij})u_{ijt}$$

where DTT_{ijt} is a dummy variable equal to 1 if an enforced DTT has been in place for 2 years or more, or where DTT-related investment provisions exist between economies i and j at year t, and the dummy variable is zero otherwise (Box 6.6).

Table 6.32 shows the results for the heterogeneous impact of BIT on FDI. The marginal impact of specific BIT provisions on Asia's FDI is examined. First, the most important provisions in Asia's BITs are TREAT and ISDM. Provisions in BIT granting for the principles of national treatment and most-favored nation status tend to increase greenfield FDI in Asia by about 7%. Likewise, provisions in BIT allowing for access to international dispute settlement mechanisms increase greenfield FDI projects into Asia by about 6%.

Second, assessing the relative importance of each provision, Asia's BITs have a significant, positive impact on FDI if they include provisions granting access to international arbitration for foreign investors (Table 6.33). These BITs tend to increase the cumulated number of greenfield FDI projects in Asia by about 53%. These

---

[68] The vector of dyadic control variables includes geographic distance, time zone difference, and the existence of a common border, language, religion, legal origin, and colonial past. The model controls for the existence of an regional trade agreement or a currency union. Because the dependent variable in this model is a count variable, i.e., it can take on nonnegative integer values , the appropriate estimation technique to use is the Poisson quasi-maximum likelihood estimation (Wooldridge 2004). To ensure robustness, we report cluster-heteroskedasticity-robust standard errors.

Box 6.6: Double Taxation Treaty with BITs and RTIAs

Using the United Nations Conference on Trade and Development bilateral investment treaty (BIT) dummy variable for the BIT data, columns (1) to (4) present that (i) BIT tends to increase the cumulative greenfield FDI projects into Asia by about 15%–19% significantly, (ii) BIT shows positive and significant impact on foreign direct investment (FDI) projects when regional trade and investment agreements (RTIAs) is controlled, and (iii) double taxation treaties (DTTs) also would likely increase greenfield FDI projects by about 14%–16%. BITs would likely drive any increase in the number of FDI projects when the impacts of RTIAs and DTT on FDIs are controlled.

Greenfield FDI and UNCTAD BIT dummy variable

	Cumulated number of greenfield FDI projects			
	(1)	(2)	(3)	(4)
BIT	0.160***	0.156***	0.152***	0.191***
	(0.058)	(0.058)	(0.058)	(0.059)
RTA		0.080***	0.078***	0.114***
		(0.026)	(0.026)	(0.027)
DTT			0.139***	0.159***
			(0.052)	(0.053)
Number of observations	18,277	18,211	18,211	18,211
Country-pairs panel	565	549	549	549

*** = significant at 1%, ** = significant at 5%, * = significant at 10%.
BIT = bilateral investment treaty, DTT = double taxation treaty, FDI = foreign direct investment, RTA = regional trade agreement, UNCTAD = United Nations Conference on Trade and Development.
Notes: Dyadic control variables and country-pair fixed effects are included in columns (1) to (3). Year fixed effects and country-pair fixed effects are included in column (4).
Sources: ADB calculations using data from Chaisse and Bellak (2015); Financial Times. fDi Markets; and United Nations Conference on Trade and Development. Investment Policy Hub. http://investmentpolicyhub. unctad.org/IIA (accessed August 2016).

Table 6.32: Greenfield FDI and Specific BIT Provisions

	Cumulated number of greenfield FDI projects				
	ENTRY	TREAT	SCOPE	PROTEC	ISDM
BIT Provision	0.083	0.070**	0.061	0.052	0.059*
	(0.054)	(0.036)	(0.039)	(0.035)	(0.035)
Number of observations	7,035	7,035	7,035	7,035	7,035
Country-pairs panel	274	274	274	274	274

*** = significant at 1%, ** = significant at 5%, * = significant at 10%.
BIT = bilateral investment treaty, FDI = foreign direct investment, ISDM = investor-state dispute mechanism, RTA = regional trade agreement.
Notes: Cluster-robust standard errors in parentheses. RTA, dyadic control variables and economyy-pair fixed effects are included in all columns. See definition of ENTRY, TREAT, SCOPE, PROTEC, and ISDM on page 161.
Sources: ADB calculations using data from Chaisse and Bellak (2015); Financial Times. fDi Markets; and United Nations Conference on Trade and Development. Investment Policy Hub. http://investmentpolicyhub. unctad.org/IIA (accessed August 2016).

results support that the principal advantages of BITs are derived from the fundamental principles of national treatment and most-favored nation status, and access to international arbitration.

Table 6.34 shows the results of the impact of each broad category of RTIA provisions on greenfield FDI projects into Asia. As with the previous results in Tables 6.32, the most important RTIA provisions are TREAT and ISDM.

TREAT provisions in RTIAs granting national treatment and most-favored nation status tend to increase greenfield FDI in Asia by about 33.3%. Likewise, ISDM provisions allowing for access to international dispute settlement mechanisms increase greenfield FDI projects into Asia by 28.5%. Both estimates are statistically significant at the 1.0% significance level.

Table 6.35 shows the relative importance of heterogeneity of RTIA provisions where RTIA increases greenfield FDI projects in the Asian region by about 18.0%, controlling for BIT and DTT among others, and TREAT provisions have a significant, positive impact on FDI projects when all provisions are considered.

If provisions to grant anti-discrimination for foreign investors in the form of the basic principles of national treatment and most-favored nation (see Table 6.35 column 2) are included, RTIAs tend to increase the number of greenfield FDI projects into Asia by approximately 33.4%.

Table 6.33: Greenfield FDI and Relative Importance of Specific BIT Provisions

	Cumulated Number of Greenfield FDI Projects	
	(1)	(2)
BIT	0.529**	
	(0.272)	
ENTRY	−0.181	−0.178
	(0.179)	(0.179)
TREAT	0.103	0.125*
	(0.074)	(0.076)
SCOPE	−0.002	−0.095
	(0.167)	(0.181)
PROTEC	−0.638	
	(0.178)	
ISDM	0.187***	0.167***
	(0.061)	(0.059)
DTT	0.101*	
Number of observations	7,035	7,035
Country-pairs panel	274	274

*** = significant at 1%, ** = significant at 5%, * = significant at 10%.
BIT = bilateral investment treaty, DTT = double taxation treaty, FDI = foreign direct investment, ISDM = investor-state dispute mechanism, RTA = regional trade agreement.
Notes: Cluster-robust standard errors are in parentheses. RTA, dyadic control variables and country-pair fixed effects are included in all columns. See definition of ENTRY, TREAT, SCOPE, PROTEC, and ISDM on page 161.
Sources: ADB calculations using data from Chaisse and Bellak (2015); Financial Times. fDi Markets; and United Nations Conference on Trade and Development. Investment Policy Hub. http://investmentpolicyhub. unctad.org/IIA (accessed August 2016).

Table 6.35: Greenfield FDI, RTIA, and Relative Importance of RTIA Provisions

	Cumulated Number of Greenfield FDI Projects	
	(1)	(2)
RTIA	0.178***	0.093
	(0.044)	(0.120)
ENTRY		0.187
		(0.265)
TREAT		0.334***
		(0.130)
SCOPE		−0.531
		(0.128)
PROTEC		−0.001
		(0.090)
ISDM		0.010
		(0.081)
BIT	0.064*	
	(0.064)	
DTT	0.092*	0.042
	(0.092)	(0.061)
Number of observations	5,901	8,150
Country-pairs panel	226	310

*** = significant at 1%, ** = significant at 5%, * = significant at 10%.
BIT = bilateral investment treaty, DTT = double taxation treaty, FDI = foreign direct investment, RTA = regional trade agreement, RTIA = regional trade and investment agreement.
Notes: RTA dyadic control variables and country-pair fixed effects are included in all columns. See definition of ENTRY, TREAT, SCOPE, PROTEC, and ISDM on page 161.
Sources: ADB calculations using data from Chaisse and Bellak (2015); Financial Times. fDi Markets; and United Nations Conference on Trade and Development. Investment Policy Hub. http://investmentpolicyhub. unctad.org/IIA (accessed August 2016).

Table 6.34: Greenfield FDI and Specific RTIA Provisions

	Cumulated Number of Greenfield FDI Projects				
	ENTRY	TREAT	SCOPE	PROTEC	ISDM
RTIA Provision	0.185	0.333***	−0.093	0.081	0.285***
	(0.126)	(0.127)	(0.091)	(0.068)	(0.110)
Number of observations	5,901	5,901	5,901	5,901	5,901
Country-pairs panel	226	226	226	226	226

*** = significant at 1%, ** = significant at 5%, * = significant at 10%.
BIT = bilateral investment treaty, FDI = foreign direct investment, ISDM = investor-state dispute mechanism, RTIA = regional trade and investment agreement.
Notes: Cluster-robust standard errors are in parentheses. BIT, dyadic control variables and country-pair fixed effects are included in all columns. See definition of ENTRY, TREAT, SCOPE, PROTEC, and ISDM on page 161.
Sources: ADB calculations using data from Chaisse and Bellak (2015); Financial Times. fDi Markets; and United Nations Conference on Trade and Development. Investment Policy Hub. http://investmentpolicyhub. unctad. org/IIA (accessed August 2016).

Policy implications

The cross sectional exponential model shows BITs and RTIAs can strongly encourage greenfield and M&A FDI projects. In the case of BITs, the presence of an investor-state-dispute mechanism (ISDM) is the only provision that appears to be significant across different model specifications. For RTIAs, foreign investors seem to be particularly sensitive to the provision expressed by TREAT, meaning that they will not be discriminated against domestic investors or other foreign investors. Provisions for national treatment and most-favored nation status in RTIAs may matter because they are possibly more comprehensive or take place alongside measures supporting international trade liberalization and the creation of regional supply chains. Overall a "pro-FDI" BIT can be expected to increase the number of FDI projects by 35.3%, or by 58.4% for a "pro-FDI" RTIA.[69] These findings suggest that IIAs which guarantee the credible protection of rights can be effective in attracting foreign investors.

To check the robustness of empirical results of the World-World BIT country pairs, panel data regressions are implemented with Asia-World BIT country pairs. The dependent variable is cumulative greenfield FDI projects into developing Asia from the world. First, interestingly, in the individual impact analyses of specific BITs and RTIAs provisions on Asian FDIs, TREAT and ISDM are the most important provisions. Second, in assessing the relative importance of each provision with other control variables, Asian BITs have a significant, positive impact on greenfield FDI projects if they include provisions that grant foreign investors access to international arbitration. In RTIA, the fundamental principles of national treatment and most-favored nation status show a significant positive effect on FDI projects. These results support our findings in the World-World BIT analysis.

Most economies have actively concluded large numbers of BITs and RTIAs with heterogeneous provisions over the decades without certainty of their impacts and long-term effects on economic variables. Particularly, our data show that developing Asian economies have

been apparently using such treaties as important policy tools for attracting FDI projects and enhancing the investment environment regardless of gaps in domestic implementation capacity.

Empirical analyses of cross-sectional and panel data find that concluding BITs and RTIAs has had significant success in attracting FDI. The two most important provisions from the analysis are ISDM in BITs and TREAT in RTIAs. Granting foreign investors international arbitration rights and guarantees of non-discrimination are particularly important for attracting FDI.

BITs and RTIAs vary in their effectiveness in encouraging FDI, depending on design and negotiation outcomes of their provisions. While no standard format for BITs and RTIAs exists, their provisions have somewhat converged over recent years. So an economy wanting to use BITs and RTIAs to promote FDI may consider its capacity for designing, negotiating, and implementing the agreed provisions as a significant potential factor in its ability to promote FDI, particularly since international arbitration mechanisms become increasingly integral to bilateral and regional trade treaties throughout the world.

---

[69] According to specification (6) of Table 6.28 and (2) of Table 6.31, via taking antilog function, the number of FDI projects would likely increase by 35.3% and 58.4%, respectively.

Annexes

Annex 6a: List of Economies for the Mode of Entry Analysis

High-income Economies	Overall WGI	Overall EoDB
Argentina	59.8	67.9
Australia	81.8	80.9
Austria	81.6	75.9
Bahrain	52.4	66.0
Belgium	76.5	73.4
Brunei Darussalam	61.1	58.9
Canada	82.5	82.7
Croatia	57.2	57.0
Cyprus	70.8	68.8
Czech Republic	67.5	62.8
Denmark	86.7	83.4
Equatorial Guinea	25.5	43.1
Estonia	70.2	75.0
Finland	88.0	80.8
France	74.0	68.0
Germany	79.0	77.9
Greece	60.7	59.7
Hong Kong, China	78.4	87.6
Hungary	66.3	65.3
Iceland	82.8	80.2
Ireland	79.6	84.6
Israel	61.2	71.5
Italy	61.8	65.1
Japan	74.0	77.5
Kuwait	53.5	60.1
Luxembourg	83.7	64.9
Malta	74.1	61.2
Netherlands	83.4	75.7
New Zealand	85.2	89.8
Norway	83.8	82.5
Oman	55.0	64.8
Poland	63.2	65.0
Portugal	71.0	71.3
Qatar	62.0	68.2
Republic of Korea	63.9	78.8
Saudi Arabia	43.0	63.8

High-income Economies	Overall WGI	Overall EoDB
Singapore	79.4	91.9
Slovak Republic	64.6	68.9
Slovenia	69.3	62.1
Spain	68.6	70.0
Sweden	85.3	80.1
Switzerland	84.4	73.2
Trinidad and Tobago	53.1	59.3
United Kingdom	78.3	84.1
United States	75.3	84.9
Average	**70.2**	**71.9**

Developing Economies	Overall WGI	Overall EoDB
Albania	43.3	57.1
Algeria	33.3	48.5
Armenia	45.2	62.6
Bangladesh	31.4	49.4
Belize	49.7	58.9
Bolivia	38.8	47.9
Bosnia and Herzegovina	42.9	51.8
Botswana	64.5	63.4
Brazil	50.5	49.0
Bulgaria	54.0	67.0
Burkina Faso	43.3	39.2
Cambodia	33.5	47.6
Cameroon	32.4	41.2
Cape Verde	58.9	53.6
Chad	23.6	28.6
Chile	73.2	68.3
Colombia	40.5	63.4
Republic of Congo	28.1	36.0
Democratic Republic of Congo	17.5	31.0
Costa Rica	61.6	54.0
Dominican Republic	42.8	59.2
Ecuador	34.3	56.1
Egypt	38.2	49.3
El Salvador	46.8	58.1
Ethiopia	30.8	45.0

continued on next page

Annex 6a continued

Developing Economies	Overall WGI	Overall EoDB	Developing Economies	Overall WGI	Overall EoDB
Fiji	41.9	67.1	Myanmar	17.8	41.5
Gabon	39.7	47.9	Namibia	56.2	61.6
Georgia	44.8	72.2	Nepal	32.5	58.5
Ghana	50.7	60.7	Nicaragua	39.2	53.2
Guatemala	37.7	56.2	Niger	37.5	37.2
Guinea-Bissau	25.8	36.2	Nigeria	26.9	43.9
Guyana	42.3	57.9	Pakistan	29.5	55.9
Haiti	25.5	38.4	Panama	51.4	62.9
Honduras	37.9	56.6	Papua New Guinea	35.7	53.7
India	44.3	46.7	Paraguay	34.7	57.2
Indonesia	37.9	54.0	People's Republic of China	39.1	54.4
Iran	29.5	54.8	Peru	43.4	67.0
Iraq	18.8	44.8	Philippines	40.6	50.5
Jamaica	49.2	60.8	Réunion	51.3	64.9
Jordan	49.5	52.3	Russian Federation	35.6	58.0
Kazakhstan	38.3	56.0	Rwanda	39.3	51.4
Kenya	35.9	55.7	Senegal	45.1	41.8
Kyrgyz Republic	32.3	57.8	Seychelles	52.6	62.1
Lao People's Democratic Republic	28.7	45.9	Sierra Leone	33.5	44.0
Latvia	63.3	73.1	Solomon Islands	37.1	56.0
Lebanon	37.6	58.0	South Africa	56.2	69.5
Lesotho	46.7	49.6	Sri Lanka	43.4	56.1
Liberia	29.0	42.9	Sudan	19.4	47.4
Libya	28.9	28.9	Suriname	48.4	40.5
Lithuania	64.4	73.8	Swaziland	37.7	55.8
Madagascar	41.8	46.2	Tanzania	41.9	52.7
Malawi	42.9	49.8	Thailand	46.4	70.2
Malaysia	56.8	73.8	Togo	30.9	37.8
Mali	41.8	41.6	Tunisia	48.1	63.5
Mauritania	37.9	40.9	Turkmenistan	48.4	63.1
Mauritius	65.5	70.8	Uganda	38.0	49.6
Mexico	48.1	68.3	Ukraine	39.0	43.1
Moldova	41.1	59.0	Uruguay	64.3	57.0
Mongolia	47.7	59.4	Venezuela	27.1	35.7
Morocco	43.5	58.6	Viet Nam	39.3	57.2
Mozambique	43.7	50.3	Zambia	42.7	57.0
			Average	**41.2**	**53.5**

EoDB = Ease of Doing Business, WGI = World Governance Index.
Note: EoDB and WGI averaged for years 2003, 2006, 2009, and 2012.
Source: World Bank (2016); World Bank. Worldwide Governance Indicators. http://data.worldbank.org/data-catalog/worldwide-governance-indicators (accessed July 2016).

Annex 6b: Data and Methodology for FDI Drivers by Mode of Entry

A more detailed description of data, model setup and specifications for the analysis of FDI drivers by mode of entry are described here. A bilateral panel dataset of greenfield and M&A is constructed, respectively, from 26 high-income economies (24 OECD members as well as Hong Kong, China and Singapore) to 97 developing economies and 45 high-income economies for 2003–2015 (see Annex 6.a for the list of economies). A gravity model is then applied to estimate the impact of institutional policy factors on FDI flows.

The World Bank's Worldwide Governance Indicators (WGI) are used to assess the host economy's institutional quality on investment inflows. These are available annually from 1996 for 215 countries and territories. The WGIs comprise six indicators: (1) voice and accountability, (2) political stability and absence of violence/terrorism, (3) government effectiveness, (4) regulatory quality, (5) rule of law, and (6) control of corruption. These aggregate indicators are based on data sources produced by a variety of organizations. Each indicator ranges from -2.5 to 2.5, with higher score for higher quality of governance/institution.[70] For easier comparison with other policy measures, the WGIs are transformed to range between 0 and 100, by adding 2.5 and then multiplying them by 20.

For measuring the policy regime of an economy, the World Bank's Ease of Doing Business Indicator (EoDB) is used. The EoDB reports have ranked ecoomies annually since 2003. The Doing Business 2016 reports include 10 components: (1) starting a business, (2) dealing with construction permits, (3) getting electricity, (4) registering property, (5) getting credit, (6) protecting minority investors, (7) paying taxes, (8) trading across borders, (9) enforcing contracts, and (10) resolving insolvency. Each indicator ranges from 0 to 100, with higher score representing better environment for doing business.

Most theoretical formulations of the gravity equation specify Y_{ijt}, flows of transactions from origin i to destination j, as the product of country/territory and bilateral-specific terms

$$Y_{ijt} = \alpha_t \frac{M_{it} M_{jt}}{D_{ijt}} \qquad (1)$$

where M_{it} and M_{jt} measure the attributes of origin i and destination j at a specific point in time t and α_t is a common time-specific factor. D_{ijt} reflects transaction costs between i and j at time t. In the application, Y_{ijt} is bilateral FDI flows (greenfield or M&A) from origin i to destination j at time t.

Two types of bilateral FDI flows are considered in the analysis: new greenfield FDI projects and new cross-border M&A deals. In the application, the host-specific terms, Mjt, are specified as

$$M_{jt} = \eta\, POLICY_{jt} + \gamma 1 \ln POP_{jt} + \gamma 2 \ln PCGD_{Pjt} + \gamma 3 \ln POP_{jt} + \gamma 4\, GROWTH_{jt} + \gamma 4\, INFLATION_{jt}$$

where POP_{jt} and $PCGD_{Pjt}$ are, respectively, the population and per capita GDP (PCGDP) of host economies and $GROWTH_{jt}$ and $INFLATION_{jt}$ are, respectively, GDP growth rate and inflation rate of host economies.[71]

It should be noted that institutional and policy variables are likely to be highly correlated with the level of economic development and hence without including a variable that captures the level of economic development, any positive relation with a policy variable and FDI flows may reflect a positive relation between economic development levels and FDI flows. Therefore, the logs of GDP per capita and population are considered separately. Population, GDP per capita, GDP growth rate, and inflation rates approximated by consumer price index (CPI) are all drawn from the World Bank's World Development Indicators.

GDP growth and inflation rates are included to capture the short-term fluctuations of macroeconomic conditions of host economies. Globerman and Sapiro (2004) find that economic growth is an important determinant of aggregate FDI, but not of the cross-border M&A flows. Higher inflation rates may suggest greater

---

[70]   For the methodology of the WGI, see Kaufmann, et al. (2011). See Thomas (2009) for a critical review.

[71]   As will be discussed in the following, the home country-specific terms, M_{jt}, will be absorbed by home-year fixed effects which account for multilateral resistance.

macroeconomic instability of the host and the currency value of the host economy may become weaker against other currencies, resulting in a lower value of local firms in terms of foreign currencies. This may increase or decrease a multinational's incentives to invest in the economy, depending on their motives (and modes) of FDI.

Also, the bilateral term is specified as

$$D_{ijt} = \beta1 \ln RTA_{ijt} + \beta2 \ln BIT_{ijt} + \theta\, PAIR_{ij} + u_{ijt}$$

where RTA_{ijt} and BIT_{ijt} indicate whether both economies are members of a bilateral/regional trade agreement or a bilateral investment treaty, respectively, and $PAIR_{ij}$ indicates bilateral fixed effects between economies i and j. PAIR includes log of geographic distance between source and host countries, a common language dummy and also a dummy for contiguity. Kogut and Singh (1988) argue that cultural factors have a more important influence on cross-border M&A than greenfield investment because unlike greenfield investment, cross-border M&A often requires the utilization of existing personnel, management, and organizational culture.

There are three main issues for a consistent estimation of the coefficients for the institutional and policy variables in the gravity framework. First, many pairs do not exert FDI flows and hence enter with zeros. Taking logs of the dependent variable would drop zero observation and result in biased estimates given that zero flows may indicate that fixed costs exceed expected variable profits (Razin et al. 2004; and Davis and Kristjánsdóttir 2010). Based on the property that the expected value of the logarithm of a random variable is different from the logarithm of its expected value (i.e., $E\,[\ln(Y)] \neq \ln E(y)$, Santos Silva and Tenreyro (2006) argue that estimating a log-linearized gravity equation by ordinary least squares (OLS) results in bias. They also argue that OLS would be inconsistent in the presence of heteroskedasticity (Lee and Ries 2016). Instead they suggest suggested that a gravity equation be estimated in its multiplicative form:

$$Yi = \exp(\chi_i\beta) + \varepsilon_i \qquad (2)$$

This formulation can be estimated using the Poisson Pseudo-Maximum Likelihood (PPML) estimator. As

PPML has received increasing recognition in estimating the gravity model, PPML is utilized in the study.[72]

The second concern relates to the endogeneity of policy variables. That is, FDI inflows may cause the policy makers of hosts to make their FDI environment more favorable to foreign investment. Three tactics override this concern. First, as an effort to reduce random volatility of FDI flows and to obtain fewer cases of zero values, the time dimension is reduced to four periods by taking the mean of the dependent variable for years 2004–2006, 2007–2009, 2010–2012, and 2013–2015. And then the dependent variable is matched with the policy variables and other explanatory variables for the preceding year of each sub-period (i.e., 2003, 2006, 2009, and 2012), thus allowing contemporaneous and lagged effects (1-2 years) of policy factors on FDI inflows to accrue.

The third concern is that "structural" gravity models consistent with theory require that estimation of a gravity equation take account of not only bilateral distance and transaction costs but also "multilateral resistance" (Anderson and van Wincoop 2003). This issue has been addressed in the empirical literature by including source-year and host-year fixed effects in panel data estimations. However, including a full set of time-varying source and host economy fixed effects is not feasible for the intended purpose because with host-year fixed effects, host economy-specific policy variables would not be measured. Therefore, only the source-year fixed effects for the sources' outward multilateral resistance are included. Arguably, FDI decisions are made by multinationals of source economies and hence host economies' inward multilateral resistance (host-year fixed effects) does not matter much.

As for the estimation of time-varying pair-specific policy variables (RTA and BIT dummy variables), a full set of time-varying source and host economy fixed effects is included, along with bilateral pair fixed effects. This specification is consistent with the "structural" gravity models of Anderson and van Wincoop (2003) and Baier and Bergstand (2007) in that it incorporates a full set of multilateral resistance effects.

---

[72] For discussions on PPML, see http://privatewww.essex.ac.uk/~jmcss/LGW.html.

Background papers

R. Desbordes. 2016. A Granular Approach to the Effects of Bilateral Investment Treaties and Regional Trade Investment Agreements on Foreign Direct Investment. Background paper prepared for Asian Economic Integration Report 2016 theme chapter on "What Drives Foreign Direct Investment in Asia and the Pacific?" Manuscript.

H.-H. Lee. 2016. Policy Factors Influencing FDI Inflows: A Comprehensive Analysis. Background paper prepared for Asian Economic Integration Report 2016 theme chapter on "What Drives Foreign Direct Investment in Asia and the Pacific?" Manuscript.

N. Ramondo. 2016. Factory Asia: The Determinants of Multinational Activity in the Context of Global Value Chains. Background paper prepared for Asian Economic Integration Report 2016 theme chapter on "What Drives Foreign Direct Investment in Asia and the Pacific?" Manuscript.

N. Ramondo. 2016. FDI Entry Mode and the Activity of Affiliates of Multinational Firms. Background paper prepared for Asian Economic Integration Report 2016 theme chapter on "What Drives Foreign Direct Investment in Asia and the Pacific?" Manuscript.

References

G. Abonyi, A. Zola, and E. Suwannakarn. 2014. *Scoping Study on Developing Border Economic Areas and Cross-border Linkages between Thailand and its Neighbours.* Manila.

_____. 2015. *Asian Economic Integration Report 2015: How Can Special Economic Zones Catalyze Economic Development.* Manila. https://aric.adb.org/pdf/aeir/AEIR2015_complete.pdf

_____. 2016. *Asian Development Outlook 2016: Asia's Growth Potential.* Manila. https://www.adb.org/publications/asian-development-outlook-2016-asia-potential-growth

_____. 2016. *The Role of Special Economic Zones in Improving Effectiveness of GMS Economic Corridors.* Manila (forthcoming).

ADB Institute. 2014. *Connecting Central Asia with Economic Centers.* Tokyo. http://www.adb.org/sites/default/files/publication/159307/adbi-connecting-central-asia-economic-centers-final-report.pdf

B. Aitken, A. Harrison, and R. Lipsey. 1996. Wages and Foreign Ownership: A Comparative Study of Mexico, Venezuela, and the United States. *Journal of International Economics.* 40 (3). pp. 345–371.

M. Aleksynska and O. Havrylchyk. 2011. FDI from the South: the Role of Institutional Distance and Natural Resources. *Working Papers.* No. 2011-05. Paris: CEPII Research Center.

L. Alfaro. 2003. *Foreign direct investment and growth: Does the sector matter?* http://www.grips.ac.jp/teacher/oono/hp/docu01/paper14.pdf

J. E. Anderson and E.van Wincoop. 2003. Gravity with Gravitas: A Solution to the Border Puzzle. *American Economic Review.* 93(1). pp. 170–192.

P. Antràs, D. Chor, T. Fally, and R. Hillberry. Measuring the Upstreamness of Production and Trade Flows. *American Economic Review: Papers & Proceedings.* 102 (3). pp. 412–416. http://scholar.harvard.edu/files/antras/files/acfh_published.pdf

P. Antràs, M. Desai, and F.C. Foley. 2009. Multinational Firms, FDI Flows and Imperfect Capital Markets. *Quarterly Journal of Economics.* 124 (3). pp. 1171–1219.

P. Athukorala. 2013. Intra-Regional FDI and Economic Integration in South Asia: Trends, Patterns and Prospects. *UNCTAD Regional Value Chains Background Paper.* Geneva: United Nations Conference on Trade and Development.

D. Aykut and S. Sayek. 2007. The Role of the Sectoral Composition of Foreign Direct Investment on Growth. In L. Piscitello and G. Santangelo eds. *Do Multinationals Feed Local Development and Growth?* London: Elsevier. pp. 35–62.

S. L. Baier and J. H. Bergstrand. 2007. Do Free Trade Agreements Actually Increase Members' International Trade? *Journal of International Economics.* 71(1). pp. 72–95.

R. Barro and J. -W. Lee. 2013. A New Data Set of Educational Attainment in the World, 1950-2010. *Journal of Development Economics.* 104. pp. 184–198.

T. Beck, A. Demirguc-Kunt, and R. Levine. 2009. Financial Institutions and Markets Across Countries and Over Time: Data and Analysis. *World Bank Policy Research Working Paper Series.* No. 4943. Washington, DC: The World Bank.

C. Bellak. 2015. Economic Impact of Investment Agreements. *Department of Economics Working Paper.* No. 200. Vienna: Vienna University of Economics and Business. http://www.cuhk.edu.hk/law/proj/BITSel/download/Christian_Bellak(2015).pdf

A. Berger, M. Busse, P. Nunnenkamp, and S. Roy. 2010. Do Trade and Investment Agreements Lead to More FDI? Accounting for Key Provisions Inside the Black Box. *WTO Staff Working Paper ERSD-2010-13.* Geneva: World Trade Organization. https://www.wto.org/english/res_e/reser_e/ersd201013_e.pdf

T. Büthe and H. V. Milner. 2014. Foreign Direct Investment and Institutional Diversity in Trade Agreements: Credibility, Commitment, and Economic Flows in the Developing World, 1971–2007. *World Politics.* 66 (1). pp. 88–122.

H.-S. Byun, H.-H. Lee, and C.-Y. Park. 2012. Assessing Factors Affecting M&As versus Greenfield FDI in Emerging Countries. *ADB Economics Working Paper Series No.293.* Manila: Asian Development Bank. https://www.adb.org/sites/default/files/publication/30058/economics-wp293.pdf

R. E. Caves. 2007. *Multinational Enterprises and Economic Analysis.* Cambridge, UK: Cambridge University Press.

J. Chaisse and C. Bellak. 2015. Navigating the Expanding Universe of International Treaties on Foreign Investment Creation and Use of a Critical Index. *Journal of International Economic Law.* 18 (1). pp. 79–115.

A. Chongvilaivan. 2012. From Inward to Outward: An Assessment of FDI Performance in Thailand. *Southeast Asian Affairs.* Vol. 2012. pp. 318–338. Singapore.

J. Coolidge and S. Rose-Ackerman. 1997. High-level rent-seeking and corruption in African regimes: Theory and cases. *Policy Research Working Papers.* No. 1780. Washington, DC: The World Bank.

J. Darby, B. Ferrett, and I. Wooton. 2013. FDI, Trade Costs, and Regional Asymmetries. *CESifo Working Paper Series.* No. 4469. Munich: CESifo Group Munich.

R. B. Davis and H. Kristjánsdóttir. 2010. Fixed Costs, Foreign Direct Investment, and Gravity with Zeros. *Review of International Economics.* 18 (1). pp 47–62.

J. H. Dunning and S. M. Lundan. 2008. *Multinational Enterprises and the Global Economy.* Cheltenham, UK: Edward Elgar.

P. Egger and P. Pfaffermayr. 2004. Distance, Trade and FDI: A Hausman–Taylor SUR approach. *Journal of Applied Econometrics.* 19 (2). pp. 227–246.

S. Globerman and D. Shapiro. 2002. Global Foreign Direct Investment Flows: The Role of Governance Infrastructure. *World Development.* 30 (11). pp. 1899–1919.

S. S. Golub. 2009. Openness to Foreign Direct Investment in Services: An International Comparative Analysis. *World Economy.* 32 (8). pp. 1245–1268.

M. Hallward-Driemeier. 2003. Do Bilateral Investment Treaties Attract FDI? Only a Bit…and They Could Bite. *Policy Research Working Papers.* Washington, DC: The World Bank. http://elibrary.worldbank.org/doi/abs/10.1596/1813-9450-3121

T. Harding and B. S. Javorcik. 2011. Roll Out the Red Carpet and They Will Come: Investment Promotion and FDI Inflows. *The Economic Journal.* 121 (557). pp. 1445–1476.

P. Harms and P. G. Meon. 2014. Good and Bad FDI: The Growth Effects of Greenfield Investment and Mergers and Acquisitions in Developing Countries. *CEB Working Paper.* No. 14/021. Bruselles: Université Libre de Bruxelles - Solvay Brussels School of Economics and Management Centre Emile Bernheim.

A. E. Harrison and J. Scorse. 2005. Do foreign-owned firms pay more? Evidence from the Indonesian Manufacturing Sector 1990–99. *Working Paper.* No. 98. Geneva: International Labour Office.

K. Head and J. Ries. 2008. FDI as an Outcome of the Market for Corporate Control: Theory and Evidence. *Journal of International Economics.* 74 (1). pp. 2–20.

K. Head, R. Jing, and D. Swenson. 2014. From Beijing to Bentonville: Do Multinational Retailers Link Markets? *Journal of Development Economics.* 110. pp. 79–92.

E. Helpman, M. J. Melitz, and S.R. Yeaple. 2004. Export Versus FDI with Heterogeneous Firms. *American Economic Review.* 94(1). pp. 300–316.

IMF. 2004. Round Tripping. *Issues Paper (DITEG) No. 13.* September. https://www.imf.org/External/NP/sta/bop/pdf/diteg13.pdf

H.L. Kee, A. Nicita and M. Olarreaga. 2009. Estimating Trade Restrictiveness Indices. *Economic Journal.* 119. pp. 172–199.

B. Kogut and H. Singh. 1988. The Effect of National Culture on the Choice of Entry Mode. *Journal of International Business Studies.* 19 (3). pp. 411–432.

H.-H. Lee and J. Ries. 2016. Aid for Trade and Greenfield Investment. *World Development*. pp. 206–218.

M. Lesher and S. Miroudot. 2006. Analysis of the Economic Impact of Investment Provisions in Regional Trade Agreements. *OECD Trade Policy Papers*. No. 36. Paris: OECD Publishing. http://www.oecd-ilibrary.org/docserver/download/5l4vwbdwmcmx.pdf?expires=1478168636&id=id&accname=guest&checksum=FCD3DA2DCC4BACA9FC37918D28971E6B

R. E. Lipsey and F. Sjöholm. 2004. FDI and Wage Spillovers in Indonesian Manufacturing. *Review of World Economics / Weltwirtschaftliches Archiv*. 140 (2). pp. 321–332. www.jstor.org/stable/40441012.

_____. 2011. The Role of South-South FDI in the Economies of Developing Asia. *ADB Economics Working Paper Series*. No. 273. Manila: Asian Development Bank. https://www.adb.org/sites/default/files/publication/29144/economics-wp273.pdf

M. J. Melitz. 2003. The Impact of Trade on Intra-Industry Reallocations and Aggregate Industry Productivity. *Econometrica*. 71 (6). pp. 1695–1725. http://web.stanford.edu/~klenow/Melitz.pdf

T. H. Moran. 2001. Parental Supervision: The New Paradigm for Foreign Direct Investment and Development. *Policy Analyses in International Economics*. No. 64. Washington, DC: Institute of International Economics.

_____ 2011. *Foreign Direct Investment and Development: Reevaluating Policies for Developed and Developing Countries*. Washington, DC: Peterson Institute for International Economics.

G. B. Navaretti and A. J. Venables. 2005. *Multinational Firms in the World Economy*. Princeton, US: Princeton University Press.

V. Nocke and S. Yeaple. 2008. An Assignment Theory of Foreign Direct Investment. *Review of Economic Studies*. 75 (2). pp. 529–557.

J. Nylander. 2015. Hong Kong Overtakes the U.S. in FDI. *Forbes*. June 25. http://www.forbes.com/sites/jnylander/2015/06/25/hong-kong-overtakes-the-u-s-in-fdi/#3751d3f537f5

N. Ramondo, A. Rodriguez-Clare, and F. Tintelnot. 2015. Multinational Production: Data and Stylized Facts. *American Economic Review Papers and Proceedings*. 105 (5). pp. 530–536.

A. Razin, Y. Rubinstein, and E. Sadka. 2004. Fixed Costs and FDI: The Conflicting Effects of Productivity Shocks. *NBER Working Paper Series*. No.10864. Cambridge, MA: National Bureau of Economic Research.

J. M. C. Santos Silva and S. Tenreyro. 2006. The Log of Gravity. *Review of Economics and Statistics*. 88 (4). pp. 641–658.

D. W. Te Velde and O. Morrissey. 2003. Do Workers in Africa Get a Wage Premium if Employed in Firms Owned by Foreigners? *Journal of African Economies*. 12 (1). pp. 41–73.

United Nations Conference on Trade and Development. 2000. *World Investment Report 2000: Cross-border Mergers and Acquisitions and Development*. Geneva: United Nations. http://unctad.org/en/Docs/wir2000overview_en.pdf

_____. 2013. *World Investment Report 2013: Global Value Chains: Investment and Trade for Development*. Geneva: United Nations. http://unctad.org/en/PublicationsLibrary/wir2013_en.pdf

_____. 2015. *World Investment Report 2015: Reforming International Investment Governance*. Geneva: United Nations. http://unctad.org/en/PublicationsLibrary/wir2015_en.pdf

_____. 2016. *World Investment Report 2016: Investor Nationality Policy Challenges*. Geneva: United Nations. http://unctad.org/en/pages/PublicationWebflyer.aspx?publicationid=1555

M. Wang and M. C. Sunny Wong. 2009. What Drives Economic Growth? The Case of Cross-Border M&A and Greenfield FDI Activities. *Kyklos*. 62 (2). pp. 316–330.

Z. Wang, S. J. Wei, and K. Zhu. 2014. Quantifying International Production Sharing at the Bilateral and Sector Levels. Paper prepared for The Third World KLEMS Conference Tokyo, Japan, May 19-20. http://www.worldklems.net/conferences/worldklems2014/worldklems2014_Wang.pdf

P. Warr and J. Menon. 2015. Cambodia's Special Economic Zones. *ADB Economics Working Paper*. No. 459. Manila.

J. M. Wooldridge. 2004. Estimating Average Partial Effects Under Conditional Moment Independence Assumptions. *CeMMAP Working Papers*. CWP03/04. London: Institute for Fiscal Studies.

World Bank. 2016. *Doing Business 2017: Equal Opportunity for All*. Washington, DC. http://www.doingbusiness.org/~/media/WBG/DoingBusiness/Documents/Annual-Reports/English/DB17-Report.pdf

7 | Statistical Appendix

Statistical Appendix

The statistical appendix is comprised of 11 tables that present selected indicators on economic integration covering the 48 regional members of the Asian Development Bank (ADB). The succeeding notes describe the regional groupings and the calculation procedures undertaken.

Regional Groupings

- Asia consists of the 48 regional members of ADB.
- Developing Asia refers to Asia excluding Australia, Japan, and New Zealand.
- European Union (EU-28) consists of Austria, Belgium, Bulgaria, Croatia, Cyprus, Czech Republic, Denmark, Estonia, Finland, France, Germany, Greece, Hungary, Ireland, Italy, Latvia, Lithuania, Luxembourg, Malta, the Netherlands, Poland, Portugal, Romania, Slovak Republic, Slovenia, Spain, Sweden, and the United Kingdom.

Table Description

Table A1: Regional Integration Indicators—Asia (% of total)

The table provides a summary of regional integration indicators for three areas: trade and investment, capital (equity and bond holdings), and people movement (migration, remittances and tourism); and for Asian subregions, including ASEAN+3 (including Hong Kong, China). Cross-border flows within and across subregions are shown as well as total flows with Asia and the rest of the world. The definition of each indicators are provided in the description below.

Table A2: Trade Share—Asia (% of total trade)

It is calculated as (tij/Tiw)*100, where tij is the total trade of economy "i" with economy "j" and Tiw is the total trade of economy "i" with the world. A higher share indicates a higher degree of regional trade integration.

Table A3: FTA Status—Asia

It is the number and status of bilateral and plurilateral free trade agreements (FTA) with at least one of the Asian economies as signatory. FTAs only proposed are excluded. It covers FTAs with the following status: Framework Agreement signed—the parties initially negotiate the contents of a framework agreement (FA), which serves as a framework for future negotiations; Negotiations launched—the parties, through the relevant ministries, declare the official launch of negotiations or set the date for such, or start the first round of negotiations; Signed but not yet in effect—parties sign the agreement after negotiations have been completed, however, the agreement has yet to be implemented; and Signed and in effect—provisions of FTA come into force, after legislative or executive ratification.

Table A4: Time to Export and Import—Asia (number of hours)

Time to export (import) data measures the number of hours required to export (import) by ocean transport, including the processing of documents required to complete the transaction. It covers time used for documentation requirements and procedures at customs and other regulatory agencies as well as the time of inland transport between the largest business city and the main port used by traders. Regional aggregates are weighted averages based on total exports or imports.

Table A5: Logistics Performance Index—Asia (% to EU)

Logistics Performance Index (LPI) scores are based on the following dimensions: (i) efficiency of border control and customs process; (ii) transport and trade-related infrastructure; (iii) competitively priced shipments; (iv) ability to track and trace consignments; and (v) timeliness of shipments. Regional aggregates are computed using total trade as weights. A score above (below) 100 means that it is easier (more difficult) to export or import from that economy compared to EU.

Table A6: Cross-Border Portfolio Equity Holdings Share—Asia (% of total cross-border equity holdings)

It is calculated as $(E_{ij}/E_{iw})*100$ where E_{ij} is the holding of economy "i" of the equity securities issued by economy "j" and E_{iw} is the holding of economy "i" of the equity securities issued by all economies except those issued in the domestic market. Calculations are based solely on available data in the Coordinated Portfolio Investment Survey (CPIS) database of the International Monetary Fund (IMF). Rest of the World (ROW) includes equity securities issued by International Organizations defined in the CPIS database and "Not specified (including confidential)" category. A higher share indicates a higher degree of regional integration.

Table A7: Cross-Border Portfolio Debt Holdings Share—Asia (% of total cross-border debt holdings)

It is calculated as $(D_{ij}/D_{iw})*100$ where D_{ij} is the holding of economy "i" of the debt securities issued by partner "j" and D_{iw} is the holding of economy "i" of the debt securities issued by all economies except those issued in the domestic market. Calculations are based solely on available data in the CPIS database of the IMF. ROW includes debt securities issued by international organizations defined in the CPIS database and "Not specified (including confidential)" category. A higher share indicates a higher degree of regional integration.

Table A8: FDI Inflow Share—Asia (% of total FDI inflows)

It is calculated as $(F_{ij}/F_{iw})*100$ where F_{ij} is the foreign direct investment (FDI) received by economy "i" from economy "j" and F_{iw} is the FDI received by economy "i" from the world. Figures are based on net FDI inflow data. A higher share indicates a higher degree of regional integration. The bilateral FDI database of the United Nations Conference on Trade and Development (UNCTAD) was updated up to 2015 using data from

ASEAN Secretariat, Eurostat, Organization for Economic Cooperation and Development, and national sources. For countries with missing data, bilateral flows from 2013 to 2015 were estimated as follows: For each economy "i", the GDP share of the FDI received from economy "j" is computed using 2012 data. This share is then multiplied to the GDP of economy "i" to get the annual amount of FDI inflow from country "j" for each year from 2013 to 2015.

Table A9: Remittance Inflows Share—Asia (% of total remittance inflows)

It is calculated as $(R_{ij}/R_{iw})*100$ where R_{ij} is the remittance received by economy "i" from partner "j" and R_{iw} is the remittance received by economy "i" from the world. Remittances refer to the sum of the following: (i) workers' remittances which are recorded as current transfers under the current account of the IMF's Balance of Payments (BOP); (ii) compensation of employees which includes wages, salaries, and other benefits of border, seasonal, and other non-resident workers and which are recorded under the "income" subcategory of the current account; and (iii) migrants' transfers which are reported under capital transfers in the BOP's capital account. Transfers through informal channels are excluded.

Table A10: Outbound Migration Share—Asia (% of total outbound migrants)

It is calculated as $(M_{ij}/M_{iw})*100$ where M_{ij} is the number migrants of economy "i" residing in economy "j" and M_{iw} is the number of all migrants of economy "i" residing overseas. This definition excludes those traveling abroad on a temporary basis. A higher share indicates a higher degree of regional integration.

Table A11: Outbound Tourism Share—Asia (% of total outbound tourists)

It is calculated as $(TR_{ij}/TR_{iw})*100$ where TR_{ij} is the number of nationals of economy "i" travelling as tourists in economy "j" and TR_{iw} is the total number of nationals of economy "i" travelling as tourists overseas. A higher share indicates a higher degree of regional integration.

Table A1: Regional Integration Indicators—Asia

	Movement in Trade and Investment		Movement in Capital		People Movement		
	Trade (%)	FDI (%)	Equity Holdings (%)	Bond Holdings (%)	Migration (%)	Tourism (%)	Remittances (%)
	2015	2015	2015	2015	2015	2014	2015
Within Subregions							
ASEAN+3 (including HKG)[1]	47.1 ▲	48.4 ▼	14.6 ▼	12.1 ▼	40.0 ▲	72.2 ▼	33.7 ▲
Central Asia	8.9 ▲	3.8 ▲	0.0 ▼	–	9.3 ▼	36.3 ▼	7.2 ▲
East Asia	36.8 ▲	47.1 ▼	11.7 ▼	8.3 ▼	34.6 ▼	60.5 ▼	35.5 ▼
South Asia	5.5 ▲	0.6 ▼	0.9 ▲	2.1 ▲	26.2 ▼	12.2 ▲	15.2 ▲
Southeast Asia	23.7 ▼	17.6 ▼	7.2 ▼	8.9 ▼	34.1 ▲	68.2 ▼	14.7 ▲
The Pacific and Oceania	6.7 ▼	17.7 ▲	5.3 ▲	1.0 ▼	56.3 ▲	19.7 ▲	30.4 ▼
Across Subregions							
ASEAN+3 (including HKG)[1]	10.7 —	4.3 ▲	3.8 ▼	6.5 ▼	8.8 ▲	5.5 ▲	6.9 ▲
Central Asia	28.6 ▲	21.3 ▲	11.6 ▼	14.6 ▲	0.8 ▼	3.0 ▲	0.7 ▲
East Asia	18.5 ▲	5.9 ▼	2.8 ▼	7.3 ▼	14.3 ▲	13.7 ▼	15.3 ▲
South Asia	32.2 ▲	38.3 ▲	22.7 ▲	10.6 ▼	5.8 ▲	32.7 ▼	5.4 ▼
Southeast Asia	45.8 ▲	35.3 ▲	36.6 ▲	25.3 ▲	14.6 ▼	23.2 ▲	13.5 ▲
The Pacific and Oceania	61.3 ▼	77.2 ▲	11.3 ▲	7.8 ▼	5.4 ▼	39.6 ▲	13.1 ▲
TOTAL (within and across subregions)							
Asia	**57.1** ▲	**52.6** ▼	**19.8** ▼	**17.9** ▼	**36.7** ▼	**72.4** ▼	**30.5** ▲
ASEAN+3 (including HKG)[1]	57.8 ▲	52.7 ▲	18.4 ▼	18.6 ▼	48.8 ▲	77.7 ▼	40.6 ▲
Central Asia	37.6 ▲	25.1 ▲	11.6 ▼	14.6 ▲	10.0 ▼	39.3 ▼	7.8 ▲
East Asia	55.3 ▲	53.1 ▼	14.5 ▼	15.6 ▼	48.9 ▼	74.1 ▼	50.8 ▼
South Asia	37.7 ▲	38.9 ▲	23.5 ▲	12.7 ▼	32.0 ▼	44.9 ▲	20.6 ▼
Southeast Asia	69.5 ▲	52.9 ▲	43.7 ▲	34.2 ▼	48.7 ▲	91.3 ▲	28.2 ▲
The Pacific and Oceania	68.0 ▼	94.9 ▲	16.6 ▲	8.8 ▼	61.7 ▲	59.3 ▲	43.5 ▼
With the rest of the world							
Asia	**42.9** ▼	**47.4** ▲	**80.2** ▲	**82.1** ▲	**63.3** ▲	**27.6** ▲	**69.5** ▼
ASEAN+3 (including HKG)[1]	42.2 ▼	47.3 ▲	79.7 ▲	81.4 ▲	51.2 ▼	22.3 ▲	59.4 ▼
Central Asia	62.4 ▼	74.9 ▼	88.4 ▲	85.4 ▼	90.0 ▲	60.7 ▲	92.2 ▼
East Asia	44.7 ▼	46.9 ▲	85.5 ▲	84.4 ▲	51.1 ▲	25.9 ▲	49.2 ▲
South Asia	62.3 ▼	61.1 ▼	76.5 ▼	87.3 ▲	68.0 ▲	55.1 ▲	79.4 ▲
Southeast Asia	30.5 ▼	47.1 ▼	56.3 ▼	65.8 ▲	51.3 ▼	8.7 ▼	71.8 ▼
The Pacific and Oceania	32.0 ▲	5.1 ▼	83.4 ▼	91.2 ▲	38.3 ▼	40.7 ▼	56.5 ▲

▲ = increase from previous period; ▼ = decrease from previous period; – = data unavailable.

[1]Includes ASEAN (Brunei Darussalam, Cambodia, Indonesia, the Lao People's Democratic Republic, Malaysia, Myanmar, the Philippines, Singapore, Thailand, and Viet Nam) plus the People's Republic of China; Hong Kong, China; Japan; and the Republic of Korea.

Trade—national data unavailable for Bhutan, Kiribati, Nauru, Palau, Timor-Leste, and Tuvalu; no data available on the Cook Islands, the Marshall Islands, and the Federated States of Micronesia.

Equity and Bond holdings—based on investments from Australia; Bangladesh (start from 2013); Hong Kong, China; India; Indonesia; Japan; Kazakhstan; the Republic of Korea; Malaysia; Mongolia; New Zealand; Pakistan; Palau (start from 2015); the Philippines; Singapore; Thailand; and Vanuatu. Data start from 2001.

Migration—share of migrant stock to total migrants in 2015 (compared with 2010).

Tourism—share of outbound tourists to total tourists in 2014 (compared with 2013).

Remittances—share of inward remittances to total remittances in 2015 (compared with 2010).

Sources: ADB calculations using data from ASEAN Secretariat; Asia Regional Integration Center, Asian Development Bank; CEIC; International Monetary Fund. Direction of Trade Statistics; International Monetary Fund. World Economic Outlook Database April 2016; Organisation for Economic Co-operation and Development; United Nations Conference on Trade and Development; United Nations. Department of Economic and Social Affairs, Population Division. International Migration Stock 2015; United Nations. World Tourism Organization; and World Bank. World Bank Migration and Remittances Data.

Table A2: Trade shares (% of total world trade, 2015)

Reporter	Asia	PRC	Japan	EU	US	ROW
Central Asia	**37.6**	**21.9**	**1.4**	**26.9**	**2.2**	**33.3**
Armenia	20.3	10.2	1.3	25.7	3.4	50.5
Azerbaijan	17.1	2.7	2.7	46.9	6.1	30.0
Georgia	26.8	7.2	2.1	31.9	3.6	37.7
Kazakhstan	32.1	20.6	1.4	33.9	1.8	32.2
Kyrgyz Republic	68.9	48.2	0.3	3.8	0.5	26.7
Tajikistan	60.1	36.0	0.1	4.6	0.9	34.4
Turkmenistan	54.6	43.3	0.2	9.6	0.8	35.0
Uzbekistan	51.4	19.6	1.5	11.9	0.9	35.9
East Asia	**55.5**	**15.6**	**6.0**	**12.2**	**13.0**	**19.4**
Hong Kong, China	78.6	51.9	5.0	8.0	7.2	6.1
Japan	55.7	21.3	0.0	10.8	15.4	18.2
Republic of Korea	55.2	23.6	7.4	11.0	11.8	21.9
Mongolia	72.0	61.2	3.9	5.6	1.1	21.2
PRC	47.1	0.0	7.2	14.6	14.3	23.9
Taipei,China	70.4	30.7	9.7	7.9	10.8	10.9
South Asia	**37.7**	**12.1**	**2.4**	**14.1**	**8.6**	**39.6**
Afghanistan	77.5	5.7	0.4	5.7	7.9	8.9
Bangladesh	42.9	13.8	3.1	23.9	7.4	25.8
Bhutan	84.3	1.2	1.8	14.4	0.7	0.7
India	34.8	10.8	2.2	13.5	9.3	42.4
Maldives	58.1	9.4	1.4	13.5	2.9	25.5
Nepal	83.4	13.9	0.9	6.4	1.8	8.4
Pakistan	43.3	22.7	2.3	12.8	6.0	38.0
Sri Lanka	52.4	4.7	6.4	11.0	5.3	31.3
Southeast Asia	**69.5**	**17.0**	**8.6**	**10.0**	**9.2**	**11.4**
Brunei Darussalam	87.6	13.6	18.8	9.1	1.4	1.9

Reporter	Asia	PRC	Japan	EU	US	ROW
Cambodia	69.1	15.5	3.9	15.3	10.4	5.3
Indonesia	70.3	15.2	10.7	8.9	8.2	12.6
Lao PDR	90.8	21.8	1.7	3.3	0.6	5.4
Malaysia	71.0	15.7	8.7	10.1	8.8	10.1
Myanmar	91.9	40.7	5.3	3.6	1.0	3.4
Philippines	69.3	13.9	14.7	10.7	12.7	7.3
Singapore	69.2	14.0	5.2	10.2	8.9	11.7
Thailand	65.4	15.6	12.3	9.5	9.1	16.0
Viet Nam	68.9	25.0	7.3	10.7	11.2	9.3
The Pacific	**69.8**	**14.9**	**11.0**	**5.2**	**2.3**	**22.7**
Fiji	68.9	10.6	3.0	8.3	6.8	16.0
Kiribati	90.5	15.2	11.8	1.1	3.1	5.2
Nauru	57.6	3.3	3.1	1.0	1.5	39.9
Palau	95.6	30.6	31.4	4.3	0.0	0.1
Papua New Guinea	66.8	14.3	13.5	4.8	1.6	26.8
Samoa	74.1	12.1	2.8	1.0	4.8	20.1
Solomon Islands	83.1	43.7	1.9	6.6	0.8	9.5
Timor-Leste	93.5	11.6	1.4	4.4	0.7	1.4
Tonga	88.6	13.3	3.2	2.3	6.9	2.2
Tuvalu	93.4	14.0	17.5	3.9	0.7	1.9
Vanuatu	79.6	14.6	19.1	4.8	1.5	14.1
Oceania	**67.9**	**26.0**	**10.6**	**12.0**	**9.0**	**11.1**
Australia	69.0	27.3	11.3	11.6	8.6	10.8
New Zealand	61.1	18.6	6.3	14.1	11.8	13.1
Asia	**57.2**	**16.2**	**6.4**	**12.0**	**11.6**	**19.2**
Developing Asia	**57.0**	**15.1**	**7.0**	**12.2**	**11.2**	**19.7**

PRC = People's Republic of China, EU = European Union, Lao PDR = Lao People's Democratic Republic, ROW = rest of the world, US = United States.
Source: ADB calculations using data from International Monetary Fund. Direction of Trade Statistics. http://www.imf.org/en/Data (accessed August 2016)

Table A3: FTA Status—Asia (2016)

Economy	Under Negotiation		Signed but not yet In Effect	Signed and In Effect	Total
	Framework Agreement signed	Negotiations launched			
Central Asia					
Armenia	0	0	0	10	10
Azerbaijan	0	0	0	10	10
Georgia	0	1	1	11	13
Kazakhstan	0	3	1	10	14
Kyrgyz Republic	0	0	0	10	10
Tajikistan	0	0	0	8	8
Turkmenistan	0	0	0	6	6
Uzbekistan	0	0	0	10	10
East Asia					
Hong Kong, China	0	2	0	4	6
People's Republic of China	0	7	0	16	23
Japan	0	8	1	15	24
Republic of Korea	0	9	0	16	25
Mongolia	0	0	1	0	1
Taipei,China	1	1	0	7	9
South Asia					
Afghanistan	0	0	0	2	2
Bangladesh	0	2	1	3	6
Bhutan	0	1	0	2	3
India	1	14	0	13	28
Maldives	0	0	1	1	2
Nepal	0	1	0	2	3
Pakistan	0	6	1	11	18
Sri Lanka	0	3	0	5	8
Southeast Asia					
Brunei Darussalam	0	2	1	8	11
Cambodia	0	2	0	6	8
Indonesia	0	7	1	9	17
Lao People's Democratic Republic	0	2	0	8	10
Malaysia	1	5	2	14	22
Myanmar	1	3	0	6	10
Philippines	0	3	1	7	11
Singapore	0	9	2	20	31
Thailand	1	8	0	13	22
Viet Nam	0	5	2	9	16

continuation on next page

Table A3 continued

Economy	Under Negotiation		Signed but not yet In Effect	Signed and In Effect	Total
	Framework Agreement signed	Negotiations launched			
The Pacific					
Cook Islands	0	2	0	2	4
Fiji	0	2	0	3	5
Kiribati	0	2	0	2	4
Marshall Islands	0	2	0	3	5
Federated States of Micronesia	0	2	0	3	5
Nauru	0	2	0	2	4
Palau	0	2	0	2	4
Papua New Guinea	0	2	0	4	6
Samoa	0	2	0	2	4
Solomon Islands	0	2	0	3	5
Tonga	0	2	0	2	4
Tuvalu	0	2	0	2	4
Vanuatu	0	2	0	3	5
Oceania					
Australia	0	5	1	12	18
New Zealand	0	6	1	11	18

FTA = free trade agreement.

Notes:

1. Framework Agreement signed: The parties initially negotiate the contents of a framework agreement (FA), which serves as a framework for future negotiations.
2. Negotiations launched: The parties, through the relevant ministries, declare the official launch of negotiations or set the date for such, or start the first round of negotiations.
3. Signed but not yet in effect: Parties sign the agreement after negotiations have been completed. However, the agreement has yet to be implemented.
4. Signed and in effect: Provisions of FTA come into force, after legislative or executive ratification.

Source: ADB. Asia Regional Integration Center FTA Database (accessed August 2016).

Table A4. Time to Export or Import—Asia (hours)

	Time to Export		Time to Import			Time to Export		Time to Import	
	2015	2016	2015	2016		2015	2016	2015	2016
Central Asia	**209**	**203**	**80**	**77**	Lao PDR	228	228	230	230
Armenia	41	41	43	43	Malaysia	58	58	82	82
Azerbaijan	69	62	73	68	Myanmar	288	288	168	280
Georgia	62	16	39	17	Philippines	114	114	168	168
Kazakhstan	265	261	8	8	Singapore	14	14	38	38
Kyrgyz Republic	51	41	73	73	Thailand	62	62	54	54
Tajikistan	141	141	234	234	Viet Nam	143	108	170	138
Turkmenistan	–	–	–	–					
Uzbekistan	286	286	285	285	**The Pacific**	**136**	**136**	**153**	**153**
					Cook Islands	–	–	–	–
East Asia	**37**	**37**	**92**	**92**	Fiji	112	112	76	76
Hong Kong, China	20	20	20	20	Kiribati	96	96	144	144
PRC	47	47	158	158	Marshall Islands	84	84	144	144
Japan	25	25	43	43	FSM	62	62	91	91
Republic of Korea	14	14	7	7	Nauru	–	–	–	–
Mongolia	230	230	163	163	Palau	–	–	–	–
Taipei,China	48	48	88	88	Papua New Guinea	138	138	192	192
					Samoa	75	75	109	109
South Asia	**158**	**152**	**331**	**324**	Solomon Islands	170	170	145	145
Afghanistan	291	276	432	420	Timor-Leste	129	129	144	144
Bangladesh	247	247	327	327	Tonga	220	220	98	98
Bhutan	14	14	13	13	Tuvalu	–	–	–	–
India	150	144	350	344	Vanuatu	110	110	174	174
Maldives	90	90	161	161					
Nepal	83	75	114	109	**Oceania**	**43**	**43**	**41**	**41**
Pakistan	141	134	294	276	Australia	43	43	43	43
Sri Lanka	119	119	130	130	New Zealand	41	41	26	26
Southeast Asia	**74**	**68**	**112**	**107**	**Asia**	**53**	**51**	**117**	**115**
Brunei Darussalam	288	280	192	188	**Developing Asia**	**55**	**53**	**124**	**122**
Cambodia	180	180	140	140					
Indonesia	125	114	243	232					

– = unavailable, PRC = People's Republic of China, FSM = Federated States of Micronesia, Lao PDR = Lao People's Democratic Republic.
Notes: Time to export (import) data measures the number of hours (for 2015 and 2016 figures) required to export (import) by ocean transport, including the processing of documents required to complete the transaction. It covers time for used up for documentation requirements and procedures at customs and other regulatory agencies as well as the time of inland transport between the largest business city and the main port used by traders. Regional aggregates are weighted averages based on total exports or imports.
Source: ADB calculations using data World Bank. Doing Business Data. http://www.doingbusiness.org/data (accessed October 2016)

Table A5: Logistics Performance Index (LPI) Scores—Asia (% EU)

	2012	2014	2016		2012	2014	2016
Central Asia	**68.5**	**68.3**	**66.4**	Lao PDR	65.7	65.8	61.8
Armenia	67.4	67.5	69.1	Malaysia	91.8	91.9	92.9
Azerbaijan	65.2	65.3	63.3	Myanmar	62.2	62.3	58.2
Georgia	72.9	73.0	64.9	Philippines	79.5	79.6	77.7
Kazakhstan	70.8	70.9	69.8	Singapore	108.4	108.6	103.6
Kyrgyz Republic	61.8	61.9	57.1	Thailand	83.5	83.6	88.7
Tajikistan	60.0	60.1	65.4	Viet Nam	79.0	79.1	81.6
Turkmenistan	–	–	59.6				
Uzbekistan	64.8	64.9	61.9	**The Pacific**	**54.9**	**56.4**	**57.0**
				Cook Islands	–	–	–
East Asia	**97.5**	**97.3**	**94.7**	Fiji	63.6	63.7	65.8
PRC	92.4	92.5	91.3	Kiribati	–	–	–
Hong Kong, China	108.3	108.4	99.0	Marshall Islands	–	–	–
Japan	103.4	103.5	101.3	FSM	–	–	–
Republic of Korea	97.1	97.2	94.8	Nauru	–	–	–
Mongolia	59.1	59.2	60.9	Palau	–	–	–
Taipei,China	97.4	97.5	96.2	Papua New Guinea	62.4	62.5	62.9
				Samoa	–	–	–
South Asia	**74.9**	**73.9**	**77.3**	Solomon Islands	63.4	63.5	66.9
Afghanistan	60.4	60.4	53.5	Timor-Leste	–	–	–
Bangladesh	–	–	66.3	Tonga	–	–	–
Bhutan	66.2	66.3	59.2	Tuvalu	–	–	–
India	80.8	80.9	79.7	Vanuatu	–	–	–
Maldives	66.9	67.0	71.1				
Nepal	53.5	53.6	66.9	**Oceania**	**96.9**	**96.9**	**97.9**
Pakistan	74.3	74.3	73.1	Australia	97.9	98.1	98.6
Sri Lanka	72.3	72.4	69.7	New Zealand	89.9	90.0	94.3
Southeast Asia	**90.3**	**89.9**	**89.3**	**Asia**	**93.4**	**93.5**	**92.1**
Brunei Darussalam	–	–	–	**Developing Asia**	**79.4**	**81.0**	**80.5**
Cambodia	67.3	67.4	70.9				
Indonesia	77.4	77.5	79.7				

– = unavailable, PRC = People's Republic of China, EU = European Union, FSM = Federated States of Micronesia, Lao PDR = Lao People's Democratic Republic.
Source: ADB calculations using data World Bank. Logistics Performance Index. http://lpi.worldbank.org/ (accessed October 2016)

Table A6: Cross-Border Equity Holdings—Asia
(% of total cross-border equity holdings, 2015)

| Reporter | Partner | | | | | |
| | Asia | of which: | | EU | US | ROW |
		PRC	Japan			
Central Asia	**11.6**	**0.1**	**8.4**	**26.4**	**52.8**	**9.1**
Armenia	–	–	–	–	–	–
Azerbaijan	–	–	–	–	–	–
Georgia	–	–	–	–	–	–
Kazakhstan	11.6	0.1	8.4	26.4	52.8	9.1
Kyrgyz Republic	–	–	–	–	–	–
Tajikistan	–	–	–	–	–	–
Turkmenistan	–	–	–	–	–	–
Uzbekistan	–	–	–	–	–	–
East Asia	**15.6**	**8.5**	**1.1**	**17.4**	**22.9**	**44.2**
PRC	30.0	0.0	5.0	17.2	36.5	16.3
Hong Kong, China	26.2	23.0	1.1	11.5	2.9	59.4
Japan	6.5	0.9	0.0	20.2	30.8	42.6
Republic of Korea	20.6	6.0	5.7	24.1	45.0	10.3
Mongolia	53.9	0.9	0.2	12.7	19.1	14.3
Taipei,China	–	–	–	–	–	–
South Asia	**23.5**	**12.9**	**0.3**	**36.8**	**24.9**	**14.8**
Afghanistan	–	–	–	–	–	–
Bangladesh	62.4	0.0	0.0	0.0	0.0	37.6
Bhutan	–	–	–	–	–	–
India	25.0	14.2	0.3	39.5	27.2	8.3
Maldives	–	–	–	–	–	–
Nepal	–	–	–	–	–	–
Pakistan	0.4	0.0	0.0	10.9	1.3	87.4
Sri Lanka	–	–	–	–	–	–
Southeast Asia	**43.7**	**13.6**	**5.0**	**10.3**	**26.5**	**19.5**
Brunei Darussalam	–	–	–	–	–	–
Cambodia	–	–	–	–	–	–
Indonesia	43.0	24.3	0.4	1.1	2.8	53.1
Lao PDR	–	–	–	–	–	–

continuation on next page

Table A6 continued

Reporter	Partner					
		of which:				
	Asia	PRC	Japan	EU	US	ROW
Malaysia	47.8	1.6	0.6	8.3	38.9	4.9
Myanmar	–	–	–	–	–	–
Philippines	11.9	0.8	0.3	32.1	53.7	2.2
Singapore	44.1	15.1	5.5	9.4	25.3	21.1
Thailand	21.2	2.3	3.0	42.7	30.0	6.2
Viet Nam	–	–	–	–	–	–
The Pacific	**–**	**–**	**–**	**–**	**–**	**–**
Cook Islands	–	–	–	–	–	–
Fiji	–	–	–	–	–	–
Kiribati	–	–	–	–	–	–
Marshall Islands	–	–	–	–	–	–
FSM	–	–	–	–	–	–
Nauru	–	–	–	–	–	–
Palau	–	–	–	–	–	–
Papua New Guinea	–	–	–	–	–	–
Samoa	–	–	–	–	–	–
Solomon Islands	–	–	–	–	–	–
Timor-Leste	–	–	–	–	–	–
Tonga	–	–	–	–	–	–
Tuvalu	–	–	–	–	–	–
Vanuatu	–	–	–	–	–	–
Oceania	**16.6**	**1.0**	**4.7**	**5.1**	**45.1**	**33.2**
Australia	13.7	1.1	4.9	4.4	47.1	34.8
New Zealand	40.3	0.3	3.7	10.3	29.8	19.6
Asia	**20.3**	**8.4**	**2.2**	**14.7**	**26.3**	**38.7**
Asia ex PRC	**19.8**	**8.8**	**2.0**	**14.6**	**25.8**	**39.8**
Developing Asia	**31.8**	**15.9**	**3.2**	**12.9**	**18.2**	**37.1**
Developing Asia ex PRC	**32.0**	**17.7**	**3.0**	**12.4**	**16.2**	**39.4**

– = unavailable, PRC = People's Republic of China, EU = European Union, FSM = Federated States of Micronesia, Lao PDR = Lao People's Democratic Republic, ROW = rest of the world, US = United States.
Source: ADB calculations using data from International Monetary Fund Coordinated Portfolio Investment Survey. http://cpis.imf.org (accessed September 2016).

Table A7: Cross-Border Debt Holdings—Asia
(% of total cross-border debt holdings, 2015)

Reporter	Partner					
	Asia	of which:				
		PRC	Japan	EU	US	ROW
Central Asia	**14.6**	**0.2**	**6.5**	**23.9**	**53.0**	**8.4**
Armenia	–	–	–	–	–	–
Azerbaijan	–	–	–	–	–	–
Georgia	–	–	–	–	–	–
Kazakhstan	14.6	0.2	6.5	23.9	53.0	8.4
Kyrgyz Republic	–	–	–	–	–	–
Tajikistan	–	–	–	–	–	–
Turkmenistan	–	–	–	–	–	–
Uzbekistan	–	–	–	–	–	–
East Asia	**16.2**	**5.0**	**1.5**	**28.5**	**39.9**	**15.5**
PRC	31.3	0.0	2.0	8.0	44.2	16.6
Hong Kong, China	51.1	29.0	8.1	15.2	21.5	12.3
Japan	7.9	0.2	0.0	32.3	43.7	16.0
Republic of Korea	20.1	5.8	3.5	26.0	35.8	18.1
Mongolia	88.1	0.6	0.0	4.7	6.4	0.9
Taipei,China	–	–	–	–	–	–
South Asia	**12.7**	**2.0**	**2.5**	**42.9**	**12.5**	**31.9**
Afghanistan	–	–	–	–	–	–
Bangladesh	11.4	2.2	2.1	46.0	13.5	29.1
Bhutan	–	–	–	–	–	–
India	42.1	0.0	0.0	44.0	13.9	0.0
Maldives	–	–	–	–	–	–
Nepal	–	–	–	–	–	–
Pakistan	26.5	0.0	7.7	4.1	0.0	69.4
Sri Lanka	–	–	–	–	–	–
Southeast Asia	**34.2**	**6.7**	**0.3**	**11.5**	**28.2**	**26.1**
Brunei Darussalam	–	–	–	–	–	–
Cambodia	–	–	–	–	–	–
Indonesia	8.4	4.0	0.1	41.4	5.2	45.0

continuation on next page

Table A7 continued

Reporter	Partner					
	Asia	of which:				
		PRC	Japan	EU	US	ROW
Lao PDR	–	–	–	–	–	–
Malaysia	65.0	2.6	0.9	7.9	10.7	16.4
Myanmar	–	–	–	–	–	–
Philippines	40.3	6.5	0.5	6.0	43.9	9.8
Singapore	31.7	5.8	0.0	11.6	30.4	26.3
Thailand	62.1	26.7	6.0	4.4	4.5	29.0
Viet Nam	–	–	–	–	–	–
The Pacific	**0.0**	**0.0**	**0.0**	**0.0**	**100.0**	**0.0**
Cook Islands	–	–	–	–	–	–
Fiji	–	–	–	–	–	–
Kiribati	–	–	–	–	–	–
Marshall Islands	–	–	–	–	–	–
FSM	–	–	–	–	–	–
Nauru	–	–	–	–	–	–
Palau	0.0	0.0	0.0	0.0	100.0	0.0
Papua New Guinea	–	–	–	–	–	–
Samoa	–	–	–	–	–	–
Solomon Islands	–	–	–	–	–	–
Timor-Leste	–	–	–	–	–	–
Tonga	–	–	–	–	–	–
Tuvalu	–	–	–	–	–	–
Vanuatu	–	–	–	–	–	–
Oceania	**8.9**	**1.4**	**4.0**	**12.6**	**31.8**	**46.7**
Australia	10.0	1.6	4.6	12.9	36.0	41.1
New Zealand	0.0	0.0	0.0	10.8	0.0	89.2
Asia	**18.3**	**4.9**	**1.6**	**24.9**	**37.8**	**19.0**
Asia ex PRC	**17.9**	**5.1**	**1.5**	**25.4**	**37.7**	**19.1**
Developing Asia	**38.3**	**14.0**	**3.8**	**14.1**	**28.7**	**18.8**
Developing Asia ex PRC	**39.0**	**15.3**	**4.0**	**14.7**	**27.2**	**19.1**

– = unavailable, PRC = People's Republic of China, EU = European Union, FSM = Federated States of Micronesia, Lao PDR = Lao People's Democratic Republic, ROW = rest of the world, US = United States.
Source: ADB calculations using data from International Monetary Fund Coordinated Portfolio Investment Survey. http://cpis.imf.org (accessed September 2016).

Table A8: FDI Inflow Share—Asia (2015)

	Partner					
	Asia	of which				
Reporter		PRC	Japan	EU	US	ROW
Central Asia	**12.5**	**7.8**	**1.2**	**42.9**	**5.8**	**38.9**
Armenia	–	–	–	51.7	0.7	47.7
Azerbaijan	1.0	–	0.1	7.8	1.7	90.4
Georgia	46.3	4.4	-3.0	39.0	2.7	12.1
Kazakhstan	12.1	8.4	1.6	49.5	6.9	31.6
Kyrgyz Republic	32.2	23.4	–	31.4	1.7	34.6
Tajikistan	100.0	100.0	–	0.0	0.0	0.0
Turkmenistan	–	–	–	–	–	–
Uzbekistan	–	–	–	–	–	–
East Asia	**66.6**	**14.6**	**6.3**	**7.3**	**-2.9**	**29.0**
PRC	77.7	0.0	6.6	2.3	2.3	17.6
Hong Kong, China	49.2	42.8	1.4	15.0	-22.2	58.0
Japan	96.6	10.7	0.0	-36.4	100.0	-60.2
Republic of Korea	53.8	2.2	37.1	14.0	19.3	12.9
Mongolia	21.9	7.6	1.1	61.6	2.0	14.6
Taipei,China	56.3	7.4	13.7	26.7	4.0	13.0
South Asia	**44.4**	**2.4**	**4.2**	**19.6**	**10.0**	**26.0**
Afghanistan	144.2	144.2	0.0	-44.2	0.0	0.0
Bangladesh	50.0	1.4	2.3	22.1	3.4	24.4
Bhutan	25.7	0.0	0.0	6.3	0.0	68.0
India	43.7	2.2	4.4	19.0	10.0	27.3
Maldives	0.0	0.0	0.0	100.0	0.0	0.0
Nepal	100.0	85.9	14.1	0.0	0.0	0.0
Pakistan	43.8	8.8	3.4	51.5	25.4	-20.7
Sri Lanka	121.6	12.0	-2.7	-32.0	0.0	10.4
Southeast Asia	**63.3**	**7.8**	**16.6**	**18.0**	**11.6**	**7.1**
Brunei Darussalam	37.1	0.0	-30.3	68.2	-5.8	0.4
Cambodia	84.5	30.7	3.0	10.3	2.3	2.9
Indonesia	96.4	1.9	29.0	-7.2	2.9	7.9
Lao PDR	93.3	61.2	7.0	2.3	0.8	3.6
Malaysia	52.9	2.4	22.0	12.1	12.5	22.5
Myanmar	92.5	1.9	3.5	7.5	0.0	0.0
Philippines	18.5	0.0	11.1	9.1	20.9	51.6
Singapore	46.5	11.6	9.7	35.3	17.3	1.0

continuation on next page

Table A8 continued

Reporter	Partner					
	Asia	of which		EU	US	ROW
		PRC	Japan			
Thailand	85.1	3.4	47.0	-4.5	11.4	8.0
Viet Nam	85.3	3.3	8.3	8.6	1.0	5.1
The Pacific	**95.6**	**3.7**	**1.2**	**4.4**	**–**	**–**
Cook Islands	–	–	–	–	–	–
Fiji	97.6	25.6	3.3	2.4	0.0	–
Kiribati	–	–	–	–	–	–
Marshall Islands	0.0	0.0	0.0	100.0	0.0	–
FSM	100.0	73.1	26.9	–	0.0	–
Nauru	–	–	–	–	–	–
Palau	100.0	0.0	100.0	0.0	0.0	–
Papua New Guinea	99.0	1.5	-0.2	1.0	0.0	–
Samoa	67.5	52.3	15.2	32.5	–	–
Solomon Islands	100.0	–	0.0	–	0.0	–
Timor-Leste	–	–	–	–	–	–
Tonga	–	–	–	–	–	–
Tuvalu	–	–	–	–	–	–
Vanuatu	90.4	10.9	-9.4	9.6	0.0	–
Oceania	**52.2**	**6.1**	**30.0**	**7.0**	**20.2**	**20.5**
Australia	48.6	6.5	32.9	4.7	22.7	24.0
New Zealand	91.7	2.4	-1.0	31.7	-6.4	-17.0
Asia	**59.3**	**10.8**	**9.8**	**13.2**	**3.9**	**23.7**
Developing Asia	**59.4**	**11.2**	**8.3**	**14.3**	**1.4**	**25.0**

– = unavailable, PRC = People's Republic of China, EU = European Union, FSM = Federated States of Micronesia, Lao PDR = Lao People's Democratic Republic, ROW = rest of the world, US = United States.
Sources: ADB calculations using data from Association of Southeast Asian Nations Secretariat; CEIC; Eurostat. Balance of Payments; Organisation for Economic Co-operation and Development; and United Nations Conference on Trade and Development. Bilateral FDI Statistics.

Table A9: Remittance Inflows Share—Asia (% of total remittance inflows, 2015)

Reporter	Partner				
	Asia	of which Japan	EU	US	ROW
Central Asia	**7.8**	**0.0**	**6.8**	**2.6**	**82.7**
Armenia	4.3	0.0	10.3	13.7	71.7
Azerbaijan	24.1	0.0	3.4	2.0	70.6
Georgia	8.9	0.0	16.7	2.4	72.0
Kazakhstan	4.0	0.0	22.2	0.6	73.3
Kyrgyz Republic	4.5	0.0	12.4	0.6	82.5
Tajikistan	12.0	0.0	4.2	0.9	83.0
Turkmenistan	–	–	–	–	–
Uzbekistan	–	–	–	–	–
East Asia	**43.0**	**18.2**	**8.9**	**27.6**	**12.7**
PRC	46.0	14.3	9.0	25.4	13.1
Hong Kong, China	22.6	0.0	11.7	30.7	35.1
Japan	39.7	0.0	13.1	34.9	12.4
Republic of Korea	16.9	156.3	4.5	44.9	7.3
Mongolia	44.9	0.0	19.6	0.4	35.1
Taipei,China	–	–	–	–	–
South Asia	**20.4**	**0.9**	**8.7**	**11.2**	**59.5**
Afghanistan	31.4	0.0	7.7	2.0	58.9
Bangladesh	35.1	0.5	5.4	3.4	55.9
Bhutan	95.0	0.0	0.0	0.0	5.0
India	18.5	0.8	8.0	15.9	57.5
Maldives	66.7	0.0	0.0	0.0	33.3
Nepal	21.0	0.0	2.9	4.8	71.3
Pakistan	16.7	1.0	12.2	6.0	65.0
Sri Lanka	16.2	3.4	18.9	3.1	61.2
Southeast Asia	**25.8**	**9.4**	**9.5**	**30.9**	**31.4**
Brunei Darussalam	–	–	–	–	–
Cambodia	67.8	0.4	7.6	21.4	3.0
Indonesia	39.0	1.8	4.6	2.8	52.9
Lao PDR	73.3	0.0	5.0	20.0	1.7

continuation on next page

Table A9 continued

Reporter	Asia	of which Japan	EU	US	ROW
	Partner				
Malaysia	88.8	0.6	4.3	3.8	2.6
Myanmar	65.9	0.0	0.7	5.4	27.9
Philippines	14.5	24.3	7.0	34.0	41.0
Singapore	–	–	–	–	–
Thailand	32.3	14.0	25.2	27.8	10.2
Viet Nam	18.0	7.7	15.4	56.4	8.8
The Pacific	**58.4**	**0.0**	**2.0**	**25.2**	**14.4**
Cook Islands	–	–	–	–	–
Fiji	59.5	0.0	3.2	23.4	14.0
Kiribati	50.0	0.0	0.0	50.0	0.0
Marshall Islands	3.7	0.0	0.0	92.6	3.7
FSM	0.0		0.0	70.8	29.2
Nauru	–	–	–	–	–
Palau	–	–	–	50.0	50.0
Papua New Guinea	90.0	0.0	0.0	10.0	0.0
Samoa	64.3	0.0	0.0	13.0	22.7
Solomon Islands	88.9	0.0	0.0	5.6	5.6
Timor-Leste	93.8	0.0	6.3	0.0	0.0
Tonga	56.8	0.0	0.0	39.8	3.4
Tuvalu	75.0	0.0	0.0	0.0	25.0
Vanuatu	21.4	0.0	10.7	3.6	64.3
Oceania	**37.3**	**6.4**	**36.6**	**13.2**	**10.5**
Australia	28.7	9.5	41.7	15.0	11.9
New Zealand	83.6	0.6	9.3	3.8	2.9
Asia	**27.6**	**10.3**	**9.1**	**19.9**	**40.5**
Developing Asia	**27.3**	**10.6**	**8.8**	**19.8**	**41.3**

– = unavailable, PRC = People's Republic of China, EU = European Union, FSM = Federated States of Micronesia, Lao PDR = Lao People's Democratic Republic, ROW = rest of the world, US = United States.
Source: ADB calculations using data from World Bank. World Bank Migration and Remittances Data. http://www.worldbank.org/en/topic/migrationremittancesdiasporaissues/brief/migration-remittances-data (accessed July 2016).

Table A10: Outbound Migration Share—Asia (% of total outbound migrants, 2015)

Reporter	Asia	PRC	Japan	EU	US	ROW
		of which				
Central Asia	**10.0**	**0.0**	**0.0**	**15.1**	**1.9**	**72.9**
Armenia	18.8	0.0	0.0	9.1	9.1	63.0
Azerbaijan	15.1	0.0	0.0	3.7	1.7	79.4
Georgia	11.9	0.0	0.0	20.4	2.9	64.8
Kazakhstan	1.6	0.0	0.0	26.8	0.6	70.9
Kyrgyz Republic	4.0	0.0	0.0	12.4	0.7	82.9
Tajikistan	7.9	0.0	0.0	5.5	0.7	85.8
Turkmenistan	2.8	0.0	0.0	4.2	0.9	92.2
Uzbekistan	23.2	0.0	0.0	3.7	1.8	71.3
East Asia	**37.0**	**3.4**	**8.5**	**9.6**	**27.5**	**14.0**
PRC	47.5	0.0	6.8	9.9	22.0	13.7
Hong Kong, China	15.9	26.0	0.0	11.9	21.5	24.7
Japan	22.0	0.9	0.0	17.0	43.3	16.9
Republic of Korea	8.9	8.0	22.3	4.2	47.7	8.9
Mongolia	32.6	0.0	0.0	27.4	0.0	40.1
Taipei,China	0.0	0.0	0.0	0.0	0.0	0.0
South Asia	**31.8**	**0.1**	**0.1**	**8.6**	**7.2**	**52.2**
Afghanistan	34.6	0.0	0.0	5.9	1.3	58.1
Bangladesh	51.8	0.1	0.1	5.3	2.6	40.1
Bhutan	89.3	0.0	0.0	4.0	0.0	6.7
India	21.8	0.1	0.1	7.7	12.6	57.7
Maldives	73.9	0.0	0.0	17.3	0.0	8.8
Nepal	52.9	0.0	0.0	4.7	4.6	37.8
Pakistan	28.6	0.1	0.2	14.3	5.5	51.3
Sri Lanka	20.7	0.3	0.6	22.0	2.9	53.5
Southeast Asia	**46.1**	**0.8**	**1.8**	**7.9**	**20.3**	**23.1**
Brunei Darussalam	75.6	0.0	0.0	14.0	0.0	10.4
Cambodia	77.0	0.0	0.3	6.1	14.1	2.6
Indonesia	43.4	1.0	0.7	4.7	2.5	47.7

Table A10 continued

Reporter	Partner					
	Asia	of which		EU	US	ROW
		PRC	Japan			
Lao PDR	80.1	0.0	0.0	3.6	14.9	1.4
Malaysia	88.0	0.3	0.4	5.3	3.5	2.5
Myanmar	88.1	0.0	0.0	0.8	3.6	7.5
Philippines	9.1	1.4	4.0	9.2	35.7	40.8
Singapore	65.1	0.0	0.7	18.5	10.0	5.8
Thailand	27.3	1.8	4.8	28.5	27.6	9.9
Viet Nam	20.7	1.1	2.8	15.2	50.9	9.3
The Pacific	**64.9**	**0.0**	**0.0**	**3.3**	**18.2**	**13.6**
Cook Islands	99.9	0.0	0.0	0.0	0.0	0.0
Fiji	63.1	0.0	0.0	3.5	19.9	13.5
Kiribati	93.5	0.0	0.0	4.3	0.0	2.2
Marshall Islands	1.9	0.0	0.0	0.1	93.9	4.1
FSM	3.4	0.0	0.0	0.5	36.7	59.4
Nauru	97.3	0.0	0.0	1.5	0.0	1.3
Palau	12.3	0.0	0.0	7.7	0.0	80.0
Papua New Guinea	46.5	0.0	0.0	33.7	0.0	19.8
Samoa	70.2	0.0	0.0	0.8	14.9	14.1
Solomon Islands	89.6	0.0	0.0	10.3	0.0	0.1
Timor-Leste	89.1	0.0	0.0	10.7	0.0	0.2
Tonga	64.7	0.0	0.0	0.8	31.3	3.1
Tuvalu	77.6	0.0	0.0	2.0	0.0	20.4
Vanuatu	22.6	0.0	0.0	12.0	0.0	65.4
Oceania	**59.2**	**0.4**	**0.9**	**25.0**	**8.2**	**6.3**
Australia	23.8	1.0	1.7	47.0	14.8	11.8
New Zealand	82.5	0.0	0.4	10.6	3.8	2.7
Asia	**34.0**	**0.8**	**1.9**	**9.6**	**13.2**	**40.5**
Developing Asia	**33.7**	**0.8**	**2.0**	**9.3**	**12.9**	**41.3**

− = unavailable, PRC = People's Republic of China, EU = European Union, FSM = Federated States of Micronesia, Lao PDR = Lao People's Democratic Republic, ROW = rest of the world, US = United States.
Source: ADB calculations using data from United Nations. Department of Economic and Social Affairs, Population Division. International Migration Stock 2015. http://www.un.org/en/development/desa/population/migration/data/estimates2/estimates15.shtml (accessed July 2016).

Table 11: Outbound Tourism Share—Asia

(% of total outbound tourists, 2014)

Reporter	Partner					
		of which				
	Asia	PRC	Japan	EU	US	ROW
Central Asia	**37.1**	**2.2**	**–**	**0.7**	**0.2**	**59.8**
Armenia	58.9	0.2	–	0.7	0.3	40.0
Azerbaijan	32.2	0.4	–	0.4	0.1	66.9
Georgia	26.8	0.3	–	2.5	0.3	70.2
Kazakhstan	29.4	5.3	–	1.0	0.3	64.0
Kyrgyz Republic	60.7	2.2	–	0.0	0.1	36.9
Tajikistan	14.5	2.1	–	0.0	0.1	83.3
Turkmenistan	16.1	2.6	–	0.2	0.2	81.0
Uzbekistan	46.7	1.1	–	0.2	0.2	51.9
East Asia	**31.0**	**39.2**	**4.0**	**5.2**	**3.5**	**17.1**
PRC	56.2	–	3.0	6.7	2.7	31.3
Hong Kong, China	4.1	86.7	1.1	0.2	0.1	7.8
Japan	43.2	12.3	–	16.5	15.5	12.5
Republic of Korea	36.1	20.5	14.2	10.2	7.5	11.5
Mongolia	8.6	73.5	1.2	0.1	–	16.6
Taipei,China	26.5	38.1	20.9	2.6	3.1	8.9
South Asia	**39.2**	**5.0**	**0.7**	**6.3**	**5.7**	**43.1**
Afghanistan	20.1	1.6	–	0.8	0.4	77.0
Bangladesh	72.4	2.9	0.4	0.1	1.6	22.4
Bhutan	86.5	2.7	–	3.1	3.0	4.7
India	36.9	5.7	0.7	9.2	8.0	39.5
Maldives	95.2	2.4	–	0.1	0.2	2.2
Nepal	60.5	9.5	3.9	0.1	2.8	23.3
Pakistan	12.8	3.6	0.3	3.6	2.3	77.4
Sri Lanka	66.1	5.0	1.4	0.2	1.7	25.6
Southeast Asia	**79.8**	**9.0**	**2.5**	**1.2**	**1.1**	**6.4**
Brunei Darussalam	98.2	0.6	0.2	0.0	0.1	0.8
Cambodia	95.5	2.9	0.6	0.0	0.3	0.7
Indonesia	77.4	6.2	1.6	1.1	1.0	12.7
Lao PDR	98.4	1.1	0.2	0.0	0.1	0.1
Malaysia	75.5	12.0	2.5	2.0	0.8	7.2

continuation on next page

Table A11 continued

Reporter	Partner					
		of which				
	Asia	PRC	Japan	EU	US	ROW
Myanmar	77.1	17.3	1.8	0.1	0.6	3.0
Philippines	55.2	16.1	3.0	1.6	3.5	20.7
Singapore	90.3	4.7	1.1	1.2	0.7	2.1
Thailand	78.9	7.2	7.2	1.4	1.1	4.3
Viet Nam	68.9	24.9	2.3	0.2	1.6	2.2
The Pacific	**80.4**	**3.9**	**–**	**0.3**	**3.5**	**12.0**
Cook Islands	97.1	–	–	0.3	0.8	1.7
Fiji	81.6	4.0	–	0.2	7.7	6.4
Kiribati	52.2	34.6	–	0.3	2.8	10.2
Marshall Islands	38.0	13.6	–	0.7	–	47.7
FSM	9.5	1.0	–	0.8	–	88.8
Nauru	90.6	5.7	–	0.6	1.8	1.3
Palau	11.0	0.9	–	1.2	–	86.9
Papua New Guinea	95.9	1.8	–	0.1	1.2	1.0
Samoa	67.7	2.7	–	0.1	–	29.5
Solomon Islands	82.3	7.1	–	2.0	2.8	5.7
Timor–Leste	86.3	7.3	–	0.7	1.6	4.1
Tonga	86.8	5.0	–	0.1	6.4	1.7
Tuvalu	62.8	29.0	–	0.9	4.1	3.2
Vanuatu	77.2	2.1	–	0.4	1.2	19.2
Oceania	**52.2**	**4.7**	**1.9**	**22.8**	**8.7**	**9.7**
Australia	48.7	4.9	2.0	25.4	8.8	10.1
New Zealand	68.2	4.0	1.3	10.9	8.1	7.5
Asia	**42.1**	**27.2**	**3.1**	**5.1**	**3.2**	**19.3**
Developing Asia	**41.4**	**29.6**	**3.4**	**3.2**	**1.9**	**20.4**

– = unavailable, PRC = People's Republic of China, EU = European Union, FSM = Federated States of Micronesia, Lao PDR = Lao People's Democratic Republic, US = United States, ROW = rest of the world.
Notes: Due to data unavailability, 2013 data for tourist arrivals in PRC is used for 2014.
Source: ADB calculations using data from World Tourism Organization. 2016. Tourism Statistics Database.

www.ingramcontent.com/pod-product-compliance
Lightning Source LLC
Chambersburg PA
CBHW061220270326
41926CB00032B/4784